PROSPECTS FOR DEMOCRACY

North, South, East, West

Edited by
David Held

Polity Press

Copyright © this collection Polity Press, 1993

Chapters 1, 2, 3, 4, 7, 8, 10, 11 & 15
© *Political Studies Association* 1992
These chapters were published originally in *Political Studies*
Special Issue, *Prospects for Democracy* (1992)

Each other chapter © the author

First published in 1993 by Polity Press
in association with Blackwell Publishers

Editorial office:
Polity Press
65 Bridge Street
Cambridge CB2 1UR, UK

Marketing and production:
Blackwell Publishers
108 Cowley Road
Oxford OX4 1JF, UK

ISBN 0 7456 0988 0
ISBN 0 7456 0989 9 (pbk)

A CIP catalogue record for this book is available
from the British Library

Typeset in 10½ on 12 pt Caslon
by Joshua Associates Ltd., Oxford
Printed in Great Britain by
T. J. Press (Padstow) Ltd, Cornwall

This book is printed on acid-free paper.

CONTENTS

ACKNOWLEDGEMENTS

The idea for this volume developed out of a request by Jack Hayward, on behalf of the Editorial Board of *Political Studies*, to edit a special issue of the journal on democracy and, in particular, on the theme of 'viable alternatives to liberal democracy'. I would like to thank Jack Hayward and the Board of *Political Studies* for the opportunity to develop the special issue (*Political Studies*, vol. XL, no. 5) and for their permission to make the special issue the basis of this book.

Chapters 1 (David Held), 2 (David Beetham), 3 (David Miller), 4 (Anne Phillips), 7 (Bhikhu Parekh), 8 (Christopher Pierson), 10 (Robert Johansen), 11 (John Keane), and 15 (Laurence Whitehead) first appeared in the journal. The other chapters were specially written for this volume and are published here for the first time.

My own chapter (chapter 1) develops themes which are part of an on-going research project sponsored by the Economic and Social Research Council (award no. R.000 23 1045). Their support is warmly acknowledged.

The intellectual support and friendship of Peter Held, Anthony Giddens, Michelle Stanworth and John Thompson remain invaluable.

Finally, I would like to thank all those at Polity, especially Rebecca Harkin, Gill Motley, Nicola Ross, Debbie Seymour, Pam Thomas and Frances Tomlinson, for their care and professionalism in the publication of this book.

DH
April 1992

THE CONTRIBUTORS

David Beetham is Professor of Politics at the University of Leeds. His publications include *Max Weber and the Theory of Modern Politics*, *Marxists in Face of Fascism*, *Bureaucracy* and *The Legitimation of Power*. He is currently working on problems of democratic theory.

Simon Bromley is Lecturer in International Political Economy in the Department of Politics at the University of Leeds. He is the author of *American Hegemony and World Oil* and co-author of *Thatcherism* (with Kevin Bonnett, Bob Jessop and Tom Ling). He is currently working on a study of the development of the modern Middle East in the international system.

Ian Budge is Professor of Government at the University of Essex. He was Visiting Professor at the University of Wisconsin (1969–70); UCI (1989), European University Institute, Florence (1982–5), Science Centre, Berlin (1990), and Universitat Autonoma Barcelona (1991). He is author and co-author of some ten books, and thirty-odd articles, mainly on elections, parties and democratic theory. He is currently Director of the Manifesto Research group engaged on comparative research on election and government programmes and their implementation.

Alex Callinicos was educated in Zimbabwe where he was born, and at Balliol College, Oxford, and the London School of Economics. He was Junior Research Fellow at St Peter's College, Oxford, 1979–81. He has taught politics at the University of York ever since. His books include *The Revolutionary Ideas of Karl Marx*, *Marxism and Philosophy*, *Making History*, *Against Postmodernism*, *The Revenge of History* and (edited) *Between Apartheid and Capitalism*.

John A. Hall is Professor of Sociology at McGill University in Montreal, Quebec, Canada. He is the author of several books, including *Powers and Liberties* and *Liberalism*, and is currently writing a book on different types of world order.

Geoffrey Hawthorn teaches sociology and politics at Cambridge University. His most recent book is *Plausible Worlds: possibility and understanding in history and the social sciences.*

David Held is Professor in Politics and Sociology at the Open University. Among his recent publications are *Models of Democracy*, *Political Theory and the Modern State* and (edited) *Political Theory Today.* His research interests focus on the changing meaning of democracy in the context of the global economic system and the evolving structures of international decision-making. He is currently writing *Foundations of Democracy: the principle of autonomy and the global order.*

Paul Hirst is Professor of Social Theory at Birkbeck College, University of London. He is the author of several books including *After Thatcher*, *Representative Democracy and its Limits* and (edited) *The Pluralist Theory of the State: selected writings of G. D. H. Cole, J. N. Figgis and H. J. Laski.* He is a member of the editorial board of *The Political Quarterly* and a member of the Council and Executive of Charter 88.

Robert C. Johansen is Senior Fellow and Director of Graduate Studies at the Kroc Institute for International Peace Studies; Professor of Government and International Studies at the University of Notre Dame (USA); author of *The National Interest and the Human Interest: an analysis of US foreign policy*; contributing editor to *World Policy Journal*; and on the Board of Directors of the Arms Control Association in Washington, DC.

John Keane is Director of the Centre for the Study of Democracy and Professor of Politics at the University of Westminster. He has taught and researched at the University of Toronto, Cambridge University, the Freie Universität Berlin, the European University Institute and the University of California, San Diego. He is the author of many essays and books, including *Public Life and Late Capitalism* and *Democracy and Civil Society.* He is currently completing a study of the life and writings of Thomas Paine and editing a three-volume *History of Democracy.*

Paul G. Lewis is Senior Lecturer in Government at the Open University. He has published in the area of comparative politics and East European studies, with particular reference to Poland. He is the editor of *Democracy and Civil Society in Eastern Europe* and is currently preparing a history of Central Europe since 1945. He is also engaged in a collaborative research

project on regime change and party development in East–Central
Europe, funded by the Economic and Social Research Council.

David Miller is Official Fellow in Social and Political Theory at Nuffield
College, Oxford. He works mainly on issues in contemporary political
theory, including social justice, market socialism and democratic theory.
His most recent publications are *Market, State and Community: theoretical
foundations of market socialism* and (edited) *Liberty.*

Bhikhu Parekh is Professor of Political Theory at the University of Hull
and was Deputy Chairman of the Commission for Racial Equality, UK
(1985–90), and Vice-Chancellor of the University of Baroda, India (1981–
4). He is the author of *Hannah Arendt and the Search for a New Political
Philosophy, Marx's Theory of Ideology, Contemporary Political Thinkers,
Gandhi's Political Philosophy* and *Colonialism, Tradition and Reform.* He has
edited, among other books, *Bentham's Political Thought, Knowledge and
Belief in Politics* and *Political Discourse.*

Anne Phillips is Professor of Politics at the City of London Polytechnic.
Her publications include *Engendering Democracy* and *Divided Loyalties:
dilemmas of sex and class.* She has recently co-edited, with Michèle Barrett,
Destabilizing Theory: contemporary feminist debates.

Christopher Pierson is Senior Lecturer in Politics at the University of
Stirling. He is the author of *Marxist Theory and Democratic Politics* and
Beyond the Welfare State?. He is currently working on problems of social
democratic renewal and market socialism.

David Potter is Professor of Political Science at the Open University. For
many years he was Chairperson of the Social Sciences Foundation
Course at that university. He is editor of the *Journal of Commonwealth and
Comparative Politics.* His research has focused on bureaucracy and politics
in India, and his publications include *Government in Rural India* and *India's
Political Administrators, 1919–1983.*

Laurence Whitehead is an Official Fellow in Politics at Nuffield College,
Oxford University. He teaches graduates in contemporary Latin
American politics and economic policy at Oxford's Latin American
Centre. In 1980/1 he was Senior Research Officer at the Latin American
Program of the Wilson Center, responsible for a large-scale comparative
project on transitions from authoritarian rule and prospects for demo-
cracy in Latin America and Southern Europe. The fruits of that research
were published in four volumes by the Johns Hopkins University Press
(*Transitions from Authoritarian Rule*, edited by Guillermo O'Donnell,
Philippe Schmitter and Laurence Whitehead).

Danilo Zolo is Professor of Political Philosophy at the University of Siena, Italy. He has been Associate Professor at the University of Florence, Research Associate at Boston University, and Visiting Fellow at the University of Cambridge, the University of Pittsburgh and Harvard University. He is a member of the Academia Europaea. His recent books include: *Scienza e politica in Otto Neurath*, *La democrazia difficile*, *Reflexive Epistemology* and *Democracy and Complexity*.

EDITOR'S PREFACE

Prospects for Democracy: North, South, East, West explores the nature and future of democracy. It has a double focus: on the strengths and limits of liberal democracy; and on the strengths and limits of alternatives to it. Faced, on the one hand, with economic, social and environmental problems which often stretch beyond the control of particular democratic polities and, on the other hand, with social movements and national forces seeking to redraw the boundaries of political life, how viable is liberal democracy in the contemporary era? How legitimate are liberal democratic institutions? What is the relationship between liberal democracy and other programmes of political change and transformation?

Addressing these questions throws into relief another pressing issue: are there any viable alternatives to liberal democracy? For all those interested in the prospects for democracy, this question carries a particular poignancy since the dramatic transformation of Eastern Europe and the Soviet Union. Liberal democracy appears triumphant across major areas of the globe and its main modern rival, Marxism, in a state of disarray. Those who have championed alternatives to liberal democracy either appear less confident than ever about these, or are engaged in a process of re-examining their merits in relationship to liberalism, democracy and other traditions of political and social thought.

The question of whether there are 'viable alternatives to liberal democracy' can be thought of in at least two ways. First, it can be interpreted as a question about ideas and principles; that is, about whether there are justifiable alternative conceptions to liberal democracy for modern states. Secondly, it can be understood as a question concerning practical realities; that is, do there exist today, or are there likely to exist, workable alternative forms of political organization? Of concern, in short, are questions about democratic ideas and principles, and their conditions of enactment.

Prospects for Democracy is, then, concerned with an appraisal of alternatives to liberal democracy as well as with an assessment of liberal democracy itself; indeed, the latter is a prerequisite of the former, and *vice versa*. The book is divided into four parts, although inevitably a number of questions cut across each part and some of the substantive concerns of particular sections overlap. Broadly, part I provides an introduction to the volume as a whole; part II focuses on current theoretical disputes about liberal democracy and competing conceptions of democratic life; part III extends the discussion by examining a number of major substantive issues which pose fundamental questions about the form and limits of democracy; and part IV assesses the opportunities and potentialities for democracy in major regions of the world.

Part I consists of a chapter by David Held. The chapter begins by contrasting the main historical models of democracy – direct or participatory democracy, liberal representative democracy and one-party democracy – and then examines the meaning and relevance of these models in the light of the intersection of political communities with each other; in the light, that is, of the growth of complex interconnections among states and societies. The chapter seeks to place new items on the agenda of democratic theory by presenting the case that democratic thought must preoccupy itself with the interconnectedness and 'cosmopolitan' basis of political associations.

Part II comprises six chapters. In the first of these, David Beetham explores the relationship between liberalism and democracy. Liberalism has provided both a foundation for modern democracy and a constraint upon it. Beetham examines this 'duality' in order to reassess what limits liberalism might place on democracy and what limits democracy should place on liberal ambitions. He concludes by reassessing the proper scope and limits of democratization. In the following chapter, David Miller contrasts the regulative ideals of liberal democracy with those of deliberative democracy, and argues strongly in favour of the latter. Comparing the liberal conception of democracy as the aggregation of individual preferences with the deliberative conception of it as a process of open debate leading to an agreed judgement on policy and other matters, Miller examines the relevance of the problems identified in social choice theory for democratic ideals and practices. He finds not only that the deliberative alternative is more attractive than liberal democracy, but that it is also less vulnerable to the objections of social choice theorists.

Examining arguments for a more actively participatory democracy, and the problems associated with representing social heterogeneity and group difference, Anne Phillips, in the fourth chapter, takes up the question of the relationship between liberal democracy and the value attached to political participation by many feminists. Phillips seeks to explore the extent to which feminism has been, and ought to be, 'at odds with liberal democracy'. She concludes that feminism 'will continue to inspire a more substantial democracy than that which is currently on offer', but that the simple juxtaposition of liberal democracy with 'alternatives' is unhelpful.

Against the background of the ruins of centralized state socialism as a political model, and the marked limits of unregulated free-market individualism, Paul Hirst outlines in chapter 5 the contribution associationalist doctrines could make to the reform of democratic governance and to the reordering of economic affairs and welfare services. Associationalism claims that liberty and human welfare are best served when as many of the activities of society as possible are organized by voluntary and democratically run associations. Exploring this central postulate, Hirst seeks to show how associationalist relationships can be built by citizens' initiatives and groups freely formed by committed individuals. Although the associationalist principle could reinvigorate and guide the democratization of states and societies, it is better thought of, Hirst cautions, as 'a supplement to and a healthy competitor for the currently dominant forms of social organization', including representative mass democracy and large-scale organizations. Associationalism is best conceived of as an 'axial principle' – a mode of organizing social relations that can be generalized, in and through successful experimentation, across an ever broader range of activities and sectors.

Throughout the last two centuries, direct democracy has generally been compared unfavourably with liberal democracy on a number of grounds, including the ground that it is simply not feasible in modern states and societies, given their size and complexity. The gathering of citizens in assemblies to debate and decide on matters of public life is an inappropriate and impractical model for contemporary democracies; it cannot be adapted to 'stretch' across space and time. However, in Ian Budge's account in chapter 6, developments in information technology, which put simultaneous two-way communication within reach, are interpreted as overturning this conventional objection. The merits of direct democracy have to be re-debated, now that its technical feasibility is at hand. Budge argues that it is unacceptable to dismiss direct democracy as if it could be realized only through 'unmediated popular voting on a take-it-or-leave-it basis'; for direct democracy can take several different institutional forms, just as liberal representative democracy does. While Budge concedes that some of these forms are open to serious reservations, he advocates a type of 'party-based direct democracy' in which the electorate would be able, in the first instance, to choose among competing parties for office and, in the second, to act like a parliamentary assembly – voting directly and regularly on proposed legislation set out and advocated by the party in office. Of course, the stability of such a political system would require a complex set of rules and procedures to be in place, but these are not in principle difficult to specify. Budge finds that many of the arguments advanced against direct democracy either relate to only one of its possible institutional forms or imply 'a distrust of democracy as such'.

Is democracy an essentially western project or is it something of wider, universal significance? Further, is the liberal democratic understanding of the person, of rights and duties, and of the nature of the significance of accountability radically limited in its value in relation to other cultures and modes of political regulation? In chapter 7, Bhikhu Parekh examines the cultural relativity of democracy. He argues that liberal democracy is specific to a particular cultural context and that we ought not to accept any claims to universal validity made on its behalf. But his argument does not lead to cultural relativism, he emphasizes. In the final part of his chapter, he suggests ways of reconciling the claims of cultural diversity with those of universalism in political thought. Political accountability can be sustained and defended, he believes, without liberal democratic presuppositions.

Part III of the volume is composed of five chapters examining some of the central issues facing the theory and practice of democracy. They focus upon the proper form and limits of democracy. Within debates about democratic theory, questions concerning whether there are necessary economic limits to democracy must surely be among the most pressing. Christopher Pierson seeks to address these matters directly in chapter 8. He begins by setting out the neo-liberal case for economic limits to democracy and counterposes this to the arguments of socialists and social democrats. In the second half of his chapter he asks whether some form of market socialism might overcome the economic limits to democracy perceived in the liberal tradition. He concludes that while there may indeed be some economic limits to democracy, 'we are still very far from reaching them'.

The revolutions which swept across Central and Eastern Europe from the end of 1989 have been taken by some – in the academy, in the press, in government and in international agencies – to indicate the imminent end of ideological conflict, a final triumph for democratic reason and

market-orientated thinking. Against this view, Alex Callinicos interprets
the East European revolutions, in chapter 9, as a victory for capitalism – a
victory which makes socialist democracy today more relevant, not less.
Defending the idea of collective self-determination and the extension of
the principle of democratic self-government to economic life, Callinicos
seeks to focus on the much-contested issue of the feasibility of such an
extension. Market socialism, he holds, is an inadequate model for a
democratic political economy, for it reproduces many of the shortcomings of capitalist markets (inefficiency, anarchic outcomes and unjust
results). The idea of a planned economy must, therefore, be defended,
although its meaning has to be rethought to avoid the serious pitfalls of
command economies (information overload and built-in scarcities, for
example). Callinicos finds positive clues for the renewal of the idea of
planning in a system of 'negotiated coordination', in which self-managing
production units would operate within parameters set down by *ex ante*
economic coordination (at international, national, industry and workplace levels). He concludes by arguing that the events of 1989 and
onward show that 'nothing has to be the way it is'. The political imagination does not have to be restricted 'to the confines imposed by the
market'. Bucking conventional wisdom, he suggests it is time to think
anew and to 'think big' about the economic limits to democracy.

The subsequent chapter by Robert Johansen explores a series of issues
which are relatively neglected in democratic thought, although they
connect directly with the arguments presented earlier by David Held for
rethinking democracy on an international basis. Johansen explores the
'severe limits' placed on democracy by the organization of the state
system and the pursuit of military policies. He argues that military values
and the system of warfare undermine democratic culture, defy public
understanding, create a decision-making process that is too often
secretive and beyond public review, skew the political process in favour of
strong sectional military interests, and damage public accountability and
democratic participation more generally. An examination of liberal
democracy in the context of military structures and the state system leads
Johansen to conclude that demilitarization and democratization require
each other.

John Keane pursues the issue of the prospects for democracy in the
context of a consideration of the media, in chapter 11. Setting out an
account of the importance of the media to democracy and elaborating a
new conception of the public service model of communications, Keane
seeks to restore to the centre of democratic debate the question of
whether the free and equal communication of citizens through the media
is a practical ideal at the end of the twentieth century. He concludes that

it is not only practical, but simply vital to the development of democracy. In addition, he sets out a defence of democracy which departs from both foundationalism and relativism. Together with the revised model of public service media, democracy, Keane holds, can become 'rule by publics' who can make and remake their judgements about the nature and quality of decisions in the political system as well as in civil society.

What is citizenship? What does democratic citizenship mean in the current era? What should it mean? Exploring the many 'diverse and confusing' meanings of citizenship, Danilo Zolo, in chapter 12, expresses scepticism about conceptions of citizenship which ascribe to it a panoply of rights and obligations which cut across all domains of activity. Such 'totalistic' conceptions of membership in a community fail to grasp the way the political sphere is necessarily differentiated in the modern world from both economic and ethical-religious realms. In contemporary industrial societies the political system is no longer undifferentiated and universal. Accordingly, modern citizenship implies 'a selective participation' of citizens in the 'artificial and partial dimension of politics'. Today, after the collapse of socialism and the assault on total or organismic conceptions of political life, the democratic task is to try 'to combine civil, political and social rights with the market economy without subordinating democratic values to the competitive and acquisitive logic of the market'. Clues as to how this might be achieved can be found, Zolo suggests, in an examination of the internal difficulties and functional tensions of modern citizenship: between, for instance, 'negative liberties' such as privacy and habeas corpus and 'acquisitive liberties' like liberty of contract and ownership of private property; between 'positive liberty' (or individual autonomy) and political liberties including freedom of association and of the press; and between the rights of the citizens of a country and the 'cosmopolitan rights' of foreign people. Exploring these tensions, and not covering them up, provides the best hope, Zolo maintains, of mapping out new possibilities for democratic politics.

The final part of *Prospects for Democracy* consists of six chapters which focus on the conditions for the successful development and consolidation of democracy, examining the changing balance of political risks and potentialities. Most of the contributors in this section agree that it is a highly appropriate time to reflect upon the future of democracy across the globe. However, they also acknowledge that these are difficult times in which to pose fundamental questions about democracy: the rapidity and drama of recent historical change leave the political analyst with uncertain terms of reference. At this juncture, political investigation must be tentative and necessarily undogmatic.

One way to compensate for the uncertainty engendered by recent events is to take an historical and comparative view of the development of democracy. Accordingly, John Hall, in the opening chapter of this part, begins by reflecting on three of the initial attempts, two successful (Britain and the United States) and one failed (Germany prior to the Second World War), at consolidating democracy. From these cases, he draws out a number of 'enabling factors' which have been central to the successful consolidation of democracies, including the 'sequence' of change (the entrenchment of liberalism, for example, prior to democratization); the dispersion of property (the higher the concentration of property, the less likely is the establishment of democratic rule); a modern state with a professional army (authoritarian rule tends to persist if it is backed by repressive forces capable of destroying dissent and if elements of these forces have an integral role within the political elite); the impact of particular international conditions and processes (from the consequences of war to the attitudes of international lending agencies); the presence of strong and independent social groups in civil society; and a culture of 'civility'. While these and related factors have often had an 'interlinked and mutually supporting' role in the development of democracy, they do not necessarily lead to its consolidation: a great deal of scope is left for 'the exercise of political skill and judgement'. Nevertheless, Hall examines the particular forms and contributions of the enabling factors in diverse settings, from Latin America to Asia. He concludes by upholding 'a careful and limited optimism' about the prospects for democracy, but recognizes the possibility of diverse and deeply contested political outcomes in different regions and contexts.

Noting that any attempt 'to predict the course of events in contemporary Eastern Europe is hazardous in the extreme', Paul Lewis in the chapter which follows examines the particular historical legacy that bears on contemporary Eastern Europe, and the dynamics both of the immediate transition from communist to non-communist rule and of the experiences of the early post-communist period. Even without fundamental problems of state formation and territorial realignment – problems facing Yugoslavia and the former Soviet Union – the obstacles to democratization are formidable. Historical experience of democratic practices has been limited; civil society remains frail and fragile; tensions persist between social forces and movements (so effective in some respects against communism) and the establishment of a pluralist and 'civil' polity; political elites are often fragmented and charged with enormous tasks they are ill prepared for (the creation of political democracy *and* a market society); and democratic political institutions – legislatures, party structures and so on – are only in the earliest stages of their entrenchment. While the political situation remains 'an unstable

one' and the process of democratization 'threatens to stall', the political
trajectories of East European countries are likely to vary, with some
facing brighter prospects for a democratic transition – notably Czechoslovakia, Hungary and Poland – than others.

The following chapter by Laurence Whitehead provides a quite
different context for reflecting on the development of liberal democracy
and alternatives to it. Whitehead notes that in Latin America a variety of
political regimes are likely to continue to be found. But he also notes that
explicitly anti-democratic ideologies and systems of government are in
retreat and seem 'unlikely to return'. Moreover, he contends that while
'consolidated' liberal democracies may well emerge, there will be many
obstacles to be overcome if they are to be sustained. In addition, he
argues, although liberal democracy may well be consolidated in Latin
America in the medium term, its meaning might vary considerably in
different countries and contexts; there will be many competing projects,
all seeking to be labelled 'liberal democracy'.

In the countries of the sub-Sahara, the establishment of the democratic
accountability of the state has been fraught with difficulties, as Geoffrey
Hawthorn illustrates in chapter 16. Where the boundaries of the state
rarely correspond to the boundaries of any state that existed before
colonization, where there is no 'established habit' of exercising central
control and accepting its role, where 'cultures of accountability' have
been provincial (found in local associations of 'those who have lived and
worked together and shared a vernacular'), and where some of the most
basic human securities have often been absent, the hopes for even a
'minimal democracy' (involving a regular competition for power, agreement on the rules of such competition and acceptance of the outcome)
are far from high. But this does not mean that there is 'no hope'.
Hawthorn argues that local associations, with their distinctive forms of
accountability, could be nurtured and developed. While the exact shape
of such a democracy is obscure, democracy might be recovered in Africa
at just that moment at which the sovereign nation-state – due to widespread acknowledgement of the limits of sovereignty and the practical
bankruptcy of many African economies – 'ceases to be the frame' in
which it is achieved. While there is a notable irony here, the situation is
not without opportunities. The prospects for democratic recovery in
Africa are better if the associations so often dismissed in pre-colonial,
colonial and post-colonial Africa as 'primordial, parochial and divisive'
are put once again at the centre of political life and strategy.

Exploring the dynamics of democratization in Asia, David Potter, in
chapter 17, seeks to show that while leadership, cultural values, chance
and error have a place in the exploration of the fate of democracy, the key

factors relate to the changing balance of class, state and transnational power structures created by the historical trajectories of capitalist development in particular countries. Distinguishing between formal democracy (including competition for political offices via regular elections, civil and political liberties, a multi-party system) and substantive democracy (including the institutions of formal democracy plus broad-based participation in rule by the majority of citizens), Potter argues that there is nothing 'automatic' about capitalist development leading in a democratic direction – of a formal let alone a substantive type. However, the social basis of authoritarian state structures, as well as the structures themselves, can be weakened by capitalist industrialization, by new patterns of class formation engendered by it, and by transnational pressures which can build on regimes committed to economic liberalization and a role in the international division of labour. Authoritarian state forms can also be weakened by economic crisis, experienced by many Asian countries from the late 1970s and early 1980s. Potter examines the effects of these and related developments through comparative evidence from all Asian polities, but considers in particular Indonesia, South Korea and India, and the democratic prospects of Asia's Communist Party mobilization regimes. He finds that although the structural context for democratization is not promising in several countries, and capitalist development is a formidable obstacle to anything more than formal democracy, 'mass organizations and participative modes of political life' may 'push democracy further', especially in post-communist regimes.

Why is there so little democracy in the Middle East? This question can only be satisfactorily addressed if, as Simon Bromley contends in the final chapter of this volume, the structural specificity of 'capitalist democracy' as a form of rule is recognized. There are two essential conditions of such democracy: first, the state apparatus must be able 'to uphold its authority and monopoly of coercion' and, secondly, there must be 'a significant degree of separation' between the institutions of political rule and the actual mechanisms by which dominant economic classes appropriate the surplus generated by direct producers. Without the differentiation of the means of administration and appropriation, dominant classes will oppose the development of 'a sovereign public sphere . . . formally responsible to elected decision-makers'. Even if these two essential conditions are present, however, democracy does not necessarily follow. In an argument similar to that of David Potter, Bromley suggests that democratic consolidation also depends on the formation of particular types of class coalition and specific patterns of economic development. Bromley proceeds to examine the formation of the social structures of the

Middle East, focusing on the ways in which such structures have been re-composed at the intersection of indigenous developments with the world market and state system. Against this background, particular projects of state construction are examined, notably in Turkey, Egypt, Iraq, Saudi Arabia and Iran. Bromley shows that the two fundamental preconditions for democratic development – concentration of the means of coercion and authority; separation of the means of administration from routine forms of economic appropriation – have been absent from much of the region for most of the post-war period. Furthermore, the scale of resources devoted 'to the imposition of state authority has often blocked the potential for future democratization'. Within this context, the changing location and role of Islam are assessed; and what is often referred to erroneously as 'Islamic fundamentalism' is argued to be, in fact, 'a form of populist mobilization . . . against foreign influence and a failed political establishment'. Bromley concludes that it is problems of state-building and economic development, rather than 'religion', which make 'the prospects for democracy in the Middle East so bleak'.

In sum, *Prospects for Democracy* provides a wide-ranging overview of the theoretical debates about democracy, of the diverse circumstances in which democracy has developed, and of the conditions which are likely to affect its future course. The explosion of interest in democracy in recent times has all too often conceived of democracy in terms of liberal democracy, assumed that democracy can only be applied to 'governmental affairs' and has no place in economic, social and cultural spheres, presupposed that the nation-state is the most appropriate locus for democracy, and taken for granted that democracy is an achievement of the west and sustainable only under the cultural conditions of western life styles. These terms of reference are all challenged in this volume. By calling them into question, *Prospects for Democracy* advances our understanding of the meaning and possibilities of democracy and shifts the debate about the future of democracy on to new ground. Of course, to challenge is not to resolve all the deep and complex difficulties, many highlighted in the chapters that follow, which stand in the way of recasting democratic theory and practice. But certainly the editor does not appear to be alone in thinking that democracy has to be extended and deepened within and between countries if it is to retain its relevance in the next century.

Part I

Introduction

1

DEMOCRACY: FROM CITY-STATES TO A COSMOPOLITAN ORDER?

David Held

Democracy seems to have scored an historic victory over alternative forms of governance.[1] Nearly everyone today professes to be a democrat. Political regimes of all kinds throughout the world claim to be democracies. Yet what these regimes say and do is often substantially different from one to another. Democracy bestows an aura of legitimacy on modern political life: laws, rules and policies appear justified when they are 'democratic'. But it was not always so. The great majority of political thinkers from ancient Greece to the present day have been highly critical of the theory and practice of democracy. A uniform commitment to democracy is a very recent phenomenon. Moreover, democracy is a remarkably difficult form of government to create and sustain. The history of twentieth-century Europe alone makes this clear: fascism, Nazism and Stalinism came very close to obliterating democracy altogether.

Against this background, it is unsettling that some recent political commentators have proclaimed (by means of a phrase borrowed most notably from Hegel) the 'end of history' – the triumph of the west over all political and economic alternatives. The revolutions which swept across Central and Eastern Europe at the end of 1989 and the beginning of 1990 stimulated an atmosphere of celebration. Liberal democracy was championed as the agent of progress, and capitalism as the only viable economic system: ideological conflict, it was said, is being steadily displaced by universal democratic reason and market-orientated thinking.[2] But such a view is quite inadequate in a number of respects.

In the first instance, the 'liberal' component of liberal democracy cannot be treated simply as a unity. There are distinctive liberal traditions which embody quite different conceptions from each other of the individual agent, of autonomy, of the rights and duties of subjects, and of the proper nature and form of community. In addition, the 'celebratory' view of liberal democracy neglects to explore whether there are any tensions, or even perhaps contradictions, between the 'liberal' and 'democratic' components of liberal democracy; for example, between the liberal preoccupation with individual rights or 'frontiers of freedom' which 'nobody should be permitted to cross', and the democratic concern for the regulation of individual and collective action; that is, for public accountability.[3] Those who have written at length on this question have frequently resolved it in quite different directions. Furthermore, there is not simply one institutional form of liberal democracy. Contemporary democracies have crystallized into a number of different types, which makes any appeal to a liberal position vague at best.[4] An uncritical affirmation of liberal democracy essentially leaves unanalysed the whole meaning of democracy and its possible variants.

This chapter seeks to address this lacuna, first, by examining the development of different models of democracy; secondly, by considering the conditions of application of these models; thirdly, by exploring the meaning of democracy in the context of the progressive enmeshment today of states and societies in regional and global networks; and finally, by assessing the proper form and scope of democracy in relation to systems of international governance. The first two sets of issues will be examined in the next section, and the second two sets in the subsequent one. It will be argued, ultimately, that democracy can result from, and only from, a nucleus, or federation, of democratic states and societies. Or, to put the point differently, national democracies require international democracy if they are to be sustained and developed in the contemporary era. Paradoxically, perhaps, democracy has to be extended and deepened within and between countries for it to retain its relevance in the twenty-first century.

If the case for rethinking democracy in relation to the interconnectedness of states and societies is established successfully, a new agenda will have been created for democratic theory and practice. It is important to be clear about the meaning of 'new' in this context. The agenda will not be new in the sense of being without precedent; others before have sought to understand the impact of the international order on the form and operation of domestic politics within democratic states. Others before have also sought to set out the normative implications of changes in the international order for the role and nature of democratic government. Nor will the agenda be new in the sense that traditional questions of democratic theory will be wholly displaced. On the contrary, questions will remain about the proper form of citizenship, the nature of individual rights and duties and the extent of participation and representation, for instance. But the agenda will be new to the extent that the case is made that a theory of democracy (whether focusing on philosophical or empirical-analytic concerns) requires a theory of the interlocking processes and structures of the global system. For a theory of democracy must offer, it will be maintained, an account both of the changing meaning of democracy within the global order and of the impact of the global order on the development of democratic associations. Democratic institutions and practices have to be articulated with the complex arena of national and international politics, and the mutual interpenetration of the national and international must be mapped. Political understanding, and the successful pursuit of democratic political theory, are dependent on the outcome of these tasks.[5] Before pursuing them, however, the concept of democracy itself requires some clarification.

Models of Democracy

Within the history of democratic theory lies a deeply rooted conflict about whether democracy should mean some kind of popular power (a form of politics in which citizens are engaged in self-government and self-regulation) or an aid to decision-making (a means of conferring authority on those periodically voted into office). This conflict has given rise to three basic variants or models of democracy, which it is as well to bear in mind. First, there is direct or participatory democracy, a system of decision-making about public affairs in which citizens are directly involved. This was the 'original' type of democracy found in ancient Athens, among other places. Secondly, there is liberal or representative democracy, a system of rule embracing elected 'officers' who undertake to 'represent' the interests or views of citizens within the framework of the 'rule of law'. Thirdly, there is a variant of democracy based on a one-party model (although some may doubt whether this is a form of democracy at all). Until recently, the Soviet Union, East European societies and many third world countries have been dominated by this conception. The following discussion deals briefly with each of these models in turn, developing concepts and issues which will be drawn upon in later argument.

The active citizen and republican government

Athenian democracy has long been taken as a fundamental source of inspiration for modern western political thought. This is not to say that the west has been right to trace many elements of its democratic heritage exclusively to Athens; for, as recent historical and archaeological research has shown, some of the key political innovations, both conceptual and institutional, of the nominally western political tradition can be traced to older civilizations in the east. The city-state or *polis* society, for example, existed in Mesopotamia long before it emerged in the west.[6] None the less, the political ideals of Athens – equality among citizens, liberty, respect for the law and justice – have been taken as integral to western political thinking, and it is for this reason that Athens constitutes a useful starting point.

The Athenian city-state, ruled as it was by citizen-governors, did not differentiate between state and society. In ancient Athens, citizens were at one and the same time subjects of political authority and the creators of public rules and regulations. The people (*demos*) engaged in legislative and judicial functions, for the Athenian concept of citizenship entailed their taking a share in these functions, participating *directly* in the affairs of 'the state'.[7] Athenian democracy required a general commitment to the principle of civic virtue: dedication to the republican city-state and the subordination of private life to public affairs and the common good. 'The public' and 'the private' were intertwined. Citizens could properly fulfil themselves and live honourably only in and through the *polis*. Of course, who was to count as a citizen was a tightly restricted matter; among the excluded were women and a substantial slave population.

The Athenian city-state – eclipsed ultimately by the rise of empires, stronger states and military regimes – shared features with republican Rome. Both were predominantly face-to-face societies and oral cultures; both had elements of popular participation in governmental affairs, and both had little, if any, centralized bureaucratic control. Furthermore, both sought to foster a deep sense of public duty, a tradition of civic virtue or responsibility to 'the republic' – to the distinctive matters of the public realm. And in both polities, the claims of the state were given a unique priority over those of the individual citizen. But if Athens was a democratic republic, contemporary scholarship generally affirms that Rome was, by comparison, an essentially oligarchical system.[8] Nevertheless, from antiquity, it was Rome which was to prove the most durable influence on the dissemination of republican ideas.

Classical republicanism received its most robust restatement in the early Renaissance, especially in the city-states of Italy. The meaning of the concept of 'active citizenship in a republic' became a leading concern. Political thinkers of this period were critical of the Athenian formulation of this notion; shaped as their views were by Aristotle, one of the most notable critics of Greek democracy, and by the centuries-long impact of republican Rome, they recast the republican tradition. While the concept of the *polis* remained central to the political theory of Italian cities, most notably in Florence, it was no longer regarded as a means to self-fulfilment.[9] Emphasis continued to be placed on the importance of civic virtue but the latter was understood as highly fragile, subject particularly to corruption if dependent solely upon the political involvement of any one major grouping: the people, the aristocracy or the monarchy. A constitution which could reflect and balance the interests of all leading political factions became an aspiration. Niccolò Machiavelli thus argued that all singular constitutional forms (monarchy, aristocracy and democracy) were unstable, and only a governmental system combining elements of each could promote the kind of political culture on which civic virtue depends.[10] The best example of such a government was, he proclaimed, Rome: Rome's mixed government (with its system of consuls, Senate and tribunes of the people) was directly linked to its sustained achievements.

The core of the Renaissance republican case was that the freedom of a political community rested upon its accountability to no authority other than that of the community itself. Self-government is the basis of liberty, together with the right of citizens to participate – within a constitutional framework which creates distinct roles for leading social forces – in the government of their own common business.[11] As one commentator put it, 'the community as a whole must retain the ultimate sovereign authority', assigning its various rulers or chief magistrates 'a status no higher than that of elected officials'.[12] Such 'rulers' must ensure the effective enforcement of the laws created by the community for the promotion of its own good; for they are not rulers in a traditional sense, but 'agents or *ministri* of justice'.

In Renaissance republicanism, as well as in Greek democratic thought, a citizen was someone who participated in 'giving judgement and holding office'.[13] Citizenship meant participation in public affairs. This definition is noteworthy because it suggests that theorists within these traditions would have found it hard to locate citizens in modern democracies, except perhaps as representatives or office holders. The limited scope in contemporary politics for the active involvement of citizens would have been regarded as most undemocratic.[14] Yet the idea that human beings should be active citizens of a political order – citizens of their states – and not merely dutiful subjects of a ruler has had few advocates from the earliest human associations to the early Renaissance.[15]

The demise in the west of the idea of the active citizen, one whose very being is affirmed in and through political action, is hard to explain fully. But it is clear enough that the antithesis of *homo politicus* is the *homo credens* of the Christian faith: the citizen whose active judgement is essential is displaced by the true believer.[16] Although it would be quite misleading to suggest that the rise of Christianity effectively banished secular considerations from the lives of rulers and ruled, it unquestionably shifted the source of authority and wisdom from this-worldly to other-worldly representatives. During the Middle Ages, the integration of Christian Europe came to depend above all on two theocratic authorities: the Roman Catholic Church and the Holy Roman Empire. There was no theoretical alternative to their account of the nature of power and rule.[17] Not until the end of the sixteenth century, when it became apparent that religion had become a highly divisive force and that the powers of the state would have to be separated from the duty of rulers to uphold any particular faith, did the nature and limits of political authority, law, rights and obedience become a preoccupation of European political thought from Italy to England.[18]

Liberal representative democracy

Modern liberal and liberal democratic theories have constantly sought to justify the sovereign power of the state while at the same time justifying limits on that power.[19] The history of this attempt since Thomas Hobbes is the history of arguments to balance might and right, power and law, duties and rights. On the one hand, states must have a monopoly of coercive power in order to provide a secure basis on which trade, commerce, religion and family life can prosper. On the other hand, by granting the state a regulatory and coercive capability, political theorists were aware that they had accepted a force that could, and frequently did, deprive citizens of political and social freedoms.

Liberal democrats provided the key institutional innovation to try to overcome this dilemma: representative democracy. The liberal concern with reason, law and freedom of choice could only be upheld properly by recognizing the political equality of all mature individuals. Such equality would ensure not only a secure social environment in which people would be free to pursue their private activities and interests, but also a state which, under the watchful eye of the electorate, would do what was best in the general or public interest. Thus, liberal democrats argued, the democratic constitutional state, linked to other key institutional mechanisms, particularly the free market, would resolve the problems of ensuring both authority and liberty.

Two classic statements of the new position can be found in the philosophy of James Madison and in the work of one of the key figures of nineteenth-century English liberalism: Jeremy Bentham. In Madison's account, 'pure democracies' (by which he means societies 'consisting of a small number of citizens, who assemble and administer the government in person') have always been intolerant, unjust and unstable.[20] By contrast, representative government overcomes the excesses of 'pure democracy' because regular elections force a clarification of public issues, and the elected few, able to withstand the political process, are likely to be competent and capable of 'discerning the true interest of their country'.

The central concern of Madison's argument is not the rightful place of the active citizen in the life of the political community but, instead, the legitimate pursuit by individuals of their interests, and government as a means for the enhancement of these interests. Although Madison himself sought clear ways of reconciling particular interests with what he called modern 'extended republics', his position signals a clear shift from the classical ideals of civic virtue and the public realm to liberal preoccupations.[21] He conceived of the representative state as the chief mechanism to aggregate individuals' interests and to protect their rights. In such a state, he believed, security of person and property would be sustained and politics could be made compatible with the demands of large nation-states, with their complex patterns of trade, commerce and international relations.[22]

In parallel with this view, Bentham held that representative democracy 'has for its characteristic object and effect ... securing its members against oppression and depredation at the hands of those functionaries which it employs for its defence'.[23] Democratic government is required to protect citizens from the despotic use of political power, whether it be by a monarch, the aristocracy or other groups. The representative state thus becomes an umpire or referee while individuals pursue in civil society, according to the rules of economic competition and free exchange, their own interests. The free vote and the free market are both essential, for a key presupposition is that the collective good can be properly realized in most domains of life only if individuals interact in competitive exchanges, pursuing their utility with minimal state interference. Significantly, however, this argument has another side. Tied to the advocacy of a 'minimal state', whose scope and power need to be strictly limited, there is a strong commitment to certain types of state intervention: for instance, to regulate the behaviour of the disobedient, and to reshape social relations and institutions if, in the event of the failure of *laissez-faire*, the greatest happiness of the greatest number is not achieved – the only scientifically defensible criterion, Bentham held, of the public good.

From classical antiquity to the seventeenth century, democracy was largely associated with the gathering of citizens in assemblies and public meeting places. By the early nineteenth century it was beginning to be thought of as the right of citizens to participate in the determination of the collective will through the medium of elected representatives.[24] The theory of representative democracy fundamentally shifted the terms of reference of democratic thought: the practical limits that a sizeable citizenry imposes on democracy, which had been the focus of so much critical (anti-democratic) attention, were practically eliminated. Representative democracy could now be celebrated as both accountable and feasible government, potentially stable over great territories and time spans.[25] It could even be heralded, as James Mill put it, as 'the grand discovery of modern times' in which 'the solution of all difficulties, both speculative and practical, will be found'.[26] Accordingly, the theory and practice of popular government shook off its traditional association with small states and cities, opening itself to become the legitimating creed of the emerging world of nation-states. But who exactly was to count as a legitimate participant, or a 'citizen' or 'individual', and what his or her exact role was to be in this new order, remained either unclear or unsettled. Even in the work of the enlightened John Stuart Mill ambiguities remained: the idea that all citizens should have equal political weight in the polity remained outside his actual doctrine, along with that of most of his contemporaries.[27]

It was left by and large to the extensive and often violently suppressed struggles of working-class and feminist activists in the nineteenth and twentieth centuries to accomplish a genuinely universal suffrage in some countries. Their achievement was to remain fragile in places such as Germany, Italy and Spain, and was in practice denied to some groups, for instance, many African-Americans in the US before the civil rights movement in the 1950s and 1960s. However, through these struggles the idea that the rights of citizenship should apply equally to all adults became slowly established; many of the arguments of the liberal democrats could be turned against existing institutions to reveal the extent to which the principles and aspirations of equal political participation and equal human development remained unfulfilled. It was only with the actual achievement of citizenship for all adult men and women that liberal democracy took on its distinctively contemporary form: a cluster of rules and institutions permitting the broadest participation of the majority of citizens in the selection of representatives who alone can make political decisions (that is, decisions affecting the whole community).

This cluster includes elected government; free and fair elections in which every citizen's vote has an equal weight; a suffrage which embraces all citizens irrespective of distinctions of race, religion, class, sex and so on; freedom of conscience, information and expression on all public matters broadly defined; the right of all adults to oppose their government and stand for office; and associational autonomy – the right to form independent associations including social movements, interest groups and political parties.[28] The consolidation of representative democracy, thus understood, has been a twentieth-century phenomenon; perhaps one should even say a late twentieth-century phenomenon. For it is only in the closing decades of this century that democracy has been securely established in the west and widely adopted in principle as a suitable model of government beyond the west.

Marxism and one-party democracy

The struggle of liberalism against tyranny, and the struggle by liberal democrats for political equality, represented a major step forward in the history of human emancipation, as Karl Marx and Friedrich Engels readily acknowledged. But for them, and for the Marxist tradition more broadly, the great universal ideals of 'liberty, equality and justice' cannot be realized simply by the 'free' struggle for votes in the political system together with the 'free' struggle for profit in the market-place. Advocates of the democratic state and the market economy present these institutions as the only ones under which liberty can be sustained and inequalities minimized. However, according to the Marxist critique, the capitalist economy, by virtue of its internal dynamics, inevitably produces systematic inequality and massive restrictions on real freedom. The formal existence of certain liberties is of little value if they cannot be exercised in practice. Therefore, although each step towards formal political equality is an advance, its liberating potential is severely curtailed by inequalities of class.

In class societies the state cannot become the vehicle for the pursuit of the common good or public interest. Far from playing the role of emancipator, protective knight, umpire or judge in the face of disorder, the agencies of the liberal representative state are enmeshed in the struggles of civil society. Marxists conceive of the state as an extension of civil society, reinforcing the social order for the enhancement of particular interests. Their argument is that political emancipation is only a step towards human emancipation: that is, the complete democratization of both society and the state. In their view, liberal democratic society fails when judged by its own promises.

Among these promises are, first, political participation, or general involvement mediated by representatives in decisions affecting the whole community; secondly, accountable government; and thirdly, freedom to protest and reform.[29] But 'really existing liberal democracy', as one Marxist recently put it, fails to deliver on any of these promises. For it is distinguished by the existence of a largely passive citizenry (significant numbers of eligible citizens do not vote in elections, for example); by the erosion and displacement of parliamentary institutions by unelected centres of power (typified by the expansion of bureaucratic authority and of the role of functional representatives); and by substantial structural constraints on state action and, in particular, on the possibility of the piecemeal reform of capitalism (the flight of capital, for example, is a constant threat to elected governments with strong programmes of social reform).[30]

Marx himself envisaged the replacement of the liberal democratic state by a 'commune structure': the smallest communities, which were to administer their own affairs, would elect delegates to larger administrative units (districts, towns); these in turn would elect candidates to still larger areas of administration (the national delegation).[31] This arrangement is known as the 'pyramid' structure of 'delegative democracy': all delegates are revocable, bound by the instructions of their constituency, and organized into a 'pyramid' of directly elected committees. The post-capitalist state would not, therefore, bear any resemblance to a liberal, parliamentary regime. All state agencies would be brought within the sphere of a single set of directly accountable institutions. Only when this happens will 'that self-reliance, that freedom, which disappeared from earth with the Greeks, and vanished into the blue haze of heaven with Christianity', as the young Marx put it, gradually be restored.[32]

In the Marxist-Leninist account, the system of delegative democracy is to be complemented, in principle, by a separate but somewhat similar system at the level of the Communist Party. The transition to socialism and communism necessitates the 'professional' leadership of a disciplined cadre of revolutionaries.[33] Only such a leadership has the capacity to organize the defence of the revolution against counter-revolutionary forces, to plan the expansion of the forces of production, and to supervise the reconstruction of society. Since all fundamental differences of interest are class interests, since the working-class interest (or standpoint) is the progressive interest in society, and since during and after the revolution it has to be articulated clearly and decisively, a revolutionary party is essential. The party is the instrument which can create the framework for socialism and communism. In practice, the party has to rule; and it was only in the 'Gorbachev era' in the Soviet Union (from 1984 to August 1991) that a pyramid of councils, or 'Soviets', from the central authority to those at local village and neighbourhood level, was given anything more than a symbolic or ritualistic role in the post-revolutionary period.

Democracy, the state, and civil society

What should be made of these various models of democracy in contemporary circumstances? The classical participatory model cannot easily be adapted to stretch across space and time. Its emergence in the context of city-states, and under conditions of 'social exclusivity', was an integral part of its successful development. In complex industrial societies, marked by a high degree of social, economic and political differentiation, it is very hard to envisage how a democracy of this kind could succeed on a large scale.

The significance of these reflections is reinforced by examining the fate of the conception of democracy advocated by Marx and Engels and their followers. In the first instance, the 'deep structure' of Marxist categories – with its emphasis on the centrality of class, the universal standpoint of the proletariat, and a conception of politics which is rooted squarely in production – ignores or severely underestimates the contributions to politics of other forms of social structure, collectivity, agency, identity, interest and knowledge. Secondly, as an institutional arrangement that allows for mediation, negotiation and compromise among struggling factions, groups or movements, the Marxist model does not stand up well under scrutiny, especially in its Marxist-Leninist form. A system of institutions to promote discussion, debate and competition among divergent views – a system encompassing the formation of movements, pressure groups and/or political parties with independent leaderships to help press their cases – appears both necessary and desirable. Further, the changes in Central and Eastern Europe after 1989 seem to provide remarkable confirmatory evidence of this, with their emphasis on the importance of political and civil rights, a competitive party system, and the 'rolling back of the state' – that is, the freeing of civil society from state domination.

One cannot escape the necessity, therefore, of recognizing the importance of a number of fundamental liberal tenets, concerning the centrality, in principle, of an 'impersonal' structure of public power, of a constitution to help guarantee and protect rights, of a diversity of power centres within and outside the state, and of mechanisms to promote competition and debate among alternative political platforms. What this amounts to, among other things, is confirmation of the fundamental liberal notion that the 'separation' of state from civil society must be an essential element of any democratic political order. Conceptions of democracy that depend on the assumption that the state could ever replace civil society, or vice versa, must be treated with caution.

To make these points is not, however, to affirm any one liberal democratic model as it stands, although many advocates of democracy appear to take this view. It is one thing to accept the arguments concerning the necessary protective, conflict-mediating and redistributive functions of the democratic state, quite another to accept these as prescribed in existing accounts of liberal democracy. Advocates of liberal democracy have tended to be concerned, above all else, with the proper principles and procedures of democratic government. But by focusing on 'government', they have drawn attention away from a thorough examination of the relation between formal rights and actual rights; between commitments to treat citizens as free and equal and practices which do neither sufficiently; between concepts of the state as, in principle, an independent authority, and state involvement in the reproduction of the inequalities of everyday life; between notions of political parties as appropriate structures for bridging the gap between state and society, and the array of power centres which such parties and their leaders cannot reach. To ignore these questions is to risk the establishment of 'democracy' in the context of a sea of political, economic and social inequality. And it is to risk the creation of, at best, a very partial form of democratic politics – a form of politics in which the involvement of some bears a direct relation to the limited participation or non-participation of others.

The implications of these points are, I believe, of considerable significance. For democracy to flourish it has to be reconceived as a double-sided phenomenon: concerned, on the one hand, with the reform of state power and, on the other hand, with the restructuring of civil society. This entails recognizing the indispensability of a process of what I have elsewhere called 'double democratization': the interdependent transformation of both state and civil society.[34] Such a process must be premised on the principles that the division between state and civil society must be a central aspect of democratic life, and that the power to make decisions must be free of the inequalities and constraints which can be imposed by an unregulated system of private capital, as Marx foresaw. But, of course, to recognize the importance of both these points is to recognize the necessity of recasting substantially their traditional connotations.[35]

In short, if democratic life involves no more than a periodic vote, citizens' activities will be largely confined to the 'private' realm of civil society and the scope of their actions will depend largely on the resources they can command. Few opportunities will exist for citizens to act as citizens; that is, as participants in public life. But if democracy is understood as a double-sided process, this state of affairs might be redressed by creating opportunities for people to establish themselves 'in their capacity of being citizens'.[36] The 'active citizen' could once again return to the centre of public life, involving him- or herself in the realms of both state and civil society. Of course, the nature of this involvement would differ in each of these realms, according to its organizational and institutional features. But opportunities will at least have been created for all those affected by the decision-making structures of their communities to participate in the latters' regulation – or so the story of democracy has so far suggested. However, democracy has another side.

Democracy, Globalization and International Governance

Throughout the nineteenth and twentieth centuries democratic theory has tended to assume a 'symmetrical' and 'congruent' relationship between political decision-makers and the recipients of political decisions.[37] In fact, symmetry and congruence have often been taken for granted at two crucial points: first, between citizen-voters and the decision-makers whom they are, in principle, able to hold to account; and secondly, between the 'output' (decisions, policies, and so on) of decision-makers and their constituents – ultimately, 'the people' in a delimited territory.

Even the critics of modern democracies have tended to share this assumption; following the narrative of democracy as conventionally told, they have thought of the problem of political accountability as, above all, a national problem. Contemporary representative structures are, they hold, insufficiently responsive to their citizens; and, in discussing various forms of participatory democracy, or contemporary interpretations of the relevance of republicanism, they place emphasis on making the political process more transparent and intelligible, more open to, and reflective of, the heterogeneous wants and needs of 'the people'.[38]

But the problem, for defenders and critics alike of modern democratic systems, is that regional and global interconnectedness contests the traditional national resolutions of the key questions of democratic theory and practice. The very process of governance can escape the reach of the nation-state. National communities by no means exclusively make and determine decisions and policies for themselves, and governments by no means determine what is right or appropriate exclusively for their own citizens.[39] To take some recent examples: a decision to increase interest rates in an attempt to stem inflation or exchange-rate instability is most often taken as a 'national' decision, although it may well stimulate economic changes in other countries. Similarly, a decision to permit the 'harvesting' of the rainforests may contribute to ecological damage far beyond the borders which formally limit the responsibility of a given set of political decision-makers. These decisions, along with policies on issues as diverse as investment, arms procurement and AIDS, are typically regarded as falling within the legitimate domain of authority of a sovereign nation-state. Yet, in a world of regional and global inter-connectedness, there are major questions to be put about the coherence, viability and accountability of national decision-making entities them-selves.

Further, decisions made by quasi-regional or quasi-supranational organizations such as the European Community, the North Atlantic Treaty Organization or the International Monetary Fund diminish the range of decisions open to given national 'majorities'. The idea of a community which rightly governs itself and determines its own future – an idea at the very heart of the democratic polity itself – is, accordingly, today deeply problematic. Any simple assumption in democratic theory that political relations are, or could be, 'symmetrical' or 'congruent' appears unjustified.

If the inadequacy of this assumption can be fully shown, issues are raised which go to the heart of democratic thought. The idea that *consent* legitimates government and the state system more generally has been central to nineteenth- and twentieth-century liberal democrats.[40] The latter have focused on the ballot box as the mechanism whereby the individual citizen expresses political preferences and citizens as a whole periodically confer authority on government to enact laws and regulate economic and social life. The principle of 'majority rule', or the principle that decisions which accrue the largest number of votes should prevail, is at the root of the claim of political decisions to be regarded as worthy or legitimate.[41] But the very idea of consent through elections, and the particular notion that the relevant constituencies of voluntary agreement are the communities of a bounded territory or a state, become prob-lematic as soon as the issue of national, regional and global inter-connectedness is considered and the nature of a so-called 'relevant community' is contested. Whose consent is necessary and whose participation is justified in decisions concerning, for instance, AIDS, or acid rain, or the use of non-renewable resources? What is the relevant constituency: national, regional or international? To whom do decision-makers have to justify their decisions? To whom should they be accountable? Further, what are the implications for the idea of legitimate rule of decisions taken in polities, with potentially life-and-death consequences for large numbers of people, many of whom might have no democratic stake in the decision-making process?

Territorial boundaries demarcate the basis on which individuals are included in and excluded from participation in decisions affecting their lives (however limited the participation might be), but the outcomes of these decisions must often 'stretch' beyond national frontiers. The implications of this are considerable, not only for the categories of consent and legitimacy, but for all the key ideas of democracy: the nature of a constituency, the meaning of representation, the proper form and scope of political participation, and the relevance of the democratic nation-state, faced with unsettling patterns of relations and constraints in the international order, as the guarantor of the rights, duties and welfare of subjects. Of course, these considerations would probably come as little surprise to those nations and countries whose independence and identity have been deeply affected by the hegemonic reach of empires, old and new, but they do come as a surprise to many in the west.

In order to explore the significance of these matters further it is necessary to examine why for most of the nineteenth and twentieth centuries democracy *in* nation-states has not been accompanied by democratic relations *among* states; why the interstate system is now coming under pressure in a way which makes the relation between democracy within borders and democracy across borders a more urgent concern; why contemporary circumstances are creating the possibility of rethinking democracy at regional and global levels; and why democracy at such levels is an important condition for the development of democracy within local and national communities. I shall endeavour to show that democracy within a nation-state or region requires democracy within a network of interwoven international forces and relations; and that such a requirement is thwarted by the 'deep structure' of the sovereign state order and the grafting on to this structure of the United Nations system in the immediate aftermath of the Second World War. None the less, one can glimpse the possibility, I shall also seek to show, of an alternative to this state of affairs.

Sovereignty and the Westphalian order

The history of the modern interstate system, and of international relations more generally, has borne little relation to any democratic principle of organization. In the arena of world politics, Hobbes's way of thinking about power and power relations has often been regarded as the most insightful account of the meaning of the state at the global level.[42] Hobbes drew a comparison between international relations and the state of nature, describing the international system of states as being in a continuous 'posture of war'.[43] A war of 'all against all' is a constant threat, since each state is at liberty to act to secure its own interests unimpeded by any higher religious or moral strictures.

In the study of international affairs, Hobbes's account has become associated with the 'realist' theory of international politics.[44] Realism posits, in the spirit of Hobbes's work, that the system of sovereign states is inescapably anarchic in character; and that this anarchy forces all states, in the inevitable absence of any supreme arbiter to enforce moral behaviour and agreed international codes, to pursue power politics in order to attain their vital interests. This *realpolitik* view of states has had a significant influence on both the analysis and practice of international relations in recent times, as it offers a convincing *prima facie* explanation of the chaos and disorder of world affairs. In this account, the modern system of nation-states is a 'limiting factor' which will always thwart any attempt to conduct international relations in a manner which transcends the politics of the sovereign state.

A concomitant of each and every modern state's claim to supreme authority is a recognition that such a claim gives other states an equal entitlement to autonomy and respect within their own borders. In the context of the rapid erosion of 'Christian society' from the late sixteenth century, the development of sovereignty can be interpreted as part of a process of mutual recognition whereby states granted each other rights of jurisdiction in their respective territories and communities. Accordingly, sovereignty involved the assertion by the modern state of independence; that is, of its possession of sole rights to jurisdiction over a particular people and territory. And in the world of relations among states, the principle of the sovereign equality of all states gradually became adopted as the paramount principle governing the formal conduct of states towards one another, however representative or unrepresentative were their particular regimes.

The conception of international order which emerged to clarify and formalize the interstate system has been referred to as the 'Westphalian' model (after the Peace of Westphalia of 1648 which brought to an end the German phase of the Thirty Years War).[45] The model covers a period from 1648 to 1945 (although some would argue it still holds today).[46] It depicts the emergence of a world community consisting of sovereign states which settle their differences privately and often by force; which engage in diplomatic relations but otherwise minimal cooperation; which seek to place their own national interest above all others; and which accept the logic of the principle of effectiveness, that is, the principle that might eventually makes right in the international world – that appropriation becomes legitimation.[47] The model of Westphalia is summarized in table 1.1.[48]

TABLE 1.1   The Model of Westphalia

1   The world consists of, and is divided by, sovereign states which recognize no superior authority.
2   The processes of law-making, the settlement of disputes and law-enforcement are largely in the hands of individual states subject to the logic of 'the competitive struggle for power'.
3   Differences among states are often settled by force: the principle of effective power holds sway. Virtually no legal fetters exist to curb the resort to force; international legal standards afford minimal protection.
4   Responsibility for cross-border wrongful acts are a 'private matter' concerning only those affected; no collective interest in compliance with international law is recognized.
5   All states are regarded as equal before the law: legal rules do not take account of asymmetries of power.
6   International law is orientated to the establishment of minimal rules of coexistence; the creation of enduring relationships among states and peoples is an aim, but only to the extent that it allows national politcal objectives to be met.
7   The minimization of impediments on state freedom is the 'collective' priority.

This framework of international affairs had a lasting and paradoxical quality rich in implications: an increasingly developed and interlinked states system endorsed the right of each state to autonomous and independent action. As one commentator has aptly noted, the upshot of this was that states were 'not subject to international moral requirements because they represent separate and discrete political orders with no common authority among them'.[49] In this situation, the world consists of separate political powers, pursuing their own interests, backed ultimately by their organization of coercive power.[50]

The consolidation of the modern states system resulted from the expansion of Europe across the globe. If the Iberian monarchies led the early wave of 'European globalization', their position was eroded in the seventeenth century by the Dutch, and subsequently by the English. Key features of the modern states system – the centralization of political power, the

expansion of administrative rule, the legitimation of power through claims
to representation, the emergence of massed armies – which existed in
Europe in embryo in the sixteenth century, were to become prevalent
features of the entire global system.[51]

While the diffusion of European power mainly occurred through the
medium of sea-going military and commercial endeavours, Europe
became connected to a global system of trade and production relationships. At the centre of the latter were new and expanding capitalistic
economic mechanisms which had their origins in the sixteenth century,
or in what is sometimes called the 'long sixteenth century', running from
about 1450 to 1640.[52] Capitalism was from the beginning an international
affair:[53] capital never allowed its aspirations to be determined by national
boundaries alone. Consequently, the emergence of capitalism ushered in
a fundamental change in the world order: it made possible, for the first
time, genuinely global interconnections among states and societies; it
penetrated the distant corners of the world and brought far-reaching
changes to the dynamics and nature of political rule.

The development of the world capitalist economy initially took the
form of the expansion of market relations, driven by a growing need for
raw materials and other factors of production. Capitalism stimulated this
drive and was, in turn, stimulated by it. It is useful to make a distinction
between the expansion of capitalist market relations based on the desire
to buy, sell and accumulate mobile resources (capital), and the formation
of industrial capitalism involving highly distinctive class relations – based
initially on those who own and control the means of production and
those who have only their labouring capacity to sell. It is only with the
development of capitalism in Europe after 1500, and in particular with
the formation of the capitalist organization of production from the
middle of the eighteenth century, that the activities of capitalists and the
capitalist system began to converge.[54] From this period, the objectives of
war became linked to economic objectives: military endeavour and
conquest became more directly connected with the pursuit of economic
advantage than they had been in earlier periods.[55]

The globalization of economic life – broadly, the growth of complex
economic interconnections among states and societies – has not by any
means been, of course, a uniform process, affecting each region and
country in a similar way. From the outset, this process has involved great
costs for the autonomy and independence of many: for example, the
progressive collapse of non-European civilizations, among them the
Moslem, Indian and Chinese; the disorganizing effects of western rule on
a large number of small societies; and the interlinked degradation of the
non-European and European worlds caused by the slave trade. In fact,

globalization has been characterized both by 'hierarchy' and 'unevenness'.[56] Hierarchy denotes the structure of economic globalization: its
domination by those constellations of economic power concentrated in
the west and north. With the decline of Europe's empires in the
twentieth century, and the end of the Cold War, economic globalization
has arguably become more significant than ever as the determinant of
hierarchy, and the front line of geopolitics. It is likely that the economic
summits of the leading industrial countries will supplant superpower
summits as the primary arena within which to discern new contours of
hierarchy and power. While there may be uncertainty about the precise
distribution of influence at the centre of the advanced industrial countries, the hierarchical structure of the economic processes of globalization firmly places the leading economic powers of the west or north in
central positions.

The other side of hierarchy is unevenness. This refers to the asym-
metrical effects of economic globalization upon the life-chances and well-
being of peoples, classes, ethnic groupings, movements and the sexes.
The contours of these processes of 'unevenness' are not difficult to
discern, although they will not be documented here. They are broadly
correlated with geography, race and gender and, accordingly, with the
clusters of poverty and deprivation found among the countries of the
south, among non-whites and among women. However, the existence of
significant poverty in the north (in Europe and the US), the persistence of
unemployment in the most advanced industrial countries (even during
periods of marked growth), and the fate of many indigenous peoples
indicate the approximate nature of conceiving of unevenness in these
terms alone. Unevenness is a phenomenon of both international and
national development. The categories of social and political stratification
must, therefore, be thought of as denoting systematic divisions within
and across territories.[57]

The effective power which sovereignty bestows is, to a significant
degree, connected to the economic resources at the disposal of a state or
people. Clearly, the resources a polity can mobilize will vary according to
its position in the global structure of economic relations, its place in the
international division of labour, and the support it can muster from
regional economic networks.[58] The growing awareness in many western
countries that their sovereignty is under pressure from a variety of
sources and forces places before them (often for the first time) issues that
have been apparent to many countries for a long time. The struggle for
sovereignty and autonomy in many third world countries was closely
related to the struggle for freedom from colonial domination. *De jure*
sovereignty has been of the utmost importance to those countries that

had previously been denied it; but *de jure* sovereignty is not of course the same thing as *de facto* or practical sovereignty. The often weak and debt-ridden economies of many third world countries leave them vulnerable and dependent on economic forces and relations over which they have little, if any, control. Although the internationalization of production and finance places many instruments of economic control beyond even the most powerful countries, the position of those at the lower end of the globalization hierarchy, experiencing the worst effects of unevenness, is substantially worse.

Political independence often provides at best only a brief respite from the processes of marginalization in the world economy. In countries such as those of the sub-Sahara, where the boundaries of the state (with two small exceptions) do not correspond to the boundaries of any states that existed before colonization, where there has been no 'established habit' of exercising central authority and accepting its role, and where some of the most elementary human securities have often been absent, independence has been fraught with many types of difficulty.[59] Against this background, the achievement of any form of democracy is significant. Nevertheless, the achievement is handicapped by vulnerability to the international economy, by a fragile resource base which is threatening to the autonomy of political organizations, and by social groups often deeply divided by extreme poverty, hardship and ill-health as well as by ethnic, cultural and other considerations. In addition, it is handicapped by the very *structure* of the international political system which leaves individual states, locked into the competitive pursuit of their own security and interests, without systematic means to pursue the accountability and regulation of some of the most powerful forces ordering national and international affairs. It is political and economic might which ultimately determines the effective deployment of rules and resources within and across borders in the Westphalian world.

The international order and the United Nations Charter

The titanic struggles of the First and Second World Wars led to a grow-ing acknowledgement that the nature and process of international governance would have to change if the most extreme forms of violence against humanity were to be outlawed, and the growing interconnected-ness and interdependence of nations recognized. Slowly, the subject, scope and very sources of the Westphalian conception of international regulation, particularly its conception of international law, were all called into question.[60]

First and foremost, opinion moved against the doctrine that international law, as Oppenheim put it, is a 'law between states only and exclusively'.[61] Single persons and groups became recognized as subjects of international law. It is generally accepted, for example, that persons as individuals are subjects of international law on the basis of such documents as the Charters of the Nuremberg and Tokyo War Crimes Tribunals, the Universal Declaration of Human Rights of 1948, the Covenants on Civil and Political Rights of 1966, and the European Convention on Human Rights of 1950.

Opinion has also moved against the doctrine that international law is primarily about political and strategic (state) affairs. According to this position, international law is concerned progressively with orchestrating and regulating economic, social and environmental matters. Linked to substantial increases in the number of 'actors' in world politics – for example, the UN, the UN Economic and Social Council, UNCTAD, the World Bank, the International Monetary Fund, the Food and Agricultural Organization and the World Health Organization – there have been many pressures to increase the scope of international law. Faced with this development, there are those who characterize the changing reach of international law as being ever less concerned with the freedom or liberty of states, and ever more with the general welfare of all those in the global system who are able to make their voices count.[62]

Finally, the influential legal doctrine that the only true source of international law is the consent of states – either their expressed consent, or their implied consent – has been fundamentally challenged. Today, a number of sources of international law jostle for recognition. These include the traditional sources such as international conventions or treaties (general or particular) which are recognized by states; international custom or practice which provides evidence of an accepted rule or set of rules; and the underlying principles of law recognized by 'civilized nations'. They also include the 'will of the international community', which can assume the 'status of law' or be the 'basis of international legal obligation' under certain circumstances.[63] The latter represents a break in principle with the requirement of individual state consent in the making of international rules and responsibilities.[64]

Although the Westphalian model of international law had its critics throughout the modern era, particularly during the ill-fated efforts of the League of Nations, it was not until after the Second World War that a new model of international law and accountability was widely advocated and accepted, culminating in the adoption of the UN Charter. The image of international regulation projected by the Charter (and related documents) was one of 'states still jealously "sovereign"', but linked together in a 'myriad of relations'; under pressure to resolve disagreements by peaceful means and according to legal criteria; subject in principle to tight restrictions on the resort to force; and constrained to observe 'certain standards' with regard to the treatment of all persons on their territory, including their own citizens.[65] Of course, how restrictive the provisions of the Charter have been to states, and to what extent they have been actually operationalized, are important questions. Before addressing them, however, leading elements of the Charter model should be sketched (see table 1.2).[66]

TABLE 1.2   The UN Charter Model

1   The world community consists of sovereign states, connected through a dense network of relations, both *ad hoc* and institutionalized. Single persons and groups are regarded as legitimate actors in international relations (albeit with limited roles).

2   Certain peoples oppressed by colonial powers, racist regimes or foreign occupants are assigned rights of recognition and a determinate role in articulating their future and interests.

3   There is a gradual acceptance of standards and values which call into question the principle of effective power; accordingly, major violations of given international rules are not in theory to be regarded as legitimate. Restrictions are placed on the resort to force, including the unwarranted use of economic force.

4   New rules, procedures and institutions designed to aid law-making and law-enforcement in international affairs are created.

5   Legal principles delimiting the form and scope of the conduct of all members of the international community, and providing a set of guide-lines for the structuring of international rules, are adopted.

6   Fundamental concern is expressed for the rights of individuals, and a corpus of international rules is created seeking to constrain states to observe certain standards in the treatment of all, including their own citizens.

7   The preservation of peace, the advancement of human rights and the establishment of greater social justice are the stated collective priorities; 'public affairs' include the whole of the international community. With respect to certain values – peace, the prohibition of genocide – international rules now provide in principle for the personal responsibility of state officials and the attribution of criminal acts to states.

8   Systematic inequalities among peoples and states are recognized and new rules – including the concept of 'the common heritage of mankind'[67] – are established to create ways of governing the distribution, appropriation and exploitation of territory, property and natural resources.

The shift in the structure of international regulation from the Westphalian to the UN Charter model raised fundamental questions about the nature and form of international law, questions which point to the possibility of a significant disjuncture between the law of nation-states – of the states system – and of the wider international community. At the heart of this shift lies a conflict between claims made on behalf of individual states and those made on behalf of an alternative organizing principle of world affairs: ultimately, a democratic community of states, with equal voting rights in the General Assembly of nation-states, openly and collectively regulating international life while constrained to observe the UN Charter and a battery of human rights conventions. However, this conflict has not been settled, and it would be quite misleading to conclude that the era of the UN Charter model simply displaced the Westphalian logic of international governance. The essential reason for this is that the Charter framework represents, in many respects, an extension of the interstate system.

The organizations and procedures of the UN were designed partly to overcome weaknesses in the League of Nations. Its 'architecture', therefore, was drawn up to accommodate the international power structure as it was understood in 1945. The division of the globe into powerful nation-states, with distinctive sets of geopolitical interests, was built into the Charter conception. As a result, the UN was virtually immobilized as an autonomous actor on many pressing issues.[68] One of the most obvious manifestations of this was the special veto power accorded to the five Permanent Members of the UN Security Council. This privileged political status added authority and legitimacy to the position of each of the major powers; for although they were barred in principle from the use of force on terms contrary to the Charter, they were protected against censure and sanctions in the event of unilateral action in the form of their veto. Moreover, the Charter gave renewed credence (through Article 51) to unilateral strategic state initiatives if they were necessary in 'self-defence', since there was no clear delimitation of the meaning of this phrase. In addition, while the Charter placed new obligations on states to settle disputes peacefully, and laid down certain procedures for passing judgement on alleged acts of self-defence, these procedures have rarely been used and there has been no insistence on compliance with them. The possibility of mobilizing the collective coercive measures envisaged in the Charter itself against illegitimate state action has, furthermore, never materialized, and even the UN's peacekeeping missions have been restricted generally to areas in which the consent of the territorial state in question has first been given.

The UN's susceptibility to the agendas of the most powerful states has been reinforced by its dependence on finance provided by its members. This position of vulnerability to state politics is underscored by the absence of any mechanism to confer some kind of direct UN status on regional and transnational functional or cultural forces (agencies, groups or movements) who often might have a significant perspective on international questions. In sum, the UN Charter model, despite its good intentions, failed effectively to generate a new principle of organization in the international order – a principle which might break fundamentally with the logic of Westphalia and generate new democratic mechanisms of political coordination and change.

None the less, it would be wrong simply to leave the argument here. The UN Charter system has been distinctively innovative and influential in a number of respects. It has provided an international forum in which all states are in certain respects equal, a forum of particular value to third world countries and to those seeking a basis for 'consensus' solutions to international problems. It has provided a framework for decolonization, and for the pursuit of the reform of international economic institutions. Moreover, it has provided a vision, valuable in spite of all its limitations, of a new world order based upon a meeting of governments and, under appropriate circumstances, of a supranational presence in world affairs championing human rights.[69] Further, some of the deficiencies attributed to the UN can be better placed at the door of the states system itself, with its deep structural embeddedness in the global capitalist economy.

It might, accordingly, be a considerable step forward in the cross-border regulation of world affairs if the UN system were to live up to its Charter. Among other things, this would involve pursuing measures to implement key elements of the rights Conventions, enforcing the prohibition on the discretionary right to use force, activating the collective security system envisaged in the Charter itself and, more generally, ensuring compliance with the Charter's main articles.[70] In addition, if the Charter model were extended – for example, by adding the requirement of compulsory jurisdiction in the case of disputes falling under the UN rubric, or by providing means of redress through a new international human rights court in the case of human rights violations, or by making a (near) consensus vote in the General Assembly a legitimate source of international law, or by modifying the veto arrangement in the Security Council and rethinking representation on it to allow for an adequate regional presence – a basis might be established for the Charter model to generate political resources of its own, and to act as an autonomous decision-making centre.

While each move in this direction would be significant, particularly in enhancing the prospects of world peace, it would still represent, at best, a movement towards a very partial or 'thin' form of democracy in international affairs. Certainly, each state would enjoy formal equality in the UN system, and regional interests would be better represented. But it would still be possible for a plethora of different kinds of political regime to participate on an equal footing in the Charter framework; the dynamics and logic of the interstate system would still represent an immensely powerful principle of organization in global affairs, especially with its military machinery largely intact; the massive disparities of power and asymmetries of resources in the hierarchical and uneven global political economy would be left virtually unaddressed; the changing structure of the global order reflected in discussion about the proper subject, scope and sources of international law would remain marginal to the model; and transnational actors, civil associations, non-governmental organizations and social movements might still have a minimal role in this governance system. It would remain, then, a state-centred or sovereignty-centred model of international politics, and would lie at some considerable distance from what might be called a 'thicker' democratic ordering of international affairs. Furthermore, it would lie at some distance from an adequate recognition of the transformations being wrought in the wake of globalization – transformations which are placing increasing strain on both the Westphalian and Charter conceptions of international governance.

Cosmopolitan democracy and the new international order

There is a striking paradox to note about the contemporary era: from Africa to Eastern Europe, Asia to Latin America, more and more nations and groups are championing the idea of 'the rule of the people'; but they are doing so at just that moment when the very efficacy of democracy as a national form of political organization appears open to question. As substantial areas of human activity are progressively organized on a global level, the fate of democracy, and of the independent democratic nation-state in particular, is fraught with difficulty.

It could be objected that there is nothing particularly new about global interconnections, and that the significance of global interconnections for politics has, in principle, been plain for people to see for a long time. Such an objection could be elaborated by emphasizing, as I have done, that a dense pattern of global interconnections began to emerge with the initial expansion of the world economy and the rise of the modern state from the late sixteenth century. Further, it could be suggested that domestic and international politics have been interwoven throughout the modern

era: domestic politics has always to be understood against the background of international politics, and the former is often the source of the
latter.[71] However, it is one thing to claim that there are elements of
continuity in the formation and structure of modern states, economies
and societies, quite another to claim that there is nothing new about
aspects of their form and dynamics. For there is a fundamental difference
between, on the one hand, the development of particular trade routes, or
select military and naval operations which have an impact on certain
towns, rural centres and territories, and, on the other hand, an international order involving the emergence of a global economic system
which stretches beyond the control of any single state (even of dominant
states); the expansion of networks of transnational relations and
communications over which particular states have limited influence; the
enormous growth in international organizations and regimes which can
limit the scope for action of the most powerful states; and the development of a global military order, and the build-up of the means of 'total'
warfare as an enduring feature of the contemporary world, which can
reduce the range of policies available to governments and their citizens.
While trade routes and military expeditions can link distant populations
together in long loops of cause and effect, contemporary developments in
the international order link peoples through multiple networks of transaction and coordination, reordering the very notion of distance itself.[72]

It needs to be emphasized that processes of globalization do not
necessarily lead to growing global integration; that is, to a world order
marked by the progressive development of a homogeneous or unified
society and politics. For globalization can generate forces of both fragmentation and unification. Fragmentation or disintegrative trends are
possible for several reasons. The growth of dense patterns of interconnectedness among states and societies can increase the range of
developments affecting people in particular locations. By creating new
patterns of transformation and change, globalization can weaken old
political and economic structures without necessarily leading to the
establishment of new systems of regulation. Further, the impact of global
and regional processes is likely to vary under different international and
national conditions – for instance, a nation's location in the international
economy, its place in particular power blocs, its position with respect to
the international legal system. In addition, globalization can engender an
awareness of political difference as much as an awareness of common
identity; enhanced international communications can highlight conflicts
of interest and ideology, and not merely remove obstacles to mutual
understanding.

In positive terms, globalization implies at least two distinct phenomena. First, it suggests that political, economic and social activity is becoming worldwide in scope. And, secondly, it suggests that there has been an intensification of levels of interaction and interconnectedness within and among states and societies.[73] What is new about the modern global system is the spread of globalization through new dimensions of activity – technological, organizational, administrative and legal, among others – each with its own logic and dynamic of change; and the chronic intensification of patterns of interconnectedness mediated by such phenomena as the modern communications industry and new information technology. Politics unfolds today, with all its customary uncertainty and indeterminateness, against the background of a world shaped and permeated by the movement of goods and capital, the flow of communication, the interchange of cultures and the passage of people.[74]

In this context, the meaning and place of democratic politics, and of the contending models of democracy, have to be rethought in relation to a series of overlapping local, regional and global processes and structures.[75] It is essential to recognize at least three elements of globalization: first, the way processes of economic, political, legal and military interconnectedness are changing the nature, scope and capacity of the sovereign state from above, as its 'regulatory' ability is challenged and reduced in some spheres; secondly, the way local groups, movements and nationalisms are questioning the nation-state from below as a representative and accountable power system; and, thirdly, the way global interconnectedness creates chains of interlocking political decisions and outcomes among states and their citizens, altering the nature and dynamics of national political systems themselves. Democracy has to come to terms with all three of these developments and their implications for national and international power centres. If it fails to do so, it is likely to become ever less effective in determining the shape and limits of political activity. The international form and structure of politics and civil society have, accordingly, to be built into the foundations of democratic thought and practice.

Three distinct requirements arise: first, that the territorial boundaries of systems of accountability be recast so that those issues which escape the control of a nation-state – aspects of monetary management, environmental questions, elements of security, new forms of communication – can be brought under better democratic control; secondly, that the role and place of regional and global regulatory and functional agencies be rethought so that they might provide a more coherent and useful focal point in public affairs; and thirdly, that the articulation of political institutions with the key groups, agencies, associations and organizations of international civil society be reconsidered to allow the latter to become part of a democratic process – adopting, within their very *modus operandi*, a structure of rules and principles compatible with those of democracy.

How might this approach to democracy be developed? What are its essential characteristics? Addressing these questions requires recalling earlier arguments about the need to conceive democracy as a double-sided process, while reappraising the proper domain for the application of this process.[76] For if the above arguments are correct, democracy has to become a transnational affair if it is to be possible both within a restricted geographic domain and within the wider international community. The possibility of democracy today must, in short, be linked to an expanding framework of democratic institutions and agencies. I refer to such a framework as 'the cosmopolitan model of democracy'.[77] The framework can be elaborated by focusing initially on some of its institutional requirements.

In the first instance, the 'cosmopolitan model of democracy' presupposes the creation of regional parliaments (for example, in Latin America and Africa) and the enhancement of the role of such bodies where they already exist (the European Parliament) in order that their decisions become recognized, in principle, as legitimate independent sources of regional and international law. Alongside such developments, the model anticipates the possibility of general referenda, cutting across nations and nation-states, with constituencies defined according to the nature and scope of controversial transnational issues. In addition, the opening of international governmental organizations to public scrutiny and the democratization of international 'functional' bodies (on the basis perhaps of the creation of elected supervisory boards which are in part statistically representative of their constituencies) would be significant.

Hand in hand with these changes, the cosmopolitan model of democracy assumes the entrenchment of a cluster of rights, including civil, political, economic and social rights, in order to provide shape and limits to democratic decision-making.[78] This requires that they be enshrined within the constitutions of parliaments and assemblies (at the national and international level); and that the influence of international courts is extended so that groups and individuals have an effective means of suing political authorities for the enactment and enforcement of key rights, both within and beyond political associations.

In the final analysis, the formation of an authoritative assembly of all democratic states and societies – a re-formed UN, or a complement to it – would be an objective. The UN, as previously noted, combines two contradictory principles of representation: the equality of all countries (one country, one vote in the General Assembly) and deference to geopolitical strength (special veto power in the Security Council to those with current or former superpower status). An authoritative assembly of all democratic states and societies would seek unreservedly to place principles of democratic representation above those of superpower politics. Moreover, unlike the General Assembly of the UN, it would not, to begin with at least, be an assembly of all nations; for it would be an assembly of democratic nations which would draw in others over time, perhaps by the sheer necessity of being a member if their systems of governance are to enjoy legitimacy in the eyes of their own populations. As such, the new assembly in its early stages can best be thought of as a complement to the UN, which it would either replace over time or accept in a modified form as a 'second chamber' – a necessary meeting place for all states irrespective of the nature of their regimes.

Of course, the idea of a new democratic international assembly is open to a battery of objections commonly put to similar schemes. Would it have any teeth to implement decisions? How would democratic international law be enforced? Would there be a centralized police and military force?[79] And so forth. These concerns are significant. But many of them can be met and countered. For instance, it needs to be stressed that any global legislative institution should be conceived above all as a 'standard-setting' institution. Although a distinction ought to be made between legal instruments which would have the status of law independently of any further negotiation or action on the part of a region or state or local government, and instruments which would require further discussion with them, implementation of the detail of a broad range of recommendations would be a matter for non-global levels of governance.[80] In addition, the question of law-enforcement at a regional and global level is not beyond resolution in principle: a proportion of a nation-state's police and military (perhaps a growing proportion over time) could be 'seconded' to the new international authorities and placed at their disposal on a routine basis. To this end, avenues could be established to meet the concern that 'covenants, without the sword, are but words'.[81]

Equally, only to the extent that the new forms of 'policing' are locked into an international democratic framework would there be good grounds for thinking that a new settlement could be created between coercive power and accountability. If such a settlement seems like a fantasy, it should be emphasized that it is a fantasy to imagine that one can advocate democracy today without confronting the range of issues elaborated here. If the emerging international order is to be democratic, these issues have to be considered, even though their details are, of course, open to further specification.

The implications for international civil society of all this are in part clear. A democratic network of states and civil societies is incompatible with the existence of powerful sets of social relations and organizations which can, by virtue of the very bases of their operations, systematically distort democratic conditions and processes. At stake are, among other things, the curtailment of the power of corporations to constrain and influence the *political* agenda (through such diverse measures as the public funding of elections, the use of 'golden shares' and citizen directors), and the restriction of the activities of powerful transnational interest groups to pursue their interests unchecked (through, for example, the regulation of bargaining procedures to minimize the use of 'coercive tactics' within and between public and private associations, and the enactment of rules limiting the sponsorship of political representatives by sectional interests, whether these be particular industries or trade unions).

If individuals and peoples are to be free and equal in determining the conditions of their own existence there must be an array of social spheres – for instance, privately and cooperatively owned enterprises, independent communications media, and autonomously run cultural centres – which allow their members control of the resources at their disposal without direct interference from political agencies or other third parties.[82] At issue here is a civil society that is neither simply planned nor merely market orientated but, rather, open to organizations, associations and agencies pursuing their own projects, subject to the constraints of democratic processes and a common structure of action.[83]

The key features of this model are set out in table 1.3. The cosmopolitan model of democracy presents a programme of possible transformations with short- and long-term political implications. It does not present an all-or-nothing choice, but rather lays down a direction of possible change with clear points of orientation (see appendix).

Would a cosmopolitan framework of democracy, assuming its details could be adequately fleshed out, have the organizational resources – procedural, legal, institutional and military – to alter the dynamics of resource production and distribution, and of rule creation and enforcement, in the contemporary era? It would be deeply misleading to suggest that it would initially have these capabilities. Nevertheless, its commitment to the extension and deepening of mechanisms of democratic accountability across major regions and international structures would help to regulate resources and forces which are already beyond the reach of national democratic mechanisms and movements. Moreover, its commitment to the protection and strengthening of human rights, and to the further development of a regional and international court system,

TABLE 1.3   The Cosmopolitan Model of Democracy

1   The global order consists of multiple and overlapping networks of
     power including the political, social and economic.
2   All groups and associations are attributed rights of self-determination
     specified by a commitment to individual autonomy and a specific
     cluster of rights. The cluster is composed of rights within and across
     each network of power. Together, these rights constitute the basis of
     an empowering legal order – a 'democratic international law'.
3   Law-making and law-enforcement can be developed within this frame-
     work at a variety of locations and levels, along with an expansion of
     the influence of regional and international courts to monitor and check
     political and social authority.
4   Legal principles are adopted which delimit the form and scope of
     individual and collective action within the organizations and associa-
     tions of state *and* civil society. Certain standards are specified for the
     treatment of all, which no political regime or civil association can
     legitimately violate.
5   As a consequence, the principle of non-coercive relations governs the
     settlement of disputes, though the use of force remains a collective
     option in the last resort in the face of tyrannical attacks to eradicate
     democratic international law.
6   The defence of self-determination, the creation of a common structure
     of action and the preservation of the democratic good are the overall
     collective priorities.
7   Determinate principles of social justice follow: the *modus operandi* of
     the production, distribution and the exploitation of resources must be
     compatible with the democratic process and a common framework of
     action.

would aid the process whereby individuals and groups could sue their
governments for the enactment of key human rights.

In addition, the establishment of regional authorities as major independent voices in world politics might contribute further to the erosion
of the old division of the world by the US and the former USSR. Likewise,
the new institutional focus at the global level on major transnational
issues would go some way towards eradicating sectarian approaches to
these questions, and to countering 'hierarchy' and some of the major
asymmetries in life-chances. Finally, new sets of regional and global rules
and procedures might help prevent public affairs from becoming a
quagmire of infighting among nations wholly unable to settle pressing
collective issues.

Of course, there would be new possible dangers – no political scheme
is free from such risks. But what would be at issue would be the beginning
of the creation of a new international democratic culture and spirit – one
set off from the partisan claims of the nation-state. Such developments
might take years, if not decades, to become entrenched. But 1989–91 has
shown that political change can take place at an extraordinary speed,
itself no doubt partially a result of the process of globalization.

Conclusion

In order to avoid possible misunderstandings about the arguments
offered above, it might be useful, by way of a conclusion, to emphasize the
terrain they occupy and the ground they reject. This can be done by
assessing critically a number of conceptual polarities frequently found in
political discourse: globalism versus cultural diversity; constitutionalism
versus politics; political ambition versus political feasibility; participatory
or direct democracy versus liberal representative democracy and global
governance from above versus the extension of grassroots associations
from below. Although these polarities provide much of the tension which
charges the debate about the possibility of democracy beyond borders,
there are good reasons for doubting their coherence.

To begin with, globalism and cultural diversity are not simply
opposites. For global interconnectedness is already forming a dense web
of relations linking cultures one to another. The issue is how and in what
way cultures are linked and interrelated, not how a sealed cultural
diversity can persist in the face of globalization.

Secondly, the juxtaposition of constitutionalism – or the elaboration of
theoretical models of principles of political organization – with politics as
a practical activity sets up another false polarity. Politics typically
operates within a framework – albeit a shifting framework – of rules.
Politics is rarely without some pattern, and is most often about the nature
of the rules which will shape and delimit political activity. For politics is
at root about the ways in which rules and resources are distributed,
produced and legitimated. The question is whether politics will be
shaped by an explicit, formal constitution or model which might, in
principle, be open and contestable, or whether politics will be subject to
an unwritten constitution, which is altogether more difficult to invoke as
a defence in the face of unaccountable systems of power.

Thirdly, the question of feasibility cannot simply be set up in opposition to the question of political ambition. For what is ambitious today
might be feasible tomorrow. Who anticipated the remarkable changes of

1989–90 in Eastern Europe? Who foresaw the fall of communism in the Soviet Union? The growing interconnectedness between states and societies is generating consequences, intended and unintended, for the stability of regimes, governments and states. While the question of political feasibility is of the utmost significance, it would be naive to juxtapose it simply with programmes of political ambition.

Fourthly, versions of participatory democracy cannot simply be opposed to liberal representative democracy. Programmes of participatory or direct democracy are fraught with complexities and questions. Likewise, liberal representative democracy does not simply mean one set of possible institutions or forms. The nature of liberal democracy is itself an intensely contested issue. So while there seem to be good grounds for accepting the liberal distinction between state and civil society, there are not equally good grounds for uncritically accepting either of these in their liberal form. The juxtaposition of participation with liberal representative democracy leaves most of political analysis to one side.

Fifthly, the problems of global governance from above cannot be solved through the extension of grassroots democracy alone. For the questions have to be posed: which grassroots, and which democracy? There are many social movements – for instance, right-wing nationalist movements or the Eugenics movement – which highlight how the very nature of a grassroots movement can be contested and fought over. Grassroots movements are by no means merely noble or wise. Like most social, economic or political forms, they can appear in a variety of shapes, with a variety of patterns of internal organization. An appeal to the nature or inherent goodness of grassroots associations and movements bypasses the necessary work of theoretical analysis.

Today, any attempt to set out a position of what could be called 'embedded utopianism' must begin both from where we are – the existing pattern of political relations and processes – and from an analysis of what might be: desirable political forms and principles.[84] If utopia is to be embedded, it must be linked into patterns and movements as they are. But if this context of embeddedness is not simply to be affirmed in the shapes and patterns generated by past groups and movements, it has to be assessed according to standards, criteria and principles. These, in my view, follow from a theory of democracy.

Finally, if the history and practice of democracy has until now been centred on the idea of locality (the city-state, the community, the nation), it is likely that in the future it will be centred on the international or global domain. It would be immensely naive to claim that there are any straightforward solutions to the problems posed by global interconnectedness, with its complex and often profoundly uneven effects; but there is, without doubt, an inescapably important set of questions to be addressed. Certainly, one can find many good reasons for being optimistic about finding a path forward, and many good reasons for thinking that at this juncture democracy will face another critical test.

Appendix
Objectives of the Cosmopolitan Model of Democracy: Illustrative Issues

Short-term	*Long-term*

Polity/governance

1 Reform of UN Security Council (to give the third world a significant voice)	1 Global parliament (with limited revenue-raising capacity) connected to regions, nations and localities
2 Creation of a UN second chamber (on the model of the EC?)	2 New Charter of Rights and Duties locked into different domains of power
3 Enhanced political regionalization (EC and beyond)	3 Separation of political and economic interests; public funding of electoral processes
4 Compulsory jurisdiction before the International Court. New International Criminal Court and new Human Rights Court for the pursuit of rights	4 Interconnected global legal system
5 Establishment of a small but effective, accountable, international, military force	5 Permanent 'secondment' of a growing proportion of a nation-state's coercive capability to regional and global institutions. Aim: demilitarization and transcendence of war system

Civil Society

1 Enhancement of non-state, non-market solutions in the organization of civil society	1 Creation of a diversity of self-regulating associations and groups in civil society

2 Introduction of limits to private ownership of key 'public-shaping' institutions: media, information, and so on

2 Systematic experimentation with different democratic organizational forms in civil society

3 Provision of resources to those in the most vulnerable social positions to defend and articulate their interests

3 Multi-sectoral economy and pluralization of patterns of ownership and possession

NOTES

1 I should like to thank Richard Falk, Anthony Giddens, Jack Hayward, Quentin Skinner, David Scott-Macnab, Saul Mendlovitz and John Thompson for many constructive comments on this chapter. It seeks to draw together and expand upon a number of themes discussed in my recent writings, particularly in *Models of Democracy* (Cambridge, Polity Press, 1987), ch. 9; 'Democracy, the nation-state and the global system', in D. Held (ed.), *Political Theory Today* (Cambridge, Polity Press, 1991); and 'Democracy and globalization', *Alternatives*, 16:2 (1991).

2 See F. Fukuyama, 'The end of History', *The National Interest*, 16 (1989) and 'A reply to my critics', *The National Interest*, 18 (1989/90). For a more detailed commentary on these texts, see D. Held, 'Liberalism, Marxism and democracy', *Theory and Society* (forthcoming).

3 I. Berlin, *Four Essays on Liberty* (Oxford, Oxford University Press, 1969), pp. 164ff.

4 See, for example, A. Lizphart, *Democracies* (New Haven, CT, Yale University Press, 1984) and R. Dahl, *Democracy and Its Critics* (New Haven, CT, Yale University Press, 1989).

5 A fuller account of the nature and scope of political theory as outlined here can be found in the 'Introduction' to Held, *Political Theory Today*, pp. 1–21.

6 See M. Bernal, *Black Athena, Vol. I* (London, Free Association Books, 1987), and P. Springborg, *Western Republicanism and the Oriental Prince* (Cambridge, Polity Press, 1992).

7 When referring to the Greek *polis*, some scholars prefer to use the term 'city-republic' on the grounds that the concept of the state was an early modern formulation. For some of the issues underpinning this preference see Held, *Models of Democracy*, ch. 2.

8 M. Finley, *Politics in the Ancient World* (Cambridge, Cambridge University Press, 1983), pp. 84ff.

9 See J. G. A. Pocock, *The Machiavellian Moment: Florentine Political Thought and the Atlantic Republican Tradition* (Princeton, NJ, Princeton University Press, 1975), pp. 64–80.

10 See N. Machiavelli, *The Discourses* (Harmondsworth, Penguin, 1983), pp. 104–11.

11 The republican view emphasizes, in short, that the freedom of citizens consists above all in their unhindered pursuit of their self-chosen ends. The highest political ideal is the civic freedom of an independent, self-governing republic.

12 Q. Skinner, 'The State', in T. Ball, J. Farr and R. Hanson (eds), *Political Innovation and Conceptual Change* (Cambridge, Cambridge University Press, 1989), p. 105.

13 Aristotle, *The Politics* (Harmondsworth, Penguin, 1981), p. 169.

14   See M. Finley, *Democracy Ancient and Modern* (London, Chatto and Windus, 1973).

15   The concern with aspects of 'self-government' in Renaissance Italy had a significant influence in seventeenth- and eighteenth-century England, France and America. The problem of how civic life was to be constructed, and public life sustained, was faced by diverse thinkers. While the meaning of the ideal of active citizenship was progressively altered – and denuded of many of its most challenging implications – threads of this ideal remained and continued to have an impact. It is possible to trace 'radical' and 'conservative' strains of republicanism throughout the early modern period. Cf. Pocock, *The Machiavellian Moment*, and G. S. Wood, *The Creation of the American Republic: 1776–1787* (Chapel Hill, University of North Carolina Press, 1969).

16   Pocock, *The Machiavellian Moment*, p. 550.

17   H. Bull, *The Anarchical Society* (London, Macmillan, 1977), p. 27.

18   Q. Skinner, *The Foundations of Political Thought, Vol. 1*, (Cambridge, Cambridge University Press, 1978), p. 352.

19   See D. Held, 'The development of the modern state', in S. Hall and B. Gieben (eds), *Formations of Modernity* (Cambridge, Polity Press, 1992).

20   J. Madison, *The Federalist Papers*, ed. R. Fairfield (New York, Doubleday, 1966), No. 10, p. 20.

21   Madison, *The Federalist Papers*, No. 10, pp. 21–2.

22   See R. W. Krouse, 'Classical images of democracy in America: Madison and Tocqueville', in D. Duncan (ed.), *Democratic Theory and Practice* (Cambridge, Cambridge University Press, 1983), pp. 58–78.

23   J. Bentham, *Constitutional Code, Book 1*, in *The Works of Jeremy Bentham, Vol. IX* (Edinburgh, W. Tait, 1843), p. 47.

24   N. Bobbio, *Democracy and Dictatorship* (Cambridge, Polity Press, 1989), p. 144.

25   See Dahl, *Democracy and Its Critics*, pp. 28–30.

26   Quoted in G. H. Sabine, *A History of Political Theory* (London, George G. Harrap, 3rd edn, 1963), p. 695.

27   See Held, *Models of Democracy*, ch. 3.

28   See N. Bobbio, *Which Socialism?* (Cambridge, Polity Press, 1987), p. 66, and Dahl, *Democracy and Its Critics*, pp. 221 and 233.

29   Bobbio, *Which Socialism?*, pp. 42–4.

30   A. Callinicos, *The Revenge of History: Marxism and the East European revolutions* (Cambridge, Polity Press, 1991), pp. 108–9.

31   K. Marx, *The Civil War in France* (Peking, Foreign Languages Press, 1970), pp. 67–70.

32   Marx, Letter 2, from the *Deutsch-Französische Jahrbücher* (Paris, 1844).

33   See, for example, V. I. Lenin, *What Is To Be Done?* (Moscow, Progress Publishers, 1947).

34   Held, *Models of Democracy*, ch. 9.

35   For texts which seek to do this, see Held, *Models of Democracy*, chs 8 and 9; Held, 'Democracy, the nation-state and the global system', pp. 227–35; and J. Keane, *Democracy and Civil Society* (London, Verso, 1988). See also Keane's chapter in this volume.

36   H. Arendt, *On Revolution* (New York, Viking Press, 1963), p. 256.

37   Held, 'Democracy, the nation-state and the global system', p. 198. Some of the material in the following paragraphs is adapted from pp. 201–5 of that essay.

38   Cf., for example, C. B. Macpherson, *The Life and Times of Liberal Democracy*

(Oxford, Oxford University Press, 1977); C. Pateman, *The Problem of Political Obligation* (Cambridge, Polity Press, 2nd edn, 1985); and B. Barber, *Strong Democracy* (Berkeley, CA, University of California Press, 1984).

39 C. Offe, *Disorganized Capitalism* (Cambridge, Polity Press, 1985), pp. 286ff.

40 R. Hanson, 'Democracy', in T. Ball, J. Farr and R. Hanson (eds), *Political Innovation and Conceptual Change* (Cambridge, Cambridge University Press, 1989), pp. 68–9.

41 Cf. Dahl, *Democracy and Its Critics*, chs 10 and 11.

42 See, for example, R. Aron, *Peace and War: a theory of international relations* (New York, Doubleday, 1966).

43 T. Hobbes, *Leviathan* (Harmondsworth, Penguin, 1968), pp. 187–8.

44 Cf. H. J. Morgenthau, *Politics Among Nations* (New York, Knopf, 1948); M. Wight, *Power Politics* (Harmondsworth, Penguin, 1986); and S. Smith, 'Reasons of state', in D. Held and C. Pollitt (eds), *New Forms of Democracy* (London, Sage, 1987).

45 See R. Falk, 'The interplay of Westphalia and Charter conceptions of the international legal order', in R. Falk and C. Black (eds), *The Future of the International Legal Order, Vol. I* (Princeton, NJ, Princeton University Press, 1969); R. Falk, *A Study of Future Worlds* (New York, The Free Press, 1975), ch. 2; and A. Cassese, *International Law in a Divided World* (Oxford, Clarendon Press, 1986), especially pp. 393ff. While the emergence of this model can be linked directly to the Peace of Westphalia, important qualifications ought also to be noted. First, the basic conception of territorial sovereignty was outlined well before this settlement (although not generally assented to). Secondly, there were few, if any, references in the classic texts of early modern political theory to an intrinsically territorial state; as T. Baldwin put it, 'political theory had still to catch up with practice'. On both these points see T. Baldwin, 'The territorial state', in H. Gross and T. R. Harrison (eds), *Cambridge Essays in Jurisprudence* (Oxford, Clarendon Press, 1993).

46 By a 'model' I mean a theoretical construction designed to reveal and explain the main elements of a political form or order and its underlying structure of relations. Models in this context are 'networks' of concepts and generalizations about aspects of the political, economic and social spheres.

47 A. Cassese, 'Violence, war and the rule of law in the international Community', in D. Held (ed.), *Political Theory Today* (Cambridge, Polity Press, 1991), p. 256.

48 These points are adapted from Falk, 'The interplay of Westphalia and Charter conceptions of the international legal order', and Cassese, *International Law in a Divided World*, pp. 396–9.

49 C. Beitz, *Political Theory and International Relations* (Princeton, N J, Princeton University Press, 1979), p. 25.

50 The resort to coercion or armed force by non-state actors is also, arguably, an almost inevitable outcome in such a world. For communities contesting established territorial boundaries have, as Baldwin succinctly wrote, 'little alternative but to resort to arms in order to establish "effective control" over the area they seek as their territory, and in that way make their case for international recognition (cf. Eritrea, East Timor, Kurdistan . . .)'. See Baldwin, 'The territorial state'.

51 See G. Modelski, *Principles of World Politics* (New York, Free Press, 1972).

52 See F. Braudel, *Capitalism and Material Life* (London, Weidenfeld and Nicolson, 1973).

53 I. Wallerstein, *The Capitalist Economy* (Cambridge, Cambridge University Press, 1979), p. 19.

54 C. Tilly, *Coercion, Capital and European States, AD 990-1990* (Oxford, Blackwell, 1990), pp. 17 and 189.

55 See M. Mann, *The Sources of Social Power, Vol. 1* (Cambridge, Cambridge University Press, 1986), pp. 510-16.

56 The following analysis is indebted to R. Falk, 'Economic dimensions of global civilization: A preliminary perspective' (working paper prepared for the Cairo meeting of the Global Civilization Project, Oct. 1990), pp. 2-12.

57 See R. W. Cox, *Production, Power, and World Order: social forces in the making of history* (New York, Columbia University Press, 1987), ch. 9.

58 I do not mean this to be an 'economistic' point. There are obviously other important factors involved in determining a state's effective power. See D. Held, *Political Theory and the Modern State* (Cambridge, Polity Press, 1989), ch. 8.

59 See G. Hawthorn's chapter in this volume. Cf. R. H. Jackson and C. G. Rosberg, 'Why Africa's weak states persist: the empirical and the juridical in statehood', *World Politics*, 17 (1982), 1-24.

60 For an overview see Bull, *The Anarchical Society*, ch. 6.

61 See L. Oppenheim, *International Law, Vol. 1* (London, Longman, 1905), ch. 1.

62 Cf., for example, B. Röling, *International Law in an Expanded World* (Amsterdam, Djambatan, 1960); W. Friedmann, *The Changing Structure of International Law* (London, Stevens and Son, 1964); and Cassese, *International Law in a Divided World*, especially chs 7-9.

63 Cf. Bull, *The Anarchical Society*, pp. 147-58; C. Jenks, *Law, Freedom and Welfare* (London, Stevens and Son, 1963), ch. 5; and R. Falk, *The Status of Law in International Society* (Princeton, N J, Princeton University Press, 1970), ch. 5.

64 It is interesting to note that the tradition of natural law thinking, which informed early modern international law in particular, recognized a certain tension between the requirement of governmental consent and the existence of international rights and duties.

65 Cassese, 'Violence, war and the rule of law', p. 256.

66 I have drawn these points from Cassese, *International Law in a Divided World*, pp. 398-400.

67 First propounded in the late 1960s, the concept of 'the common heritage of mankind' has been enshrined in two notable treaties: the Convention on the Moon and Other Celestial Bodies (1979) and the Convention on the Law of the Sea (1982). The concept has been proposed as a device to exclude a state or private right of appropriation over certain resources and to permit the development of these resources, where appropriate, for the benefit of all, with due regard paid to environmental protection.

68 See Falk, *A Study of Future Worlds*, pp. 69-72; R. Falk, *A Global Approach to National Policy* (Cambridge, MA, Harvard University Press, 1975), pp. 169-96; Cassese, *International Law in a Divided World*, pp. 142-3, 200-1, 213-14 and 246-50.

69 Cf. R. Falk, 'Reflections on democracy and the Gulf war', *Alternatives*, 16:2 (1991), p. 272.

70 In making these proposals I do not wish to imply that the UN Charter itself is a fully coherent document. It includes some contradictory stipulations and procedures; some of its clauses are vague at best; and some of its recommendations can generate conflicting priorities. It is, in short, open to conflicts of interpretation which would have to be addressed thoroughly if it were to take on a more robust role.

71 P. Gourevitch, 'The second image reversed: the international sources of domestic politics', *International Organization*, 32 (1978).

72 Or, as Anthony Giddens usefully put it, globalization can be defined as 'the intensification of worldwide social relations which link distant localities in such a way that local happenings are shaped by events occurring many miles away and vice versa', in *Consequences of Modernity* (Cambridge, Polity Press, 1990), p. 64.

73 See A. McGrew, 'Conceptualizing global politics', in A. McGrew, P. Lewis et al., *Global Politics* (Cambridge, Polity Press, 1992), pp. 1–28.

74 C. W. Kegley and E. R. Wittkopf, *World Politics* (Basingstoke, Macmillan, 1989), p. 511.

75 I have discussed these processes and structures in 'Democracy, the nation-state and the global system', pp. 207–27 and at greater length in *Foundations of Democracy: the principle of autonomy and the global order* (Cambridge, Polity Press, forthcoming).

76 See above, pp. 23–5.

77 In previous publications I have referred to this as 'the federal model' but given the current controversy about 'federalism' in Europe the term has become unhelpful in conveying my intentions. I would like to thank Daniele Archibugi for pressing this point. A central theme of my forthcoming work, *Foundations of Democracy*, is what I now prefer to call 'the cosmopolitan model of democracy' or, better still, of 'democratic autonomy'. Of course, anyone who seeks to use the term 'cosmopolitan' needs to clarify its meaning, especially in relation to Kant's thought. I seek to do this in *Foundations*.

78 It is beyond the scope of this chapter to set out my particular conception of rights, which I link to the notion of a 'common structure of action': the necessary conditions for people in principle to enjoy free and equal political participation. See Held, 'Democracy, the nation-state and global system', pp. 227–35, and, particularly, Held, *Foundations of Democracy*.

79 Among other difficulties to be faced would be the rules determining the assembly's representative base. One country, one vote? Representatives allocated according to population size? Would major international functional organizations be represented? Cf. I. McLean, 'Forms of representation and systems of voting', in D. Held (ed.), *Political Theory Today* (Cambridge, Polity Press, 1991), pp. 190–6, and J. Burnheim, *Is Democracy Possible?* (Cambridge, Polity Press, 1985), pp. 82–124.

80 European Community law embodies a range of relevant distinctions among legal instruments and types of implementation which are helpful to reflect on in this context. However, I leave open these complex issues in this chapter.

81 Hobbes, *Leviathan*, p. 223.

82 The models for the organization of such spheres are, it must be readily acknowledged, far from settled. See D. Held and C. Pollitt (eds), *New Forms of Democracy* (London, Sage, 1986).

83 The proposed European Social Charter embodies principles and rules which are compatible with the idea of generating elements of a common structure of action. If operationalized it would, in principle, alter the structure and functioning of market processes in a number of ways. While the Charter falls considerably short of what I have in mind as a common structure of action, and its details require extensive consideration which I shall not offer here, it is a useful illustration of the possibility of legislation to alter the background conditions and operations of the economic organizations of civil society.

84 Cf. R. Falk, 'Positive prescriptions for the near future' (Princeton, NJ, Princeton University, Center for International Studies, World Order Studies Program Occasional Paper, No. 20, 1991), pp. 8–10.

Part II

Contesting Democracy: Theoretical Disputes

2

LIBERAL DEMOCRACY AND THE LIMITS OF DEMOCRATIZATION

David Beetham

Democracy I take to be a mode of decision-making about collectively binding rules and policies over which the people exercise control, and the most democratic arrangement to be that where all members of the collectivity enjoy effective equal rights to take part in such decision-making directly – one, that is to say, which realizes to the greatest conceivable degree the principles of popular control and equality in its exercise. Democracy should properly be conceptualized as lying at one end of a spectrum, the other end of which is a system of rule where the people are totally excluded from the decision-making process and any control over it. Disputes about the meaning of democracy which purport to be conceptual disagreements are really disputes about how much democracy is either desirable or practicable; that is, about where the trade-off should come between democratic and other values, or at what point along the spectrum a given set of institutional arrangements for realizing the principle of control by equal citizens is in practice sustainable. In other words, we should distinguish between the *concept* of democracy, which in my view is uncontestable, and whose point of reference lies at one end of a spectrum of possibilities; and different *theories* of democracy, which involve contestable claims about how much democracy is desirable or practicable, and how it might be realized in a sustainable institutional form.[1] Of any existing set of political arrangements it is thus meaningful to ask how they might be made more democratic. And the concept of 'democratization' expresses both a clear direction of change along the spectrum, and a political movement or process of change, which can apply to any given system, not only change from authoritarian or dictatorial forms of rule.

If we now add to this concept of democracy the idea of liberalism, as in the portmanteau construct 'liberal democracy', we find a relationship that is both one of mutual necessity and a source of tension or antagonism. On the one hand, certain key assumptions and institutions characteristic of classical liberalism have proved quite indispensable to the maintenance of democracy at the level of the nation-state in the nineteenth and twentieth centuries, to such a degree that attempts to abolish them, or do without them, have proved disastrous for democracy. On the other hand, liberalism has also served as a constraint upon the process of democrat-ization, and the same two centuries have witnessed an almost continual struggle between liberals and various types of democrat over the extent and form that democratization should take. So liberalism has historically provided both a necessary platform for democracy and a constraint upon it.[2] And it is this paradoxical conjunction that makes it so difficult to give a straightforward answer to the question: are there any viable alternatives to liberal democracy? As I shall suggest, the question should rather be rephrased as follows: how far can the constraints that liberalism has historically placed upon the process of democratization be overcome, without undermining the basis of democracy itself?

Paradoxes of the Liberal Democratic Conjunction

Let me examine each side of this paradoxical conjunction of liberal democracy in turn. Of the different components of liberalism that have proved to be indispensable to democracy at the level of the nation-state I would distinguish five.

1   The securing of the freedoms of expression, of movement, of associa-
    tion and so on, as individual rights subject to special legal or
    constitutional protection. Of course not all individual rights are
    democratic rights, but without the guaranteed right of all citizens to
    meet collectively, to have access to information, to seek to persuade
    others, as well as to vote, democracy would be meaningless.
    Democratic rights, in other words, are those individual rights which
    are necessary to secure popular control over the process of collective
    decision-making on an ongoing basis, and which need protection
    even when (or especially when) their exercise involves opinions or
    actions that are unpopular, whether with the government or with
    society at large.
2   An institutional separation of powers between executive, legislature
    and judiciary, without which the idea of the 'rule of law' and all that is

embraced by that idea would be illusory: the protection of individual rights themselves, the guarantee of a fair trial and due process, the subordination of state officials to the law, the possibility of legal redress against maladministration or abuse of office.

3 The institution of the representative assembly, elected on a geographical basis through open competition for the popular vote, with powers to approve all taxation and legislation and to scrutinize the actions of the executive. In comparison with the direct assembly of all citizens, the representative assembly finds its justification as the most effective device for reconciling the requirements of popular control and political equality with the exigencies of time and the conditions of the modern territorial state.

4 The principle of the limited state, and a separation between the public and private spheres, whether the 'private' be defined in terms of an autonomous civil society, of the market and private property, of the family and personal relations or of individual conscience. The relevance to democracy of this distinction is to be found in an interrelated set of considerations: for example, that democracy cannot in practice subsist without an autonomous sphere of citizen will-formation separate from the state, or without a pluralism of power centres, or if the state takes on too much of the task of social coordination, or if all social relations are politicized. Together these considerations imply that the democratic state has in practice to be a limited state, though there is considerable room for disagreement about where precisely the limits should be drawn.

5 The epistemological premise that there is no final truth about what is good for society, belonging to the domain of revelation or special knowledge, and that the only criterion for the public good is what the people, freely organized, will choose, not what some expert or prophet decrees on the basis of superior knowledge. The anti-paternalism of democracy is here the direct descendant of the anti-paternalism of liberalism, and rests on the same epistemological foundation.

We have, then, a number of principles and institutions characteristic of liberalism in its classical period and established prior to the extension of the suffrage, which have proved necessary to the survival of democracy in the era of mass politics. One thing we have learnt by the end of the twentieth century is that attempts to abolish these liberal features in the name of a more perfect democracy have only succeeded in undermining the democracy in whose name they were attacked. Thus the very idea of individual rights has been attacked in the name of the popular will, the collective good or the realization of a higher form of freedom; the separation of powers has been eroded in the name of people's justice; the powers of a representative parliament have been neutered in the name of direct democracy, or functional representation, or soviet power; the separation between the public and the private spheres has been abolished in the name of bringing all aspects of social life under democratic control; and the pluralism of ideas about the common good has been dismissed as a source of error and confusion in the face of established truths about the ends of human life or the future course of history. Whatever the good intentions or popular credentials of such projects, they have typically succeeded in cutting the democratic ground from under their feet.

The reason for this is that democracy as a method of government is not whatever the people at a given moment may happen to decide, but a set of arrangements for securing their control over the public decision-making process on an ongoing basis. And to these arrangements the distinctive developments of the classical liberal era, whether we call them 'bourgeois' or not, have made an indispensable contribution, whose relevance to democracy is to be found in liberalism's own struggle to subject the absolutist state to some public accountability and societal control. In this sense there is no serious democratic alternative to liberal democracy, if by that we understand democracy underpinned by these distinctive liberal components. There may be non-democratic alternatives which are able to achieve legitimacy, though their range has been considerably reduced with the collapse of the communist model.[3] But there is no serious democratic alternative.

However, that is only one side of the story if we look back from the vantage point of the 1990s. The other side of the conjunction 'liberal democracy' is a history of successive struggles between liberals and various types of democrat over the extent and form of democratization. The reason is that there are other aspects of the classical liberal legacy which have been profoundly hostile to democracy as I have defined it: as the control of collectively binding rules and policies by equal citizens. It is notorious that when classical liberals spoke about the popular control of government they did not include all the people in that designation. Thus Locke talked of the active consent of the propertied and the tacit consent of the rest.[4] And the constitution-makers of the first National Assembly in France drew a distinction between 'active' and 'passive' citizenship: between the enjoyment of legal rights, which was universal, and the exercise of political rights, which was limited to taxpayers.[5] Furthermore, almost all of the classical liberals excluded women from citizenship on the grounds that they could be sufficiently represented, and their interests be protected, by either their husbands or their fathers.[6] In each case it was the commitment of liberals to the defence of a key social institution – that of private property on the one hand, and the family with its hierarchical division of labour on the other – that formed the basis of their resistance to the extension of the suffrage. So the first site of struggle between liberals and democrats came over the suffrage, and to establish the principle that the basic requirement for active citizenship was not the possession of property, or the headship of the household, or the level of formal education, or whatever, but the capacity to take responsibility for decisions about one's own plan of life, and by extension to share responsibility for decisions about the collective life – a capacity which all adults, whatever other differences between them, must be assumed to share equally.

Most subsequent struggles between liberals and democrats have revolved around the same social institutions of private property and the family. Thus socialists and social democrats have argued that the formal equality of political rights is of only limited value if private wealth can be used as a political resource to control or influence access to public decision-making, and if major economic decisions are taken by private institutions unaccountable to either the public or their own employees.[7] In a parallel manner feminists have argued that the hierarchical division of labour established within the family compromises equality at the formal political level, and that gender relations themselves constitute a crucial arena for democratization.[8] In each case what has been challenged is not so much the liberal distinction between the public and the private spheres as the way in which liberalism has defined the boundary between them, to exclude in the one economic relations, in the other gender power, from the sphere of the political, and thus from the scope of democratization. Of course in the zeal to shift the boundary between the public and the private as established by liberalism there has been a danger that the distinction itself has been jeopardized; and one of the key issues about the limits of democratization, to which I shall return, is how far the boundary can be shifted without also being eroded.

So where the first set of struggles between liberals and democratizers was over the extension of the suffrage, the second has been over the kind of social agenda necessary to make the principle of political control by equal citizens properly effective – something which arguably cannot be done if we take too narrow a view of what is political, or if we overlook the capacities and opportunities that people need if they are to exercise their legally established rights.

A final source of conflict between liberals and democratizers is less easy to characterize, since it has permeated the others, and has not been identified with any single definable set of social agents. It has focused upon the institution of representation, and upon the way this has served not only as a necessary instrument of accountability, but also as a means of keeping the people at arm's length from the political process, and establishing a division of labour between an elite of professional politicians engaged in politics as a specialized activity on the one side, and a depoliticized, privatized citizenry on the other. This has reflected tendencies deep within the liberal tradition (though not shared by all liberals): of prioritizing the activities and relationships of civil society, especially the market, and of regarding politics as a necessary evil to be limited to those problems the market cannot solve on its own; or else of treating politics as an arena for the exercise of leadership by the superior few, who merit protection from interference at the hands of the masses.[9] Against these assumptions have been arrayed a variety of democratizers: from those who have defined the public sphere as something qualitatively different from, and morally superior to, the private, through those who have sought to subject representatives to the constraints of strict delegation and recall, to the advocates of expanded political participation and direct democracy.[10]

My conclusion so far, then, is that the conjunction 'liberal democracy' is paradoxical, because the relationship between liberalism and democracy has been a deeply ambiguous one. Liberalism has provided not only the necessary foundation for, but also a significant constraint upon, democracy in the modern world. This ambiguity in turn makes a democratic critique of liberalism both necessary and also problematical, in so far as it threatens the conditions of liberal democracy itself. The question we should address, therefore, is not so much what alternatives there might be to liberal democracy, but rather: how far is it possible to carry the process of democratization, in the sense of both extending popular control and equalizing the conditions for its exercise, without undermining the conditions for democracy itself? In short, what are the limits to democratization? The remainder of the chapter will examine two key components of liberal democracy – the institution of representation, and the principle of the limited state – and consider what sort of constraint they impose, in the one case upon demands for a more direct or participatory form of democracy, in the other upon the social agendas for democratization that socialists and feminists have demanded.

Representation and the Economy of Time

Before proceeding to consider the institution of representation it is necessary first to examine the grounds on which democracy can be justified and democratization advanced, since clarifying what democrat-ization means is not sufficient to establishing that its promotion is desirable, for all that we tend to regard democracy as a self-evident good. If the core meaning of democracy is the popular control of collective decision-making by equal citizens, then the key value in terms of which it can be promoted and justified is that of autonomy or self-determination, both of a people collectively and of citizens in so far as they share in the exercise of that control. To be able to shape the course or conditions of one's life through sharing control over collective decisions is a necessary counterpart to exercising such control at the personal or individual level.[11]

The justification for democracy on the grounds of autonomy is more compelling than that based on the protection of interests, in at least two respects. The first is that collective, like individual, decision-making involves the articulation of values, principles or ideals as well as the defence or promotion of interests. Since it does not specify the content of decisions, but only how they are to be made, the concept of autonomy is able to embrace both types of consideration. Certainly, the experience of having one's interests disregarded provides a most powerful incentive to demand a say in decision-making, but having a say is rarely just about defending one's own interests. In the second place, if the idea of interest-maximization is to deliver a defence of democracy, rather than of paternalist forms of rule, then it must contain the implicit assumption that people are the best judges of their own interests; that is it must embody a concept like that of autonomy, on which it is in effect parasitic.[12]

Justifying democracy on the grounds of autonomy or self-determination rather than the protection or maximization of interests brings a theory of democracy closer to that of the so-called 'participation' theorists. However, it is important to clarify on what grounds political participation is to be advanced. Sometimes its advocates speak as if participation in public affairs is an end in itself, a part of the good life, so to say. Yet the point of participation, surely, is to have some say in, and influence upon, collective decisions; and its value is principally to be judged by how far it contributes to this end, and for whom. Communist systems, notoriously, required much more political participation than liberal democracies, yet they were very short on popular control of major collective decisions, of 'high' rather than 'low' politics, as Bialer calls it.[13] Theorists of participa-tion also talk about its educative value,[14] but again this is an inadequate justification. It is an argument that can only be advanced on behalf of others, typically when they are being denied participation on the grounds of their unreadiness for it;[15] it is hardly a consideration that people will

advance on their own behalf. At most, therefore, the educative value of
participation can only be a side-effect, a consideration secondary to that
of achieving more control over the circumstances of one's life and the
decisions that affect these. This is not to say that the education of its
future citizens is not an important concern for any democratic society;
only that it cannot be the primary justification for extending and
equalizing the conditions for popular control over collective decisions.

Drawing a parallel between the concept of autonomy at the individual
and the collective levels, between a condition of determining the
priorities for one's own personal life and sharing in decisions about
priorities for the collectivity, should make us suspicious of theories that
privilege the one over the other, whether in the name of 'negative' or
'positive' freedom, since the justifications for individual liberty and for
democratic participation are at root one and the same. Of course there
are also important differences between the two levels. Taking part in
collective decision-making involves a recognition that decisions are the
result of a process of interaction, in which no one person or group gets all
they wanted at the outset of the process. Autonomy here can only mean
having the right to take part in the process as an equal, and under
procedures of debate and decision-taking acknowledged as fair. This is a
less strenuous condition than the ultra-individualist criterion for autonomy
demanded by R. P. Wolff in his *In Defense of Anarchism*, according to
which my autonomy is infringed whenever a binding decision is made
whose content I do not agree with.[16] Such a criterion simply refuses to
recognize the necessary compromises and give-and-take that are an
inescapable feature of social living, and that make collective necessarily
different from individual decision-making.

However, to specify that autonomy requires the right to take part in
collective decision-making as an equal is still a sufficiently tough condition to call into question one of the key institutions of liberal democracy,
that of representation. Representation involves the surrender of control
over decisions to others, so that any control is only exercised indirectly; it
constitutes a condition of inequality, whereby only a few are entitled to
take part in decision-making and the vast majority are excluded. How is
such a surrender conceivably compatible with autonomy? To argue that
citizens retain their autonomy in so far as they willingly consent to such a
surrender presupposes that a satisfactory mechanism for giving such
consent can be identified. Even then, this could not be a sufficient condition for preserving autonomy, since the same argument could prove the
compatibility of autonomy with dictatorship, if people were ever to
consent to that. And dictatorship, like slavery, is a paradigmatically
heteronomous condition, however arrived at. On the other hand, to

argue that the vast majority of people are inherently incapable of making principled choices in matters of policy or legislation, and that at best they must select others to do it for them, would be to abandon the terrain of democratic argument itself, since it is a basic postulate of democracy that the prioritization of competing values involved in decisions over public policy, though it requires expert advice, is not itself a subject of special expertise and lies within everyone's capacity.

The conclusion is unavoidable that the institution of representation constitutes a substantial surrender or diminution of citizens' autonomy, one that can only be justified by the overriding practical consideration of time. The spatial difficulty of having millions of citizens deliberating in one place could now be overcome by communications technology, if applied with sufficient ingenuity and determination. Yet an electronic voting button operated alongside a special television channel in every living room would not overcome the problem that the work of legislation requires full-time attention if the issues are to be fully debated and understood, just as the work of supervising a full-time executive also requires continuous attention. Any society with similar requirements to our own in terms of production and reproduction (including the work of domestic care) could only afford to have a relatively small number devoted full time to this activity. These few are prevented from forming an oligarchy to the extent that their positions are effectively open to all, and that their tenure of them is systematically dependent upon the votes of the rest, to whom they are accountable for the exercise of office. To the rest falls the task that is compatible with their more limited time span: deciding between the broadest priorities for policy and legislation that are embodied in competing electoral programmes, and assessing the calibre of those responsible for implementing them. No doubt most people could afford some more time for politics than this; but this is a minimum that all can be presumed to have available *equally*.

Is such equality, however, merely an equality of heteronomy, as Rousseau asserted? Are the people of England free only once every five years when choosing whom they will be subservient to?[17] Such a judgement is echoed by those participatory theorists who complain that putting a cross on a ballot once every so often is a trifling amount of participation. Two points can be made in response. First, from the standpoint of popular control, elections exert an effect well beyond the time when they are actually taking place. This is due to the well-known law of anticipated reactions: power is operative even when it is not being exercised. The fact of the vote casts a long shadow in front of it, as it were. It acts as a continuous discipline on the elected, requiring them to give public account of their actions and to take constant notice of public opinion through its various channels of expression – media comment, opinion polls, party meetings, lobbying activity and so on. In the economy of political time, voting delivers a considerable degree of control for a small outlay, to an extent that is liable to be overlooked if we concentrate on the act alone and ignore all that it causes to happen.

Of course the popular control that is underpinned by elections could be both more rigorous and more equal between citizens. Here lies a substantial agenda for democratization, including a more effective control of the executive (for example, through a sufficiently independent parliament, guarantees of open government, individual redress against abuse); ensuring a more representative legislative assembly (through equalizing the value of each vote and the effective opportunity to stand for election); making the electoral process less open to manipulation by those in office, and so forth. Different priorities will be relevant to different countries, but the direction in which democratization points should be clear.

The second point to make is that a representative democracy not only allows its citizens a much greater level of political activity than the minimum involved in the vote; it also requires it if it is to function effectively – through membership of political parties, pressure groups, trade unions, campaigning organizations, protest meetings and suchlike. From one point of view this activity can be seen as the natural outgrowth of the freedom of association that is necessary to the electoral process. It is also a response to the acknowledged limitations of that process, whereby the choices offered to the electorate lie between broad constellations of policies which they cannot disaggregate. Having available a more narrowly focused medium for the mobilization of opinion and the exertion of influence on specific issues of concern as they arise is an essential complement to the bluntness of the electoral process. In this respect the Schumpeterian account of the division of labour between the electors and the elected, whereby the former 'refrain' from all political action once they have cast their vote, far from being realistic as is claimed, is simply inaccurate.[18] It represents more a yearning for an untrammelled form of elective dictatorship than a realistic account of how liberal democracies actually operate, or what is required for them to work effectively.

From a democratic point of view, the problem with a representative democracy in practice is not so much that it restricts political activity to the vote as that the opportunity for a more extensive involvement, and the degree of influence with government which it carries, are dependent upon a variety of resources – of time, of money, of learned capacity – that are distributed unevenly between different sections of the population. The freedoms of speech and association not only provide the guarantee of a more extensive political activity than the vote; they are also the means whereby the inequalities of civil society are transmitted to the political domain. A minimum agenda for democratization at this point, therefore, would include measures to moderate the political impact of these inequalities: on the one side, by limiting the scope that wealth gives to individuals and powerful corporations to purchase political influence through ownership of the media, sponsoring or 'retaining' elected representatives, or financing election campaigns; on the other, by improving access to the policy process of the socially marginalized and those who represent them. It is here, too, that the more substantial social agenda for democratization to be considered in the next section has its rationale.

Let me summarize the argument so far: the institution of representation involves a significant limitation of citizens' autonomy, but one that is justifiable by considerations of time consistent with political equality; voting nevertheless delivers a more continuous control than might appear from its frequency or time span, and one that is complemented by opportunities for more extensive political activity and influence; and this control could be made both more stringent and more equal between citizens. It follows, further, that if representation offers both an effective and an improvable form of popular control consistent with the economy of time, then the electoral process could be extended to other institutions, private as well as public, local and neighbourhood as well as national and supranational.[19] Democratization, in sum, should be sought through a deepening and extending of representative institutions which, while setting bounds to citizen participation, also provide the necessary framework for it.

Finally, however, if the institution of representation constitutes one of the limits to the process of democratization, as I have argued, then it is not enough for a theorist to demonstrate how it might be reconciled with the retention of a measure of autonomy; it has also to be agreed to by citizens themselves. Here we need a more adequate medium of consent than voting in an election, which cannot be taken to imply agreement with the institutional arrangements within which the election takes place.[20] At the minimum, consent would require a written constitution, including a constitutional document setting out the rights and obligations of the citizen, with their limitations, to which individuals would be required formally to agree upon reaching majority or acquiring citizenship; and which would therefore be associated with a systematic agenda of political education. Moreover, these rights would have to include the right for a given number of citizens to require parliamentary or other appropriate consideration of amendments to the same constitution, if that consent was to be other than a formality. It is difficult to see how otherwise the surrender of autonomy involved in representation might be not only kept to a minimum but also made subject to the explicit authorization that autonomy requires.

The Limited State and the Social Agenda of Democratization

I have already touched on the social inequalities that qualify or compromise political equality and argued that reducing their political salience forms part of any agenda for democratization. However, many socialists and feminists would contend that the kind of measures so far suggested are at best remedial ones and do not go to the source of inequalities in the economy and the family, in the relations of production and of reproduction, and that a strategy for democratization must extend to these areas directly. In particular, such a strategy should not be bound by the liberal distinction between the public and the private spheres, whereby democratic norms are confined to the former while hierarchical relationships continue unattended in the latter. This is not only because of the impact that the relations of civil society have on the formally 'political' sphere; it is also because the institutions of civil society, in view of their salience for people's lives, constitute a critical arena for democratization in their own right. The question I now wish to address is whether, or how far, such strategies risk eroding distinctions or over-stepping limits that are necessary to the maintenance of representative democracy itself. Since the areas of property and gender raise different issues, for all the parallels that can be drawn between them, I shall treat them separately in what follows.

At first sight the questions of how much the state should do, and who can or should control it, would seem to belong in quite different theoretical domains. Surely the extent and the distribution of political power are two separate issues? Yet both liberals and socialists have argued that they are connected. Among the many issues in contention between them about the organization of economic life (justice, freedom, efficiency), not least is its implications for democracy. The liberal contention is that representative democracy has to be capitalist democracy, because only capitalism ensures the necessary limitation of state power that enables it to be democratically controlled. It is possible to distinguish a number of different arguments here, two about private property, two about the market, and a more general one about the pluralism of power. I shall set them out in propositional form to facilitate analysis and comparison.

L1   If the state owns and controls all productive property, it will be able to deny resources and even a livelihood to those campaigning against its policies. Political opposition requires secure access to the means of organizing, campaigning and disseminating information, and such access can only be guaranteed by the institution of private property.[21]

L2   A system of socialized property of whatever kind will necessarily have to outlaw private ownership of the means of production, and, for its own survival, prevent political parties emerging which might campaign for its restitution. Socialism's tendency towards single-party rule is thus no historical aberration, whereas capitalism's ability to tolerate forms of social ownership in its midst (co-operatives, collective welfare organizations and so on) provides a secure basis for multi-party competition.[22]

L3   If the state takes over the task of economic coordination from the market, replacing its voluntary and lateral relations with a compulsory hierarchy of administrative planning, it will create a bureaucratic monster that no one can control, and stifle all independent initiative within society.[23]

L4   From the standpoint of the citizen, the market is experienced as a much more democratic device than the polity, since it allows maximum individual choice and power to the consumer, in comparison with the monopolistic and insensitive provision of the public sector, where collective choices necessarily disregard minority preferences. Democracy therefore requires that the scope of the latter be restricted to an absolute minimum.[24]

L5   The political liberties intrinsic to democracy depend upon a plurality of power centres capable of checking one another, among which the separation of power between the political and economic spheres and within each, such as capitalism guarantees, is the most critical.[25]

These propositions, taken together, do not entail that capitalism always produces political democracy, only that it is necessary to it; and more careful liberals will make this distinction clear. 'History suggests only that capitalism is a necessary condition for political freedom', writes Milton Friedman; 'clearly it is not a sufficient condition'.[26] In other words, there can be both capitalist democracies and capitalist dictatorships; but there can be socialist dictatorships only. On this view a fourth quartile (socialist democracy) is necessarily a historically empty category.

To each of these liberal propositions can be counterposed a corresponding socialist assertion.

S1   Private ownership makes democratization of the workplace impossible, since management must account to its shareholders rather than to its workers. The subordination of the latter in a key area of their lives is not only a major infringement of autonomy; it also discourages the exercise of autonomy at the wider political level.[27]

S2   Capitalism's 'tolerance' of socialist experiments in its midst is very limited, since they are forced to operate under conditions which hamper their effectiveness. The historical record shows that, if a socialist movement or party gathers sufficient support to threaten the interests of private property, capitalists will back a dictatorship to eliminate the threat.[28]

S3   To leave key economic decisions to market forces is to surrender a crucial sphere of collective self-determination to the haphazard play of private choices and to powerful institutions that owe no accountability to the public at large.[29]

S4   Exercising choice in the consumer market depends upon income derived from the capital and labour markets, and here the character of the market is to intensify the inequalities of resource that people bring to it. The freer the market, the more repressive the state has to be to control the dissatisfactions of market losers.[30]

S5   Capitalist society's pluralism is a highly constrained one, given the many modes of capitalism's integration into the state. Socialist pluralism would be more diverse, since it would not be tied to class conflict at the point of production.[31]

Each of the ten propositions above merits a volume of commentary in itself, but I shall confine myself to making a few points that can be drawn from a comparison between them. First, although the liberal and socialist theses can be said to correspond to one another, they are not symmetrical. Whereas the thrust of the socialist five is that socialism is necessary to the *full* realization of democracy, the liberal case is that capitalism is necessary to the preservation of any democracy *at all*. In keeping with the characteristically sceptical temper of liberalism comes the advice to democrats to limit their ambitions: half a loaf is better than none.

Secondly, however, it is evident that not all liberalism's propositions carry the same weight against different versions of socialism. While all five can be arrayed against a command economy of the Soviet type, only one (L2) has any force against a form of market socialism with diversified social ownership.[32] On the other hand, social democrats for their part can appeal to proposition S4 against neo-liberals to argue that, whatever other conditions democracy needs, it cannot be secure without a substantial welfare state. The balance sheet, in other words, is more complex than appears at first sight.

Thirdly, one of socialism's own propositions (the second part of S2) underlines what has proved a key historical dilemma for democratic socialists: whenever they have successfully mobilized popular support against private property, they have jeopardized the existence of representative democracy through the threat of capitalist reaction. Although the prospect of such support looks highly improbable in socialism's present nadir, it would be foolish to exclude the re-emergence of such support for ever, given that the end of the communist experiment does not signal the end of the problems of capitalism which gave it its initial impetus, least of all in the developing world. It is not enough, therefore, for socialists to show how a future socialist society might *guarantee* as well as extend democracy. They must also provide a credible strategy for realizing such a society within the framework of liberal democratic institutions.

It is this dilemma of transition, in conclusion, that justifies those strategies of economic democratization that work with the grain of private property rather than against it. Creating special representative bodies at the regional and national level to control the investment of pension funds, on the one side; requiring a percentage of profits in individual firms to be set aside as shares for the collective control of employees, on the other: these could provide the basis for a thorough-going democratization of economic life. The former would give workers the control over their own property that they now patently lack; the latter would ensure a progressive accumulation of ownership rights to accompany codetermination within enterprises. Unlike liberal proposals for wider share-ownership, however, such rights would have a crucial collective as well as individual dimension and would give the idea of a 'property-owning democracy' a more genuinely democratic content through the equalization of control over collective decisions they would bring.[33]

In contrast to socialism, feminist strategies for democratization do not threaten to undermine the principles of the limited state or of political pluralism in the way that at least some forms of socialism have done. For this reason I shall give them only brief consideration here. This is not to say that their proposals are not significant or far-reaching; only that, while they challenge the bases of male power and privilege, in doing so they do not threaten the defining features of liberal democracy as I have characterized them. Feminists have always been much more suspicious of the state than have socialists, and much more conscious of the ways in which political movements of the subordinate can generate new hierarchies of power and privilege. Furthermore, although the power of gender has even more ramifications than the power of property, it is hard to envisage an organized last-ditch defence on the part of masculinity which would threaten the democratic order. Precisely for these reasons, feminism offers a more plausible prospect for the progressive transformation of social relations consistent with democracy than socialism has achieved this century.

This judgement assumes that the feminist purpose in challenging the liberal distinction between the public and private spheres, and in its slogan 'the personal is the political', is not the total politicization of every aspect of life, so that there remains no private sphere left in which it is not the state's business to intervene. It involves rather the claim that the private sphere is *already* political, in the sense that it is a key site of power relations, and that these condition both the character of, and the mode of access to, the politics of the public domain.[34] The agenda of feminist democratization, then, is far-reaching, but not totalizing. It extends from a redistribution of the time and burdens of domestic caring at one end, to a reform of parliamentary and electoral processes at the other, through a variety of modes of political engagement and instrumentality.[35] Unless one takes the implausible view that none of this agenda can be effected without the prior abolition of capitalism, it is difficult to see how it can be incompatible with the premises of liberal democracy. It involves a redefinition of the private and public spheres and of their interrelationship, certainly, but not the elimination of every boundary between them. It offers an alternative to liberal democratic politics as these have historically been practised, to be sure, but not an alternative to liberal democracy itself.

Conclusion

In this chapter I have offered a theory of liberal democracy through an analysis of the relation between its component concepts, which provides us with a definition, a strong theoretical claim, an account of its history and a practical question. The definition of liberal democracy incorporates the five elements of the liberal legacy outlined at the start of the chapter, which can be read as its defining characteristics. The strong theoretical claim is that, without these elements, no popular control over collective decision-making at the level of the modern state is sustainable. Within the framework provided by these elements, however, there has been a history of repeated struggle between democratizers, seeking the extension and more equal distribution of popular control, and those other features of liberalism that have historically served to limit it. The practical question, finally, that derives from both the theoretical claim and the account of history is how far this democratization can proceed without threatening one or other of the basic conditions of the democratic order itself.

Like all practical questions, this one can only ultimately be resolved in practice. However, I have suggested good reasons why representation, despite the limits it imposes on autonomy, is an irreducible necessity; and I have considered the points at which a social agenda of democratization might infringe the principle of the limited state. Here I have been exploring what might be termed the limits of democratization. Within these limits, however, there remains a large scope for further extending and equalizing the opportunities for popular control. The history of liberal democracy, in conclusion, has not yet come to an end. The struggle for democratization both will, and should, continue.

NOTES

1   This distinction is similar to that made by Keith Graham between a general *concept* of democracy and rival *conceptions* of it, in K. Graham, *The Battle of Democracy* (Brighton, Wheatsheaf Books, 1986), p. 8. The distinction is confused by many writers on democracy; see, for example, J. Schumpeter, *Capitalism, Socialism and Democracy* (London, Unwin University Books, 1947), chs 21–2.

2   The ambivalence of the relationship is explored in B. Holden, *Understanding Liberal Democracy* (Oxford, Philip Allen, 1988), ch. 1; and in a more historical way in A. Arblaster, *The Rise and Decline of Western Liberalism* (Oxford, Blackwell, 1984), especially chs 10, 11 and 15.

3   For the legitimacy of alternatives to liberal democracy see D. Beetham, *The Legitimation of Power* (London, Macmillan, 1991), chs 5 and 6.

4   J. Locke, *Two Treatises of Government* (Cambridge, Cambridge University Press, 1967), pp. 365–81.

5   J. H. Stewart, *A Documentary History of the French Revolution* (New York, Macmillan, 1951), pp. 129ff.

6   For example J. Mill, *An Essay on Government* (Oxford, Blackwell, 1937), p. 45.

7   For recent examples see P. Green, *Retrieving Democracy* (London, Methuen, 1985), and S. Bowles and H. Gintis, *Democracy and Capitalism* (London, Routledge and Kegan Paul, 1986).

8   For example, C. Pateman, 'Feminism and democracy', in G. Duncan (ed.), *Democratic Theory and Practice* (Cambridge, Cambridge University Press, 1983), pp. 204–17; S. Rowbotham, 'Feminism and democracy', in D. Held and C. Pollitt (eds), *New Forms of Democracy* (London, Sage, 1986), pp. 78–109; A. Phillips, *Engendering Democracy* (Cambridge, Polity Press, 1991).

9   The complexity of the liberal tradition is explored in C. B. Macpherson, *The Life and Times of Liberal Democracy* (Oxford, Oxford University Press, 1977); see also

D. Beetham, 'Max Weber and the liberal political tradition', *Archives Européennes de Sociologie*, 30 (1989), 311–23.

10 Recent examples are provided by B. Barber, *Strong Democracy* (Berkeley, CA, University of California Press, 1984); J. Burnheim, *Is Democracy Possible?* (Cambridge, Polity Press, 1985); C. C. Gould, *Rethinking Democracy* (Cambridge, Cambridge University Press, 1988).

11 For a fuller discussion of autonomy see D. Held, *Models of Democracy* (Cambridge, Policy Press, 1987), ch. 9.

12 For a discussion of the limitations of interest-based justifications for democracy see Graham, *The Battle of Democracy*, ch. 2.

13 S. Bialer, *Stalin's Successors* (Cambridge, Cambridge University Press, 1980), pp. 185ff.

14 See C. Pateman, *Participation and Democratic Theory* (Cambridge, Cambridge University Press, 1970).

15 This is its context in the writings of J. S. Mill. See the discussion in Macpherson, *The Life and Times of Liberal Democracy*, ch. 2.

16 R. P. Wolff, *In Defense of Anarchism* (New York, Harper and Row, 1970), ch. 1.

17 J-J. Rousseau, *The Social Contract* (London, Dent, 1913), p. 78.

18 J. Schumpeter, *Capitalism, Socialism and Democracy*, p. 295.

19 'When we pose the question whether democracy has made any progress . . . we must enquire how many more spaces there are where the citizen can exercise the right to vote'; See N. Bobbio, *The Future of Democracy* (Cambridge, Polity Press, 1987), p. 56.

20 See C. Pateman, *The Problem of Political Obligation* (Cambridge, Polity Press, 1985), ch. 5; Gould, *Rethinking Democracy*, ch. 8.

21 M. Friedman, *Capitalism and Freedom* (Chicago, University of Chicago Press, 1962), ch. 1.

22 'The socialist society would have to forbid capitalist acts between consenting adults'; See R. Nozick, *Anarchy, State and Utopia* (Oxford, Blackwell, 1978), p. 163.

23 F. A. Hayek, *The Road to Serfdom* (London, Routledge and Kegan Paul, 1944), especially chs 5–7.

24 A. Seldon, *Capitalism* (Oxford, Blackwell, 1990), ch. 5; D. Usher, *The Economic Prerequisite to Democracy* (Oxford, Blackwell, 1981).

25 This classical liberal thesis was given a sociological reformulation by Mosca and Weber as a warning against the dangers of socialism. See G. Mosca, *The Ruling Class* (New York, McGraw-Hill, 1939), pp. 285ff., and M. Weber, *Economy and Society* (Berkeley, CA, University of California Press, 1978), pp. 1401ff.

26 Friedman, *Capitalism and Freedom*, p. 10.

27 G. D. H. Cole, *Self-Government in Industry* (London, Bell and Hyman, 1917); A. J. Topham and K. Coates, *Industrial Democracy in Great Britain* (London, MacGibbon and Kee, 1968).

28 This proposition can be traced back to Marx's analysis of Bonapartism in 'The Eighteenth Brumaire of Louis Bonaparte', in K. Marx and F. Engels, *Selected Works Vol. 1* (Moscow, Foreign Languages Publishing House, 1935). Cf. A. Gramsci, 'Democracy and fascism', in Q. Hoare (ed.), *Antonio Gramsci: selections from prison writings 1921–1926* (London, Lawrence and Wishart, 1978), pp. 267–72; H. J. Laski, *Democracy in Crisis* (London, Allen and Unwin, 1933).

29 A. Arblaster, *Democracy* (Milton Keynes, Open University Press, 1987), ch. 10.

30 A. Gamble, 'The free economy and the strong state', in R. Miliband and J. Saville (eds), *Socialist Register 1979* (London, Merlin Press, 1979), pp. 1–25.

31 R. Miliband, *The State in Capitalist Society* (London, Weidenfeld and Nicolson, 1969); H. Breitenbach, T. Burden and D. Coates, *Features of a Viable Socialism* (London, Harvester Wheatsheaf, 1990), ch. 7.

32 See D. Miller, *Market, State and Community* (Oxford, Clarendon Press, 1990), part 3; also C. Pierson's chapter in this volume.

33 Similar proposals are discussed in R. A. Dahl, *A Preface to Economic Democracy* (Cambridge, Polity Press, 1985), chs 3 and 4. A cautious review is provided by W. L. Adamson in 'Economic democracy and the expediency of worker participation', *Political Studies*, 38 (1990), 56–71.

34 See, however, the discussion in J. Siltanen and M. Stanworth, 'The politics of private woman and public man', in *Women and the Public Sphere* (London, Hutchinson, 1984), ch. 18.

35 See A. Phillips's chapter in this volume.

3

DELIBERATIVE DEMOCRACY AND SOCIAL CHOICE

David Miller

If we are in the business of thinking about liberal democracy and possible alternatives to it, we must begin by drawing a distinction between institutions and their regulative ideals. Liberal democracy may be taken to refer to the set of institutions – free elections, competing parties, freedom of speech – that make up the political system with which we are familiar in the west; or it may refer to the conception of democracy that underlies and justifies that system. The relationship between institutions and regulative ideals is not necessarily simple or one-to-one. The same institution may be justified from different points of view, although characteristically those who favour contrasting regulative ideals will aim to shape the institution in different ways. Thus, to take a familiar case, the practice of electing representatives to a legislative assembly may be seen as a way of subjecting legislators to popular control; alternatively, it may be seen simply as a means of removing visibly corrupt legislators from office. Which of these views you take will affect your preferences as to the form of the practice. (How frequent should elections be? Should the voting system be first-past-the-post or something else? And so forth.)

The argument that follows has mainly to do with competing regulative ideals of democracy. In comparing liberal democracy with what I shall call deliberative democracy, my aim is to contrast two basic ways of understanding the democratic process. In favouring deliberative democracy, therefore, I am not recommending wholesale abolition of the

I should like to thank Joshua Cohen, David Held, Iain McLean, William Riker and Albert Weale, as well as the participants in the *Political Studies* conference on Alternatives to Liberal Democracy, for their very helpful comments on earlier versions of this paper.

present institutions of liberal democracy but rather a reshaping of those institutions in the light of a different regulative ideal from that which I take to be prevalent now. I shall only address the institutional questions briefly. My main aim is to bring out what is at stake between liberal and deliberative democracy, particularly in the light of social choice theory, which appears to challenge the cogency of anything beyond the most minimal of democratic ideals.

Let me now sketch the contrast between liberal and deliberative democracy as regulative ideals. In the liberal view, the aim of democracy is to aggregate individual preferences into a collective choice in as fair and efficient a way as possible.[1] In a democracy there will be many different views as to what should be done politically, reflecting the many different interests and beliefs present in society. Each person's preferences should be accorded equal weight. Moreover, preferences are sacrosanct because they reflect the individuality of each member of the political community (an exception to this arises only in the case of preferences that violate the canons of liberal democracy itself, such as racist beliefs that deny the equal rights of all citizens). The problem then is to find the institutional structure that best meets the requirements of equality and efficiency. Thus liberal democrats may divide on the question of whether majoritarian decision-making is to be preferred, or whether the ideal is a pluralist system which gives various groups in society different amounts of influence over decisions in proportion to their interest in those decisions. This, however, is a family quarrel in which both sides are guided by the same underlying ideal, namely how to reach a fair and efficient compromise given the many conflicting preferences expressed in the political community.

The deliberative ideal also starts from the premise that political preferences will conflict and that the purpose of democratic institutions must be to resolve this conflict. But it envisages this occurring through an open and uncoerced discussion of the issue at stake with the aim of arriving at an agreed judgement.[2] The process of reaching a decision will also be a process whereby initial preferences are transformed to take account of the views of others. That is, the need to reach an agreement forces each participant to put forward proposals under the rubric of general principles or policy considerations that others could accept. Thus even if initially my aim is to support the claims of a particular group to which I belong or which I represent, I cannot in a general discussion simply say 'I claim that group A - farmers, say, or policemen - should get more money'. I have to give reasons for the claim. These might be that the group in question has special needs, or that it is in the common interest to improve the living standards of the group. By giving these reasons, however, I am committing myself to a general principle, which by implication applies to any other similarly placed group. Thus I am forced to take a wider view, and either to defend the claim I am making when applied not only to my group but to groups *B*, *C* and *D*, which are like *A* in the relevant respects, or else to back down and moderate the claim to something I am prepared to accept in these other cases too. Although finally when a decision has to be reached there may still need to be a vote taken between two or more options, what participants are doing at that point is something like rendering a judgement or a verdict on the basis of what they have heard. They are expressing an opinion about which policy best meets the various claims that have been advanced, or represents the fairest compromise between the competing points of view that have been expressed.

The deliberative view clearly rests on a different conception of 'human nature in politics' from the liberal view. Whereas the latter stresses the importance of giving due weight to each individual's distinct preferences, the former relies upon a person's capacity to be swayed by rational arguments and to lay aside particular interests and opinions in deference to overall fairness and the common interest of the collectivity. It supposes people to be to some degree communally orientated in their outlook. It also seems to be more vulnerable to exploitation, in the sense that the practice of deliberative democracy can be abused by people who pay lip-service to the ideal of open discussion but actually attempt to manipulate their colleagues to reach decisions that serve private interests.[3] We shall shortly see, however, that liberal democratic procedures are themselves vulnerable to political manipulation. At this stage, therefore, we must take it as an open question which of the two democratic ideals is more likely to be subverted by manipulative individuals or groups.

In presenting my account of deliberative democracy, I mean to distinguish it not only from liberal democracy but from what has been called 'epistemic' democracy.[4] The epistemic conception of democracy sees the aim of democratic procedures as being to arrive at a correct answer to some question facing the political community. It is assumed here, in other words, that there is some objectively right or valid answer to the question that has been posed, but because there is uncertainty as to what the answer is, a decision-procedure is needed, and democracy, in the form of majority voting, is the procedure most likely to produce the right answer. This was, for instance, the view of Condorcet,[5] and it has also been attributed to Rousseau,[6] although my own belief is that Rousseau's view is ambiguous as between deliberative and epistemic conceptions of democracy.[7]

I believe the epistemic conception sets an unrealistically high standard for political decision-making. Although occasionally a political community may have to decide on some question to which it is plausible to suppose a correct answer exists (say some scientific question in circumstances where there is complete consensus on the ends which the decision should serve), it is much more likely that the issue will concern competing claims which cannot all be met simultaneously in circumstances where no resolution of the competition can be deemed objectively right. In the deliberative conception, the aim is to reach agreement, which might be achieved in different ways. One way is for the participants to agree on a substantive norm, which all concur in thinking is the appropriate norm for the case in hand. Another way is to agree on a procedure, which abstracts from the merits of the arguments advanced by particular claimants. (Thus suppose the question is how an available resource such as a tract of land should be allocated as between several groups that lay claim to it. One possibility would be to agree on a principle such as that the resource should go to the group which needs it most or which could use it most productively, and then on the basis of the arguments advanced decide which group that was. Alternatively the deliberating body might feel that it was not competent to make such a judgement, and opt instead for a procedural solution, such as sharing the resource out equally between the groups, rotating it between them, or deciding by lot.) In either case, the outcome is a decision which all the parties involved may feel to be reasonable, but this does not entail its reflecting any transcendent standard of justice or rightness. The emphasis in the deliberative conception is on the way in which a process of open discussion in which all points of view can be heard may legitimate the outcome when this is seen to reflect the discussion that has preceded it, not on deliberation as a discovery procedure in search of a correct answer.[8]

My aim in this chapter is to see whether deliberative democracy may be less vulnerable than liberal democracy to the problems posed by social choice theory for democracy in general. In arguing in this way, I am apparently reversing a common opinion that social choice obliges us to abandon 'populist' models of democracy, in which democratic decisions are represented as expressions of 'the people's choice' or the 'popular will', in favour of 'liberal' models, in which democratic elections are construed merely as a safeguard against the emergence of tyrannical rulers. Democracy on this view is a matter of the voters having the right, at periodic intervals, to remove from office governments which they have come to dislike. Any notion that the voters should in some more positive way determine public policy is misguided. This argument plays some role in the classical defences of liberal democracy by Schumpeter and Dahl[9] and has more recently been developed at length and with great intellectual force by William Riker.[10]

From my perspective, however, both liberalism and populism as understood by Riker count as variants on the liberal ideal of democracy. For populism is the view that individuals' preferences should be amalgamated, by voting, to yield a general will which then guides policy. Liberalism in Riker's sense is less ambitious in that it sees the purpose of elections in negative terms as involving the removal of unpopular leaders. Both views see democracy as a matter of aggregating voters' preferences: they differ over the question of whether policy can be chosen in this way, or only the personnel of government. The idea that democratic decisions are not a matter of aggregating preferences at all but of reaching agreed judgements is foreign to both.

Let me now remind readers of the challenge which social choice theory poses for these liberal views of democracy. Suppose a voting public has to decide between a number of policy options – suppose, to take a concrete case, that the issue is how Britain should generate its electricity, and the public has to choose between coal-fired, oil-fired, gas-fired and nuclear power stations. The message of social choice theory, and in particular its most celebrated constituent, Arrow's general possibility theorem,[11] is that one cannot devise a mechanism for making such decisions which simultaneously meets a number of quite weak and reasonable-sounding conditions that we might want to impose (such as monotonicity or the requirement that if a voter raises the position of one option in his or her own personal ranking, this cannot have the effect of lowering it in the social ranking).

This, one might say, is *the* problem posed by social choice for democracy – that is, in general there is no fair and rational way of amalgamating voters' preferences to reach a social decision – but it entails two more specific problems. The first is the arbitrariness of decision rules and the second is the near-unavoidability of strategic voting, or more strictly of opportunities for strategic voting. Decision rules fall broadly speaking into two classes, which following Riker we may call majoritarian and positional methods of selecting a preferred outcome. Majoritarian rules proceed by offering voters a series of binary choices and, depending on which option wins which encounters, identify an overall winner. So, in our example, voters would be asked to choose between coal and oil for generating electricity, between coal and gas, and so forth. There would be a series of majorities on the questions asked, and then some rule for discovering the overall choice. Positional rules ask voters to rank the available options and then compute a winner using all or part of this fuller information. Thus voters might be asked to rank the energy options from 1 to 4 on their ballot papers, and then a winner could be found by some rule such as giving an option two points each time it is someone's first choice and one point each time it comes second.

The problem of arbitrariness arises because it is not clear which of the many possible rules best matches our intuitive sense of 'finding the option which the voters most prefer'; or, to put the point another way, for any given rule it is possible to give examples where using that rule produces an outcome that seems repugnant to our sense of what a democratic decision should be. Among majoritarian rules, a strong contender is the Condorcet rule that any option which beats all the others in a series of binary choices should be the social choice. But there is no guarantee in any particular case that such a Condorcet winner can be found, so the rule is incomplete. Thus gas might beat coal and oil but lose to nuclear power, which in turn was beaten by one of the other options. If the rule is to be complete it has then to be extended to cope with this possibility, but there is no extension that is obviously the right one.[12] Among positional rules, the one most often favoured is the Borda count, which scores each option according to the place it holds in each voter's ranking, so that my top option gets n points, my second option $n-1$ points and so on right the way down. One problem with this is that it may make the decision among quite popular options depend upon the way some voters rank way-out or eccentric options if these are on the ballot paper. Finally, it is an embarrassment that the Condorcet and Borda rules do not necessarily converge; that is, a Condorcet winner may exist, but a different option may be selected by use of the Borda count. This might occur where the Condorcet winner – nuclear power, let us say – was the first choice of a fair number of people but tended to be ranked very low by those who were against it, whereas another option – gas, let us say – was the first preference of just a few, but ranked second by quite a lot. Here it is not at all clear which way we should jump. There is a case for the option with most first preferences, and a case for the compromise proposal which comes reasonably high in most people's rankings.

The second problem is strategic voting, which means misrepresenting your true preferences when you vote with the aim of increasing the chances of your favoured option. Obviously the success of this depends on your having some knowledge of the preferences of other voters. It can be shown that there is virtually no decision rule that is not vulnerable to strategic manipulation if some voters choose to act in this way.[13] Again a couple of examples may help to bring this out. Suppose we are using a majoritarian decision rule. It is possible by strategic voting to block the emergence of a Condorcet winner. Thus suppose in our example nuclear power is the Condorcet winner if everyone votes sincerely. I am not particularly averse to nuclear power, but I am very strongly committed to coal-fired stations. I cannot prevent nuclear power defeating coal in a run-off between these options, but if others think like me we can stop the nuclear bandwagon by voting insincerely for gas when the choice between gas and nuclear power is posed, thus preventing the emergence of nuclear power as a Condorcet winner and triggering whatever subsidiary rule is being employed in the hope that coal will win. Equally, if a Borda count is being used and I know that gas, say, is the likely winner, then I can boost the chances of coal by insincerely pushing gas down into fourth place. There is of course no guarantee that my strategy will work, since my opponents may behave strategically too. But this only serves to underline the arbitrariness of the eventual decision which in these circumstances would have very little claim to be called anything like a popular will.

So the challenge posed by social choice to democratic theory can be reduced to two basic claims: that there is no rule for aggregating individual preferences that is obviously fair and rational and thus superior to other possible rules; and that virtually every rule is subject to strategic manipulation, so that even if it would produce a plausible outcome for a given set of preferences if everyone voted sincerely, the actual outcome is liable to be distorted by strategic voting.

Working from within the liberal view of democracy, pessimists such as Riker respond to this challenge by reducing the significance of the electoral process to that of providing a safeguard against what Riker calls 'tyranny'. But even this safeguard is quite weak, since if the outcome of elections is to some degree arbitrary (as the social choice analysis shows), it is not apparent why they should pick out for removal unpopular or 'tyrannical' leaders. Coleman and Ferejohn put this point well:

> Nonreasoned removal from office is precisely what follows if Riker is correct in interpreting the instability results of social choice theory as demonstrating the meaninglessness of voting. If outcomes are arbitrarily connected to the preferences of the electorate, we cannot infer from his removal from office that an officeholder's conduct was in fact disapproved of by the voters. This is hardly the ideal of officeholders being put at risk by elections that we associate with liberalism.[14]

Social choice theory seems to undermine the liberal view of democracy in a systematic way, regardless of the precise function that is assigned to the act of voting in elections.

Can the problems of social choice be avoided altogether by switching to the deliberative ideal of democracy? Social choice theory postulates voters with given preferences over outcomes, and it is sometimes suggested that, once we allow that voters' preferences may alter in the course of decision-making, its results no longer apply.[15] But this response is too simple-minded. So long as there is a problem of amalgamating the voters' wishes at the point of decision – so long, to be more precise, as three or more policy outcomes are still in play and there is no unanimous preference for one of these outcomes – the social choice results apply. A decision rule must be found and this is potentially vulnerable to the problems of arbitrariness and strategic manipulation. In my account of deliberative democracy I indicated that, although full consensus was the ideal guiding discussion, it would be quite unrealistic to suppose that every instance of deliberation would culminate in unanimous agreement. Votes will still have to be taken, and where voting occurs so, potentially, will social choice problems.

Rather than sweeping away social choice theory at a stroke, my aim is the more limited one of showing that deliberative democracy has the resources to attenuate the social choice problems faced by the political community. The case I shall make has two main aspects. The first concerns the way in which deliberation may limit the range of preferences that have to be amalgamated in the final judgement. The second concerns the way in which knowledge of the structure of opinion in the deliberating body may influence the choice of decision rule.

The first part of the argument addresses one of the axioms of Arrow's original theorem, namely the requirement that the social choice procedure should be able to accommodate any possible set of individual rank orderings of outcomes. This axiom may indeed seem self-evident; it appears to pick up the liberal idea that each person is entitled to express whatever preferences he or she chooses, so that any limits on individual rank orderings would be discriminatory (as Riker puts the point, 'any rule or command that prohibits a person from choosing some preference order is morally unacceptable (or at least unfair) from the point of view of democracy'[16]). But rather than some external prohibition of possible ways of ranking alternatives, the possibility I wish to contemplate is that some initial sets of preferences might spontaneously be transformed through the process of deliberation, so that the final set of rankings from which a decision had to be reached was much smaller than the original set. If this were so, we could drop Arrow's unrestricted condition in favour of the weaker requirement that the social decision procedure should be able to cope with all possible sets of *post-deliberation* rankings.

I shall shortly suggest how this might help to resolve the social choice problems we have identified. But first we need to consider why some initial preferences might be eliminated in this way. The most straightforward case is that of preference orders that are irrational because they are based on false empirical beliefs. To use the energy policy example, someone might judge energy sources entirely on the basis of environmental soundness and begin with the rank order coal, gas, oil, nuclear power. However, in the course of debate strong evidence is produced about the atmospheric effects of coal-burning power stations which decisively pushes coal below gas and oil from an environmental point of view. This is not to say that the original rank order is completely untenable because there may be other value stances from which it remains appropriate. But then again it may be that no one or virtually no one holds these value stances, so the effect of debate is to crystallize the rank orderings into a smaller number of coherent patterns.

A second case is that of preferences that are so repugnant to the moral beliefs of the society within which the decisions are being made that no one is willing to advance them in a public context. This seems to be roughly the position with racist beliefs in contemporary Britain: a number of people hold them privately, but it is generally recognized that they cannot be articulated in political forums like Parliament. And this does constrain the set of policies that can be supported. You may favour immigration restrictions for racist reasons, but the fact that you cannot present these reasons publicly means that the policies you advocate have to be general in form; that is, they cannot explicitly discriminate between black and white immigrants.

The most important way in which deliberation may alter initial preferences, however, is that outlined in my original description of the deliberative ideal. Preferences that are not so much immoral as narrowly self-regarding will tend to be eliminated by the process of public debate. To be seen to be engaged in political debate we must argue in terms that any other participant could potentially accept, and 'It's good for me' is not such an argument. Or as Bob Goodin has put the point, when we adopt a public role, we must launder our preferences so that only public-orientated ones are expressed.[17] I discount here the possibility of people expressing one set of preferences in debate and voting according to another set at decision time. If voting is public, this could only occur at the cost of immediate loss of future credibility, and this may be a good reason for having an open voting system under conditions that approximate to deliberative democracy, as Brennan and Pettit have recently argued.[18] However, even under a secret ballot, it seems to me quite unlikely that we would witness widespread hypocrisy such as is involved in arguing for one position and then voting for another. This is a claim about human psychology: it says that if you have committed yourself to one position publicly you would find it demeaning to retreat to a more selfish posture at the point of material decision.[19] I do not say this is universally true, but I think it is widely true.

Since this claim about the moralizing effect of public discussion is crucial to my argument about deliberative democracy, I would like at this point to illustrate it with some empirical evidence, although not alas drawn directly from the field of politics. The first piece of evidence comes from psychological experiments which try to simulate the behaviour of juries.[20] In these experiments, a number of subjects are shown a video recording of a trial in which the evidence for and against the accused is fairly evenly balanced. They are then asked to give their private guilty/ not guilty verdict, and on the basis of this they are formed into a number of mock juries divided evenly between the two views. The question is: which verdict will the jury eventually reach? *A priori* one would predict some hung juries, and then equal proportions of guilty and not-guilty verdicts. In fact, however, there is a marked tilt towards the not-guilty side, which the researchers attribute to the presence of a 'leniency norm'. That is, where the presence of conflicting opinions suggests that there is real doubt as to the guilt or innocence of the accused, you should give the accused the benefit of that doubt by returning a not-guilty verdict. Now the leniency norm is always present to some degree, but the point to which I want to draw attention is that allowing the 'jurors' a period of discussion before asking them to give their collective verdict shifted the outcome noticeably in the not-guilty direction. The best explanation seems to be that the effect of discussion was to activate the norm so that some participants who went in thinking 'Yes, he did it' ended up thinking 'We can't agree on this, so I'd better give him the benefit of the doubt.' In other words, the effect of discussion was to shift at least some people from a particular judgement to a general norm which people in liberal societies tend to apply to cases of this sort.

I want, however, to claim not only that discussion can activate norms but also that it can create norms by inducing participants to think of themselves as forming a certain kind of group. Broadly speaking, discussion has the effect of turning a collection of separate individuals into a group who see one another as cooperators. Perhaps I can again illustrate this with some experimental evidence, this time involving groups confronting a classic Prisoner's Dilemma. Each member is given a small sum of money and told that he or she can either keep it him- or herself, or donate it to a common pool whereupon it will be doubled in value and shared equally among all members of the group. Obviously if everyone donates, everyone doubles their income, but the individually rational thing to do is to hold back the money. In the experiment I am describing, a ten-minute period of discussion more than doubled the rate of cooperation, from 37.5 per cent to 78.6 per cent.[21] Exactly what the normative mechanism at work here is may be open to question, but plainly the effect of debate was to generate a norm of cooperation within the group strong enough in the great majority of cases to override individual self-interest. A group of friends would have no difficulty extricating themselves from a Prisoner's Dilemma – they would trust one another already. Talking to one another appears to be a fairly effective way of simulating friendship in this case.

The upshot of this argument is that we have good reason to expect the deliberative process to transform initial policy preferences (which may be based on private interest, sectional interest, prejudice and so on) into ethical judgements on the matter in hand; and this will sharply curtail the set of rankings of policy outcomes with which the final decision procedure has to deal. How does this help to eliminate the social choice problems we identified earlier? Take first the indeterminacy problem, and our observation that the Condorcet rule may be defeated by the existence of voting cycles (where, say, majorities favour gas over coal, coal over nuclear power, and nuclear power over gas in two-way comparisons). Here I wish to appeal to the well-known finding that cycles of this kind (and the Arrow problem more generally) can be avoided on condition that voters' rank orderings are 'single peaked'.[22] That is to say, the alternatives can be arrayed on a continuum such that if, say, a voter ranks the alternative on the left the highest, he or she does not rank the alternative on the right above that in the centre.[23] Where preferences are single peaked in this sense, one option must be the Condorcet winner and it would be possible to find this by repeated binary votes.

What does single-peakedness reveal about voters' preferences? It shows that they understand the choice before them in the same way, even though they adopt different positions on the spectrum. Thus suppose in the example we are using that coal is the cheapest of the three fuels but environmentally the most harmful; that oil is the most expensive but environmentally the best; and that gas stands between coal and oil in both respects. Then we might see the choice facing the voters as essentially that between economic cost and environmental soundness, and they would naturally divide into economizers (who put coal first but prefer gas to oil), greens (who put oil first but prefer gas to coal) and moderates, who favour gas as the best trade-off between the two values. A single dimension of choice underlies the various positions, and this is sufficient to guarantee that the rank orderings will be single peaked.

In many cases we may expect ethically informed judgements to display this property: the policy options represent a choice between two values, and different groups of voters weight these values differently.[24] However, it is still possible for single-peakedness to fail even where ethical judgements are involved. For an example of this consider the following. Suppose nuclear power replaces oil as the third possible source of energy, and the facts about it are these: it is moderately cheap, it is environmentally sound in general, but it carries with it the risk of a major accident. We might then have three groups of voters: economizers, whose ranking is (1) coal, (2) nuclear power and (3) gas; pessimistic greens, whose ranking is (1) gas, (2) coal and (3) nuclear power; and a more optimistic group of greenish voters who believe that the risk of a nuclear accident can be borne in the light of the all-round benefits of nuclear power, and whose ranking is therefore (1) nuclear power, (2) gas and (3) coal. As a moment's inspection shows, if no group of voters forms a majority we have a voting cycle in which each energy option can defeat one of the others.

How has this come about? There are two dimensions of disagreement underlying the decision in this case. One is the balance to be struck between cost and environmental safety; the other is the relative weighting to be given to predictable pollution as against the risk of a nuclear accident *within* the fold of environmental concern. The economizers think the issue is only about costs; the out-and-out greens think it is only about environmental safety; the third group think it is about both, but they also disagree with the greens about what environmental safety consists of. It is this condition of cross-cutting disagreement that produces rank orders that are not single peaked and threatens to produce a voting cycle.

Now consider how such a choice might be handled within the context of deliberative democracy. Participants in the debate, aiming to convince others to support the alternative that they favour, must inevitably give grounds for their preference. As the various views are articulated, one thing that will be revealed is whether there is just a single dimension of disagreement underlying the original set of alternatives, or more than one dimension. If there is more than one dimension, then it may be possible to split the original decision into components. I say 'may be' here because it is of course possible that the original alternatives were discrete and irreducible. Consider again the choice between types of power station. It looks as though this might be a case where the alternatives are discrete (a station must be *either* coal or gas fired and so on), whereas many possible dimensions of disagreement underlie the choice: relative costs, levels of employment, issues of environmental safety and so on. However, I do not think that the choice is really so discrete. For instance, coal-fired stations might in general be favoured on cost grounds, but there could be a separate issue as to whether they should be fitted with filters to reduce emissions of sulphur or carbon dioxide at the cost of some loss of output. If it became clear in the course of debate that the major reason why some speakers were opposing coal-fired stations was their polluting emissions, then the obvious solution would be to have two votes, or series of votes, one concerning the basic technology, another concerning the environment/efficiency trade-off given that technology.

Such a solution is obvious in the sense that it enables a final outcome to emerge that can reasonably be regarded as the majority's choice, even in cases where it is not a Condorcet winner.[25] Here one is taking an Olympian perspective and saying what ought to happen. From the point of view of the participants, some may have an incentive to prevent the issues being disaggregated because they envisage that the alternative they favour will lose when this is done.[26] Indeed they may have an incentive artificially to yoke issues together – I am not a student of Labour Party politics, but I suppose this is the art of compositing as practised at party conferences; that is, running together motions to create artificial majorities encompassing the particular position you are interested in. However, the conditions for this technique to work appear to be that there is a group of people who are in a privileged position to manipulate the agenda in the sense of deciding which decisions will be taken separately and which together; and that this group also has a better sense of the pattern of preferences among ordinary participants than those participants do themselves. In a deliberative democracy the pattern of opinion – the extent to which opinions on one issue correlate or fail to correlate with opinions on others – should become public knowledge as different speakers argue for and against the various composite proposals on the table. It would then be difficult to make a public argument against the disaggregation of decisions where it was clear that the original choice was multidimensional. In cases where it was not so clear, speakers might of course try to bamboozle their fellows into choosing simply between composite proposals in the hope that their favoured composite might win.

Let me try to summarize the point I have just made. I have suggested that the major reason apart from empirical error why preference orders are likely not to be single peaked is that the issue under discussion amalgamates separate dimensions of choice to which different voters attach different weights. I am claiming that it is a virtue of deliberative democracy (unlike, say, simple opinion polling) that it will reveal this to be the case. Unless a lot of people are prepared to behave strategically, there should be a general willingness to break the decision down along its several dimensions, on each of which we should expect to find a winning position. Putting the bits together again, we would have an overall result which can fairly be said to represent the will of the majority, since it follows the majority's judgement on each dimension of policy choice.

In the foregoing discussion the Condorcet criterion has been used as the test of a democratic choice. Starting with preference orders that produce cycles, we have looked at ways in which the process of discussion might be expected to change either the preference orders or the decision agenda so that non-cyclical majorities emerge. However, earlier in the chapter I observed that majoritarian methods of decision-making competed with positional methods as represented, for example, by the Borda count, and this particular dilemma has still to be addressed.

The Condorcet criterion invites us to look for the policy option that can win a majority vote against any other, if one can be found. The Borda count invites us to look at voters' complete rank orderings and to choose the alternative with the highest overall score. What is at stake in the choice between these potentially conflicting decision rules? I think the question can best be brought into focus by citing Michael Dummett's case for preferring the Borda count to majoritarian methods of decision-making:

> The question turns on whether it be thought more important to please as many people as possible or to please everyone collectively as much as possible. The latter is surely more reasonable. The rule to do as the majority wishes does not appear to have any better justification than as a rough-and-ready test for what will secure the maximum total satisfaction: to accord it greater importance is to fall victim to the mystique of the majority.[27]

What is noticeable about this is that it treats political decisions as delivering variable amounts of satisfaction to those who vote for them. Now some decisions approximate to this stereotype. If, say, we have to take a vote on what dish is to be served at the annual college feast, then Dummett's argument that it matters much more that overall satisfaction is maximized than that a majority's will prevails seems a good one, and it would be perfectly sensible to use a Borda count to decide this matter. Equally, though, many other decisions are better represented as judgements about what is the right thing to do – say a decision about whether to impose the death penalty for a particular crime – and here it would be very odd to defend the Borda count in the way that Dummett does. Indeed it seems here that the natural procedure would be to use one of the majoritarian methods, since what seems important is that whatever is done is done by the will of the majority – if possible what the majority wills in preference to all other options.[28]

If that intuition is right, then the best and fairest decision procedure to use will depend on the issue at hand. Now one virtue of deliberative democracy here is that the process of deliberation will reveal what sort of issue is at stake if indeed that is not obvious from the outset. In my presentation of the deliberative model, I focused on its most distinctive aspect, namely the process whereby individual preferences are transformed into ethically based judgements about matters of common concern. However, in any real democracy there are going to be other issues that come closer to the college-feast stereotype in the sense that personal preferences should reasonably play a large role in deciding them. This will be true of many ordinary public goods, for instance. If we have to make a budget allocation as between football pitches and the swimming pool in the local park, the main consideration is likely to be the general direction and strength of preference between these options. So here, once the alternatives are identified, it would be sensible to use a Borda count to find the most satisfactory way of allocating funds, and if no other considerations intervene, the final decision would simply amount to ratifying that result. This is a case where the role of deliberation is to identify a procedure for making a decision rather than to arrive at a substantive agreed judgement.

What we have seen here is that standard social choice theory invites us to pick a mechanism for aggregating preferences regardless of the content of those preferences; whereas deliberative democracy, precisely because the content of people's preferences emerges in the course of deliberation, can in theory select the decision procedure most appropriate to the case in hand. Now clearly once we allow that the decision procedure might be flexible in this way, we open the door to manipulation by those who opt for a procedure not on grounds of its appropriateness to the issue but because they believe it enhances the chances of their preferred policy being adopted. This highlights the point that, for deliberative democracy to work well, people must exercise what we might call democratic self-restraint: they must think it more important that the decision reached should be a genuinely democratic one than that it is the decision that they themselves favour. This depends in turn on the level of trust that exists in the deliberating body: people will tend to behave in a democratic spirit to the extent that they believe that others can be trusted to behave likewise. Here the evidence cited earlier, showing that discussion itself is a good way of building up trust among the participants, is relevant. But this evidence, obtained from research in small group contexts, does also raise the question of the scale on which deliberative democracy can be expected to operate.

It is a mistake to think that the deliberative ideal requires us to treat the citizens of a modern nation-state as a single deliberating body. Although it is a requirement of democracy that every citizen should have the opportunity to participate in collective decision-making in some way, this requirement can be met in a system embodying a high degree of pluralism. Pluralism may work in either or both of two ways: decisions may be parcelled out to the sub-constituencies that are best placed to make them, or most affected by the outcome; or else lower-level deliberating bodies may act as feeders for higher-level ones, with arguments and verdicts being transmitted from one to the other by representatives. Thus one might, for instance, envisage primary assemblies at town or city level making decisions on local matters, and at the same time debating issues of national concern in the presence of their parliamentary representatives: the latter would not be bound by the outcome, since they would themselves be involved in a deliberative process in which new arguments might be presented, but part of their job would be to convey the sense of the local meeting to the national body.[29]

For citizens to be directly involved in deliberation even at local level poses major problems of organization, although recent technological developments can help us see how relatively large bodies of people might be brought together to engage in something we would recognize as common debate.[30] Nor do I want to consider the question of whether citizens will be sufficiently motivated to take part in debating assemblies if these are brought into existence. Clearly these are key issues when considering the extent to which the deliberative ideal can be realized in a large society. My focus here has been on what I take to be a key weakness in the liberal conception of democracy – the vulnerability of preference-aggregating procedures to problems of social choice – and the way in which deliberative democracy can overcome that weakness. If we take social choice seriously, as I do, then rather than retreating to a minimal form of liberalism, we can seek to shift democratic practice towards the deliberative ideal, encouraging people not merely to *express* their political opinions (through opinion polls, referenda and the like), but to *form* those opinions through debate in public settings.

NOTES

1   This is how liberal democracy, *qua* regulative ideal, will be understood for the purposes of the chapter. Some liberals may protest at this appropriation of the term. However, although my interpretation fastens upon only one strand of liberalism – the importance it attaches to individual preferences and their expression – I take it to be an important strand. It is also the strand that prevails in contemporary liberal societies, where democracy is predominantly understood as involving the aggregation of independently formed preferences.

2   The ideal of deliberative democracy has recently been advocated and discussed
    by a number of political theorists. The most incisive presentation is probably
    J. Cohen, 'Deliberation and democratic legitimacy', in A. Hamlin and P. Pettit
    (eds), *The Good Polity* (Oxford, Blackwell, 1989). See also B. Manin, 'On legitimacy
    and political deliberation', *Political Theory*, 15 (1987), 338–68; J. Drysek, *Discursive
    Democracy* (Cambridge, Cambridge University Press, 1990); and my own earlier
    discussion in D. Miller, *Market, State and Community* (Oxford, Clarendon Press,
    1989), ch. 10.

3   This point is well made in J. Elster, *Sour Grapes* (Cambridge, Cambridge
    University Press, 1983), ch. I.5.

4   See J. Coleman and J. Ferejohn, 'Democracy and social choice', *Ethics*, 97 (1986–
    7), 6–25, for this view.

5   See H. P. Young, 'Condorcet's theory of voting', *American Political Science Review*,
    82 (1988), 1231–44.

6   See B. Barry, 'The public interest', in A. Quinton (ed.), *Political Philosophy*
    (London, Oxford University Press, 1967); B. Grofman and S. L. Feld, 'Rousseau's
    General Will: a Condorcetian perspective', *American Political Science Review*, 82
    (1988), 567–76.

7   Some of the ambiguities are brought out in the exchange between D. Estlund,
    J. Waldron, B. Grofman and S. L. Feld, 'Democratic theory and the public inter-
    est: Condorcet and Rousseau revisited', *American Political Science Review*, 83
    (1989), 1317–40.

8   This is not to deny that deliberation tends to improve the quality of decisions. It
    may indeed be part of the process of reaching a decision that alternatives which
    initially find favour with some people are eliminated because these preferences
    rest on empirical misapprehensions which discussion exposes (I give an example
    of this later on). But it is wrong to suppose that this is the only or in many cases
    the main purpose of deliberation.

9   J. A. Schumpeter, *Capitalism, Socialism and Democracy* (London, Allen and Unwin,
    5th edn, 1976); R. A. Dahl, *A Preface to Democratic Theory* (Chicago, University of
    Chicago Press, 1956). Schumpeter wrote before Arrow had stated his theorem,
    but I believe it is informally anticipated in some of Schumpeter's remarks. Dahl
    refers explicitly to Arrow.

10 W. H. Riker, *Liberalism Against Populism* (San Francisco, W. H. Freeman, 1982).

11 K. J. Arrow, *Social Choice and Individual Values* (New York, Wiley, 2nd edn, 1963).

12 See Riker, *Liberalism Against Populism*, ch. 4.

13 This is the so-called Gibbard–Satterthwaite theorem, after A. Gibbard,
    'Manipulation of voting schemes: a general result', *Econometrica*, 41 (1973), 587–
    601, and M. Satterthwaite, 'Strategy-proofness and Arrow's conditions', *Journal of
    Economic Theory*, 10 (1975), 187–217.

14 Coleman and Ferejohn, 'Democracy and social choice', p. 22. See also the
    discussion in J. Cohen, 'An epistemic conception of democracy', *Ethics*, 97 (1986–
    7), 26–38, especially pp. 29–31.

15 The literature of social choice theory may give the impression that voters'
    preferences are taken as immutable, with apparent changes being explained in
    terms of changes in the choice set. But in fact a social choice theorist can quite
    readily concede that preferences vary, are subject to social influences and so
    forth, so long as for any particular decision or set of decisions they are taken as
    fixed and identifiable. The shift of approach occurs when we see preferences as
    altering within the process of decision-making itself, so that individuals end up

making judgements which do not necessarily correspond to their initial preferences.

16 Riker, *Liberalism Against Populism*, p. 117. Arrow himself, however, concedes that the condition may be too strong, and indeed in his original proof of the Possibility Theorem used a somewhat weaker version; see *Social Choice and Individual Values*, pp. 24–5 and 96–7.

17 R. Goodin, 'Laundering preferences', in J. Elster and A. Hylland (eds), *Foundations of Social Choice Theory* (Cambridge, Cambridge University Press, 1986).

18 G. Brennan and P. Pettit, 'Unveiling the vote', *British Journal of Political Science*, 20 (1990), 311–33.

19 Jon Elster argues along similar lines in *Sour Grapes*, p. 36.

20 See J. Davis, M. Stasson, K. Ono and S. Zimmerman, 'Effects of straw polls on group decision-making: sequential voting pattern, timing and local majorities', *Journal of Personality and Social Psychology*, 55 (1988), 918–26.

21 J. M. Orbell, A. van der Kragt and R. Dawes, 'Explaining discussion-induced co-operation', *Journal of Personality and Social Psychology*, 54 (1988), 811–19.

22 This idea was first introduced and explored in D. Black, *The Theory of Committees and Elections* (Cambridge, Cambridge University Press, 1958).

23 Suppose the alternatives are coal, gas and oil and they are arranged from left to right in that order. For single-peakedness to obtain, each voter must rank them in one of the four following ways: (1) coal, (2) gas, (3) oil; (1) gas, (2) coal, (3) oil; (1) gas, (2) oil, (3) coal; or (1) oil, (2) gas, and (3) coal. Conversely, no voter may have (1) coal, (2) oil, (3) gas or (1) oil, (2) coal, (3) gas. The requirement is not that voters should agree, but that there should be a certain logic to their disagreement.

24 Arrow himself accepts that if decisions are made on impartial, rather than self-interested grounds, voting cycles are less likely to occur. 'If voters acted like Kantian judges, they might still differ, but the chances of coming to an agreement by majority decision would be much greater than if voters consulted egoistic values only.' See K. J. Arrow, 'Tullock and an existence theorem', in *Collected Papers of Kenneth J. Arrow, Vol. I* (Oxford, Blackwell, 1984), p. 87.

25 The majority position on the two dimensions may still be defeated when run against the minority position on both. Thus suppose the first issue is whether to have coal- or oil-fired stations and the second is whether to fit pollution filters or not. Majorities may judge that coal is preferable to oil and that filters are desirable; yet if we were to take a vote between coal-with-filters and oil-with-no-filters, the latter might still win by attracting the support of enough people strongly committed to oil together with people strongly opposed to filters. In my view we should still regard coal-with-filters as the majority choice in these circumstances.

26 This is so even where their support for that alternative is based on ethical beliefs: convictions as well as interests may give people a motive to manipulate democratic procedures.

27 M. Dummett, *Voting Procedures* (Oxford, Clarendon Press, 1984), p. 142.

28 The assumption here is that we have an issue about which reasonable people may disagree, but on which some collective decision is needed: in such a case the decision with the greatest democratic legitimacy will be that which follows the will of the majority, which points us towards the Condorcet criterion. If, however, we took the epistemic view – that is, we thought that there was indeed a right answer to the question being posed, and justified democratic decision-making as

the most likely means of finding it – then with more than two options on the table the best method would probably be to take a Borda count. See Young, 'Condorcet's theory of voting', for this result.

29   This is not the only way in which deliberative institutions might be created, and advocates of deliberative democracy disagree to some extent about the best institutional setting for their ideal. Tocqueville, one of the founders of this tradition, pointed to voluntary associations as well as to town meetings as sites of public debate. Others have emphasized the role of political parties as institutions within which policies are put together in coherent packages, enabling ordinary voters to arrive at more rational decisions. See Manin, 'On legitimacy and political deliberation' and J. Cohen and J. Rogers, *On Democracy* (New York, Penguin, 1983), ch. 6 for the latter view.

30   For a good discussion, see I. McLean, *Democracy and New Technology* (Cambridge, Polity Press, 1989).

4

MUST FEMINISTS GIVE UP ON LIBERAL DEMOCRACY?

Anne Phillips

Feminism has often found itself at odds with liberal democracy: indeed feminist judgements in this area have usually been harsher than our judgements on liberalism *per se*. Despite many and much-rehearsed limitations, liberalism can at least claim credit in the historical development of the feminist tradition, and it enjoys today its double legacy as founding inspiration and favourite target of attack. Liberal *democracy*, by contrast, does not even inspire us. The prolonged exclusion of women from the most basic right to vote turned out to be the merest tip of the iceberg: a discouraging hint at deeper structures that keep women politically unequal. Whatever its claims in other fields of endeavour, liberal democracy has not served women well.[1]

Within this generally damning perspective, there are none the less two discernible strands.[2] The first stems from the politics of the contemporary women's movement, which emerged out of a period of widespread dissatisfaction with the banalities of liberal democracy and shared with virtually all radical groupings of the 1960s and 1970s a vision of a more active, participatory democracy. In the practices of most women's groups, this translated into a distrust of hierarchy and leadership, a concern with sharing expertise and influence and time, and a preference for the direct democracy of the meeting rather than the anonymity of the vote. The relationship between these principles of self-organization and the principles that should govern the polity as a whole were hardly a matter of urgent concern, but under the broad slogan of 'the personal is political', feminists developed an analysis of power as all pervasive and democracy as everywhere significant. The women's movement then became associated with the values of local, decentralized democracy, with the idea that democracy matters wherever there are relations of power, and with the importance of organizational forms as prefiguring ultimate goals.

The theorization of feminist perspectives on democracy lagged considerably behind, and as these developed (largely in the course of the 1980s) they moved on to what might seem the more respectable ground of citizenship and political equality.[3] Where the first moment in feminist thinking had coincided with an explosion in participatory democracy, the second occurred at a time of growing disdain for the 'fetish of direct democracy',[4] and resurgent confidence in the procedures of liberal democracy. This confidence has not on the whole been shared by feminists, but the transition from participation towards citizenship none the less mirrors the movement in radical thought as a whole. In the first phase, feminists concerned themselves with what we might call the micro-level of democracy inside a movement, and democracy in everyday life. In the second phase, we have turned to the macro-level of women's membership in the political community: exploring questions of inclusion and exclusion, and dampening down the universalizing pretensions of modern political thought.[5] The first moment almost sidelined more conventional democratic debates. Perhaps the second will in its turn be sidelined, but in associating itself with the language of citizenship, it occupies more central ground.

There are reasons behind this shift that are distinctive to feminism, but it also reproduces a division that has characterized all the critical literature on liberal democracy. For many democrats, the decisive weakness of liberal democracy is the way it has restricted the scope and intensity of citizen engagement, retreating so far from classical ideals of democracy as to cast some doubt on the use of the term. The more ambitious practices of active and equal involvement in decision-making have given way to a minimalist, or in Benjamin Barber's term, a 'weak' democracy[6] that offers little more than protection against the excesses of what governments might do. The central principle of contemporary democracy is that governments must subject themselves to periodic recall: there must be enough freedom of association and information to promote the organization of a variety of political parties and there must be regular elections in which all adults are permitted to vote. Those who query the limits of this typically argue for more democracy and democracy in more places. The earlier practices of the women's movement fell broadly within this school.

The second major line of attack focuses on the failure to deliver on the promise of political equality. Liberal democracy tends to regard this as adequately met by the equal rights to vote and to stand for election, and in doing so it abstracts from the social and economic conditions that would make this equality effective. Even setting aside issues of gender and race, our unequal access to economic resources combines with our unequal access to knowledge, information and political skills to render us politically (not just socially) unequal. Robert Dahl clearly acknowledges this in his recent magisterial restatement of his views on democracy, and goes so far as to question whether political equality is compatible with the market economy.[7] But as this very example indicates, the promise of political equality has provoked an extensive literature on the obstacles that might stand in its path, and many defenders of 'actually existing democracy' will admit at least some part of the problem. Certainly since the post-war development of the welfare state, most of those societies that would appear in the roll-call of liberal democracies have come to address various social or economic rights that may be necessary to make citizenship effectively equal. This poses important questions to the current analyses of women and citizenship. Is the differential political treatment of women and men part of the sorry history of liberal democracies, or built into their very foundations? Does liberal democracy have to turn itself into something *other* – an alternative to liberal democracy – in order to deal with sexual inequality? Or can the inadequacies and inequalities be redressed within some future, but still *liberal*, democracy?

I explore here the powerful critiques that feminists have developed under the three broad headings of citizenship, participation and heterogeneity, under each heading querying whether the arguments add up to a case against liberal democracy. The preoccupation with liberal democracy as a totalizing system we must be either 'for' or 'against' proves relatively unhelpful, for it attributes to liberal democracy a greater theoretical fixity than is confirmed by its subsequent history.[8] The 'democratization' of liberal democracy has already moved it a long way from its founding moments; so far indeed that the neo-liberals and neo-conservatives of the 1970s and 1980s cried out against what they saw as an all too successful democratic subversion.[9] If the precise character of liberal democracy can be formed and reformed in a process of political contestation, then feminists may have quite enough on their hands in engendering democracy without also worrying about whether the results are still 'liberal democracy'.

Citizenship

Recent explorations of women and citizenship share considerable common ground with other critiques of liberal democracy, in that they

address the substantive conditions that would make political equality
more than a nice choice of words. The most obvious point of entry here is
the extraordinary under-representation of women in the world's political
assemblies. All versions of liberal democracy link the right to vote with
the right to stand for election – and few are as cavalier as Joseph
Schumpeter, who noted in a brief footnote that we are free to compete
for political leadership 'in the same sense in which everyone is free to
start another textile mill'.[10] It is, however, in considering the imbalance
between the proportion of women in the citizen body and the proportion
elected to power that the vacuous nature of this particular right is most
starkly revealed.[11] The caring responsibilities that most women carry in
relation to the young, the sick and the old – not to mention the able-
bodied men – act as a powerful practical barrier to their political
involvement; while the cultural constructions of politics as primarily a
matter for men work to disadvantage those women who still put
themselves forward. The results are entirely predictable: with the
important exception of the Nordic countries, the women elected to the
world's national assemblies make up 2–12 per cent of the whole.

The solutions to this fall roughly into three categories. Some of the
problems relate to the sexual division of labour in production and
reproduction and will only be finally resolved when men and women
share equally in the full range of paid and unpaid work. Others are
associated with the working conditions of politicians and require major
modification to accommodate people who are active parents as well.
Others again relate to the 'boys' club' prejudices of party selectorates or
voters, which require affirmative action (such as quotas) to boost the
election of women. The importance feminists currently attach to the
third reflects our sadly realistic assessment of the time it will take to alter
the first two, though this may be a case of dealing with the symptoms
rather than tackling the underlying cause. It is worth noting, meanwhile,
that the literature on women's (under-) representation rarely addresses it
as something intrinsic to the nature of liberal democracy.

The unique move made by recent theorists is to consider the broader
collection of rights and responsibilities that *already* underpin liberal
democratic notions of citizenship and the ways in which these have been
gendered. Feminists have drawn attention, for example, to the relationship between citizenship and the defence of one's nation, or between
citizenship and the work that one does, noting that in both instances the
status of women as citizens appears profoundly ambiguous. In much of
the late nineteenth- and early twentieth-century battle for women's
suffrage, the fact that women did not fight to defend the realm was
regarded as a definitive argument. Carole Pateman has noted that part of

the counter-argument for extending the vote to women was that in their role as mothers and educators women too were performing a public service: that the women who died in childbirth were sacrificing their lives to the nation just as much as the men who died in battle; that the women who devoted their lives to bearing and rearing children were performing tasks without which no society could survive; that this seemingly private activity was as much a qualification for citizenship as going out to work or defending the nation.[12] The troubling legacy from this, she argues, is that men and women were then incorporated into citizenship in decisively different ways: men primarily as soldiers and workers, women primarily as mothers.

Similar points have been made in relation to the development of the welfare state. In most post-war liberal democracies, the meaning of citizenship was expanded to embrace what are classed as 'social rights', so that a citizen could legitimately expect to be provided with access to education, employment and, failing that, a living income. Yet the welfare state that supposedly encapsulated this wider citizenship was typically founded on a model of the male as breadwinner responsible for dependent wife and children, and social security provision in Britain, for example, was organized around this conception. Despite subsequent – in my view, largely trivial – changes, the household remains the unit for calculating social entitlement, and within this household there is a primary/secondary divide. Such practices reflect and help sustain a profoundly gendered division of labour.

The novelty of this argument lies not so much in what is being said about the sexual division of labour as in the links being forged between the gendered distribution of paid and unpaid labour and the gendered distribution of political status and power. Under the rubric of citizenship, feminists are now exploring issues that used to be dealt with as economic or social policy, and the strategic significance of this is that it lifts the arguments over sexual equality from the private to the public realm. Part of the traditional critique of liberal democracy is that it concedes only the formality of political equality, while ignoring or indeed condoning the social inequalities that are associated with the market economy. The standard riposte is that any of the measures that might be proposed to deal with these 'other' inequalities will come into conflict with liberties that are also part of the democratic tradition: that there is a tension between freedom and equality and that a balance must be struck between the two.[13] Political equality may not meet all the requirements of an egalitarian society – but then half a cake is always better than none. The more challenging point made in recent feminist explorations is that membership of the political community is itself profoundly gendered. It is not a matter of political equality being *inadequate* – as if this equality has been won, but should now be extended from the political to the social realm – but that our 'political' status as citizens is premised on arrangements of sexual inequality. If men 'earnt' their citizenship as soldiers and workers, while women 'earnt' their citizenship as mothers and educators of their children, then the political settlement has already legitimated the sexual division of labour. The inequalities are intrinsic to the politics, not an extraneous, additional concern.

When equality in the household or at work is conceived as an 'additional' question, then the staunchest supporter of liberal democracy can feel justified in refusing to consider the case. Political equality is one thing; all these other kinds of equality are quite another. No right-thinking democrat would now argue for inequalities in political rights; but democrats can take any position they fancy on what are seen as a range of additional concerns. The demarcation line helps close down discussion of more substantial notions of equality – and as those following events in East-Central Europe have noted, this has particularly disastrous consequences for women. The 1989 revolutions created or restored the rights of citizens to elect their governments; but this has been associated with a reinstatement of women as primarily mothers, with moves to criminalize abortion, shut down child-care facilities or encourage women out of their full-time jobs.[14] The differential basis on which men and women are incorporated into citizenship is not some historical oddity but all too alive and well.

These are powerful arguments, but they leave open the question as to how far they challenge the basic principles of liberal democracy. They shift the boundaries between what are public and what are private concerns, and they query the particular point at which this division has been drawn. But while liberal democracies insist on some such boundary (otherwise what does it mean to put 'liberal' in front?), they have proved reasonably flexible in their definitions of where this boundary should lie. Partly under the impact of labour and social democratic parties, liberal democracies have extended the legitimate scope of government interference to include extensive regulation of the workings of the market. And partly under the impact of feminism, they have entered more decisively into the regulation of sexual violence, as in the growing recognition of rape within marriage as a crime. Meanwhile, the work of Scandinavian feminists suggests the scope for a new 'social citizenship' that builds care work into the responsibilities of the state.[15] The analysis of unequal citizenship remains as a major and urgent task for anyone concerned with sexual equality. But unless it can be demonstrated that liberal democracy is founded – and not just historically, but in some sense in its very logic – on the differential treatment of women and men, then the work of dealing with this difference may not alter its basic parameters. To argue otherwise would be to establish some central and defining principle that cannot be made compatible with sexual equality. This case is not yet established and remains an important, but open, question.[16]

Participation

The second major ground for feminist dissatisfaction lies in the critique of liberal democratic minimalism and the contrast drawn between this and more active participation. Here too there are problems in considering whether the criticisms add up to a case *against* liberal democracy, or more modestly compute as an argument for more democracy within broadly liberal democratic norms. There is an additional difficulty, for women's experience provides evidence on both sides of the argument. While I regard the positive case as stronger, this has to be considered within a balance sheet that moderates the enthusiasm of earlier years.

Let me start with the downside. In a recent overview of feminist writing on citizenship, Kathleen Jones notes that 'feminist ideas about political institutions stress participation almost to the point of obsession';[17] the very phrasing reveals ambivalence towards this kind of obsession. In the course of a powerful argument for a more actively participatory democracy, Iris Marion Young none the less warns against the uncritical retention of 'an anarchist, participatory democratic communitarianism to express our vision of the ideal society',[18] and notes the almost overwhelming pressures towards homogeneity that such a politics can bring in its train. As these and other comments indicate, the early practices of direct democracy in the women's movement lent themselves to an overly consensual – indeed illiberal – politics, which made it peculiarly difficult for feminists to agree to disagree. The emphasis on face-to-face meetings encouraged more active and equal participation, but women's groups found it hard to develop the mechanisms for coping with conflict, and particularly in the early years (much less so later on) expected women to discover how fundamentally their interests were shared. The false unities of 'sisterhood' imposed tremendous pressure towards reaching a common consensus, while the almost familial model of political activity exacted 'a toll that is not always consistent with the feminist stress on autonomy and self-development'.[19] Sceptics will recognize this as one of the standard points made in contrasts between liberal and participatory democracy, for liberalism will accept disagreement as inevitable – and certainly not anyone's fault. The more active engagement of participatory democracy often tends towards the opposite, for instead of taking people and their interests as given, it looks forward to a process of discussion, transformation and change. This is not to say that participatory democracy necessarily anticipates convergence on some 'general will', but in the early years of the contemporary movement such tendencies were undoubtedly strong.

This is one problem feminists have encountered in developing a more active and engaged democracy, serving not so much as a reason for dropping all such ambitions but as a reminder of the problems that direct democracy can bring. The second arises from female rather than feminist experience, and relates to the pressures on women's time. The founding inspiration for all visions of democracy lies back in the fifth century BC, when the citizens of Athens (and other Greek city-states) participated in an extraordinarily rich and engaged political life. Citizens did indeed rule, sharing, in however minor a way, in the administrative responsibilities of the city and deciding central matters of legislation and policy in the frequent citizen assemblies. The very intensity of the engagement was, however, at odds with political equality, and the citizen body was severely restricted in size. The most fervent admirer of classical democracy can hardly ignore the premise on which it was founded: the citizens were 'freed' for politics by a vast army of women and foreigners and slaves.

The obvious point made by any contemporary democrat is that citizen assemblies and rotation of duties work only in the context of tiny communities and do not translate easily to the modern nation-state which counts its citizens by the million. In feminist literature, the issue is posed even more starkly, for the very notion of the active citizen presumes someone else is taking care of the children and doing the necessary maintenance of everyday life. In one of the earliest contributions to the now substantial body of feminist political theory, Susan Moller Okin notes that 'if women were to be politically equal, they, too, would have to spend a considerable amount of time in political meetings and other public activities', which would mean either revising downwards what could be expected of any active citizen, or else substantially socializing the conditions under which child-rearing takes place.[20] Current feminist preferences have veered away from purely socialized solutions towards a mixture of increased social provision and equal parenting between women and men. Although this would significantly reduce the burdens on women's time, it is hard to see how anyone would then be 'freed' for citizenship in its grander sense.

Set in this context, the alliance between feminism and participatory democracy looks strained, and considering the intense pressures on women's time, it is remarkable that feminists have been so wedded to a politics of meetings. We might more readily expect male politicos to warm to a politics of continuous meetings and discussion and debate, all of them held conveniently outside the home and away from the noise of the children. But most women have been so grounded by responsibilities for children and parents and husbands and house that they could well have settled for the less arduous democracy of casting the occasional vote. From Oscar Wilde through to Michael Walzer, people have recurrently worried that activism involves too many meetings: that whatever the excitements of politics, people also want to 'take long walks, play with their children, paint pictures, make love, and watch television'.[21] Add on to this rather delightful list the more mundane maintenance that swallows up so much of women's time, and it is astonishing that early feminists sought out the most demanding of democratic forms.

The point can be made more generally to stress the potentially inegalitarian implications of a politics that relies on meetings. Once reformed to include genuinely universal suffrage (and let us not forget how recently this was accomplished), liberal democracy claims to weight all its citizens as equals. In the moment of voting each of us counts only as one. As Philip Green has so acutely observed, this then serves as the definitive answer to any pretensions to greater democracy, for each reference to direct action, to mass protest, to more substantial meeting-based participation, exposes itself to the thorny question: who elected *you* to decide?[22] The higher the demands placed on participation, the more inevitable that it will be unevenly spread around; the more active the democratic engagement, the more likely it is to be carried by only a few. The two forms of political participation that are most equally distributed across the populations of contemporary democracies are voting in elections and signing petitions – the two activities, significantly, that demand the least of our time. All other moments of democratic engagement involve groups that are largely self-selecting and have not been authorized to speak for the rest. In considering what counts as fair and equal representation, the very weakness of liberal democracy then turns into its strength. Precisely because it sets its demands so low, asking only that we turn up at the polling booth to register an occasional vote, it can anticipate majority involvement. 'In this way the liberal pluralist tradition tends to make elections into virtually absolute trumps: the only legitimate method of ascertaining the will of the only definable cast of characters known as "the People".'[23] All further extensions of democracy can be criticized as unrepresentative.

This is where we must turn to the counter-arguments that press feminism to a more participatory engagement. Liberal democracy takes the high ground of requiring the sanction of the popular vote, but in doing so it fails to engage with the inadequacies of voting as an expression of our interests or needs. Through centuries of contestation, democrats have pointed out that voting once every five years hardly counts as a substantial expression of popular control, that choosing between alternatives that may vary only in detail does not give citizens much of a choice, that choosing between vaguely expressed and all too frequently abandoned programmes leaves the decisions to the political elites. The further problem relates to the vote as an expression of interests. In the analysis of female identity and interests, feminism adds considerable weight to those who have queried this connection.

One of the defining characteristics of women's movement politics was the importance attached to 'consciousness-raising' and the widely shared sense that women were grappling with a contradictory identity they had in some sense been forced to assume. In Simone de Beauvoir's classic statement, 'one is not born a woman, one becomes one', and part of this social construction is precisely a culture of passivity and self-denial. Women have felt the need to 'unlearn' the lessons of their past: hence the otherwise odd experience of having to 'discover' that women were oppressed. What made this possible was of course the contradictory nature of women's experiences and consciousness, the feeling that things did not fit. But the political problem that flows from this is not so much that women know what they want and have been unable to make themselves heard; even more pervasive and damaging are the difficulties in articulating one's needs. A key implication in terms of democracy is the transformative significance of meetings, discussion, talk. Interests are not already 'there', pre-given or fixed. Democracy is not just about registering (however occasionally) one's existing preferences and views. For women in particular, there is a prior and continuing process of creating one's identity, constructing one's interests and forming one's political views.

Feminists have built on such arguments to query the very notion of a 'women's interest' that can be simply mobilized and expressed;[24] and if in the earlier years there was a common perception of stripping away the accretions of centuries to find the 'real' person beneath, contemporary theory speaks almost with one voice in regarding female identity as multiple, unstable, something to be created and recreated, rather than simply uncovered. The further one goes in this direction, the more crucial is that vision of wider participation that informs critics of liberal democracy. The inadequacy of the vote is not just that it occurs so infrequently and provides no substantial popular control; as important is its presumption that interests are pre-given, and the way this works to sustain the status quo.[25] The social construction of femininity (by implica-tion, masculinity as well) is such that we cannot simply accept initial positions as expressions of people's interests and needs. The opinions that are registered through elections, referenda or the seemingly endless plethora of opinion polls and attitude surveys are not to be taken as the first and last word, for when gender so profoundly structures our sense of our selves and our interests, these original positions are ambiguous and suspect.

This first part of the argument for a more active democracy combines with the second point: that feminist analysis of oppression goes beyond material inequalities of income or occupation to focus on women's marginality and lack of power. If sexual inequality reduced itself to the distribution of income and work (too little of the first and far too much of the second), it would in principle lay itself open to remedies from above. Armed with the crucial democratic weapon of the vote, women could work to elect a government more responsive to women's poverty, one committed to a fuller programme of equal pay for equal work, combined with a set of welfare policies that would cater for women's needs. But the problems of oppression are not resolved through redistribution alone, for they involve not merely an unequal end-state in the distribution of goodies, but an institutional context that limits our ability to participate and the development of our own capacities.[26] The kind of autonomy and self-respect that feminism seeks to develop can only be arrived at when women shake off their status as dependants, and this in turn happens only through the activity of women themselves.

For both these reasons, feminism remains committed to a politics of participation, to women's more active involvement in making decisions for themselves. But once again, the question arises: is this an argument against the principles of liberal democracy, or for further democratization within the framework of liberal democracy? Women's acute sensitivity to the pressures of time joins with feminist experience of the pitfalls of direct democracy to block too polarized an alternative between more meetings and just going out to vote, encouraging us to combine the strengths of both traditions rather than setting up one as superior to the other. The problem with liberal democracy may then lie not so much in its being intrinsically incapable of extending forms of citizen participa-tion, as in the complacency with which it claims to have met all legitimate democratic aspirations. Not that this makes it so much easier to deal with. The closure may be historically contingent rather than logically determined, but at a period in history when liberal democrats feel they have won all the political battles, this complacency is a powerful obstacle to further democratization.

Heterogeneity and Group Difference

The final area of contention may prove the most difficult for liberal
democracy to swallow, for it takes issue with the individual as the basic
unit in democratic life. If we consider liberal democracy as an amalgam of
certain key principles from the liberal and democratic traditions, what it
takes from liberalism is an abstract individualism which may note the
differences between us, but says these differences should not count. At its
best, this is a statement of profound egalitarianism that offers all citizens
the same legal and political rights, regardless of their wealth, status, race
or sex. At its worst, it refuses the pertinence of continuing difference and
inequality, pretending for the purposes of argument that we are all of us
basically the same. Feminists working on issues of legal or economic
equality have noted how difficult this can make it for women to press for
any differential treatment that may be necessary for significant equality.
Feminists working on issues of democratic representation have come up
against the same kinds of problem, most notably in arguing that the sex
of our representatives matters.

As recent experience in the Nordic countries has shown, the under-
representation of women is entirely open to remedy – and even without
that much needed upheaval that would redistribute work more equally
between women and men. With sufficient political will, aided by formal
party quotas to ensure a 40 per cent minimum for either sex, the numbers
of women elected as political representatives can be dramatically raised.
That political will materializes, however, only when gender is acknowledged as a salient political factor. The abstract individualism of liberal
democracy is a powerful impediment to this, for it encourages a notion of
the 'individual' and 'citizen' as a character of indifferent sex. In societies
that are thoroughly saturated by gender, such indifference to sex can only
reinforce the position of men.

Recent feminist work has pushed this insight further, building on the
analysis of sexual difference to develop far-reaching arguments that deal
with the multiple group differences of heterogeneous societies, and the
ways these can be represented and expressed. The starting point, for
example, of Iris Young's critique of existing democracy is that it fails to
admit the pertinence of group differentiation.[27] Liberal democracy
presumes a continuing plurality of opinions and beliefs (as its insistence
on multi-party competition confirms), but with the exception of what
have come to be known as consociational democracies, it does not see
this plurality as relating to different, and unequal, social groups. Political
parties address us as people with varying opinions on the major national

issues of the day, and though these parties will frequently draw their support from distinct class groupings, the aggregate has to be broad enough (and vague enough) to contest a national election. Pressure groups can of course mobilize on a more particular social basis (black parents for better schools, students for higher grants, farmers for larger subsidies), but then the very particularity works against them, for they are only one among many competing interests. The question raised in Iris Young's work is whether political equality can be meaningful without formal mechanisms for representing group difference.

The vitality of democracy, she argues, cannot wait on us to settle whether such group differentiation is desirable or inevitable (though she herself believes it is both of these things). 'Our political problem is that some of our groups are privileged and others are oppressed.'[28] Existing mechanisms deliver effective power to the dominant groups, and while their dominance may be dressed up in the trappings of an impartial general perspective, or presented as just the majority decision mobilized through a national vote, the consequence is the continued suppression of any marginalized, disadvantaged voice. Democracy cannot continue to proceed on the assumption of an undifferentiated humanity, or the complacent assertion that voices are equally weighted by their equal right to participate in the vote.

The alternative agenda she proposes would provide for public funding to promote the self-organization of oppressed groups, a requirement on policy-makers that they take into consideration the policy proposals that then emanate from such groups and, most controversial of all, a veto power over specific policies that most directly affect any of these groups. I do not present this as a blueprint for the future – the debate on it has barely commenced – and indeed have several reservations on the notion of group representation. These include the difficult problems of group closure (people coming to define themselves politically through what is only one frozen, single aspect of their lives), the question of who is to legislate on which groups qualify for additional group representation, and the almost insuperable obstacles to establishing what any group wants. I have dealt with these at greater length elsewhere;[29] the most pertinent in this context is how to develop acceptably democratic procedures for mobilizing any group voice. At the end of the day, we have only two tried and tested procedures. People can cast their votes in some anonymous ballot, or they can turn up at meetings in order to express their views. The first seems particularly inappropriate to the development of a hitherto marginalized perspective, for how are we to identify all the relevant constituents, and how do we make sure they are voting with that particular part of their identity in mind? (One could feasibly organize all women on to a women's register, but could not expect them all to be voting *as women*, rather than as Catholics or as socialists or as people with some other axe to grind. With smaller, and less visible, sub-groupings, it is hard even to know who makes up the group.) The alternative is to rely on the meeting, which has the double advantage of leaving it to the group members to identify themselves and enabling them to develop a group perspective. But the slightest acquaintance with studies of political participation confirms what most of us know already from personal experience of meetings: that those who go to meetings are a pretty unrepresentative bunch.

The issue of group inequality is far too serious to be brushed aside by any such reservations as these. The questions of democracy and difference are ones that lie at the heart of contemporary dilemmas in democracy – and on an international scale have their counterpart in the fragmentation of older empires into smaller nationalities, and the rising threat to national minorities. People do not define themselves just as citizens of a nation but, either through choice or necessity, often identify with some smaller sub-group. Where this reflects a history of systematic ill-treatment for particular minorities, it cannot be summarily dismissed as an irrelevant basis for democratic organization. But the mechanisms we are offered to deal with systemic group difference and inequality often look like the old interest-group politics dressed up in more radical guise. Iris Young's vision of an active and grassroots representation for oppressed groups looks a good deal more promising than the elitist practices of consociational democracies, but it still does not resolve all problems. As those who speak in the older language of civic republican-ism rightly remind us, democracy also includes a vision of people coming to perceive the limits of their own specific interests and concerns, learning to recognize the potential conflicts between their own position and that adopted by others, and acknowledging the wider community to which we all ultimately belong.[30] This vision has usually failed – it has never proved comprehensive enough to embrace all specific group interests or articulate all grassroots concerns – but this is not enough to dislodge it from its place in the democratic tradition. Perhaps the worst legacy of the Thatcherite years in Britain has been the way they legitimated a politics of individual and narrow group interest, scorning the idealism of all those who contributed to the more generous visions of the modern welfare state. And while this lays itself open to a powerful critique in terms of the *other* interests that have been discarded or denied – primarily those in the lowest income brackets in society – it is even more fundamentally at odds with any notion that there might be common concerns.

Feminists have their own experience of this, which surfaces in exasperation that we must continue to articulate 'the women's point of view' when this is only one of many burning concerns. What inspires this is not just a fear of being kept on the sidelines (the fear expressed by many women politicians throughout this century who have resisted association with 'women's issues' as something that would keep them from the centres of power) but a more profound sense that politics is about a whole range of issues and visions, which do not reduce to group interest or need. In this sense, one of the major problems in developing a feminist vision of democracy is how to resist the pressures towards subsuming women under the supposedly gender-neutral 'man', without thereby capitulating to the narrowness of merely group interest or need – or to put it the other way round, how to retain a vision of human beings working democratically together in pursuit of their shared concerns, without falling into the complacency that dismisses the systematic inequalities between groups.

What is important here is that liberal democracy as currently practised makes it hard even to address this dilemma, for it recurrently returns us to the individual as the basic unit in political life, blocking serious consideration of the empowerment of disadvantaged *groups*. This is perhaps the point of most marked divergence between feminist and liberal democratic perspectives, and as feminist theorists pursue the complex and difficult implications of a 'politics of difference', we can anticipate considerable resistance from those who see democracy in relentlessly individual terms. The question then is whether these hardy individualists exhaust the possibilities of liberal democracy, whether such individualism is intrinsic to its nature? It is hard to give a definitive 'yes'. Michael Walzer has recently reformulated the communitarian critiques of liberalism as a debate *within* liberalism;[31] Will Kymlicka has set out an impeccably liberal case for recognizing group rights;[32] while the current practices of consociational democracies already provide institutionalized representation for communities as well as individuals. Unless we define these theoretical and political initiatives as outside the scope of liberal democracy, then liberal democracy has already made gestures towards recognizing the pertinence of the group.

Feminism and Liberal Democracy

These three areas indicate both the extent of feminist dissatisfaction with existing liberal democracy, and the problems in resolving whether this adds up to an alternative view. Feminist explorations of citizenship raise

major questions about the basis on which women have been included in
the political community and consider the substantive conditions that
have to be met in order to qualify for political equality. The weight
feminism attaches to women being able to transform their identity and
sense of themselves highlights the continuing importance of active
involvement in collective discussion and action. The critique of
dependency as a crucial part of sexual inequality puts feminism firmly in
the camp of a strong democracy, where what matters is empowerment as
well as the ultimate policy results. The analysis of systemic inequalities –
not only between women and men, but more generally between
oppressed and dominant social groups – raises important questions about
empowering people not only as individuals but as members of specific
groups.

Each of these pinpoints what has been a recurrent feature of liberal
democracy, and the arguments combine in an enduring and radical
critique of the limits of existing democracy. Yet none of them can be
presented as a decisive alternative to liberal democracy, partly because of
the difficulties in disentangling what are historical origins from what is
defining essence. Origins do not shape all subsequent developments, and
establishing either the historical or, as feminists are well able to do, the
contemporary associations between liberal democracy and sexual
inequality does not prove a necessary or intrinsic connection. A richer
and more equal democracy may still be possible within the broad
framework liberal democracy implies.

When the world is littered with the skeletons of 'alternatives' to liberal
democracy, it is particularly difficult to present one's critique as leading to
a qualitatively different political form. Thus feminists may – I believe
should – associate themselves with the impetus towards a more active
and engaged democracy, but we cannot afford to present this as an
alternative to holding elections. Feminists have always challenged, and
will continue to challenge, the way that particular divisions between the
public and private secure the exclusion and oppression of women, but few
would want to build on this to argue for dissolving all such distinctions.
Feminists are rightly extending the analysis of sexual difference into a
wider consideration of the systematic differences between unequal social
groups, but the requirements of democratic accountability combine with
the reservations over 'merely' group interest and need to set some
cautionary limits to this.

Caution is of course the watchword of the moment, and the more
likely danger for the immediate future lies less in the risk of non-
democratic alternatives to liberal democracy than in the complacency of
those who feel they have reclaimed the political agenda. In both its

theory and its practice, liberal democracy has largely failed to engage with sexual equality, and it would be a sorry outcome for democracy in general if the extraordinary political events of the 1980s and 1990s ushered in a period of unquestioning celebration of the limited democracy we currently enjoy. It is indeed against this background that I worry about the shift in emphasis from participation towards citizenship. However shaky the democracy of the meeting, however exposed to the taunt that too few people will go, the more active and engaged democracy that was practised in the early years of the women's movement cannot be dislodged from feminist notions of a better and fuller democracy. The trump card of elections, of guaranteeing the numerical equality that gives each individual an equal weight, has to be seen in this context. It serves as a crucial reminder of the founding and abiding principle of democracy – that in democracy we are meant to be equals – and introduces a necessary caution into all our discussions about developing and deepening democracy. But premised as it still is on a notion that interests or preferences are unproblematic, and working as it always does to discourage more radical innovation, it cannot be taken as the simple last word. It does not help to discuss these issues in terms of an 'alternative' to liberal democracy, but for all the reasons outlined above, feminism will continue to inspire a more substantial democracy than that which is currently on offer.

Notes

1   Among the critical literature, see C. Pateman, 'Feminism and democracy', (1983) reprinted in Pateman, *The Disorder of Women* (Cambridge, Polity Press, 1990); S. Rowbotham, 'Feminism and democracy', in D. Held and C. Pollitt (eds), *New Models of Democracy* (London, Open University and Sage, 1986); A. Phillips, *Engendering Democracy* (Cambridge, Polity Press, 1991).

2   I restrict myself here to feminist engagement with liberal democracy over the 25 years since the contemporary women's movement was born. Other stories can be told of earlier feminist engagements.

3   For an overview of more recent literature, see K. Jones, 'Citizenship in a woman-friendly polity', *Signs*, 15:4 (1990).

4   N. Bobbio, *Which Socialism?* (Cambridge, Polity Press, 1986), p. 78.

5   For feminist critiques of universalizing theory, see C. Pateman, *The Sexual Contract* (Cambridge, Polity Press, 1988); essays in L. Nicholson (ed.), *Feminism/ Postmodernism* (London, Routledge, 1990); A. Phillips, 'Universal pretensions in political thought', in M. Barrett and A. Phillips (eds), *Destabilizing Theory: contemporary feminist debates* (Cambridge, Polity Press, 1992).

6   B. Barber, *Strong Democracy: participatory politics for a new age* (Berkeley, CA, University of California Press, 1984).

7   'If democracy is to exist and citizens are to be political equals, then will democracy not require something other than a market-orientated, private

enterprise economy, or at the very least a pretty drastic modification of it?'
R. Dahl, *Democracy and Its Critics* (New Haven, CT, Yale University Press, 1989),
p. 326.

8 I am indebted to David Beetham for the remarks that finally liberated me from
this preoccupation.

9 This is argued in Ernesto Laclau and Chantal Mouffe, *Hegemony and Socialist
Strategy* (London, Verso, 1985), ch. 4.

10 J. A. Schumpeter, *Capitalism, Socialism and Democracy* (London, Allen and Unwin,
1954), p. 272n.

11 For a recent overview of conditions throughout the world, see V. Randall, *Women
and Politics* (Basingstoke, Macmillan, 2nd edn, 1987). For a fuller discussion of the
issues of representation, see Phillips, *Engendering Democracy*, ch. 3.

12 C. Pateman, talk on work in progress to Gender Group, London School of
Economics, 26 April 1991.

13 Steven Lukes has argued persuasively that this formulation is inadequate, that
the trade-offs are not between equality on the one hand and liberty on the other,
but between different combinations or interpretations of both. See 'Equality and
liberty: must they conflict?', in D. Held (ed.), *Political Theory Today* (Cambridge,
Polity Press, 1991).

14 See for example, B. Einhorn, 'Women's rights in East Central Europe: back to
Cinderella?', in V. Moghadam (ed.), *Perestroika and Women* (Cambridge,
Cambridge University Press, 1992).

15 See B. Siim, 'Towards a feminist rethinking of the welfare state', in K. B. Jones
and A. G. Jonasdottir (eds), *The Political Interests of Gender* (London, Sage, 1988).

16 This parallels that other major question that must be put to liberal democracy:
what is the relationship between democracy and the market? Is the market
historically contingent or a condition without which liberal democracy cannot
possibly thrive? See C. Pierson's chapter in this volume.

17 Jones, 'Citizenship in a woman-friendly polity', p. 788.

18 I. M. Young, 'The ideal of community and the politics of difference', in
L. Nicolson (ed.), *Feminism/Postmodernism* (London, Routledge, 1990), p. 301.

19 Jones, 'Citizenship in a woman-friendly polity', p. 808. For further discussion of
the 'paradoxes of participation' see Phillips, *Engendering Democracy*, ch. 5.

20 S. M. Okin, *Women in Western Political Thought* (London, Virago, 1980), p. 278.

21 M. Walzer, 'A day in the life of a socialist citizen', in Walzer, *Obligations: essays on
disobedience, war and citizenship* (Cambridge, MA, Harvard University Press, 1970),
p. 234.

22 P. Green, 'A review essay of Robert A. Dahl *Democracy and Its Critics*', *Social Theory
and Practice*, 16:2 (1990).

23 Green, 'A review essay of Robert A. Dahl', p. 238.

24 See R. Pringle and S. Watson, '"Women's interests" and the post-structuralist
state', in M. Barrett and A. Phillips (eds), *Destabilizing Theory: contemporary feminist
debates*.

25 There is a parallel here with the arguments developed in Barber's *Strong
Democracy*, which similarly emphasizes the transformative significance of active
participation through meetings. Note, however, that aspects of his argument
have been roundly criticized from a feminist perspective by Iris Young in her
essay on polity and group difference (see below, note 27).

26 I. Young, *Justice and the Politics of Difference* (Princeton, NJ, Princeton University
Press, 1990).

27 Young, *Justice and the Politics of Difference*; see also I. M. Young 'Polity and group difference: a critique of the ideal of universal citizenship', *Ethics*, 99 (1989).
28 Young, 'Polity and group difference', p. 261.
29 A. Phillips, 'Democracy and difference: some problems for feminist theory', *Political Quarterly* (1992). For a critical analysis of the closest approximations to group representation in British politics, see H. Cain and N. Yuval-Davis, 'The "equal opportunities community" and the anti-racist struggle', *Critical Social Policy*, 29 (1990).
30 For a related argument, see D. Miller's chapter in this volume.
31 M. Walzer, 'The communitarian critique of liberalism', *Political Theory*, 18:1 (1990).
32 W. Kymlicka, *Liberalism, Community and Culture* (Oxford, Clarendon Press, 1989).

5

ASSOCIATIONAL DEMOCRACY

Paul Hirst

Ideas can be compared to animal species: having lost out to the dominant doctrines and surviving in marginal niches, they may enjoy a new period of evolutionary advantage as selection pressures shift and their hitherto powerful competitors totter toward extinction. This may be the case with associationalism. This chapter outlines the contribution that associationalist doctrines can make to the reform of democratic governance and to the organization of economic affairs and welfare services in western societies.[1] Associationalism may be loosely defined as a normative theory of society the central claim of which is that human welfare and liberty are both best served when as many of the affairs of society as possible are managed by voluntary and democratically self-governing associations. Associationalism gives priority to freedom in its scale of values, but it contends that such freedom can only be pursued effectively if individuals join with their fellows.[2] It is opposed to both state collectivism and pure free-market individualism as principles of social organization.

New Times for Old Ideas

Associationalism is the most neglected of the great nineteenth-century doctrines of social organization. It lost out to collectivism and individualism, and it lacked advocates who attained the political influence of Marx or the Webbs, Smith or Spencer. At the end of the twentieth century, however, associationalism may yet come into its own as a principle of reform and renewal of western societies. Centralized state socialism is clearly dead and with it much advocacy of lesser species of socialist collectivism. The collapse of Soviet-style socialism has destroyed the credibility of this political model for a generation at least. Unregulated free-market individualism is also close to ruin as a political model. It has wreaked havoc on the societies that were foolish enough to follow those right-wing and Labour leaders who saw it as a principle of renewal: the US, Britain, Australia and New Zealand.

One might think that left space for pragmatism. Yet that is hardly possible, for in the twentieth century 'pragmatism' has generally meant some synthesis of liberalism and social democracy. Unfortunately, social democracy in the form of 'Keynesian' national economic management and bureaucratically administered mass welfare is close to failure too.[3] Keynesian macro-economic strategies are no longer effective in the new international economic conjuncture. Without full employment and sustained growth the costs of state-funded mass welfare raise serious distributional issues. Furthermore, bureaucratic welfare is all too often so inefficient and so demeaning of its clients that this lesser form of collectivism can hardly survive long as a model of social organization rather than as an administrative necessity in the absence of an alternative.

The distribution of economic success and failure since the end of the great post-war boom in 1973 shows that those societies that have fared best have managed to balance cooperation and competition, and have been able to draw on sources of social solidarity which have mitigated the effects of individualism and the market on the manufacturing sector.[4] Japan, with its construction of a capitalistic community within the enterprise and thick, quasi-corporatist networks between industry and the state, has achieved, in a strongly business-orientated form, an effective simulation of the cooperative and coordinative economy advocated by associationalists.[5] That tends to indicate that associationalist institutions and relationships may prove highly competitive, if they can be developed. What was West Germany offers a similar business-orientated synthesis: between a responsible social democratic labour movement and a pragmatic, corporatistically inclined management, between an efficient manufacturing sector and the anti-inflationary monetarism of the *Bundesbank*.[6] Neither case, before or after 1973, much resembles the supposedly 'classic' post-war combination of Keynesianism and welfarism, whether in its social-democratic British or 'liberal' US variants. Japan and Germany are difficult models to copy, and in both cases they may be models on the verge of crisis. The 'Anglo-Saxon' countries (Britain and the US) have failed to develop or sustain these quasi-collectivist and corporatist forms of social solidarity. Given the failure of these formal structures of collectivist intervention, they have tried deregulating markets and have found that this has accelerated rather than checked decline.[7] Such societies need a principle of social renewal that does not trade on legacies of consensus they cannot renew or hardly possess, that is anti-collectivist while ensuring social welfare, and yet is consistent with strongly individualist values and an activist civil society based on voluntary associations. That principle is associationalism.

Associationalism began in the nineteenth century as a critique of a purely competitive market society and of the concentrated and centralized state power that was necessary to protect that realm of private transactions from foes without and preserve it from social strife within. In this task it was in competition with and was challenged by state socialism and reformist social engineering, and it was defeated by them. Associationalism had several distinct sources: the decentralist utopian socialism of Pierre-Joseph Proudhon; the English advocates of industrial and social cooperation like Robert Owen and George Jacob Holyoake; the English political pluralists John Neville Figgis and Harold J. Laski; and English Guild Socialism, whose greatest exponent was G. D. H. Cole.[8]

Associationalism failed not because it was inherently impractical and utopian, but because as a political movement it could not compete in given political conditions with collectivism and centralism. The great wars of this century stimulated both of these tendencies as the major states mobilized all social resources to pursue industrialized conflict. In doing so, they decisively reinforced the commitment of the European labour movements to statism. It is possible that in the west centralizing pressures are now lessening steadily. Western states no longer face major military competitors. Class war has for long been a vanished threat. With the lessening of the scope for national macroeconomic management by centralized agencies and the decline of hierarchical and centralized Fordist production organization, so too have the economic imperatives for large-scale concentrated administration lessened markedly.[9]

The main threats to western societies are no longer external and organized but internal and diffuse. They are none the less real for that, but centralized bureaucratic structures cope so badly with these more amorphous threats of crime and drug addiction, for example, that this can hardly provide them with a convincing *raison d'être*. The real problems stem from the failure to sustain full employment and from the side-effects of collectivist welfare. In the US, in Britain, even in Germany we face the growing reality of a two-thirds versus one-third society. The notion of an 'underclass' is both graphic and yet absurd, since its members will not accept their 'place' at the bottom. A differentiated society cannot work if elementary freedoms of movement and association for all are to be preserved. Unless effective work and welfare are offered, in a way that both targets *and* empowers the members of this 'class', then the way is open to an escalating conflict between crime and deviance and disablingly authoritarian measures which aim at the protection of the majority. The members of the 'underclass' are not stupid. They know that wealth and success are in part capriciously distributed; that is, that they depend on the chances of social position and geographical location. Property will never be legitimate unless it offers real welfare – that is, a stake in society – to all in return. That is in large measure what Proudhon meant when he said 'property is theft'. The retreat to pure police protection of the property of the 'haves' is ineffective and the theft of opportunity from the 'have nots'. They cannot overthrow society, but they can make it unliveable in.

The only answer to this problem is a mixture of social crusading by those 'haves' who care and empowerment of the 'have nots'.[10] That can only be achieved by effective and committed voluntary associations in partnership with the poor and excluded. Only by resourcing associations that help the poor to organize themselves and then funding the projects for transformation of ghettos and slums can the state help to reverse this corrosive process of social decline. Socialists have by and large written themselves out of this task, by identifying welfare with state provision for the better part of this century. Religious groups, community self-help groups and so on are the ones to see the need for activism and cooperation to create a 'civil society' for the poor.

The labour movement and its political parties long ago retreated from this role. In Britain it gave up the hard and slow task of building socialism *in civil society* for the apparently quicker and more effective route of imposing it through the state. Friendly societies for welfare, cooperation in distribution and production, the voluntary principle and mutual aid as the basis for social organization – all were gradually discarded and diminished in favour of state provision and bureaucratic administration.[11] It turns out that voluntary relationships are tenacious and effective: they tend to endure as forms of social organization, where they are funded and supported by the right kinds of law and institutions. Bureaucracies are, by contrast, fragile and rigid; they easily lose impetus and their officials quickly lose *esprit de corps* in the face of crises of funding and function. Had the labour movement built socialism in civil society, alongside the efforts of other voluntary groups like churches, the disaster that has overtaken the health, education and welfare sector in Britain, for example, could never have occurred.

Centralized state power in Britain has allowed deregulation and privatization. It has also permitted rigid control of welfare institutions by a *Nomenklatura* committed to hierarchy, destabilizing 'reform' and the

appropriation of control by managers from 'doers'. Top-down management in welfare institutions is the creature of and the reflection of
centralized state power. It is the enemy of all real welfare, of all real
education, of all real healing. Each activity depends on the willingness of
those who provide such services to act without strict reference to time
and money. Each activity only survives as well as it does in the British
welfare sector because there are still many such people who have not
learned the calculus of utilitarian self-interest and who insist on keeping
remote bureaucracies alive by acting on the principles of service and
mutual aid.

Associationalism seems less incredible after the experience of the
1980s, when it is clear what tyrannical power over society is offered to the
governors of apparently 'liberal' states. We need a principle of renewal
that will offer extensive and equitable welfare, but is prey to fewer of the
authoritarian dangers of collectivism. Whether power is held by the
extreme left or the radical right matters less than the existence of institutions that make such concentrated power possible. That is the real lesson
of the 1980s, and one that many on the left failed to see because they
were mesmerized by their traditional battle with the right.

The need for renewal is becoming apparent. The collapse of the Soviet
system has produced an entirely new situation. Yet in the face of it,
western triumphalism has quickly evaporated. In both Britain and the
United States in particular there is deep and widespread dissatisfaction
about both economic performance and the health of democracy. Conventional representative democracy has become little more than a plebiscite
that chooses and legitimates the rulers of a big governmental machine
that is out of control, in that it is largely unaccountable and cannot tackle
major social problems. The crisis of citizen participation and of effective
accountability of government to society is all too obvious. Democracy
needs to be renewed. It needs to be more inclusive, to give voice not only
to those who are excluded by poverty and discrimination but to many
other citizens as well who see politics as a professional spoils system
beyond their control and concern. With the end of the Cold War the
rationale for defending the status quo in the west has lessened. It is no
longer a legitimation of our flawed democracy to point out that it is far
better than the system that produced Stalin and his successors.

The way is open for the advocacy of a programme of reform that would
supplement and extend rather than destroy representative democracy.
That supplement would involve a growth in the scope of governance
through associations.[12] Associational institutions are in keeping with the
fundamental principles of western liberalism; they are libertarian and
consistent with fundamental human rights. Associational governance

would lessen the tasks of central government to such an exten[t] greater accountability of both the public power and of the de[...] associational agencies would be possible. The main political objective of modern associationalism is to decentralize and devolve as much of the affairs of society as possible to publicly funded but voluntary and self-governing associations.

Such associations are widely regarded in modern democratic theory as the social foundation for plural political interests, as the cement of the 'civil society' that sustains the liberal state. Associationalism, however, treats such self-governing voluntary bodies not as 'secondary associations' but as the *primary* means of organizing social life. In this doctrine, a self-governing civil society becomes primary, and the state becomes a secondary (if vitally necessary) public power that ensures peace between associations, protects the rights of individuals and provides the mechanisms of public finance whereby a substantial part of the activities of associations are funded. The activities of the state, central and local, are thus greatly reduced in scope. Large areas of governance of social affairs come to depend either on associations directly or on processes of coordination and collaboration between associations. In this way what the state does becomes more readily accountable. As its work is increasingly regulatory, so the legislature and judiciary rise in importance relative to the executive, reversing the strong trends in the other direction of this century in both Britain and the US.

Representative democracy thus becomes viable, providing oversight of a government which is a guardian rather than a service provider. As the state ceases to be both provider of services and the guarantor of the standard of those services, it can begin to perform the latter role adequately. It thus inspects and oversees associations, and ensures their compliance with democratic norms in their internal governance and their conformity to commonly agreed community standards of service provision. Associationalism is thus eventually capable of accomplishing that reduction of the extent of the state's service provision activity that conservative anti-collectivists have sought and failed to achieve by means of privatization and the market. Unlike their efforts, associationalism attains this without a reduction in either the scope of social governance or the extent of publicly funded welfare, for neither of these domains is abandoned to unregulated market mechanisms. The scope of public provision is not reduced, but the form in which it is provided ceases to be directly administered by the state.

An Answer to 'Ottomanization'?

Associationalist ideas developed primarily on the left and on the part of religious social activists. Associationalism is not, however, a doctrine confined in its appeal to socialists or social Christians. It may be acceptable to groups far away in their beliefs from these intellectual origins, and whom the originators of these ideas could hardly have imagined. John Neville Figgis would find it hard to comprehend the gay movements in the US, for example. This is simply an illustration of the extent to which western societies are subject to a process of pluralization of social norms and styles of life. This is most marked in the US – where the divergence of ethnic, social, religious and life style groups has produced a virtual process of 'Ottomanization', in which plural communities coexist side by side with very different rules and standards.[13]

One notices this most when such groups clash over the prevailing laws and mores: gays vs. Christian fundamentalists, pro- and anti-choice campaigners on abortion issues, blacks vs. Hassids in New York, and so on. The centralized state does not prevent and cannot check this process of pluralization. Indeed, it is hardly able to contain the violent antagonisms arising from it. Such tendencies toward divergence are almost inevitable in societies in which the range of social and personal choice is extended by mass affluence, by geographical and social mobility, and by the decline of prescriptive community standards in the face of the personal autonomy that the former factors make possible. At the same time, old and new foci of identity compete to bind individuals' choice of communities of association – religion, language, gender and ethnicity. For those left at the bottom these may appear as classes used to; that is, as communities of fate and resistance. For others, however 'traditional' and communitarian they claim to be, old and new identities are reshaped to be sources of social solidarity around *chosen* standards.

Communities of choice and the associations representing them may be no less disruptive for being recent social constructs than are ancient feuds between 'traditional' communities. Common national standards of personal conduct may be fewer and thinner, groups may have divergent mores and ideals of the good life, but most groups act in and make claims on the public realm in remarkably similar ways. Groups make similar claims to freedom of action, seek to have their own chosen objectives made into 'rights' and also seek to criminalize or deny public funding for behaviour of which they disapprove. This applies to both the born again and the politically correct.[14] In the end such antagonisms between groups and such attempts to annex the public power to their own exclusive interests are corrosive of the public sphere and of any common political life. This is exaggerated in the US by weak and non-ideological political parties.

Surely in such circumstances associationalism is a cure that is worse than the disease, since it just endorses an entirely negative pluralism and permits groups to opt out of a common political culture? I believe the opposite to be the case. Associationalism offers the only clear way in the absence of enforced 'common' standards – to make such pluralism a going concern.[15] That way is to reduce inter-group antagonism by the acceptance of a substantial measure of self-regulation, at the price of mutual tolerance. No group could impose its vision on all, most groups could regulate themselves. Clearly, there would be limits to this process: a common morality is not *that* thin – paedophiles are not likely to enjoy rights of self-regulation, nor are rich white neighbourhood associations that exclude black residents. In other cases the likelihood of mutual tolerance is small. Pro- and anti-choice lobbies on abortion issues can hardly be expected to agree to coexist, even geographically in separate states, any more than could slave and free states. Outside of such irreconcilable and competing claims to rights and moral regulation, the parallel and socially competitive social governance by associations would be possible more often than not.

In an associationalist society, given sufficiently varied and overlapping planes of social identity and cleavage, most conflicts between groups could be contained by being 'parcellized'. The coexistence of standards would enable the associations representing groups to regulate those who chose to join them and to remain. Most groups would have a strong interest in preserving the associationalist system because it would secure them the chance of public funding for their welfare activities, an enhanced role in social governance within their own sphere, and protection of their legitimate autonomy from predation by other groups, through the defence of group and individual rights by the public power. Laws regulating all persons and groups would remain, and so would certain common core standards. This core would be narrow but strongly subscribed to – the born again and the politically correct both abhor armed robbery, embezzlement of charity funds and child beating.

The advantage of a measure of localized regulation by groups and associational self-governance is that it would permit the reduction of the extent and complexity of the laws and regulations of the central public power. Framework legislation might be sufficient, if it set the goals of self-governance and the standards by which to measure it. This is true not only of associations in the social and moral sphere, but also, for example, of joint management–worker safety committees in the area of occupational safety and health. The result might be that laws might once again become almost comprehensible to the citizen, rather than filling kilometres of shelf-space. A society that spews forth more and more regulations, because its political institutions are centralized and it purports to cover all aspects of life, does not attain comprehensiveness and uniformity in regulation – quite the contrary. Hence it may be just as well to accept the inevitable diversity that will come with self-governance. Provided the institutions in question are reasonably democratic and that there are protections for basic individual rights, such diversity can be healthy. A legal system whose rules are by their very bulk and complexity unintelligible to the citizens and whose regulatory processes often seem opaque to specialist lawyers is in danger of undermining the rule of law in its search to perfect it.

The essential checks imposed on such self-regulatory associations are that they must submit to certain minimum common standards of democratic self-governance and that they must not prevent exit by dissatisfied members.[16] Exit is not only a powerful solvent of oligarchy; it also limits the extent to which groups may sanction the loyalty of their members. There is no point in pluralizing the state only to create totalitarianism potentialities and authoritarian practices at the level of associations. Associationalism is a vital supplement to liberal democracy and *not* a substitute for it.

The Politics of Decentralization

Our discussion above is a negative thought experiment. It has envisaged an extremity of group divergence and value pluralism. In doing so it has drawn on tendencies that are evident in the US. Other societies are more cohesive, but even in these there are strong reasons for decentralization and associational self-government, other than the dampening of inter-group conflict. Not the least of these reasons are the dangers of centralized state power and the failures of bureaucratic welfare collectivism I discussed at the beginning of this chapter. Moreover, even in circumstances of strong pressures toward group divergence, associational governance may actually *help* to rebuild ties between groups and facilitate the construction of national, regional or social foci of common identification. Associationalism hands over great powers and responsibilities to groups. But most associations will not be exclusive groups that enclose the whole of their members' social lives. A self-governing association cannot stand against all the world – if it did it would be a *de facto* 'sovereign' state. Associational law, as we shall see, would limit certain acts as *ultra vires* – in particular, it would forbid trade unions to own firms directly and it would require associations (such as churches, welfare bodies and so on) to create special organizations for each domain in which they were in receipt of public funds (such as schools, hospitals and so on).[17] Thus the purposes and powers of most associations, and certainly the organizations they create for public welfare, would be limited, in the former case by their own choice in the main, and in the latter by law. The members of most associations would also be members of others too. Moreover, for many purposes associations or their organizations would need to coordinate and collaborate with others in like spheres of activity – if only to build coalitions of mutual convenience when funds were distributed or common standards set. Associations might thus gradually create a network of formal and informal relations, which would enable society to enjoy both diversity in social governance and a substantial measure of coordination.[18]

As far as individual citizens are concerned, associational institutions might actually reduce the negative sources of identification with groups and dispose them to regard neighbouring groups in a more tolerant light. Greater democratic governance through voluntary associations means greater control over his or her affairs by the citizen. The possibility of diverse standards of social governance on the part of associations representing groups at least ensures that among those with whom one has chosen to live certain values will prevail. The combination of a reduction in powerlessness in the control of one's own affairs and the removal of the fear of being at the mercy of hostile moral legislators might well promote more widespread feelings of security on the part of citizens and a consequent lessening of hostility toward others. Fear of others' moral politics can be acute where the state is both centralized and claims a plenitude of power in the recognition and regulation of groups and their actions. In such a state moral minorities compete to control or influence power and then compel others to live in a certain way: the state is then either for or against gay rights, either militantly anti-clerical or the upholder of a compulsory religion.

Associationalism is an explicitly normative theory. It starts from the premise that voluntary self-governing associations are the best way of organizing human affairs that combines liberty with social obligation. But it is not merely a doctrine that makes judgements based on values; from this basic value premise, associationalist thinkers have developed powerful theoretical and practical criticisms of the centralized 'sovereign' state, of bureaucratic collectivism and of the individualism of unregulated markets. They have also developed practical models of how to organize the economy and welfare on associationalist lines.

For this reason associationalism is the political theory best able to give effective expression to the feelings of unease that many have about contemporary social organization, but in a more coherent form than moral unease or protest. For example, associationalism provides a rationale for the decentralization of administration and a practical means of accomplishing it. Interest in decentralization, regionalism and 'subsidiarity' is strong and growing right across the political spectrum: thus many conservatives genuinely want to roll back the state in the interests of greater accountability and not for mere financial advantage; Greens evidently want a less hierarchical and centralized economic system; and the left are desperately seeking some alternative to central planning. But this advocacy and aspiration lacks a coherent political theory; it is less effective as a result, and the different parts of the political spectrum are more conscious of their differences than of the means to hold their divergent aspirations in common. Decentralization and localism are strong and widely shared value preferences, responses to the remoteness and impersonality of big administrative machines, but they tend to be dismissed because they run counter to the apparent efficiency gains of large-scale organizations. Anyone who has seen the mess made by English local government since the 1960s by a series of centralizing 'reforms' will know that these goals are more often promised than delivered.[19] Decentralization will accomplish little if the lesser units are as large and as bureaucratic as, say, London boroughs or English area health authorities. The need is to explain how and why things could be different.

Here English political pluralism is particularly valuable as a component part of associationalist doctrine. Proudhon in *Du principe fédératif* argued strongly against centralized power and defended the thesis that all power should be delegated *upwards* rather than the other way around, as is customary in hierarchical organizations. But he develops a utopian scheme in which communes give limited grants of power to higher bodies. Harold Laski is in this respect more practical and pragmatic, recognizing that centralized states will have to *devolve* power. In 'The problem of administrative areas', he writes to persuade political leaders and state officials of the need to recognize functional agencies and to devolve power to them.[20] He is interested in a crafting of pluralism by reform, in which the state surrenders elements of sovereignty while exercising it. Like Proudhon, however, he starts from the premise that all power is by its nature federative. This is the case *de facto*, whatever the claims of the state *de Jure*. There are fundamental geographical and social divisions that must be respected in the organization of government. If they are not, then not only is liberty put at risk by excessive centralization, but also those wellsprings of association and cooperation that make a society truly efficient are threatened. Laski argued that the art of good government is to identify these discrete units to give them appropriate powers, and to respect the degree of autonomy necessary for them to function. He saw that they were both geographical and functional, and that both types should enjoy self-government: 'the railways are as real as Lancashire'.

John Neville Figgis argued that not only is good government decentralizing, but that the most effective form of government is the self-government of associations freely formed of citizens. The state should leave such associations to their own evolution by the decisions of their own democratic bodies. He argued that the claim of 'sovereignty' – integral to the existence of centralized and concentrated state power – must deny this right to associations and treat all freedom of action of an agency as a concession sanctioned by representatives of the sovereign and revokable by legislation. Whether such 'sovereign' power is democratically legitimated or not, it still has the potential for both tyranny and inefficiency. Indeed, being able to point to the support of a mass electorate made oppression easier. Figgis, in *Churches in the Modern State*, well before the advent of modern totalitarian regimes, saw these dangers inherent in modern centralized state power, drawing the lessons from Bismark's *Kulturkampf* and French republican anti-clericalism.[21] We can see the same lessons today, for example, in the abolition of the democratically elected government of London in 1986 despite widespread opposition by local citizens.

The autonomy of local and regional government is relatively well understood and respected in at least some states – Switzerland being the most notable example. Less well recognized, still – and the English pluralist writings are all but forgotten – is the need for democratic self-government by *function*.[22] The problem here is that functional government can mean little if the great mass of economic affairs is conducted by privately owned and hierarchically managed firms, and the bulk of public services by state-funded and state-directed large bureaucracies. The space for real functional government is then tiny, within the existing voluntary sector and on the margins of social life. If these institutions persist unreformed, then the role of 'democracy' is restricted in the one case to shareholders (at least nominally) electing directors and, in the other, to citizens electing representatives who have nominal direction over the heads of public bureaucracies. Noberto Bobbio in *The Future of Democracy* remarks that democracy has stopped short of 'the two great blocks of descending and hierarchical power in every complex society, big business and public administration. And as long as these blocks hold out against the pressures exerted from below, the democratic transformation of society cannot be said to be complete.'[23] The key test of democracy now is not '"who votes" but "where" they can vote'.[24] But the issue is not where in the literal sense, but in what *kind* of institution and for what *kind* of authority.

The problem is that such hierarchical and large-scale organizations cannot easily be democratized. Voting will change them much less than might be supposed. Indeed, it will legitimate their governing elites if hierarchy persists. Moreover, who is the constituency to vote in such organizations? Critics of industrial democracy have argued that the very idea of self-government here acts against the accountability of such institutions to society – it empowers the employees or providers of a service with a measure of control over its delivery. This was the Fabian critique of administrative and industrial syndicalism, for example – that it enabled the producers to govern themselves at the expense of the consumer.

If such large hierarchical organizations are not readily democratizable by the mere voting of their members, then the present situation remains highly unsatisfactory; for large firms and bureaucracies are not well stewarded by existing 'democratic' mechanisms. The firm as a republic of shareholders is a fiction; the management of firms is only notionally elected by and accountable to the shareholders (it is 'answerable' to the stock market and to major institutional investors, but that is another matter, and the economic consequences are far from satisfactory). Large welfare bureaucracies are only nominally accountable to ministers or councillors; for most practical purposes senior officials make detailed policy and junior ones have a large measure of administrative discretion with regard to clients. The concentration of economic power in large corporations and the concentration of social welfare and social control in large bureaucracies acts against that dispersal of social power and influence that liberal democratic theorists have seen as essential to the preservation of liberty. The sphere of civil society and secondary associations shrinks in the face of bodies that are in effect compulsory (one has to seek work, and large bureaucracies amount to a significant share of the labour force; the unemployed are subject to welfare tutelage) and which are not open to the *social* or *political* influence of the average citizen.[25] As a worker the citizen cannot of right make company policy; at best he or she can only disrupt the service the firm supplies by industrial action to modify that policy. As recipient of state benefits or services the citizen has no political rights or mutual ties in the capacity of claimant.

This is all the more absurd when one recalls that companies, while controlled by a few, are financed through the funds of the many – through insurance policies, pension funds, unit trusts and bank deposits.[26] The great mass of capital comes from the pockets of ordinary citizens, often in the form of necessary or compulsory saving. It is also absurd that while public welfare agencies are funded by citizens' social insurance and taxes (even by welfare recipients in the case of indirect taxes), citizens are treated like supplicants when seeking discretionary funds or actions from public officials.

Roads to Economic Democracy

The only answer to these problems is a long-term one: to restore the scope of civil society by converting both companies and state welfare service agencies into self-governing associations. This will be a long haul, and in the interim the most realistic policies are those which boost the cooperative economy and the voluntary sector in welfare. The need for the democratization of companies is widely perceived. The most accomplished of modern political theorists, Robert A. Dahl, in his *A Preface to Economic Democracy* argues strongly for the development of a worker-owned cooperative sector as a way of checking the unhealthy concentration of corporate control over the economy that has grown up in the US in this century.[27] Democracy requires the diffusion of ownership. Revisionist socialists have espoused market socialism, an explicit model of an economy that marries cooperation and neo-classical economics.[28] The economic units are to be worker cooperatives and they are linked one with another and with consumers through market transactions.

The problem with views like the latter is that they treat the economy as if it were reducible to its component parts, to enterprises. Get ownership and control within the enterprise into the right balance, add to it an effective competition and anti-monopoly policy to prevent firms getting too big, and then the distribution of rewards will be fair and markets will also operate as efficient allocative mechanisms. Market economies, however, depend for their substantive outcomes on non-market social factors that the firm cannot easily create within itself.[29] Those factors are, for example, the achieving of an effective balance between cooperation and competition among firms that ensures an adequate supply of necessary 'public goods' to firms (suitably trained labour, market information and so on), and the creation of a structure of publicly regulated financial institutions that provide a range of sources of investment finance at suitable rates and terms for the sustained development of the economy. These are but two examples of the ways in which successful market economies are embedded in a social context that the market cannot supply and cannot reproduce. The problem is that reformers focusing on one level, the enterprise, propose changes that make sense at that level, but at another level they ignore the ensemble of social conditions necessary to a democratic and decentralized society in which markets play a contained but constructive role.

Such balances between cooperation and competition are struck more satisfactorily in some national and regional economies than others.[30] But they may not be struck on terms that are favourable to openness, to democracy or to equality of influence between core economic actors and other parts of the society. This is why it is not possible to follow those wholly business-orientated commentators who advocate learning from Japan, even if we could manage to reproduce Japanese institutions.[31] The great advantage of associationalism is that it provides principles and concepts for assessing the range of institutions that make a balance between cooperation and competition possible, and for establishing which are most consistent with extended democratic governance in civil society. It does this is in three ways. First, by insisting on the devolution of governmental functions to the lowest level at which they can be efficiently performed, it provides a *political* rationale for the tendencies toward local and regional economic regulation. Secondly, by emphasizing the principles both of organizing social activities through voluntary organizations and of voluntary cooperation between them, it provides political rationales for economic governance through open, inclusive bodies like trade associations, and for firms to cooperate in developing the industrial 'public sphere' of a region or locality. Thirdly, by emphasizing the principle of mutuality, it encourages enterprises and other agencies to develop ongoing relationships and offer one another help in a range of ways (from the informal, such as the established customs of firms sharing work and information, to the formal, such as industrial credit unions).

The control of the concentration of ownership cannot be checked by state regulation alone, if, that is, the whole thrust of the economy is towards greater agglomeration of capital and if the operation of financial markets facilitates this. Associationalism would help to check concentration by strengthening the small- and medium-sized-firm sectors' capacity to resist, and by providing such firms with a supportive regional and local institutional context, a local industrial public sphere that makes such firms politically tenacious and economically able to share many of the benefits size confers on their larger competitors.[32] Associationalism would foster the development of, in particular, institutions to encourage the localization and regionalization of capital. Evidence suggests that where capital can be both generated and recycled within a region, the chances for that region to enjoy a measure of autonomy and economic success are greater if it is dependent on small and medium-sized firms. Combined with effective local economic regulation and strong patterns of association between firms, this factor helps to make localities into publicly aware and responsive entities that take charge of their economic fate. Local financial institutions and relationships of mutual borrowing and lending help to provide both the material means of autonomy and the foci of effective 'intimate knowledge' of the region, which enable key actors to exercise strategic direction over its development.[33] In the case of the majority of British regions, concentration of ownership means that decisions about local firms are taken in London boardrooms or the City. British small and medium-sized firms are isolated in purely competitive and market relationships. Local government is denied the fiscal and policy autonomy for local economic regulation by Westminster. The result has been economic decline, and the absence of local political and financial resources to combat it.

Worker-owned cooperatives are superficially an attractive way to ensure both the greater diffusion of economic ownership and economic democracy, through the diffusion of control. However, as the Guild Socialists like G. D. H. Cole were well aware (even more so than the Fabians, who favoured professional management in both public bodies and private concerns), industry is a service to society and this service is by no means ensured by giving its control of enterprises exclusively into the hands of their workers.[34] Guild Socialism, at least in its moderate version, was critical of syndicalism for this very reason. In *Guild Socialism Re-Stated*, Cole outlines how this service would be organized through national guilds.[35] This institutional design is clearly now obsolete in a world of international competition, rapidly changing technologies and shifting divisions of labour. But the need for extended accountability beyond the firm and for institutions that link firms in both the locality and the industrial sector are points that can be taken over from Cole into modern associationalism.

There are more stakeholders in industry than just the immediate producers. Economic democracy certainly requires that workers enjoy extensive rights of participation within a company, the right to acquire a share in its ownership and representation on its governing body.[36] But other interests have a right to be represented too – principally the providers of capital and the local community. Where the economy is regulated by regional or local collaborative and public institutions, where relations of capital provision are mutualized, then this tripartite relationship of stakeholders in company governance becomes credible. It also ensures that these three interests are each knowledgeable about business conditions and capable of ensuring that the firm is both competitive and profitable and yet provides a decent service. The creation of local or regional mutual financial institutions – local industrial savings banks, industrial credit unions for firms, and locally controlled pension funds – reduces the distance between capital providers and the company. Whether the capital be provided as shares, bonds or loans, whether the representation of capital as stakeholder takes the form of electing representatives through shareholdership or through interlocking directorships, matters less if financial institutions are local, accountable in diverse ways to the community and committed to the long-term success of the region or locality. Such patterns will develop differently as regions and localities evolve their own patterns of regulation, and this is preferable to prescribing one model in law. Local mutual institutions will be more effective stewards of citizens' money and more active stakeholder representatives on companies' governing bodies than are national or international absentee fund managers, who watch the stock market and little else.

In a similar way, the fact that companies are enmeshed in substantial local and regional relationships with other firms, trade associations and public bodies will make it much easier for them to choose for themselves or accept from outside representatives of the community-as-stakeholder. Assuming a tightly integrated and collaboratively governed local or regional economy makes it easier to see how one will find 'community' representatives who are not mere nominees of either labour or capital, and who possess real knowledge and commitment to the firm and the local economy. Such tripartite representation in its governance helps to make the firm accountable to its members and to society at large: it has real stakeholders rather than the notional 'shareholders' (who in the main are only interested in a marketable financial asset). At the same time, because the firm is embedded in society by this community representation and other links, the local community will feel responsible for it and will try to ensure that it stays in business to provide work and profit for local people.

A model of this kind that tries to balance cooperation and competition between firms, that tries to regulate as far as possible by means of trade associations, representative forums and mutually owned agencies, and that seeks to preserve the economic and social integrity of localities, is thus quite different from either the advocacy of collective ownership and planning or unregulated market individualism. Such a perspective, indeed, amounts to a relatively coherent concept of a 'third way' between the two. Such a perspective emphasizes economic decentralization and explains how to get it through regional and local economies regulated through private–public partnerships. Not only does this associationalist theory encourage economic relationships of manageable scale, it also links to the political doctrine by showing how the firms involved in these relationships are easier to make accountable to employees and communities than are very large national and multinational firms. There is a great deal of evidence from studies of existing regional economies and industrial districts that such mutualist and associational economic relationships are possible, that they are not inimical to productive efficiency (quite the contrary), and that not all production and distribution need be conducted on a large scale in order to match national and international competitors.[37]

It should be obvious that such economies can only develop by genuine local initiative and cooperation, given a favourable institutional and fiscal climate that encourages such experiments rather than one which crushes them, as in the UK at present. Economic democracy must be built out of two kinds of partnership, one between employees, managers and owners within the firm, and the other between firms themselves and the locality. Modern associationalist economic doctrine accepts that the route to economic democracy is complex and that it cannot take the form of a single 'industrial democracy' statute as envisaged by Labour radicals in Britain the 1970s.[38] Company law must, indeed, be reformed and it must include strong inducements for firms to move in the direction of collaborative governance. Legislation that is permissive and incremental can then follow along these avenues of advance. Clearly, the idea of imposing 'workers' control' by law is an absurdity and the statute would fall on the deaf ears of reluctant, ill-educated and often cynical workforces with low loyalty to their firms and poor motivation. Even if it were politically possible in countries like Britain and the US, it would not be desirable. This may be a reflection of the policies of so many British and American firms' management, but it is an insuperable obstacle to the centralist and legalist conception of a single reform to impose industrial democracy – even if there were no opposition from business or unions. For workers in the majority of firms to be motivated to participate on an extended scale, a long period of human relations initiatives, training and worker capital acquisition incentives supportive of greater collaboration would be necessary.

The model of the development of an associational economy may not be at all like that envisaged by the Guild Socialists, in which it grew out of the efforts of the labour movement and was strongly worker-orientated. Rather, it is more likely to grow up from the coalescence of a series of concerns that concentrate on the preservation and construction of industrial districts and of local and regional economies. Classes used to be considered communities of fate; now for many people – including entrepreneurs, managers and skilled workers whose non-financial assets or labour are not easily relocated on national or international markets – it is the region that is a community of fate. It may well be that more collaborative relationships *within* firms, and the financial institutions necessary to fund cooperatives, will develop from partnerships *between* firms, and between them and the local public agencies and organized labour. The Guild Socialists believed that the contest for political power was at best a diversion; society was to be changed by the labour movement pressing on capital and shifting the frontier of control irreversibly towards labour. This political naivety, which it shared with syndicalism, led to its political marginalization and to the disregard of such ideas by the Labour Party.[39] However anti-statist modern associationalism may be, it cannot ignore the reality of the modern state, and it knows that private initiatives must go hand in hand with – indeed, may depend on – public reforms. Legal and institutional changes would be necessary to facilitate the rapid growth of associational governance.

An Associationalist Strategy for Reform

How might that happen? In the economic sphere one can argue that if industrial districts, organized regional economies, and collaborative relationships that balance cooperation and competition can survive competitive pressures from large firms, they can serve as a political model. The hope would then be of the gradual diffusion of localization and mutuality through its regional success stories, promoting both emulation from below and pressure for the reform of national laws to permit the diffusion of such developments. Similarly, in the welfare sector, the gradual growth of voluntarism as a remedy for and a supplement to state collectivism may create models to be emulated and diffused. Above all, what is needed is a *concept* that ties these various, often popular, ideas together and shows their practicality – political decentralization and governance through associations, new regional economies, and confederalism and voluntarism in welfare. That concept has been missing, not because it was not available, but because political activity and circumstances have only just caught up with long-neglected ideas. The only route to the success of associationalism demands a clear concept, because that will tie together organizationally and attitudinally separate efforts working in different localities and social spheres toward similar ends. Local unionists and the owners of small firms, Christian voluntary workers in the inner cities, ecological groups seeking both a more human scale and a sustainable environment may all profit from this knowledge.

The model of them all coming together in a single political party that attains power by persuading the electorate of the virtues of its programme and then enacts that plan into the simultaneous reform of the whole society is quite inappropriate. That is possible as a dream for collectivists and for those who wish to decollectivize through deregulation and privatization – both accept centralized sovereign state power and do not wish to change it. Associationalists have to rely on the multiplication of diverse efforts. Associationalist relationships have to be built by citizens' initiative and bodies freely formed by committed individuals. Unless such relationships arise from genuine cooperation they will be of little value – the idea of being *compelled* to join a voluntary association for any purpose is an absurdity (but that is what a statutory 'big bang' approach to an associationalist system of welfare would imply). The role of legislation must be permissive and gradual, not prescriptive and peremptory. Fortunately there is some hope that this process of diffusion of the associational model may begin to happen: if nation-states continue to become less effective loci of economic regulation, if highly concentrated corporate power becomes less legitimate to citizens as it seems less and less the only route to industrial efficiency, and as the secret of supply-side success comes to be seen as a diffuse set of public and private commitments to the effective functioning of firms, networks and supportive public institutions. The ultimate legitimations of large scale are now economic; if they falter, then the case for more decentralized institutions will grow in strength.

But it would be foolish to talk ourselves into a process of transition to an associationalist wonderland, the substitute object for the workers' fatherlands of yore. The associational principle can democratize and reinvigorate societies as a supplement to and a healthy competitor for the currently dominant forms of social organization: representative mass democracy, bureaucratic state welfare and the big corporation. Not all economic activities can be carried out by cooperative small and medium-sized firms (however efficient), nor can all economic regulation be collaborative or regionally based. Some elements of public welfare cannot be entrusted to voluntary agencies (however sophisticated the mechanisms for devolution of functions and funding): in the last instance, rights of entitlement, standards of service and principles of equity must be maintained by the public power at the federal level. National states and international agencies of a regulatory nature (world public powers) will remain necessary and, in the latter case, will become more important. No serious associationalist imagines that global warming or Third World poverty can be tackled (if they can be tackled at all) solely by voluntary agencies.

It is best to envisage associationalism not as 'the society of the future', a system complete in itself, but as an axial principle of social organization; that is, as a pattern of organizing social relations that can be generalized across sectors and domains of social activity, which is not a localized institution or pattern of customary action. In this it resembles the market and bureaucratic administration. Such principles compete for dominance in modern societies: a mixture of the prevailing social conditions and the availability of a credible and effectively presented conceptual model decide whether a principle will play a major or a subsidiary role in a given period. In each case part of the role of a conceptual model is to show how the axial principle in question can be elaborated as the practical and credible basis for social organization. Such models as Smith's *The Wealth of Nations* or the Webbs' advocacy of bureaucratic collectivism have proved efficacious in aiding the spread of the market and state welfare principles. Associationalism needs a similar elaboration to show its widespread applicability and effectiveness. What it has too often had are 'blueprints', turning models into utopian actualities. Whether associationalism can act as a supplement to our failing institutions now depends not on restating the principle, but on working out the detail of credible models of associational governance in the economy and the welfare sectors. That is now the main task of associationalist theory.

NOTES

1   I have tried to examine in greater detail elsewhere the theoretical case for associationalism and political pluralism: see P. Hirst, *Representative Democracy and its Limits* (Cambridge, Polity Press, 1990), chs 1, 4, 5 and 6, and P. Hirst (ed.), *The Pluralist Theory of the State: selected writings of G. D. H. Cole, J. N. Figgis and H. J. Laski* (London, Routledge, 1989), Introduction, pp. 1–45. This chapter concentrates more on the current political situation and how associative democracy may contribute to democratic renewal than on expounding associationalist political theory. That theory is most usefully developed by working out the institutional framework of associationalism in sufficient detail to show how such relationships would work as one of the main means of social organization. Space prohibits trying to do this here: I have developed a model of an associationalist confederal welfare state in which voluntary service provision agencies are publicly funded but in which there is extensive consumer choice, and yet the system relies very little on either central administrative discretion in allocating funds or on markets: see P. Hirst, 'Associationalism and a confederal welfare state – thin collectivism, thick welfare', *Birkbeck Public Policy Centre Papers* (1992). I am grateful to both the members of the Anglican Association for Social Responsibility and the A. E.

Havens Centre, University of Wisconsin, Madison, for the opportunity to present my ideas to critical audiences who contributed considerably to my definition of the institutional problems of associationalism.

2 'Unless groups are allowed free development the self-development of individuals will be hindered.' J. N. Figgis, *Churches in the Modern State* (London, Longman Green and Co., 1913), p. 12.

3 On the limits of Keynesian strategies today, see M. Piore and C. Sabel, *The Second Industrial Divide* (New York, Basic Books, 1984), and F. Scharpf, *Crisis and Choice in European Social Democracy* (Ithaca, NY, Cornell University Press, 1991). On the constraints of the failure of Keynesianism for welfare, see A. Cutler, K. Williams and J. Williams, *Keynes, Beveridge and Beyond* (London, Routledge, 1986). As an example of left dissatisfaction with collectivist welfare and of alternative market-orientated thinking, see J. Le Grand, 'Rethinking welfare: a case for quasi-markets', in B. Pimlott et al. (eds), *The Alternative* (London, W. H. Allen, 1990).

4 On the mechanisms whereby cooperation and competition are balanced, see P. Hirst and J. Zeitlin, 'Flexible specialisation and the competitive failure of UK manufacturing', *The Political Quarterly*, 60:2 (1989), 164–78, and C. Sabel, 'Studied trust: building new forms of cooperation in a volatile economy', *Paper No. 11*, Conference on Industrial Districts and Local Economic Regeneration, ILO, Geneva (1990).

5 On Japan, see R. Dore, *Taking Japan Seriously* (London, The Athlone Press, 1986).

6 On the former West Germany, see Scharpf, *Crisis and Choice*, especially ch. 7.

7 On Britain's failure to develop a collaborative and interventionalist system of economic regulation, see D. Marquand, *The Unprincipled Society* (London, Cape, 1988), and for the US, L. Thurow, *The Zero-Sum Society* (New York, Basic Books, 1980).

8 For selected writings of Cole, Figgis and Laski, see Hirst, *The Pluralist Theory of the State*. For Proudhon, see S. Vincent, *Pierre-Joseph Proudhon* (New York, Oxford University Press, 1984), and Proudhon's *The Principle of Federation*, intro. R. Vernon (Toronto, University of Toronto Press, 1979). For R. Owen, see K. Taylor, *The Political Ideas of the Utopian Socialists* (London, Frank Cass, 1982), and for G. J. Holyoake, see his *The Cooperative Movement Today* (London, Methuen, 1891), and P. Gurney, 'George Jacob Holyoake: socialism, association and cooperation in nineteenth-century England', in S. Yeo (ed.), *New Views of Cooperation* (London, Routledge, 1988).

9 See P. Hirst and J. Zeitlin, 'Flexible specialisation vs. post-Fordism: theory, evidence and policy implications', *Economy and Society*, 20:1 (1991), 1–50, and Piore and Sabel *The Second Industrial Divide*.

10 This may sound like nineteenth-century philanthropy. Actually nineteenth-century voluntary action has been largely misrepresented: working-class mutual aid within voluntary agencies (outside the labour movement) was very important and there was substantial popular financial support for voluntary causes. Hence one should not assume charity was a 'middle-class' imposition on the poor or that it was a failure: it appears to have contributed greatly to relieving distress and it was less demeaning and disabling of its recipients than much modern state welfare. For a major reinterpretation, see F. Prochaska, *The Voluntary Impulse* (London, Faber and Faber, 1988).

11 A great deal of this switch from voluntarism and mutualism in the British labour movement occurred very late on in the twentieth century. In the 1920s, employers, unions and state officials still preferred a voluntary and employer-based system of

welfare to a uniform state system. Beveridge was still strongly in favour of the voluntary principle in his 1942 Report: see K. Williams and J. Williams, *A Beveridge Reader* (London, Allen and Unwin, 1987), ch. 5.

12   Arguments for democratic renewal are numerous. Examples of arguments to make interest group representation more inclusive through institutional reform are P. Schmitter, 'Corporative democracy: oxymoronic, just plain moronic? or a promising way out of the present impasse?', unpublished ms (1988), and J. Cohen and J. Rogers, 'Secondary associations in democratic governance', *Politics and Society*, November (1992).

13   This refers to the devolved structure of communal self-governance in Ottoman cities. See R. Davidson, 'The *Millets* as agents of change in the nineteenth century Ottoman Empire', in R. Braude and B. Lewis (eds) *Christians and Jews in the Ottoman Empire*, Vol. 1 (New York, Holmes and Meyer, 1983).

14   On competing rights claims with reference to the abortion issue, see E. Kingdom, *What's Wrong with Rights?* (Edinburgh, Edinburgh University Press, 1991).

15   This strategy of plural self-governance does not stem from the premise that all value standards are relative. On the contrary, a pluralistic associational society requires a limited common core of widely supported beliefs and standards and, moreover, there must be strong grounds for those beliefs that the community feels it can justify: see P. Hirst, 'An answer to relativism', *New Formations*, 10 (1990), 13–23.

16   A. O. Hirschman, *Exit, Voice and Loyalty* (Cambridge, MA, Harvard University Press, 1970).

17   See P. Hirst, 'From statism to pluralism', in B. Pimlott et al. (eds), *The Alternative* (London, W. H. Allen, 1990), and Hirst 'Associationalism and a confederal welfare state'.

18   See W. Streek and P. Schmitter, 'Community, market, state and associations', *European University Institute Working Paper No. 94*, Florence (1984).

19   See R. Rendell and C. Ward, *Undermining the Central Line* (London, Chatto and Windus, 1989).

20   This essay is to be found in H. J. Laski, *The Foundations of Sovereignty and Other Essays* (London, Allen and Unwin, 1921), pp. 30–103.

21   London, Longman Green and Co., 1913.

22   See K. Knight, 'The myth of functional democracy', Ph.D. thesis, University of London (1990).

23   N. Bobbio, *The Future of Democracy* (Cambridge, Polity Press, 1987), p. 57.

24   Bobbio, *The Future of Democracy*, p. 56.

25   See H. Belloc, *The Servile State* (originally published 1913; reprinted Indianapolis, Liberty Classics, 1977).

26   On the dominance of institutional investment, see G. Thompson, *The Political Economy of the New Right* (London, F. Pinter, 1990), ch. 6, pp. 144–6.

27   New Haven, CT, Yale University Press, 1985.

28   See J. Le Grand and S. Estin (eds), *Market Socialism* (Oxford, Oxford University Press, 1989), especially ch. 2.

29   On the balance between cooperation and competition and the failure of the market to secure this, see Piore and Sabel, *The Second Industrial Divide*, and note 4.

30   On the significance of industrial districts and regional economic regulation, see C. Sabel, 'The flexible specialisation and the re-emergence of regional economies', in P. Hirst and J. Zeitlin (eds), *Reversing Industrial Decline* (Oxford, Berg, 1989), pp. 17–71, and J. Zeitlin, 'Industrial districts and local economic

regeneration: models, institutions and policies', *Paper No. 10*, Conference on Industrial Districts and Local Economic Regeneration, ILO, Geneva (1990).

31 For a stinging critique of Japanese institutions, a necessary if overdone corrective to Japan-worship, see K. von Wolferen, *The Enigma of Japanese Power* (London, Macmillan, 1989).

32 For the concept of an 'industrial public sphere', see Hirst and Zeitlin, 'Flexible specialisation and the competitive failure of UK manufacturing'; for the benefits of cooperation to secure the equivalent economies of scale, see S. Brusco, 'Small firms and the provision of real services', *Paper No. 4*, Conference on Industrial Districts and Local Economic Regeneration, ILO, Geneva (1990).

33 'Intimate knowledge' is a concept used by Alfred Marshall in *Industry and Trade* (London, Macmillan, 1919) to describe a crucial part of the 'industrial atmosphere' that made traditional industrial districts function. See G. Becattini, 'The Marshallian industrial district as a socio-economic notion', in F. Pyke et al. (eds), *Industrial Districts and Inter-firm Cooperation in Italy* (Geneva, International Institute for Labour Studies, 1990).

34 On this aspect of Cole, see P. Hirst, 'Guilding the factory', *Samizdat*, 10: special issue on 'The Radical Tradition', May/June (1990), pp. 6–7.

35 London, Leonard Parsons, 1920.

36 For attempts to show how workers might establish a substantial measure of ownership and control by gradual change, see J. Mathews, *The Age of Democracy* (Melbourne, Oxford University Press, 1989), ch. 3; J. Cornford, 'A stake in the company', *Economic Study No. 3*, London Institute of Public Policy Research (1990); and S. Turnbull, 'Re-inventing corporations', *Human Systems Management*, 10 (1991), pp. 169–86.

37 For studies of two modern industrial districts, both of which have proved strongly competitive in the 1980s, see: for Baden-Württemberg, C. Sabel et al, 'Regional prosperities compared: Massachusetts and Baden-Württemberg in the 1980s', *Economy and Society*, 18:4 (1989), pp. 374–404, and Hubert Schmitz, 'Industrial districts: model and reality in Baden-Württemberg', *Paper No. 5*, Conference on Industrial Districts and Local Economic Regeneration, ILO, Geneva (1990); and, for Emilia-Romagna and Italy generally, S. Brusco, 'The Emilian model: productive decentralisation and social integration', *Cambridge Journal of Economics*, 6:2 (1982), pp. 167–84, and C. Trigilia, 'Italian industrial districts: neither myth nor interlude', *Paper No. 8*, Conference on Industrial Districts and Local Economic Regeneration, ILO, Geneva (1990).

38 For a criticism of those *dirigiste* Labour proposals of the 1970s, see P. Hirst, *Law Socialism and Democracy* (London, Allen and Unwin, 1986), ch. 6.

39 On the failure of Guild Socialism, see S. T. Glass, *The Responsible Society* (London, Longman, 1966), and N. Carpenter, *Guild Socialism: an historical and critical analysis* (New York, D. Appleton, 1922).

6

DIRECT DEMOCRACY: SETTING APPROPRIATE TERMS OF DEBATE

Ian Budge

Introduction

As a method of democratic decision-making, direct voting has received little consideration from political theorists, largely because it has been dismissed as impracticable from the start. The traditional reaction to the idea of populations voting directly on decisions that affect them has been that in principle it is a fine thing, but impossible to bring about, owing to the size of modern communities which rules out anything like the popular assembly of all citizens in the classical Greek cities. Without the ability to meet together for face-to-face discussion, direct democracy is impossible, so some form of representation must be introduced. With representation, the debate switches to the proper balance of powers between representatives and represented, and how the former may be held accountable without fettering their proper initiative and autonomy.

Opinions have certainly been expressed in the debate on representation which have considerable relevance for its direct equivalent. Arguments for popular control over the representative being restricted because of the lack of knowledge or the apathy of the masses would be even stronger if applied to their direct participation in decision-making. It is the aim here to take some of these arguments along with others less widely applied to systems of representation, and to consider their relevance for direct democracy.

A first sketch of some of the arguments in this chapter appeared as 'L'impatto politico delle tecnolologie informatiche: partecipazione o autoritarismo?', *Teoria Politica*, V (1989), pp. 67–84, following a conference organized by the journal *Quaderni del Circolo Rosselli* in Florence, 12 December 1986. I wish to thank Alfio Mastropaolo for his help: also, at later stages of the chapter, Geraint Parry, David Held and Onora O'Neill.

Such an enterprise makes sense only if we are discussing some system of government which has a certain possibility of being implemented. The first thing to note about direct democracy in the contemporary world is that modern technology has transformed its prospects of realization. While citizens of modern states clearly cannot meet directly together, they can communicate at a distance and in complex networks by electronic means. This is possible even at the present time through linkages of telephone, radio, television and computer. During the next decade these will in all likelihood be combined within a unified device, which will respond to vocal instructions and facilitate two-way or multiple communication with an ease undreamt of up to now.[1]

Objections to the quality of electronic debate are certainly pertinent. The type of discussion and the nature of the decisions we make are affected by a change from face-to-face discussion to telephone or electronic mail, for example. It is a moot point, however, whether they would be as much affected by a change in the means of communication used as by a change in the natural language in which they were conducted (switches from English to German or Greek, for example, have a considerable potential for altering the import of political words and the level of abstraction of the discussion).

Surely, however, popular debate and decision-making have certain characteristics which make them recognizably the same in whatever way they are conducted. A telephone conversation differs from face-to-face conversation but both are conversations. Similarly one might claim that an electronically based debate – provided (an essential point) that it permitted interaction and dialogue – allowed for decisions to be made on broadly the same lines as in actual popular assemblies. Both can therefore be regarded as variants of direct democracy.

Direct Democracy: Differing Institutional Forms

Before discussing the forms which direct democracy might take, we need first to identify the common characteristics which all its variants share and which differentiate it from representative democracy as such. In the abstract, direct democracy can be characterized as a regime in which the population as a whole votes on the most important political decisions. Operationally we can translate this abstract stipulation into the practical requirement that the body of adult citizens vote directly on most of the matters on which, in representative democracies, Parliament votes. Even within such a definition there is a variety of institutional forms which direct democracy can take, just as there is for representative democracies.

We list two polar types below, though clearly there are many half-way houses between them – all of them different types of direct democracy.

Unmediated popular voting

This is often (erroneously) thought to be the only form of direct democracy. In such a situation all political initiatives would be put to the popular vote, so the executive would have more or less of a routine administrative role. There would be no political parties, no advisory bodies and no entrenched rights: propositions would be put to the sovereign people for immediate decision after popular debate, transmitted through the electronic media discussed above. All political decision-making would thus approximate to nothing so much as the referendum campaigns waged in systems with substantial forms of popular initiative and recall, like those of Switzerland and California. Politics would be a perpetual referendum, where the sovereign people were urged to vote for or against a variety of issues, technical and otherwise, ranging from ecology to nuclear war, budgetary provisions to education, morality to penology. There would be no constraints on these expressions of popular will (unlike Switzerland and California today) – not even from their own past decisions.

It is easy to see how such a set-up could confirm the worst fears of critics and opponents of direct democracy, who argue that decisions are often inconsistent with each other and ill considered. One alternative is often carried on a great wave of emotion at one point of time, only to be partially abrogated or contradicted in another measure months later – or abrogated altogether once the implications become clearer. Budgetary constraints are not considered, partly because proposals are voted on separately so that everything tends to be regarded as desirable and attainable, rather than any realistic rank ordering of expensive policies being made.

These problems are often confounded, moreover, by the fact that causes are covertly promoted and indeed initiated by interest groups, whose machinations are only revealed too late. Referenda often stimulate a temporary influx of ill-informed and normally apathetic electors whose participation adds further unpredictability to the result and introduces greater inconsistency and incoherence to the process of decision-making. An additional fear is that popular majorities would not limit themselves, so that minorities would be disregarded and even suppressed before they had the opportunity of transforming themselves into future majorities.[2]

On the positive side, supporters of the system argue for the self-improving and educative effects of debate and decision-making,[3] which might in the long run lead to majorities themselves imposing limits on their actions. Whether the educational influence of participation would be great or widespread enough to counteract the defects listed above, however, is debatable. To whatever degree one may accept the morally beneficial effects of debating and voting on one's own destiny, some institutional constraint seems necessary to safeguard against the appeals of demagogues, or to guide the populace through highly technical legislation, or even to ensure an acceptable level of participation so that decisions are not taken, effectively, by a small and probably self-interested minority.

In making a fair assessment of the claims of direct democracy, however, it is vitally important to realize that some of its other forms are perfectly capable of providing for institutional safeguards, and that these meet many of the criticisms sketched above. Unmediated voting of the kind just described is usually focused upon by opponents as though it were the only possible institutional embodiment of direct democracy. It is in fact very important for informed debate to recognize that there are many other ways it could be institutionalized, starting with the party-based direct democracy we examine next.

Party-based direct democracy

It is easy to understand why both proponents and critics of direct democracy instinctively identify it with the unmediated system described above. If the impulse towards direct participation is impatience with institutions which clog and divert the popular will from directly expressing itself, the natural response is to sweep them all away as impediments to popular sovereignty.[4]

Suppose, however, that the impulse for change is less idealistic and more pragmatic. Within this perspective, representative institutions appear as products of a particular historical conjuncture when the mass societies produced by industrialization had not yet produced a communications and information technology appropriate to their needs. Neither were their populations sufficiently educated or informed to use more efficient means of communication adequately. All these circumstances have now changed. The level of education, of sophistication and of 'civility' among the population has vastly increased: means for simultaneous communication are either in place or being developed. Why should we not now review and reform political institutions which seem increasingly ill adapted to modern conditions, given the nineteenth-century premises on which they rest?

From the essentially pragmatic point of view of adapting institutions to the social changes which have taken and are taking place, there is no necessity to sweep away or replace existing institutions which are functioning adequately (or which might be usefully redefined so as to function better). The central institutions of contemporary democracy are not so much parliaments as political parties, which have taken over the role of mediation between populace and government. Within the more pragmatic approach to direct democracy, there is no reason why parties should not function as policy-initiating and clarifying bodies substantially as they do today. Nor is there any good reason why parties should not adopt substantially the same role in guiding and organizing popular voting as they do now for legislative voting.

Certainly parties could not function entirely in the same way in regard to the population-as-legislative-assembly as they do now in regard to representative parliaments. Their stance might well be midway between the one they now adopt at elections and the one they adopt inside the assembly. One cannot argue that a change from representative democracy to direct democracy would be without its effects on parties. Conceding this is far from envisaging their disappearance, however, or even the supercession of their essential mediating role between population and government. One can indeed envisage a type of direct democracy in which there is a party-based government, chosen by elections in exactly the way they function in practice today. This government would put important legislative bills and other political decisions to popular votes, just as it does with legislative votes under representative democracy.

There is clearly a greater possibility of government measures being defeated by popular vote than by legislative voting with strong party discipline. This raises the possibility, at the extreme, of a totally disrupted and inconsistent programme being enacted.[5] Within the institutional framework we are discussing there are, however, a variety of ways to avoid this possibility:

1 Measures already included in the ruling party's or parties' programme at election might require a qualified (perhaps two-thirds) majority against to be rejected.

2 Any measure which the government chose to make a vote of confidence could require a qualified (60 per cent? two-thirds?) adverse majority to be rejected (in the first year or two years of the government? for its whole term? – all are possibilities).

3 Governments could be fixed term or variable term. In the latter case various entrenched measures such as 1) or 2) above could be adopted to ensure them a reasonable life.

4   Measures would not need, of course, to be passed by one vote. There could be first, second and third readings as in contemporary legislatures. Votes themselves need not be yes or no except in urgent cases: they could include other alternatives, as suggested by Barber,[6] such as 'leaving back for consideration in six months'.

All these possible institutional variations are perfectly compatible with a system in which a popular vote substitutes for a parliamentary one. Parliamentary voting is far from unmediated and unconstrained, and popular voting might be institutionally constrained in precisely the same way without departing from direct democracy in a general sense.

Critics might well object that institutions cannot be expected to function in the same way that they do in the parliamentary setting: and in particular the political parties could not maintain their internal cohesion in the face of voting whose outcomes they could not ultimately control through the imposition of party discipline. As against this one can point to existing systems such as the American presidency in relation to Congress: or the Italian parliament, where party discipline in the representative assembly itself is weak and the possibility of adverse outcomes always present. The numerous minority governments of continental Europe also face the possibility of defeat unless they can build voting coalitions, often on a measure-by-measure basis. Parties have different characteristics in these contexts to those they assume under tightly focused, highly disciplined single-party governments. But they are still recognizably political parties. There is no reason, therefore, to anticipate that parties facing popular rather than legislative voting would lose their essential characteristics or their usefulness in focusing and mediating popular concerns.

In some ways the two systems of direct democracy which we have sketched are polar opposites of each other, thus accurately reflecting the different motivations which call them into being. Unmediated voting reflects the plebiscitory urges of those who believe in a unified general will – which, if only allowed to express itself, will sweep away unnecessary and manipulated conflicts and assert the common good. This form of continuous unmediated plebiscite is usually taken, both by supporters and critics, as the only possible way direct democracy could be institutionalized. But this is quite fallacious. If one's motivations are pragmatic – above all to make decision-making reflect more efficiently the needs and aspirations of citizens (the main justification of democracy in any of its forms) by re-examining nineteenth-century processes and institutions – the kind of direct democracy proposed will be quite different and far from unmediated. Even though it accepts a leading argument from theorists of participation, in regard to the educational and moral benefits of involvement in political processes, this is far from saying that the citizens' decision-making can express itself without guidance, or without some degree of institutionalization and binding procedures. These might have to include entrenched provisions safeguarding the communications process itself or minority rights.[7]

Clearly there are many institutional 'mixes' between unmediated forms of direct democracy and highly institutionalized forms such as those described.[8] However, what is clear is that if critics want to deliver a conclusive blow to the moral and practical arguments for direct democracy, they need to concentrate on the institutionalized form rather than the unmediated one. The former is highly resistant to the traditional arguments used against direct democracy, while the latter has so many undesirable features that in spite of some abstract appeal it functions as a kind of straw man, easily knocked down by practical objections. The time has surely come, particularly in light of recent technical developments, to consider the political alternatives offered by the other form of direct democracy seriously.

Arguments against (Direct) Democracy?

The point of the perhaps provocative heading of this section is that most contemporary arguments against direct democracy seem on closer examination to be objections to any kind of popular involvement in politics at all, thus ending up as criticisms of representative democracy to an only slightly lesser degree than of direct democracy. It seems very difficult to draw the line, in arguing for the bad effects of increased popular decision-making, so as not to criticize (at least implicitly) the extent to which it takes place now.

If this indeed turns out to be the case, either better arguments need to be found or we ought, if we truly believe in the superiority of democratic forms, to be planning for an extension of direct decision-making. By this somewhat negative but quite powerful route we arrive at a consideration, in the next section, of the key questions of rationality and information and of the role of the specialist in democratic politics, compared to that of politicians and citizens. Then in the following section we consider a variant of this, namely the idea that populations are inherently better able to judge governments than policies. First, however, we turn to a general review of the leading arguments for and against direct forms.

Direct voting is often opposed on the grounds that popular majorities are fickle and shifting and provide no basis for a permanent executive or consistent policies. Clearly this argument has a point, since if one thing emerges from the comparison of popular and parliamentary voting it is that the same disciplines cannot be applied to the former as to the latter. Decision-makers cannot count on patronage or ideological gratifications keeping the populace as loyal as they do their supporting legislators.

On the other hand, parties, as pointed out above, do organize electoral majorities and in many legislatures have to rely on uncertain support – parliamentary coalitions which form and reassemble round particular measures, sometimes bringing the government down with them. Reliance on popular majorities would not involve too much of a transition in many systems. This is particularly true if the safeguards built into the institutionalized form of direct democracy are introduced. It is not unreasonable that they should be; and they do not detract from the 'direct' nature of the system in the sense defined above. Fears about shifting majorities stem particularly from projects for an uninstitutionalized direct democracy in which the population substitutes not only for Parliament but to all intents and purposes for the government too. Again we have a case in which criticisms attach particularly to one type of direct democracy rather than to the concept as such. But it would hardly be fair, for example, to criticize the 'Westminster model' of strict single-party majority government for failing in sensitivity to minorities, and to regard this as a conclusive criticism of representative democracy as such, ignoring the greater number of minority-sensitive coalition governments which exist under this general type.

To present a balanced argument, however, we should not speak only of the limits on what popular majorities can do; for one can certainly see them as making a positive contribution to the very characteristics which make democracy an attractive political system. If majorities do shift it is not necessarily because they are inherently fickle but because they are communicating something: either that different problems are coming to the fore or that the government is not meeting current ones. In either case it is surely good that they should communicate the message. Institutional arrangements can, as we have said, be built in to ensure that the government has a reasonable stability. But if it persists in going counter to majority wishes consistently over a longer time period, should it not be forced to demit?

This is often the juncture at which considerations of balance get raised. Popular voting is likely to be shifting and unstable: however, it does provide messages to the governors about popular reactions to their policies, which the prospect of coming elections forces them to take into account. The development of public opinion polls provides continuing evidence about popular reactions which was hard to get in the past: so do phone-ins and chat-shows. Representative democracy from this point of view has accommodated modern developments in information techno-logy and pre-empted the opening point made in this chapter. In this way it can balance the necessarily uninformed and inconsistent reactions of the public with the expertise of legislators and party politicians, to get a blend of responsive but also informed and firm decision-making. It is in this sense that it constitutes a superior system to any in which one of these elements gets out of hand.

The point that virtue is found in the middle goes back to Aristotle. One could argue, however, that the party-based forms essential to the working of representative democracy today are hardly in the middle of a continuum between pure democracy and authoritarianism but are tilted to the latter, allowing popular reactions only a little chink to let themselves, possibly, be felt. The existence of a legislative buffer and infrequent elections in conjunction with a competitive party system puts a positive premium on deceiving and manipulating the public, by altering policy in the run-up to the election in order to produce prosperity and gain another term, then imposing unpopular measures immediately afterwards when elections are far away.[9]

The difficulty with public opinion is, as participatory theories often argue, that it is irresponsible and uninformed because people are asked to make judgements without debate, and decisions without immediate responsibility for the way they will affect themselves and their associates. If it is necessary to emasculate expressions of popular opinion and to build so many safeguards against them, why, again, is it necessary to have them at all? Or, if they provide essential information, why not substitute polls for elections, since wise representatives and politicians will take popular opinions into account anyway? What is the unique virtue of elections if they merely tempt politicians from their considered courses of action, which are better for everyone than simply pandering to popular whims?

If the special expertise of political professionals is discounted, however, would the institution of direct democracy not destroy the political parties? These are often criticized from the viewpoint of direct democracy as diverting and manipulating the popular will, along the lines mentioned above. Would any system of direct democracy not necessarily do without them, or at least weaken them, thus knocking out the major modern political innovation which organizes and forms opinion and helps it operate responsibly?

We have already largely answered this question in the second section above. A direct, unmediated form of direct democracy would indeed knock out the parties, like every other political institution and constraint.

But as we have argued before, this is not the only form direct democracy need take. In a pragmatically organized direct democracy, parties would be invaluable for exactly the reasons mentioned. The critique just made of parties, in the context of legislative buffers against popular reactions, is of their operation in the particular case of representative democracy with occasional elections, and does not relate to what they might do if they were made continuingly responsive to popular reactions.

Mention of the parties brings us to the role of the professional politicians staffing them, the men and women living off as well as for politics in Weber's sense.[10] Distrusted as full-time organizers of conflict and agitators till the early twentieth century, they have come to be seen as just as essential to politics as are their counterparts in the economic sphere – speculators, financiers and entrepreneurs – to the smooth operating of the market. And for the same reasons: they are the people who, to take their profits, persuade, organize and get things done, who smooth the way to bills and administrative measures, bring together disparate groups, often creating a consensus but in any case facilitating the collective action which would otherwise not be undertaken.

Granting all these points, it follows from what has been said about parties that professionals can still play an important role in institutional-ized forms of direct democracy (if not also in unmediated forms – even the Athenians had Pericles). Popular voting would require facilitators more, if anything, than legislative voting. Only, they might be more wary of becoming obliged to special interests when operating in a public arena.

Or perhaps not. One argument often brought against popular voting, even in representative systems, is that it is ill informed and apathetic. Would this not lead to a situation in which, after the first novelty wore off, 'popular voting' actually degenerated to voting by small self-interested groups very open to manipulation by professionals with an axe to grind?

This is a clear danger but not necessarily insuperable, for the following reasons:

1 Where parties retained a role, it would be in their interest to organize the vote and stimulate turnout and argument – in short, to do all the things that parties normally do under present systems of representa-tion.

2 A minimum voting level could be required for measures to pass. This would make it even more important for parties to stimulate participa-tion.

3 From a participatory point of view, greater opportunities for debate and participation stimulate greater engagement. Representative democracy can well be seen as institutionalizing popular inertia

through its limitation of such opportunities. It would be unwise to claim there would be a magical transformation of popular attitudes after the extension of voting, but combined with suitable civic programmes in colleges and on the media, some increase in popular attention and interest is surely to be expected.

4 Voting could of course be compulsory. Far from 'forcing people to be free', this has been a feature of many post-war representative democracies (Italy, The Netherlands) – though of course compulsory voting once every four years is a different matter from voting weekly or monthly.

This last point, however, immediately opens the way to another criticism of direct participation – should decisions be swayed by the views of uninformed apathetics, pushed into voting solely by coercion? Does not this vision immediately discredit all the claims of direct democracy to higher moral standing? Does it not clearly demonstrate the superior merits of representative democracy where decisions can be made by informed, dedicated professionals able to assess the arguments of specialists properly and to handle them correctly?[11]

Here is perhaps the nub of the whole argument against direct democracy: the mass of the citizens are not qualified to decide high policy, so they can be allowed to influence it only indirectly, by choosing those who are to decide rather than deciding themselves.[12] This objection can be considered from several aspects: in the first place, that of the contrast between individual qualities and collective decision-making; in the second, that of the question of the rights of the ill-informed – for example, is it self-evident that they should be excluded from decision-making for the whole society? Thirdly, the terms of the question itself should be examined – what do we mean by knowledge and information in the political context?

It is of course by no means clear that politicians and legislators are invariably well informed. The mode by which legislators specialize in different areas and defer to each other's opinions in areas where they are ignorant is well known. It is the self-corrective built in through its tolerance of debate and argument that makes democracy a superior political system – but in that case, where is the objection to extending it?

Clearly, on an overall average comparison, legislators will show up as more generally informed and politically aware than citizens. However, there is an important distinction to be drawn here between the individuals involved and the collective process which leads to decision. The individual competence of the legislator hardly counts in representative systems with strict party voting: what matters is the capacities of the party leadership.

In a direct democracy with parties, therefore, the quality of decision-making would hardly vary from that of current parliaments, since both depend heavily on leadership. Parties would have more difficulty getting popular majorities for their policies, but not insuperable ones. Indeed, the necessity of meeting and overcoming criticism and debate might even improve the quality of the policies initially put forward. While the proportion of the educated, informed and politically engaged in the population is lower than in the legislature, the absolute number is of course vastly greater. On the argument that the quality of a decision is improved by expertise, opening it up to participation by more experts should surely help.

However, this means also that large numbers of ill-informed, unsophisticated elements in the population will be given access to the debate too. Some commentators have taken this as such a self-evident defect of proposals for direct democracy as to invalidate it from the start. Better a representative system in which popular opinion can be read off from polls and enter as an element into the decision by professionals than one in which the ignorant can directly affect policies. They have no moral right to participation and could only degrade the quality of the decisions.

Taking the last point first, it does rather assume that no important decisions are ever taken by majorities of ignorant legislators and that the quality of current decision-making *could* be significantly lowered within a continuing democratic context. If parties continue as prime movers so that policy is essentially party policy, participation by the uneducated and unsophisticated is unlikely to alter things very much.

A wider question is that of their right to participation. Should the ignorant be *ipso facto* excluded from political decisions bearing upon them? The justification for doing so surely rests on some idea of their own and society's best interests being served by this – a generally better decision will be reached without them. However, this ignores two significant considerations. In the first place, political ignorance is not a static quality: people can be educated; and educated through debate. The interest aroused by decision-making on matters touching their immediate well-being is likely to increase the motivation for learning, which educational research shows to be the most important single factor in improvement. Secondly, the definitions of general interest and 'best interest of a specified group' are problematic and debatable, and shaped by the perceived interests of those making the decision. One justification of the extension of rights to all, and also of pluralistic interpretations of democracy, is that all groups should have a voice to ensure that the decision reflects something of everyone's interests. As the uneducated, ignorant and unsophisticated are unevenly distributed over social groups, they are very likely to lose out by their exclusion.[13]

Advocates of representation point out that they are able to vote for parties under existing democratic forms and that this gives them a certain leverage – but at the same time the party and legislative buffer prevents them destabilizing or rendering inconsistent the content of decisions. Again, however, these terms themselves are hardly fixed objectively: what may be stability and consistency to those whose interests are served by current decisions may be misery and exploitation to those excluded from them.

Once again, the argument against direct democracy in this context lends itself easily to general anti-democratic stances. If certain elements should be excluded from direct decision-making because of ignorance, why should they even participate in the selection of decision-makers? And if there are arguments for them choosing decision-makers, are these not the same arguments for them contributing to decisions?

The point has been made above that many political concepts, particularly concepts of interest, are themselves debatable. Here we should underline that terms like 'political ignorance' and 'expertise', 'uneducated', 'unsophisticated' and 'apathetic' are all controvertible from differing points of view. This is particularly true when they are regarded as static and unresponsive to changes in political circumstances. As we shall expand on this point in the next section we wish only to summarize it here, underlining one particular consequence. To accept that these characteristics are not static and that they change with political circumstances is to accept the thesis of participatory theorists, namely that an extension of opportunities will itself change the political nature of many citizens from the apathy and lack of interest, which produce withdrawal and ignorance, to involvement and interest, which produce more sophistication and information.

Obviously debate can be carried much further. We cannot be exhaustive here but simply point to the fact that it needs to be deepened and that some traditional arguments are untenable. Two major criticisms, which we have not had space to consider adequately above, do need to be presented in more detail, however, so the last two sections are devoted to their elaboration.

The next section deals with the ground on which so many criticisms of direct democracy base themselves: the lack of information and expertise of the public, which render their opinions on many subjects quite valueless. This section looks more closely at what is meant by the terms 'informed' and 'ignorant' and the role of professionals and experts as compared to the average citizen. The following section follows through this point, by seeing whether publics are inherently confined to reviewing personalities and past record rather than voting on policy alternatives because of the inbuilt instability of their decision-processes.

'Information' and 'Expertise' as Criteria of Inclusion

A major argument of authors as disparate in other respects as Schumpeter, Plamenatz and Sartori[14] is that ordinary citizens are incapable of making everyday political decisions and should for that reason be confined to passing judgements on their representatives in elections. The reasons for this vary: for Schumpeter it is total lack of interest and disinvolvement in politics; for Plamenatz it is the different criteria used by voters in deciding between parties compared to the expertise involved in decisions (one may sensibly choose between solicitors to represent one in complete ignorance of law); for Sartori it is this and also the extreme technicality of political problems, which make them difficult for professional politicians let alone ordinary citizens to understand.

While the reasons for excluding citizens vary, they are not con-tradictory and indeed in some ways are mutually reinforcing. Lack of interest in the public sphere, as we have pointed out, removes a major motivation for acquiring knowledge, which may well then lead to citizens making decisions on different criteria from those used by legislators. Sartori's criticism of the cognitive incompetence of ordinary citizens is more forceful in that it is seen as irremediable, given the complexity of modern decisions and their susceptibility only to technical and expert analysis. Experts are *de facto* acquiring more power, or at least more standing and influence, than ever before, and on this ground alone it is inappropriate to argue for more direct citizen judgements on policy.

There are of course problems with this approach, as specialists in one area are lay people in others. Perhaps a bridge is to be found in professional politicians. Sartori's argument, however, is that even they are 'living beyond their intelligence'. So what hope is there of the ordinary citizen exerting control?

One answer suggested by Parry[15] is that knowledge is not of one piece and therefore cannot be the monopoly of one group of specialists. There is no one objective assessment to be made of nuclear risk, for example: the standard basis of comparison – number of past deaths per unit of output – can be challenged on the grounds that future conditions (and generating plants) are different from those in the past, so this cannot be projected. The nuclear industry as a whole is a good source of examples of highly challengeable assumptions, made by specialists, which have been shown to be matters of opinion more than anything else. For instance, British nuclear generating costs were for many years shown as cheaper than those of conventional fuel. This, however, was because they were based on the first generation Magnox stations, pushed many of the initial research and development costs on to the military nuclear programme, and ignored the prospects of increasing breakdown with age and ultimate decommissioning. Only when private business refused to purchase the nuclear part of the industry were alternative cost estimates made (as had been consistently urged by environmentalists and coal-miners).

Such examples demonstrate that the unchallengeability of technical judgements is itself an element of political debate, and subject to challenge. The relatively uninformed may not be able to make technical judgements directly, due to their lack of relevant expertise, but they can always find or hire their own experts to challenge the original judgement and to suggest alternative tests or criteria. Sartori's view on the inevitable prevalence of technical experts ignores the fact that science and engineering are not closed bodies of knowledge. They are very open to new ideas and to debate. In order to be applied to political arguments, scientific findings have in any case to be embodied in a fairly long train of politically relevant assumptions and consequences (perceived need for some benefit, like electricity, for example). Thus there is no hermetically sealed body of expert knowledge which overrides political judgement. The claim of 'expert knowledge' to be so is itself an element in political debate and can always be queried. This frees political professionals from subordination to experts. And what it does for them it does also for the average citizen, with his or her increasing access to media channels tuned in to debates between experts, documentaries and educational pro-grammes. Far from being relatively less informed than in the past, the citizen is, *vis-à-vis* specialists and professionals, better informed.

That said, most – perhaps the vast majority of – citizens are clearly not going to match the professional politicians in their ability to handle and organize facts. They have less need to, as in some forms of direct democracy at least they would have professional politicians to do it for them. In such circumstances ordinary citizens may well simplify decisions through devices like those specified by Plamenatz. That is, they will project the past behaviour and ideology of a party on to what they might do in an unpredictable future: thus a vote for a left-wing party might be given, not on the basis of what it currently promises to do, but on the projection that whatever happens, it will always keep up levels of welfare more than its rival(s).[16]

Plamenatz interprets this as a different form and basis of judgement from that applied by the political elite, though not less rational. Given the complexity and volume of the information available, however, it is clear that everyone uses calculating and simplifying rules of this kind. The specialist cannot be equally expert over the whole of his or her narrow field, still less over the whole of science. An easy way to decide on the balance of probabilities for a particular finding in a vaguely known but relevant field is to count the relative frequency of findings on the one side as opposed to others – hardly much different from the citizen adding up salient issues which 'belong' to one party or another and voting for the one with the majority that he or she supports. The politicians consistently voting for their party in legislatures are using another simplifying rule. Nobody can operate without such rules – not even scientists with citation indices.

Citizen ignorance and inconsistency are often summed up in the example of a majority of electors wanting tax cuts at the same time as a majority want welfare increased. Both alternatives were clearly endorsed by a majority.[17] The original investigators interpreted this as political naivety – how else could welfare be paid for but by tax increases? To this a modern answer might be: by defence cuts, inflation, joining the European Community, and economic growth. There are a lot of strategies, any or all of which might be pursued, but pervasive uncertainty about which might work. Electors are, after all, not so naive. It is the tendency of experts and professional politicians to codify knowledge, to pretend or convince themselves that there is only one possible course of action, which makes them appear so – though often, of course, this is a political strategy, adopted to impose a solution, rather than evidence of lack of sophistication on the part of citizens.

Enough has been said, however, to indicate that knowledge is not the prerogative of specialists and politicians. Through education and the media it is widely and increasingly diffused. Simplified calculating strategies are used at all levels, not just that of electors: they are not products of ignorance and lack of sophistication but rational ways of coping with a complex and confusing world. There is, in short, no knowledge barrier looming between population and elite which inevitably debars the former from full political participation. The population are well able to calculate and simplify in ways not essentially different from those used by specialists and professionals, and not inferior to them. Moreover, the longer a debate goes on, the more citizens absorb specialist knowledge and the less certain specialists are likely to be about the incontrovertible standing of their own opinions. Knowledge is not static, but subject to both expansion and change from general discussion. The latter is much less likely to impoverish it than to enrich it.

Voting Cycles, Instability and Majority Decision: A Brick Wall for Direct Democracy?

In discussing the differences in knowledge and information between citizens and their representatives, Sartori makes the point that the former have unstable opinions on most general matters but enough personal experience of how they themselves and the groups with which they identify are doing under a government to judge the representatives' performance. We have dealt with some of the relevant arguments above. By a somewhat different route two other authors, Riker and McLean, have arrived at essentially the same conclusion, drawing on social choice theory.[18] We need to consider their argument, because if popular voting on policies, no matter how well informed, is inherently unstable and shifting and thus unable to reflect true majority opinion, this is clearly a conclusive rebuttal of the possibility of direct democracy, even in the institutionalized form which we have been mainly discussing.

The argument takes its start from the well-known Paradox of Voting. Succinctly put, it states:

> a rational individual who prefers A to B to C must prefer A to C . . . it is always possible that majority rule is intransitive. In the simplest case, if voter 1 prefers A to B and B to C, voter 2 prefers C to A and A to B, and voter 3 prefers C to A and A to B, there is a majority for A over B, a majority for B over C, and a majority for C over A. Transitive individual preferences lead to an intransitive social ordering, otherwise known as a cycle.[19]

It is easy to see how this pattern of voting might generalize over large populations, and how it could occur often enough to cast doubt on the pretension of any popular vote to reflect true majority opinion. It would be equally likely, on the basis of these arguments, to reflect an arbitrary placement of topics on the agenda, or even deliberate manipulation of it.

McLean uses this proof to suggest that direct democracy at a national level is unattainable, as it could provide no guarantees against occurrence of the Paradox. Riker argues that popular voting is best confined to passing judgement on the representatives' record, as this does not involve cycles and the Paradox. In this way both support Sartori, Schumpeter and Plamenatz, who reach the same conclusion on the basis of the citizens' limited inherent capacities for political decision-making. It is indeed clear that to support representative democracy against direct democracy on the one hand and against more authoritarian alternatives on the other, one has to argue to a similar conclusion: citizens are capable of judging representatives but not of deciding policy. The argument from inherent limitations on intellectual capacity having been shown to be suspect, the one from cycles and inability to find a true majority emerges as crucial.

But is it an argument against direct democracy as such rather than against the very possibility of majority decision-making at all, under any form of democracy? On the face of it, paradoxes and voting cycles seem just as likely to emerge under representative democracy and in legislatures as in large populations. Indeed, they may be *more* likely to emerge in legislatures rather than populations, given the tendency for the less informed to use simplified decision procedures which do not involve the preference orderings over all alternatives needed to generate the Paradox.[20] It is very puzzling to work out why McLean, for example, seems to think the possibility of voting cycles is more of a problem for direct democracy than for representative democracy. The very tendency of ordinary citizens to consider each issue separately (to consider preferences on welfare, for example, separately from preferences on taxation) tends to rule out cycles and Paradoxes.[21] Schofield has additionally pointed out that forming a majority judgement on government record involves much the same possibilities of voting cycles and paradoxes as does the formulation of preferences on a particular issue.[22] This seems a conclusive argument against any attempt to attribute more inherent difficulties to direct popular voting on policies than on the election of representatives. The attempt to mobilize social choice theory against direct democracy seems to encounter the familiar pitfall of arguing against the possibility of democracy as such, rather than any particular form of it.

Conclusions

In this analysis we have shown that direct democracy cannot now be dismissed on grounds of impracticability alone, given increasing opportunities for two-way communication between citizen and citizen, citizen and opinion-former, and between these and governments. Unmediated voting with the citizenry acting as both legislature and executive is not the only form that it need take: there is no reason why popular voting should not be guided and organized by political parties just as legislative voting is now. Recognition of this last possibility subverts many arguments against direct democracy. Those which remain perforce take on a radical tinge, basing themselves more and more on a critique of the citizen's capacity for making any informed collective decision – an argument which in the end ranges these arguments against representative democracy as well as against direct democracy.

In particular, the attempt to draw a strict barrier between specialists' knowledge and that of the ordinary person was shown to be based on a static and utopian conception of specialist knowledge which is essentially untenable in the light of modern analysis, while voting paradoxes, if they exist, apply to all voting processes and not just popular ones.

The discussion demonstrates that better and more refined arguments need to be found against direct democracy if they are to stick. More than that, however, it shows that the main gulf opens up between supporters of democracy in any of its forms and supporters of elitist and other alternatives, which seek to exclude ordinary citizens as much as possible from any form of decision-making. Perhaps the time has come for 'representative' and 'direct' democrats to bury their specific differences and work together for the opening up of existing regimes, recognizing that what they have in common is much more than what separates them. Something like Barber's *Strong Democracy* (1984) is perhaps an acceptable meeting point here. What is clear is that democracy as a system cannot rest where it is. Either the many elitist and undemocratic elements of existing western regimes will get stronger, or better procedures for reflecting popular interests and preferences need to be introduced. Third alternatives seem increasingly implausible.

NOTES

1   For a recent optimistic discussion of technological developments from this point of view, see I. McLean, *Democracy and New Technology* (Cambridge, Polity Press, 1990).

2   G. Sartori, *The Theory of Democracy Revisited* (Chatham, NJ, Chatham House Publishers, 1987), pp. 115–20.

3   C. Pateman, *Participation and Democratic Theory* (Cambridge, Cambridge University Press, 1970); B. Barber *Strong Democracy: participatory politics for a new age* (Berkeley, CA, University of California Press, 1984).

4   J-J. Rousseau, *The Social Contract and Discourse*, tr. G. D. H. Cole, J. Brumfitt and J. C. Hall (London, Dent, 1973).

5   Sartori, *The Theory of Democracy Revisited*, p. 148.

6   Barber, *Strong Democracy*, p. 284.

7   Onora O'Neil, 'Practices of Toleration', chapter 5 of *Democracy and the Mass Media*, ed. Judith Lichtenberg, (Cambridge, Cambridge University Press, 1990).

8   Barber, *Strong Democracy*, eloquently presents a detailed scheme for one of these.

9   E. Tufte, *Political Control of the Economy* (Princeton, NJ, Princeton University Press, 1978).

10 Max Weber, *From Max Weber*, tr. H. H. Gerth, and C. Wright Mills (New York, Oxford University Press, 1958); A. Mastropaolo, *Il politico professionale* (Turin, Einaudi, 1988).

11 Sartori, *The Theory of Democracy Revisited*, pp. 431–9.

12 Sartori, *The Theory of Democracy Revisited*, pp. 116–18.

13 G. Parry, 'Democracy and amateurism: the informed citizen', unpublished ms, Department of Government, University of Manchester (1989).

14 J. Schumpeter, *Capitalism, Socialism and Democracy* (New York, Harper, 1942); J. Plamenatz, *Democracy and Illusion* (London, Longman, 1973); Sartori, *The Theory of Democracy Revisited*.

15 Parry, 'Democracy and amateurism'.

16 I. Budge and D. J. Farlie, *Explaining and Predicting Elections* (London, Allen and Unwin, 1983), ch. 2.

17 McLean, *Democracy and New Technology*, p. 109.

18 Sartori, *The Theory of Democracy Revisited*, pp. 106–10; W. H. Riker, *Liberalism against Populism* (San Franciso, Freeman, 1982); McLean, *Democracy and New Technology*, p. 123.

19 I. McLean, 'Rational choice and politics', *Political Studies*, XXXIX (1991), pp. 496–512.

20 I. Budge, 'Rational choice is more than economic theorising', unpublished ms, Department of Government, University of Essex (1992).

21 P. C. Ordeshook, *Game Theory and Political Theory* (Cambridge, Cambridge University Press, 1986), p. 250.

22 N. Schofield, *Social Choice and Democracy* (Berlin, Springer-Verlag, 1985), pp. 292–9.

7

THE CULTURAL PARTICULARITY OF LIBERAL DEMOCRACY

Bhikhu Parekh

In the aftermath of the collapse of communism in the erstwhile Soviet Union and Eastern Europe, many in the west have begun to argue that western liberal democracy is the best form of government discovered so far and ideally suited to the modern age. Some even think that as the 'moral leader' of the world the west has a duty to encourage its spread and to create a new world order on that basis. This western triumphalism has aroused deep fears in the fragile and nervous societies of the rest of the world, especially those which were until recently at the receiving end of the western civilizing mission. The nature and universalizability of western liberal democracy have thus become a subject of great philosophical and political importance. My intention in this chapter is two-fold: to elucidate the inner structure of liberal democracy and to assess the validity of the universalist claims made on its behalf.

In the history of the west, Athenian democracy, which flourished between 450 BC and 322 BC, was the first and for nearly two millennia almost the only example of democracy in action. This period of approximately 130 years saw many institutional changes and revealed both the good and ugly aspects of democracy. During its glorious period it produced stable governments, brought out the best in its citizens and fostered great developments in all areas of life. Towards the end it lost its vitality and lacked stability, creative imagination and political modera-tion. It thus left behind a mixed legacy, which was interpreted and assessed differently by different writers. The Athenian experience as described by Herodotus and Thucydides and theorized by Plato, Aristotle and others gave rise over time to a tradition of discourse on democracy.

Liberal democracy is a historically specific form of democracy arriving on the scene nearly two millennia after the disappearance of its Athenian cousin. Although democracy preceded liberalism in western history, in the modern age liberalism preceded democracy by nearly two centuries and created a world to which the latter had to adjust. Liberal democracy is basically a liberalized or liberally constituted democracy; that is, democracy defined and structured within the limits set by liberalism. Liberalism is its absolute premise and foundation and penetrates and shapes its democratic character.

Liberalism is a complex body of ideas which began to gain intellectual and political ascendency in different parts of Europe from the seventeenth century onwards. Unlike the Greeks, and indeed all the pre-modern societies which took the community as their starting point and defined the individual in terms of it, liberalism takes the individual as the ultimate and irreducible unit of society and explains the latter in terms of it. Society 'consists' or is 'made up' of individuals and is at bottom nothing but the totality of its members and their relationships. The view that the individual is conceptually and ontologically prior to society and can in principle be conceptualized and defined independently of society, which we shall call individualism, lies at the heart of liberal thought and shapes its political, legal, moral, economic, methodological, epistemological and other aspects.

The concept of the individual is obviously complex and presupposes a theory of individuation. By the very conditions of his or her existence, every human being is inseparably connected with other human beings and nature. To individuate a person is to decide where to draw the boundary between that person and other persons and nature. Individuation is thus a matter of social convention, and obviously different societies individuate human beings and define the individual differently. The ancient Athenians saw the human being as an integral part of nature and society; they believed that a man taken together with his land and political rights constituted an individual. Almost until the end of the Middle Ages a craftworker's tools were believed to be inseparable from the person; they constituted the craftworker's 'inorganic body' and were just as much an integral part of the person as were hands and feet – to deprive a craftsman of his tools was to mutilate him, and he was not free to alienate them. For the Hindus the caste into which a person is born is not an accident but a result of his or her actions in a previous life. It is an integral part of the person's identity and determines his or her rights and duties as well as the value of the person's life. The Chinese view of the family as an indissoluble organism linking ancestors and descendants into a living union gives rise to a highly complex conception of the individual.

For reasons which we cannot here consider, liberalism defines the individual in austere and minimalist terms. It abstracts the person from all his or her 'contingent' and 'external' relations with other people and nature, and defines the person as an essentially self-contained and solitary being encapsulated in, and unambiguously marked off from the 'outside' world by his or her body.[1]

In the liberal view each individual is distinct and easily distinguishable from others, is unassimilable, and leads a separate existence. Individuals define their individuality in terms of their separateness from others and feel ontologically threatened and diminished when the boundary of their individuality gets blurred or their selves overlap with those of others. Their constant concern, therefore, is to preserve their separateness, to construct all kinds of high protective walls around themselves, and to ensure that nothing enters, let alone settles, in their being without their knowledge and scrutiny. In one form or another the idea of self-enclosure, of a bounded self accessible and available to others only to a severely limited degree, is an integral part of the liberal view. Liberal individuals seek to run their lives themselves, to make their own choices, to form their own beliefs and judgements, to take nothing for granted or as given. Since they necessarily begin life as socially conditioned beings, their goal is gradually to decondition themselves, to become ontologically transparent, to reconstruct and recreate themselves, and thus to become autonomous and self-determining. They are therefore suspicious of, and feel nervous in the presence of, feelings and emotions, especially those that are deep and powerful and not fully comprehensible to reason or easily brought under its control. Not warm emotional involvement, which leads to overlapping selves and compromises autonomy, but the relatively cold and distant principle of mutual respect is the liberal's preferred mode of governing the relations between individuals.[2] How an open society can be created out of closed selves is a paradox to which no liberal theorist has paid much attention. Unless the self learns to open itself up to the thoughts and feelings of others and maintains *both* an open mind and an open heart, thereby creating the basic preconditions of a genuine dialogue, society can never be truly open.

In one form or another the idea of self-ownership is also inherent in the liberal conception of the individual. Since individuals are defined as choosers, they must obviously be separated from their choices, including their values, goals and ways of life, raising the question as to how they are related to them. Again, in the kind of society imagined by the liberal, individuals must be able to alienate their labour, capacities and skills without alienating themselves and becoming another's property during the period of alienation. They must therefore be separated from their labour and the rest, and the consequent self-bifurcation or inner duality raises the question of the nature of the self's relationship with them. Individuals' capacities, qualities of character, deepest beliefs, goals, loyalties and allegiances obviously cannot be conceived as their modes of being, their ways of existing for themselves and for others, but only as their properties, as their primary or secondary qualities rather than the constituents of their innermost being or substance. For the liberal the individual is a 'master' or 'mistress' of himself or herself, owning his or her body and having proprietary rights over its constituents. As such, individuals' lives are their own to do what they like with, and the products of their labour are theirs to enjoy as they please. Individuals relate to their thoughts, feelings, opinions, rights and so on in similar proprietary terms, and define liberty, equality, justice and obligation accordingly.

Since in the liberal view the individual is conceptually prior to society, liberty is conceptually prior to morality. Individuals are moral beings because they are choosing beings, and it is their choices that give their conduct a distinctly moral as distinct from a 'merely' conventional or customary character. Since morality, including moral rules, principles and ways of life, is a matter of choice, there is and can be no substantive general agreement on the kind of life the individual and the community ought to live. In liberal thought, morality therefore comes to centre around secondary and behaviourally orientated virtues, which tell human beings not what they should ultimately value and what ends they should pursue, but rather how they should pursue whatever ends they choose. The individual's central moral concern is two-fold, to maintain his or her personal independence and autonomy and to live peacefully with others by respecting theirs. Each leads to a complementary set of secondary virtues. The former calls for such qualities of character as self-discipline, self-reliance, prudence, the ability to live within the limits of one's moral and emotional resources, planning, foresight, moderation and self-control; the latter calls for such qualities as reliability, cooperation, the keeping of promises, the conscientious discharge of one's obligations, the spirit of compromise, civility, respect for the law and tolerance. Some liberal writers did stress the need to cultivate refined feelings, a 'beautiful' soul free of mean and petty impulses, the spirit of self-sacrifice and the pursuit of noble ideals, but they had difficulty grounding them in their conception of the human being, demonstrating their social relevance, and integrating them with the secondary virtues. The proper relation between the right and the good, and at a different level between liberty and morality, has continued to elude liberals and explains the inner tensions of their thought.

Although different individuals value different things and pursue different ways of life, the liberal thinks that they share several interests derived from their common nature. These include the security of life, liberty, property and so on, and, at a different level, the development and exercise of their powers of reason, will and autonomy. Since these interests are deemed to be inherent in our humanity and demanded by our nature, they are considered basic or fundamental. Some liberals called them natural rights, while others eschewed that language, but all alike were agreed on their vital importance. For liberals the concept of interest overcomes the vast distance they postulate between the self and the other, and build bridges or bonds between otherwise unrelated men and women. The civil society, the liberals' greatest invention and deeply cherished by them, is the realm of interest and choice *par excellence*. It stands for the totality of relationships voluntarily entered into by self-determining individuals in the pursuit of their self-chosen goals. It is a world created by individuals who, though strangers to one another, have nevertheless found enough in common to bring and to hold them together for varying lengths of time and with varying degrees of mutual commitment.

For the liberal the state shares some of the characteristics of civil society, but it is basically quite different. Like civil society it is based on interest and has largely an instrumental value. However, unlike civil society, the state is a coercive and compulsory institution, coercive because it enjoys the power of life and death over its members, compulsory because its citizens are its members by birth and may not leave it, and outsiders may not enter it, without its approval. The state is also a formal and abstract institution. In civil society human beings meet as bearers of multiple and changing identities. In the state they are expected to abstract away these identities and to meet only as citizens; that is, as equal bearers of formal and state-derived rights and obligations and being guided solely by the interest of the whole. The abstract state and the abstract citizen complement and entail each other.

For the liberal, the government's primary task is to create and maintain a system of rights and to undertake activities required by this. Under no circumstances can it be justified in pursuing large-scale social, economic and political goals, such as creating a classless, egalitarian, fully human or compassionate and caring society. Different liberals advance different arguments in support of this view, but the following five are most common. First, the government owes its existence and authority to the fact that its subjects are self-determining agents wishing to pursue their self-chosen goals under conditions of minimal constraints. Its task therefore is to maximize *their* liberties and to facilitate *their* goals, which by definition it cannot do if it pursues large-scale goals of its own.

Secondly, citizens of a liberal society do not all share a substantive conception of the good life. There is therefore no moral source from which the government can derive, and in terms of which it can legitimize, its substantive goals. Whatever goals it chooses to pursue are bound to be disowned by, and thus to violate the moral autonomy of, at least a section of them. An attempt to create a 'better' or 'more humane' society flounders on the fact that its citizens deeply disagree about the underlying criteria. A government that goes beyond laying down the necessary framework of formal and general rules therefore compromises its subjects' humanity and risks committing a moral outrage.

Thirdly, a government engaging in a programme of large-scale economic redistribution or radical transformation of the social order uses some of its citizens as instruments of its will and treats their interests as less important than others', violating the principles of human dignity and equality. Since it is unlikely to enjoy their consent, it is also bound to be oppressive and risks forfeiting its legitimacy. Fourthly, a programme of economic redistribution implies that the government has something to distribute, that it is the owner of what it seeks to redistribute. For the liberal the assumption is wholly false, for property belongs to its owners and not to the government, and is a product of their labour and not its. It is entitled to claim from them, with their consent, only that portion of their property which is necessary to help it undertake its legitimate and collectively agreed activities.

Finally, for the liberal almost all social institutions are grounded in and propelled by specific natural desires. This is as true of the economy as of the others. People work hard, exert themselves, accept privations, and save up for the future because they are driven by self-interest and the desire to better their condition. The dynamic interplay of these impulses creates the complex economic world with its own autonomous logic. Government interference with the economy, as with other social institutions, runs up against the inescapable limits of human nature and the inexorable logic of the economy, and is ultimately counter-productive.

All this does not mean that the liberal government is committed to a policy of *laissez-faire*. Liberals' attitudes to the government's economic role have varied greatly over time. Almost all of them have agreed that it has a variously derived duty to help the poor and the needy, and some have gone much further. But all of them, including the interventionists, remain deeply hostile to the radical redistribution of wealth, to the curtailment of the right to private property, to the restriction of individual choices, to measures likely to weaken the ethic of self-discipline and self-help or to interfere with the basic structure and processes of the economy, and to the attempt to subordinate the economy to the larger considerations of moral and political good. Thanks to this hostility, which is built into the very structure of liberal thought, even those liberals who are deeply critical of, and morally embarrassed by, the social, cultural and other consequences of capitalism have been able to do little.

Having briefly and rather hurriedly sketched some of the basic features of liberalism, we may ask why and how democracy as traditionally understood on the basis of the Athenian experience enters the liberal world-view and whether the latter has a conceptual space for it. Liberalism obviously represents a very different view of human beings and society to the one lying at the basis of the Athenian democracy. The latter was grounded in a sense of community; liberalism is individualist and finds it difficult to offer a coherent account of the community. The Athenians were keen to deserve well of their community and to enrich it by giving it their best; liberal citizens are anxious to pursue their self-chosen goals and cherish privacy. The Athenian democracy was informed by a view of freedom that demanded active political participation as its necessary expression. The liberal defines liberty in individualist rather than communal terms and sees little value in active political involvement. Democracy in the Athenian sense does not satisfy liberal individuals' deepest aspirations and has at best only a marginal place in their conception of the good life. The Athenian democracy trusted the masses; as we shall see, the liberal is deeply suspicious of them. For these and other reasons liberalism neither can accommodate nor has a need for classical democracy.

Yet it does need *some* kind of democracy, for at least two reasons. First, in the liberal view all individuals are free and equal 'by nature' and masters or mistresses of themselves, and no one can have authority over others without their consent. A liberal polity therefore needs some mechanism by which the people can give their consent to the government and thereby confer on it the authority to govern them. Secondly, as we saw, the liberal expects the government to set up and maintain a system of rights based on the principle of maximum liberty. But the government might not set up such a system or, having set it up, might violate it. A liberal polity therefore needs a mechanism by which the people can control and compel the government to fulfil its trust.

The liberal turns to democracy to provide both these mechanisms and defines it in terms of them.[3] Democracy is seen not as a form of collective existence, but as a mode of constituting and controlling public authority. That is, it is not a way of life but a form of government. For the classical Athenians, democracy was grounded in a passionate desire for freedom defined in participatory and communal terms. For the liberal it is grounded in an equally passionate desire for liberty defined in protective or negative and individualist terms. For the classical Athenians democracy was a vehicle of collective self-expression and self-determination. For the liberal it is a device for keeping others at a safe distance and protecting the individual in the exercise of his or her self-chosen goals within a legally secured private space. For the liberal, democracy therefore basically means a form of government in which the people wield the ultimate political authority, which they delegate to their freely chosen representatives and which they retain the right to withdraw if the government should grossly violate its trust.

Since democracy as understood by the liberal is grounded in, and derives its legitimacy from, sovereign individuals, it is conceptually prevented from violating individual rights as defined by the liberal. Thus a government violating the right to liberty, property or freedom of expression is considered not only illiberal but also undemocratic. In other words liberalism is built into the conceptual structure of liberal democracy. Liberalism specifies what rights are basic and inviolable and must be guaranteed by law. The majority may have altogether different views on the subject, but these have no relevance and are to be fought if they fall foul of liberalism. In a liberal democracy liberalism is the dominant partner and exercises a hegemonic role. Moral paternalism and some form of political authoritarianism lie at the heart of liberal democracy.

Democracy as defined by the liberal raises two important questions. First, who constitute the people and wield the ultimate political authority? Secondly, what is the relationship between the people and their representatives? The answers to the two questions are closely related.

As for the first question, liberals were for a long period deeply uneasy about granting the universal franchise. Some of their arguments were the same as those of the Greek opponents of democracy; others were new. First, liberals argued that the masses, mostly consisting of the poor, were hostile to the rich and to the institution of private property in general. The association of the universal franchise with some form of socialism was also shared by socialists, including Marx. Secondly, some liberals argued, especially after the publication of de Tocqueville's *Democracy in America*, that the masses sought equality in all spheres of life and that their rise to power was bound to lead to cultural homogeneity, intolerance of diversity and the tyranny of public opinion. Thirdly (a variation of the second argument), the masses preferred the sleep of ignorance and habit to the light of critical reason and were hostile to the spirit of critical enquiry, freedom of expression and the pursuit of truth, all of which liberals cherished both as intrinsically valuable and as vehicles of progress. The death of Socrates at the hands of the Athenian democracy was frequently invoked in this context. Fourthly, the right to vote presupposed and could only be granted to those possessed of rationality, the capacity for reflection, knowledge of social and political affairs, and so forth. Since the masses lacked these, they could not be entrusted with the conduct of public affairs. Finally, in a democracy the community as a whole was in charge of its collective destiny, whereas universal suffrage limited political power almost exclusively to the 'brute' majority, thereby virtually disenfranchising the minority. Democracy implied that all significant social groups and bodies of opinion should enjoy access to power. Far from being identical with democracy, the universal franchise threatened it. A 'truly' democratic polity must establish parity between the majority and the minority by either restricting the franchise or somehow compensating the minority for its numerical inferiority. Hence the popularity of such ideas as plural votes for the elite, some form of proportional representation, and a suitably strengthened upper chamber among a large number of nineteenth-century liberals.[4]

Once the liberals realized that the democratic tide was irreversible, they turned to finding ways of containing it, evolving a tripartite strategy. First, they developed such devices as constitutionally guaranteed rights which virtually put them beyond the reach of the majority, parliamentary as opposed to popular sovereignty, elitist theories of representation and political parties. Secondly, they turned to state-sponsored and often state-controlled compulsory education as a way of suitably educating the masses into the principles of liberalism. And thirdly, they sought to extend the fruits of capitalism and the gains of colonialism to the masses in order to give them a stake in the capitalist economy.

As for the second question, the relationship between the people and their representatives, two different answers were possible. It could be argued that since the people cannot directly run their affairs in the large modern state, they should do so indirectly through their elected representatives. They should give clear instructions to their representatives, keep a keen eye on them, and in general treat them as their delegates. This is 'representative' or 'indirect democracy'; that is, popular self-rule through the mediating agency of the elected representatives. Such a representative or indirect democracy was unacceptable to the liberals. As J. S. Mill put it, the 'substitution of delegation for representation is the one and only danger of democracy'.[5] Since the liberals did not trust the masses, they saw in this type of democracy a serious threat to all they valued, including and especially private property. Besides, the atomized and fragmented liberal society lacked the communal basis necessary to enable people to form coherent collective views on public affairs. Furthermore, representative democracy required a participatory culture noticeably absent in the liberal society.

For these and other reasons (especially the first) the liberals, including the most enlightened among them, opted for representative *government*; that is, a government of the people *by* their representatives. Representatives were to be elected by the people, but once elected they were to remain free to manage public affairs as they saw fit. This highly effective way of insulating the government against the full impact of the universal franchise lies at the heart of liberal democracy. Strictly speaking liberal democracy is not representative *democracy* but representative *government*. As J. S. Mill put it, liberals advocate a 'well-regulated' or 'rational democracy', one ruled by 'an enlightened minority accountable to the majority in the last resort'. The elitism of Mill and other liberal leaders sat ill at ease with, and emasculated, the significance of their advocacy of political participation.[6]

Liberal democracy, then, represents a highly complex theoretical and political construct based on an ingenious blend of liberalism and democracy. It is democracy conceptualized and structured within the limits of liberalism. Broadly speaking, liberalism constitutes its theory of the state and democracy its theory of government. Liberalism determines the nature of the state (formal, abstract), its structure (separate from the autonomous civil society, a clear separation between public and private), its rationale (protection of the basic rights of its citizens) and its basic units (individuals rather than groups or communities). Democracy specifies who constitutes the legitimate government and wields the authority inherent in the state (the elected representatives), how they acquire authority (free elections, choice between parties) and how they are to exercise it (in broad harmony with public opinion). Although in liberal democracy liberalism is the dominant partner, democracy, which has its own independent tradition and internal logic, has from time to time revolted against the liberal constraints. People have demanded new or different kinds of rights or questioned the degree of importance given to the rights to liberty, property and the freedom of enquiry and expression. They have also questioned the separation between the state and the economy and the individualist basis of the state. No liberal democracy therefore is, or has ever been, without tensions. By and large, however, liberal democracy has managed to retain the structural design it evolved in the latter half of the nineteenth century and to keep the democratic impulse under check.

The liberalization of democracy occurred differently in different western societies, depending on their history, traditions and social structures. Hence liberal democracy has taken different forms in different countries. In some, such as Britain, liberalism has long been a most dominant partner and democracy has more or less accepted its subordinate status, while in France democracy gave in less easily and not without extracting significant concessions. The US, Canada, Germany, Sweden, the Netherlands, Australia and others represent yet other forms of liberal democracy. In spite of their differences they are all constituted along liberal democratic lines and have in common such features as individualism, elections, majority rule, multiple political parties, a limited government, the autonomy of the civil society, fear of political power and the familiar mechanisms for regulating it, the absence of mediating institutions between the individual and the state, the law as the central means of social regulation, the abstract state and its correlative the abstract citizen.

Although liberal democracy bears some resemblance to its Athenian counterpart, the two are, as we saw, quite different in their ideological bases, structures and central concerns. Since each arose within a specific historical context and culture, this is hardly surprising. Liberal democracy cannot therefore be considered a degenerate form of 'true' democracy, as the nostalgic Hellenophiles maintain. Athenian democracy can be a source of inspiration and a useful corrective for us, but neither a model nor even a standard of judgement. Like all new historical forms, liberal democracy both misses out some of the important insights of its classical cousin *and* adds new ones of its own. It rightly fears unrestrained popular sovereignty but goes to the other extreme and disempowers the people. It rightly stresses the importance of non-political interests but fails to appreciate the true significance of public life. It rightly cherishes individuality and privacy but ignores the communal soil in which alone the individual can flourish. Although it fragments the community, it gives democracy the element of universality it had hitherto lacked. One person, one vote is basically a liberal idea. Even when the liberals resisted it in practice, they knew that it was inherent in their individualist view of humanity.

Although liberalism defines rights in narrowly individualist, elitist and bourgeois terms, it gives democracy moral depth by insisting on the inviolability of basic human rights and on the protection of minorities and dissenting individuals. While it fails to appreciate the creative potential of political power, it is intensely alive to its pathology and guards against it in a way that classical democracy did not. As many of its critics have pointed out, liberal democracy is open to serious criticisms.

But if the criticisms are not to be anachronistic, they must be grounded not in its alleged failure to conform to the classical 'model', but in its inability to satisfy the deepest urges and aspirations of the *modern* human being and to meet the challenges of the *modern* age.

Having briefly highlighted the basic features of liberal democracy, we may ask if the liberal democrat is right to claim universal validity for it and to maintain that all political systems failing to measure up to it are to that extent improperly constituted and defective.

As we saw, liberal democracy defines democracy within the limits of liberalism and represents one way of combining the two. There is no obvious reason why a political system may not combine them differently. It might assign them *equal* importance and use each to limit the excesses of the other. While continuing to insulate the government against popular pressure, it might provide ways of making it more responsive. Without damaging the government's right to govern, it might provide a greater network of channels for popular participation. And while recognizing the importance of protecting basic human rights, it might define and limit them in the light of a constantly evolving democratic consensus.

Or a political system might be democratically liberal rather than a liberal democracy, making democracy the dominant partner and defining liberalism within the limits set by it. Like liberal democracy, such a political system cherishes and respects individuals, but defines them and their rights in social terms. It establishes a healthier balance between the individual and the community, aims at a fairer distribution of the opportunities required for full citizenship, extends participation to major areas of economic and political life, and opens up new centres of power. The early socialists, the young Marx, C. B. Macpherson and many European socialist parties today advocate such a democratically constituted liberal polity in preference to liberal democracy. Democratic liberalism is fairly close to social democracy and represents a partial transcendence of liberalism.

How a polity combines liberalism and democracy or how liberal and democratic it chooses to be depends on its history, traditions, values, problems and needs. A polity is not a chance and fluctuating collection of individuals but has a history and a character, and needs to work out its political destiny in its own distinct way. As we saw, the Athenian democracy could not be revived in the modern age, and modern western societies had to evolve their own distinct forms of democracy. What is true of the west is equally true of the rest of the world. To insist on the universality of liberal democracy is to deny the west's own historical experiences and to betray the liberal principles of mutual respect and love of cultural diversity. It imposes on other countries systems of government unsuited to their talents and skills, destroys the coherence and integrity of their ways of life, and reduces them to mimics, unable and unwilling to be true either to their traditions or to the imported alien norms. The cultural havoc caused by colonialism should alert us to the dangers of an over-zealous imposition of liberal democracy.

Liberal democracy is a product of, and designed to cope with, the political problems thrown up by the post-seventeenth-century individualist society. As such there are at least two types of polity where its relevance would seem to be considerably limited, namely cohesive polities with a strong sense of community and multi-communal polities. Let us take each in turn.

There are polities in the world which have a strong sense of community based on a widely shared and deeply held conception of the good life. Saudi Arabia, Kuwait and several Middle Eastern and African polities belong to this category. They define the individual in communal terms and do not regard the atomic liberal individual as the basic unit of society. A poignant recent example illustrates the point well. A middle-aged Bangladeshi entitled to settle in Britain had two sons whom he was at liberty to bring into the country. When the immigration officer asked him if they were his sons, he replied in the affirmative. It later transpired that they were his dead brother's sons. Since they were not *his* children, the officer accused him of making a fraudulent claim. The Bangladeshi argued that his dead brother was not 'really' separate from him, that their children had all grown up together as brothers and sisters entitled to the equal attention and affection of all adults, that each adult in the family had a moral obligation to look after the children of all them, that this was how his society was constituted, and that he had additionally given a pledge to his dying brother to treat his children as his own. Since he saw no difference whatsoever between his own and his brother's sons, he chose to bring in the latter. When the bemused officer proved unrelenting and insisted that the Bangladeshi could only bring in his own two sons, the latter offered to bring in one of his own and one of his dead brother's sons. Since the quota of two children was not exceeded, he could not understand why it mattered to the British government how it was made up. He also argued that his 'selfishness' would not be forgiven by his community and his dead brother's family, and nor would he be able to live with himself, if he did not bring in at least one of his dead brother's sons. In this conflict between the two different conceptions of the self, neither side could make sense of the other. Being used to the liberal view which he regarded as self-evident, and convinced that it was his duty to enforce the law, the immigration officer deported the Bangladeshi back to his country with the instruction that he was never to be allowed into Britain.

The point of this example is that different societies define and individuate people differently. They also therefore define freedom, equality, rights, property, justice, loyalty, power and authority differently. For example, in a traditional Moslem society every man is required to consider a portion of his property as belonging to others. He has a duty to use it for their benefit and is not allowed to deny food or shelter to a hungry man or to a stranger. The latter does not have a *right* to food or shelter, but the host has a most stringent *duty* to provide these. No one talks of rights, yet almost everyone's needs are met. No one uses the language of 'justice', a term for which some of these societies have no equivalent words, but most of their members receive their due and the distribution of goods is generally equitable. In short, the liberal principle of individuation and other liberal ideas are culturally and historically specific. As such a political system based on them cannot claim universal validity.

The non-liberal but not necessarily illiberal societies we are discussing cherish and wish to preserve their ways of life. Like most pre-modern societies they are communally orientated and believe that their members' 'rights' may be legitimately restricted in the larger interest of the traditional way of life. Most of them allow freedom of speech and expression, but not the freedom to mock and ridicule their sacred texts, practices, beliefs and rituals. They restrict the right to property and to trade and commerce lest it should undermine the ethos of social solidarity and the ethic of communal obligation lying at the basis of their ways of life. They restrict travel, immigration and the freedom to buy and sell land for basically the same reasons. Liberals find such restrictions unacceptable, but most members of traditional societies do not. Unless we assume that liberalism represents the final truth about human beings, we cannot indiscriminately condemn societies that do not conform to it. This is particularly so today when the liberal societies are themselves beginning to wonder if they have not carried individualism too far, and how they can create genuine communities without which individuals lack roots and stability. Community implies shared values and a common way of life, and is incompatible with the more or less unrestrained rights of its members to do as they please. It is striking that many a communitarian theorist has suggested restrictions on pornography, freedom of expression and immigration that are not very different from those characteristic of traditional societies.

It is, of course, true that some traditional societies have grossly outrageous practices and customs which obviously need to be changed, preferably by internal and, when necessary, by a judiciously applied external pressure. The question we are considering, however, is not how to improve their ways of life but whether they must adopt, and be condemned for refusing to adopt, liberal democratic institutions. It is difficult to see how this question can be answered in the affirmative. As long as their forms of government are acceptable to their people and meet the basic conditions of good government, to which we shall return later, they must be at liberty to work out their political destiny themselves.

We have so far talked about cohesive communities. We may now briefly consider multi-communal societies; that is, societies which comprise several cohesive and self-conscious communities each seeking to preserve its traditional way of life. Several Third World countries belong to this category. Neither the Athenian model, which presupposes a community, nor the liberal model, which presupposes none, applies to such multi-communal societies, with the result that the theoretical problems raised by their experiences have received little attention in much of western democratic theory.

The point will become clear if we look at the case of India, one of the most ethnically and religiously diverse societies in the world. The colonial state in India left the long-established communities more or less alone, accepted their 'laws' and practices, and superimposed on them a minimal body of mainly criminal laws. Unlike its European counterpart, it permitted a plurality of legal systems and shared its 'sovereignty' with the autonomous and largely self-governing communities.

Post-independence India only partially rationalized the colonial state and remains a highly complex polity. It has a uniform body of criminal but not civil laws. Moslems continue to be governed by their own civil laws, which the state enforces but with which it does not interfere. The tribals too are governed by their separate laws, and the state has committed itself to making no changes in the practices and laws of the Christians without their explicit consent and approval. The Parsis are subject to the same civil laws as the rest of non-Moslem Indians, but the interpretation and application of the laws is in some cases left to their *panchayats* or community councils. Thus the ordinary civil courts will hear a Parsi divorce case, but leave it to the Parsi *panchayat* to decide on the machinery of reconciliation and the amount of alimony. The Indian state is thus both an association of individuals and a community of communities, recognizing both individuals and communities as bearers of rights. The criminal law recognizes only individuals, whereas the civil law recognizes most minority communities as distinct legal subjects. This makes India a liberal democracy of a very peculiar kind.

It is tempting to say, as many Indian and foreign commentators have said, that the Indian state is too 'deeply embedded' in society and too 'plural' and 'chaotic' to be considered a properly constituted state or a state in the 'true' sense of the word. But such a view is obviously too superficial and ethnocentric to be satisfactory. There is no reason why we should accept the view that the modern western manner of constituting the state is the only true or proper one, and deny India and other non-western societies the right to indigenize the imported institution of the state and even to evolve their own alternative political formations. Rather than insist that the state *must* be autonomous and separate from society, and then set about finding ways of restoring it to the people, we might argue that it should not be separated from society in the first instance. And rather than insist that a state *must* have a uniform legal system, we might argue that it should be free to allow its constituent communities to retain their different laws and practices, so long as these conform to clearly laid down and nationally accepted principles of justice and fairness. Thus the law might require that a divorced wife must be provided for, but leave the different communities free to decide whether the husband, his family, or his community as a whole should arrange for her maintenance, so long as the arrangements are foolproof and not open to abuse and arbitrary alternation. If the multi-communal polities are to hold together and to avoid the all too familiar eruptions of inter- and intra-communal violence, they need to be extremely sensitive to the traditions, values and levels of development of their constituent communities, and may find the institutions and practices developed in socially homogeneous liberal societies deeply subversive.

Like the concepts of the individual, right, property and so on, such institutions as elections, multiple political parties, the separation of powers and the abstract state too cannot be universalized. Elections of the western type impose a crushing financial burden on poor countries and encourage the all too familiar forms of corruption. In an ethnically and religiously diverse society lacking shared values, or in a society unused to discussing its differences in public and articulating them in neat ideological terms, elections might also prove deeply divisive, generate artificial ideological rigidities, release powerful aggressive impulses and channel them into dangerous and unaccustomed directions. Such societies might be better off sticking to or evolving consensual and less polarized ways of selecting their governments and conducting their affairs. What is true of elections is equally true of other liberal democratic institutions and practices.

This is not to say that liberal democratic institutions have no value for non-western societies, rather that the latter have to determine the value themselves in the light of their cultural resources, needs and circumstances, and that they cannot mechanically transplant them. As a matter of fact, many third world countries have tried all manner of political experiments, some successful and others disastrous. Thanks to the profoundly mistaken belief, partly self-induced and partly encouraged by western governments and developmental experts, that their experiments were 'deviations' from the 'true' liberal democratic model and symptomatic of their immaturity and backwardness, they often undertook them without much zeal and self-confidence and abandoned them prematurely. Their political predicament is very like their linguistic predicament. They abandoned their traditional languages, which they well knew how to speak, in favour of the 'proper' and 'respectable' languages of their colonial rulers, which they could never adequately master.

It would appear that the democratic part of liberal democracy, consisting in such things as free elections, free speech and the right to equality, has proved far more attractive outside the west and is more universalizable than the liberal component. Millions in non-western societies demand democracy, albeit in suitably indigenized forms, whereas they tend to shy away from liberalism as if they instinctively felt it to be subversive of what they most valued and cherished. This is not because it leads to capitalism, for many of them welcome the latter, but because the Third World countries feel that the liberal view of the world and way of life is at odds with their deepest aspirations and self-conceptions. As they understand it, liberalism breaks up the community, undermines the shared body of ideas and values, places the isolated individual above the community, encourages the ethos and ethic of aggressive self-assertion, rejects traditional wisdom and common sense in the name of scientific reason, and weakens the spirit of mutual accommodation and adjustment. Non-western societies wonder why they cannot import such western technology and expertise as they need while rejecting some of its liberal values and suitably indigenizing some of its democratic practices. They might be proved wrong and may suffer as a result. But forcing them into the standard liberal democratic mould is not without its heavy human cost either.

To reject the universalist claims of liberal democracy is not to endorse the crude relativist view that a country's political system is its own business and above criticism, and that western experiences have no relevance outside the west. In an increasingly interdependent world every country's internal affairs impinge on others and are a matter of general concern. The dissidents, the oppressed minorities and the ill-treated masses the world over appeal to international public opinion for support, and we cannot respond to them without the help of general principles to guide our judgements and actions. Thanks to the widening of our moral consciousness, we feel morally concerned about human suffering even when our help is not directly asked for. And thanks to the increasing demystification of the modern state, we are beginning to realize that its citizens are not its property, that it is accountable to humankind for the way it treats them, and that it must be opened up to external scrutiny. All this calls for a body of moral and political principles that are both universally valid and capable of accommodating cultural diversity and autonomy. We need to work out the minimum conditions or principles of good government and leave different countries free to evolve their own appropriate forms of government compatible with these regulative principles.

Since we cannot here pursue this large and complex question, a few general remarks will have to suffice. Universally valid regulative principles cannot be laid down by western governments, let alone by a philosopher, both because they are bound to be infected by an ethnocentric bias and because they can have no authority over the rest of humankind. It is easy to be prescriptive, but such prescriptions have no meaning and force unless they resonate in the lives of, and evoke sympathetic responses in the minds of, those affected by them. The principles of good government can be genuinely universal (in their scope and content) *and* binding only if they are freely negotiated by all involved and grounded in a broad global consensus. It would be wholly naive to imagine that all governments and all men and women everywhere will ever agree on them. What we can legitimately hope and strive for is a broad cross-cultural consensus commanding varying degrees of universal support. As individuals and groups in different parts of the world invoke it in their internal struggles, and as the rest of the world responds to them, the consensus acquires depth and vitality, becomes an acceptable political currency, strikes roots in popular consciousness, and acquires new adherents. This is broadly how almost all our moral principles have evolved and acquired authority. And this is also how the 1948 United Nations Declaration of Human Rights has acquired its current appeal. A pious statement of good intentions when first formulated in the aftermath of the Second World War, it was increasingly invoked by the leaders of colonial struggles for independence and oppressed minorities, and over time became an important part of domestic and international morality.[7]

The UN Declaration is a complex document and articulated at three different levels. First, it lays down the general principles every government should satisfy. Secondly, it translates these principles into the language of rights and lists different kinds of rights. Thirdly, it lays down institutions and practices that alone in its view can guarantee and protect these rights. The last two parts of it have a liberal democratic bias, the second part because of its use of the language of rights and the kinds of rights it stresses, and the third because the recommended institutions and practices presuppose and are specific to liberal democracy.

As for the general principles of the UN Declaration, they fall into two categories. Some are distinctly liberal and culturally specific; for example, the more or less unlimited right to freedom of expression and to private property, and the insistence that marriages must be based on the 'free and full consent' of the intending spouses. Other principles relate to vital human interests valued in almost all societies and have a genuinely universal core, such as respect for human life and dignity, equality before the law, equal protection of the law, fair trial and the protection of minorities. Liberalism does, of course, deeply cherish and place great value on these principles, but they are not unique to it. They are found in classical Athens and Rome and many a medieval kingdom, are emphasized in the sacred texts of all great religions, and were widely practised in many non-western societies. Indeed the record of some non-western societies in such areas as respect for human life and the protection of minorities, including Jews, is not only as good as but even better than that of the liberal west.

Evidence that the second category of principles laid down by the UN Declaration commands considerable universal support is three-fold. First, the UN Declaration was signed by a large number of governments representing different cultures, geographical areas and political systems. Secondly, when the newly liberated Asian and African countries joined the UN they demanded amendments to its Declaration, which were accepted after much debate and embodied in the two International Covenants of 1966. The latter documents rejected the right to property and to full compensation in the event of nationalization, toned down the individualistic basis of the 1948 Declaration, and endorsed the occasional need to suspend individual rights in the national interest. However, they not only left untouched but even strengthened what I have called the genuinely universal principles of the 1948 Declaration. Thirdly, people the world over have frequently appealed to these principles in their struggles against repressive governments. For their part the latter have almost invariably preferred to deny the existence of unacceptable practices rather than shelter behind relativism and cultural autonomy. In their own different ways both parties are thus beginning to accept the principles as the basis of good government, conferring on them the moral authority they otherwise cannot have. In other words, the principles are increasingly becoming 'a common standard of achievement for all peoples and nations' as the UN Declaration itself had hoped. As such they provide a most valuable basis for a freely negotiated and constantly evolving consensus on universally valid principles of good government.

Within the limits set by these principles, different countries should remain free to determine their own appropriate forms of government. They may choose liberal democracy, but if they do not their choice deserves respect and even encouragement. After all, liberals have always held, and rightly, that diversity is the precondition of progress and choice, and that truth can only emerge from a peaceful competition between different ways of life.

NOTES

1   That human beings have the capacity to rise above their circumstances and critically to reflect on themselves is not in question. What is in question is the liberal view that this capacity alone constitutes human essence and that everything else is merely contingent. Michael Sandel is right to criticize this view, but goes to the other extreme. Although he does not deny the human capacity for self-transcendence, he treats it as a free-floating faculty and assigns it no ontological or moral role, with the result that his concept of the self remains unstable and even incoherent. Besides, how does the self know that it is radically situated? And how does its capacity for self-transcendence impinge on and restructure its social identity? See his *Liberalism and the Limits of Justice* (Cambridge, Cambridge University Press, 1982), ch. 1. See also Bhikhu Parekh, *Marx's Theory of Ideology* (Baltimore, MD, Johns Hopkins University Press, 1982), ch. 2.
2   Unlike almost all pre-modern writers, hardly any liberal has given emotions an ontological and epistemological status; that is, regarded them as constitutive of humanity and playing a vital creative role in the constitution and pursuit of knowledge.
3   This was how John Locke first formulated the problem. If Hobbes has the honour of being the first to articulate the philosophical basis of *liberalism*, Locke must be credited with first formulating the basic structure of liberal *democracy*.
4   For a good discussion of this peculiar and ideologically biased view of democracy, see J. Roper, *Democracy and its Critics* (London, Unwin Hyman, 1989), pp. 145 ff.
5   G. Himmelfarb (ed.), *Essays on Politics and Culture by John Stuart Mill* (New York, Anchor Books, 1962), p. 197.
6   For a valuable discussion, see A. Gutman, *Liberal Equality* (Cambridge, Cambridge University Press, 1980), pp. 48ff.
7   For a discussion of universal rights, see J. W. Nickel, *Making Sense of Human Rights* (Berkeley, CA, University of California Press, 1987). For a cross-cultural perspective, see L. Rouner (ed), *Human Rights and the World's Religions* (Notre Dame, University of Notre Dame Press, 1988), especially parts III and IV. For a good discussion of the problems of minorities in a plural society, see W. Kymlicka *Liberalism, Community and Culture* (Oxford, Clarendon Press, 1991). See also Bhikhu Parekh, 'The Rushdie Affair: research agenda for political philosophy', *Political Studies*, 38:4 (1990), 695–709.

Part III

---

*Substantive Issues: The Scope and
Limits of Democratic Politics*

8

DEMOCRACY, MARKETS AND CAPITAL: ARE THERE NECESSARY ECONOMIC LIMITS TO DEMOCRACY?

Christopher Pierson

Of the many disputes which have surrounded the theory and practice of democracy, few have been more contentious than those that concern the proper *limits* of democratic decision-making. While these arguments have often concerned the restrictions placed upon membership of the *demos* or the constitutional limits within which a democratic majority may impose its will upon a resistant minority, just as frequently and fiercely they have been debates about the *economic* limits of democracy. For many liberal theorists of democracy, there has been an aspiration to hold the economic and the political apart, or to insulate the economic sphere from immediate control by the *demos*, so as to protect either 'the primacy of the political' or else 'the sanctity of private property rights'.[1] For many socialists, by contrast, democracy which is confined to the 'purely political' sphere is, at best, 'limited' and, at worst, a 'sham'.[2] The terms of some of these debates may now seem rather archaic. But in fact the issue of the economic limits to democracy lies at the heart of the contemporary debate about the viability of alternatives to liberal democracy and is fundamental to the renewed political and intellectual authority of neo-liberalism.

Neo-liberalism and the Economic Limits of Liberal Democracy

Neo-liberal commentators have always made much of the (exclusive) historical affinity in modern times between democracy and capitalism.[3]

However, just as frequently, they have insisted that this happy co-incidence is dependent upon the ways in which the jurisdiction of democracy is strictly delimited. This was a persistent theme in the literature on 'overloaded government' that blossomed in the 1970s.[4] It is also a central concern of those public choice theorists who have set out to show that individually rational decision-making under established democratic procedures will always tend to generate collectively sub-optimal outcomes.[5] But perhaps the most sophisticated statement of the neo-liberal view is that developed by Friedrich Hayek in the three volumes of *Law, Legislation and Liberty*.[6]

Although Hayek would doubtless have considered himself a democrat (of a very particular kind), he was still more an advocate of individual freedom, and certainly an opponent of the ideas of sovereign and unlimited government frequently associated with the rise of democracy.[7] A free and just society, he insisted, can only be secured on the basis of 'catallaxy', the neologism Hayek used to describe 'the special kind of spontaneous order produced by the market through people acting within the rules of the laws of property, tort and contract'.[8] He insisted that 'a condition of liberty in which all are allowed to use their knowledge for their purposes, restrained only by rules of just conduct of universal application, is likely to produce for them the best condition for achieving their aims'.[9] Hayek ascribed a correspondingly limited role to the (democratic) state. 'Only limited government can be decent government', he argued, 'because there does not exist (and cannot exist) general moral rules for the assignment of particular benefits.'[10] The duty of the public authority is not to pursue its own ends but rather to provide the framework (of 'the Rule of Law') within which 'catallaxy' may develop. Those functions for which the state may properly raise taxation are correspondingly limited to the maintenance of collective security against external threats, the preservation of the Rule of Law, provision for that limited number of public goods which cannot be efficiently delivered by the market and the relief of destitution.

In practice, democratic government as it has developed over the past hundred years has systematically broken these constitutional limits. Most damaging has been the working through of 'the pernicious principle of parliamentary sovereignty'.[11] Where parliament is sovereign, govern-ments become the plaything of organized sectional interests. Principles and 'the national interest' are abandoned in the attempt to mobilize a majority-creating coalition of particular interests against the *genuinely* common or public interest.

These vices of unlimited government have been peculiarly damaging in the hands of socialists and social democrats. First, socialists set out to adjust the spontaneous order generated by market transactions, a project which Hayek depicted as hopeless, given the impossibility of adequate centrally organized knowledge of the infinity of market-like decisions. Interventions in the market will *always* have sub-optimal outcomes and *always* lessen general social welfare. Secondly, social democrats' sponsorship of the welfare state and of particularistic legislation, most notably to confer privileges upon its allies in the organized labour movement, represents a break with Hayek's insistence that the law must be confined to rules of 'just conduct of universal application'. Thirdly, socialists and social democrats intervene in the market and its outcomes to promote 'social justice'.[12] Justice, Hayek insisted, is strictly *procedural* and can only refer to the proper enforcement of general rules of universal application without regard to its particular results. 'The mirage of social justice' which the socialists pursue is, at best, a nonsense and, at worst, pernicious and itself unjust. It means undermining the justice of the market, confiscating the wealth of the more successful, prolonging the dependency of the needy, entrenching the special powers of organized interests and overriding individual freedom. Indeed, it is 'irreconcilable with the rule of law' and in seeking to press state intervention beyond its legitimate minimum, the socialists have been the principle offenders in 'giving democracy a bad name'.[13]

In response, Hayek proposed a number of constitutional reforms. These include the division between a (fundamental) law-making and a more prosaic 'legislating' assembly, the election of representatives (who must have reached the age of 45) to single 15-year periods of office and, possibly, some sort of constitutional constraint to protect against the 'intellectual error' of slipping into socialism. All of these measures are intended to underwrite what Hayek understood to be an appropriately and necessarily limited democracy by insulating the economic sphere from control by the *demos*.[14]

Socialism and the Limits of Liberal Democracy

Historically, the most influential criticism of the limitations of liberal democracy has come from socialists and social democrats. They have always rejected these sorts of constraint upon democratizing the economy. In various ways, they suggest that market outcomes cannot be presumed to be just, that government intervention can generate outcomes which are to be preferred to those given by the market and that democracy is not to be understood as just 'a utilitarian device for safeguarding internal peace and individual freedom' but, wherever practicable, as a preferred principle for all collective decision-taking.[15] Since the allocation of scarce means and resources is probably the single most important determinant of people's well-being and defines their most essential interests, it seems perverse to exclude precisely these most fundamental issues from democratic control. Socialists have frequently insisted, in the sharpest contrast to Hayek's constitutional recommendations, that representative democracy can *only* work if representatives or delegates are under the most immediate control of their constituents (through frequent elections, recall and mandating). I do not want here to develop this socialist response. Our present purposes will be adequately served by a brief reconstruction (without supporting arguments) of a typical statement of the socialist case against the *economic* limitations of liberal democracy:

1 Democracy is the appropriate institutional mechanism to be deployed whenever important collective decisions are to be taken.
2 Decisions about economic life are of fundamental importance to every member of society; accordingly, all those involved should have an equal say in economic decision-making.
3 The existing division of political and economic spheres under liberal democracy protects the unjustified power and the unmerited wealth of the private owners of capital and excludes the majority from effective decision-taking.
4 Therefore, new institutional arrangements must be installed through which the economic power of private capital can be replaced by the democratic decision-making power of the whole community.

Of course, such a synopsis abstracts from many of the arguments for democracy which have been most important to socialists (including, for example, arguments about participation, equality and autonomy). It does, however, identify the core of traditional socialist hostility to the limitations of liberal democracy and places at the heart of the socialist cause the institutional arrangements for ensuring democratic control over economic decision-making.

The 'Failures' of Socialist Democracy

What has seemed for many commentators to be fatally damaging to this socialist argument is the continuing failure to generate a satisfactory model for the democratic control of economic life. This objection seems even more compelling now in the light of the recent experience of the two most prominent and quite divergent forms which 'real socialism' took in the twentieth century – the Soviet model and western social democracy, both of which are seen to have 'run out of steam' at the same time. While there are certainly dangers in conflating the experiences of 'socialism – east and west', in both spheres the problems of socialism have been prominently attributed not just to economic under-performance but also to the failure of socialists to democratize economic decision-making.

While the practices of socialism in east and west have been profoundly different, both were motivated (or at least sanctioned) by an under-pinning belief that the 'anarchy of production' under capitalist imperatives could be replaced by democratic control of the economy. Models for controlling the economy were very different in east and west. While the economies of Eastern Europe (even excluding Yugoslavia) have been quite varied, the essence of the Soviet model was a centrally planned economy, which in its more extreme forms could embrace the forced direction of labour and the rationing of consumer goods.[16] In the west, while some industrial undertakings were taken into 'public ownership', it was essentially the Keynesian model, in which government control of a few macroeconomic levers would yield effective control over the wider economy, which described the preferred form for the (indirect) management of the economy. Both the Soviet model (and the derivative 'reform' models of Eastern Europe) and Keynesianism now stand condemned for having failed (literally) 'to deliver the goods' and having concentrated economic power in the hands of state bureaucrats rather than dispersing it among the general population. The past and, one suspects, the future of socialism in east and west are quite different. Yet both of the major twentieth-century variants of the socialist tradition are seen to have failed to deliver on their promise to democratize economic life and this failure, in turn, is seen to have considerably enhanced the authority which neo-liberal accounts of the economic limits of democracy have enjoyed in recent years.

Problems of the Democratization of Economic Life

We can think about the challenge that this presents to the traditional socialist aspiration for the democratization of economic life under two heads. First, there are problems in the political economy of socialism. Of these perhaps the most important are the failures of planning and of Keynesian demand management. These are not perhaps as universal as is now widely believed. None the less, there is a broad consensus (even *on the left*) that, particularly within the developed economies of the present period, both centralized economic planning and traditional forms of Keynesian macro-management may be extremely difficult to sustain. These objections are not solely concerned with efficiency. It is also very widely argued that economic planning has proven to be undemocratic. This is not perhaps an especially contentious argument in respect of the experience of Soviet planning.[17] Meanwhile, of state economic intervention in the west, it has been argued that socialists and social democrats in (perhaps properly) using state power to counteract the outcomes of purely capitalist markets were naive (or disingenuous) about the ways in which state power could be made democratically accountable. Social democrats in their enthusiasm for taming 'the excesses of capitalism' neglected to recognize that the instruments of state policy that they used for this purpose, albeit that they were in a formal sense democratically legitimated, might be as alienating and hierarchical as those very market structures which they sought to control.[18]

A second set of difficulties for the socialist politics of economic democratization arise from the changing circumstances in which such policies must be pursued. Thus, it is argued that even if traditional socialist remedies of centralized planning or demand management were desirable they would be extremely difficult to pursue in the context of a new world economic order (variously described as 'post-Fordism' or 'disorganized capitalism'). Since so much has been written about these developments elsewhere, I shall confine myself to outlining some of their consequences for the traditional social democratic politics of economic intervention.[19] In essence, those circumstances that permitted the pursuit of Keynesian interventionist economic management in the post-war period are said to be 'withering away'. Traditional Keynesian policies depended, among other things, upon the capacity of a national government (within certain international limitations) to establish its own fiscal and monetary policy, to control the major parameters of its own economic development and to negotiate about these with the leaders of 'national' capital and 'national' organized labour. Economic planning required that the national economy could be sufficiently insulated from the surrounding world economy to allow governmental controls to be at least minimally effective. But the contemporary global political economy is in fact witnessing a decline in the integrity of 'national' economies, the intensified globalization of a capitalist world market and the heightened mobility of capital. It has seen the growth of multinational corporations and of multi-site industrial production, a new international division of labour in which manufacturing is increasingly transferred to low-waged economies in the third world and the growing authority of supra-national economic and political institutions (the EC, the Organization of

American States, the World Bank, the IMF).[20] Under these circumstances, it is very unclear that the minimum requirements for effective national economic planning still obtain.[21]

'Democratizing the economy' defended

How might critics of liberal democracy, particularly those who are principally concerned about the extension of economic democracy, respond? One argument is to insist that since the societies of neither Eastern nor Western Europe may properly be described as socialist, it is inappropriate to describe the failures of their planning experience as 'failures of socialism'. This is a central contention of Mandel's 'In defence of socialist planning' and of Alex Callinicos's *The Revenge of History*.[22] A second response is the call to reinstate the classical socialist ambition for the direct socialization of production but in a new form, a position which has achieved its most developed and articulate expression in plans of the Swedish social democratic left for *wage-earners' funds*.[23]

Market Socialism

Here I want to focus upon a third response and consider the recent revival of interest in *market socialism*. At its simplest, market socialism describes an economic and political model which combines the principles of social ownership of the economy with the continuing allocation of commodities (including labour) through the mechanism of markets. In one of the most comprehensive recent treatments, David Miller describes 'the pure model of market socialism' thus:

> The key idea is that the market mechanism is retained as a means of providing most goods and services, while the ownership of capital is socialized ... all productive enterprises are constituted as workers' co-operatives, leasing their operating capital from an outside investment agency. Each enterprise makes its own decisions about products, methods of production, prices, etc., and competes for custom in the market. Net profits form a pool out of which incomes are paid. Each enterprise is democratically controlled by those who work for it, and among the issues they must decide is how to distribute income within the co-operative.[24]

In fact, market socialism has a comparatively long history, retraceable at least to the development of the cooperative movement in the nineteenth century. Its modern origins are often identified with the 'Socialist

Calculation Debate' of the inter-war period and particularly with the contributions of Oskar Lange and Abba Lerner.[25] The details of the Lange–Lerner scheme and its historical reception need not concern us here, though it is worth noting that their model did not seek to limit the (extremely extensive) powers of the state, but rather to secure a market-mimicking device which would permit the rational calculation of the prices of capital and production goods under state ownership.

By contrast, in the more recent advocacy of market socialism, we find not so much a concern with overcoming allocational problems under centralized planning, but rather the expectation that the market can be used within a socialized economy as a way of extending effective economic democracy for the mass of the working population. Market socialism is seen not only as a promising response to the failures of planning, but also as a way of overcoming the bureaucratic deformation of economic reform and the limitations of state-administered forms of socialism (in both east and west). It is said to afford new structures for democratic control of the economy which are impossible within the limitations of existing forms of liberal democratic capitalism.[26] It is with this claim, that a form of market socialism can overcome the limitations placed upon economic democracy under existing liberal democratic regimes without experiencing the 'deformations' of more traditional forms of socialism, that I am centrally concerned.

In practice, there are many models of market socialism, and the term has been employed to describe societies as different as China, Hungary, Austria and even Singapore.[27] The following representative (though far from exhaustive) summary is derived from one of the earliest and most influential of texts in the revival of Western European interest in market socialism, Alec Nove's *The Economics of Feasible Socialism*.[28] Nove identifies the characteristic features of a market socialist economy thus:

1 State, social and cooperative property would predominate, and there would be no large-scale private ownership of the means of production.
2 An authority responsible to an elected assembly would consciously plan major investments of structural significance.
3 Central management of current micro-economic affairs would be confined to sectors (and to types of decision) where informational, technological and organizational economies of scale, and the presence of major externalities, render this indispensable.
4 There would be a preference for small scale, as a means of maximizing participation and a sense of 'belonging'. Outside central-ized or monopolized sectors, and the limited area of private enterprise, management should be responsible to the workforce.

5   Current output and distribution of goods and services should whenever possible be determined by negotiations between the parties concerned. There should be explicit recognition that this implies and requires competition, a precondition for choice.

6   Workers should be free to choose the nature of their employment and given every opportunity to change their specialization. If they prefer it, they could opt for work in cooperatives, or on their own account (for instance in a family farm, workshop or service agency).

7   As an unlimited market mechanism would in due course destroy itself and create intolerable social inequalities, the state would have vital functions in determining income policies, levying taxes (and differential rents), intervening to restrain monopoly power and · generally setting the ground-rules and limits of a competitive market. Some sectors (education, health, and so on) would naturally be exempt from market-type criteria.

8   It is recognized that a degree of material inequality is a precondition for avoiding administrative direction of labour, but moral incentives would be encouraged and inequalities consciously limited. The duty to provide work would override considerations of micro-profitability.

9   The distinction between governors and governed, managers and managed, cannot realistically be eliminated, but great care would have to be taken to devise barriers to abuse of power and the maximum possible democratic consultation.

Market Socialism and Economic Democratization Assessed

Nove's is neither the most radical nor the most conservative statement of the market socialist case.[29] Rather than investigate these many variations, in the second half of this chapter, I want to consider whether market socialism offers a model for democratization of the economy which avoids the shortcomings identified in more traditional forms of socialist policy. I shall concentrate upon four potential problem areas: the possibility of 'markets under socialism', the nature of the state under market socialism, the international context of market socialism and the question of its feasibility.

Economic democracy in the socialist market

We have seen that socialists have traditionally insisted that the market is a radically anti-democratic institution. Only by confining democratic practices to the less influential sphere of the formally political – and allowing authoritarian powers to private capital within the market – can the illusion of democracy within market economies be sustained. At the heart of their response is the insistence that it is not markets but *capitalist* markets that are undemocratic. There are two principal elements in defending this claim. First, where economic power is concentrated in the hands of private capitalist concerns, the controllers of this capital will be able to exercise an undue influence upon democratically elected govern- ments. In this way, political life, which within the rubric of liberal democracy should properly be under popular control, is usurped by the dominant power of capital. A second objection to capitalist market societies is that 'democracy stops at the factory gates'. Thus, decision- taking *within* economic enterprises, even where these are in public ownership, is explicitly hierarchical and authoritarian.[30]

Market socialists claim to be able to resolve both of these weaknesses within a system of 'markets under socialism'. First, the undue influence of private capital upon the democratic process is simply removed by eliminating large-scale private holdings of capital. We may anticipate that, as a part of the legitimate process of political bargaining, enterprises and organized interests will continue to seek to represent their interests before government. However, the *undue* influence which derives from concentrated and coercive economic power will be eliminated by replacing traditional forms of capitalist ownership with new forms of social ownership. The second issue of a lack of democracy *within* economic enterprises is to be addressed by the similarly bold strategy of replacing the capitalist enterprise with workers' cooperatives. While the precise form of this internal democracy may be unspecific, and does not necessarily mean the elimination of (an elected) managerial authority, the overall intention, which is to deliver control over the conduct of the enterprise to all its workers, is clear.

If we ignore, for the moment, the legion difficulties which might be thought in practice to militate against the socialization of capital and its replacement with an economy of workers' cooperatives, to what extent would the market socialists' model satisfy traditional socialist objections to the impossibility of democracy under market arrangements? The projected socialization of capital and the inauguration of a cooperative economy do in principle meet several of the major objections that socialists have traditionally voiced against the anti-democratic element in capitalist markets. The objection to the unwarranted power of private capital must, by definition, be removed, where capital is no longer in private hands, and enterprises which are democratically controlled by all those who work for them are likely to recommend themselves to most socialists in preference to a system that entrenches the unqualified powers of capitalist management.

Yet while this model promises a much more extensive democratic determination of economic decision-taking than the neo-liberals are ready to allow, it is still quite clearly a *limited* form of democratization that is on offer. Thus market socialism promises a form of economic democracy *within* the enterprise but not *between* enterprises, where market competition will still apply. It promises economic enfranchisement to those who are employed, but not to the growing numbers in all advanced societies who find themselves (for all sorts of reasons) *outside* the paid/employed population. It promises greater democratic control over micro-economic decision-taking, but little prospect of greater democratic control over the economy *as a whole*. Those who see the rational and democratic management of social and economic life *in general* as central to the realization of democracy will be disappointed by the market socialists' mixture of (a measure of) direct democracy within the enterprise and (a largely unreformed) representative democracy at the level of the state. Again, the market socialist model does offer some encouragement to enthusiasts of more direct forms of democracy. Workers' cooperatives are an institutional form in which many of the demanding criteria for direct democracy (small scale, permanent involvement of all members of the *demos*, no division between legislative and executive functions) might be satisfied. But once again there is a 'trade-off', in the insistence that at the *societal* level, governance will still be through representative forms, and that, within the enterprise, certain forms of authority and decision-making are likely to be devolved to (albeit accountable) professional managers.

Indeed, market socialism generally is a compromise between democratic economic decision-making and the unplanned and unsystematic dictates of the market. While market socialists resist the neo-liberal enthusiasm for the market as a kind of 'permanent referendum' in which consumers use their money to 'vote' for particular packages of goods and services, they do clearly understand a reformed market as an arena of choice and freedom, in which consumers' judgements of their own best interests should normally take precedence over collective evaluations of social need. Yet traditionally socialists have been profoundly sceptical about these sorts of claims once applied to 'real world markets', and many

of the choices about the provision of goods and services which the
market socialists would prefer to see governed by consumer sovereignty,
more conventional socialists have claimed for the *demos*.[31]

Perhaps the most skilful attempt to reconcile the market socialist
account of economic democratization with these sorts of reservation is
that offered by David Miller. Familiarly, a first move is to argue that
some of the alienating features that socialists have identified with the
market should more properly be attributed to *capitalist* markets. Yet this
can only be a partial response, given that much of this criticism is
directed against markets *in any form*. Miller isolates three such criticisms
in Marx's account of the alienating consequences of the market: 'Under
the market economy, the relationship between production and human
need is distorted by the intervention of exchange value; human interactions take on a detached and potentially hostile character; and the
whole economic system slips out of people's theoretical and practical
grasp.'[32] Miller's response is to argue that the sort of developed
individuality to which Marx aspired under communism can only
effectively be secured through the mechanism of a market economy. But
how is this to avoid the attendant problems of alienation and a loss of
human (and potentially democratic) control over economic activity?
Miller's answer is that where the use of a market mechanism is itself the
result of a reasoned and collective choice, much of its alienating and
anti-democratic quality is dissipated. Thus, for example, it may be true
that in a market *particular* outcomes are unintended and to that extent
beyond human agency. None the less, we may choose the market (with
its unanticipated outcomes) as the best available means of attaining
some particular end (maximizing output or choice, for example). As
developed individuals, we are capable of living with relationships that
have the dual character of being in part competitive and in part cooperative (Miller employs the analogy of a game of tennis between
friends). 'Under market socialism ... work would appear to be merely
instrumental ... but at an underlying level would be seen to be
communal, because everyone would understand that the system of
exchange led to beneficial results.'[33] Inasmuch as the use of the market
process is itself a conscious, deliberate and democratic choice of the
community, its outcomes need not be seen as lying outside the (non-
alienating) control of human agency.

   This is an ingenious argument and Miller may well be right to suppose
that what he proposes is the closest to a communal form of economy that
those concerned with developed individualism might wish to come.
However, it is not clear that 'choosing a non-democratic form of resource

allocation' is properly redescribed as a surrogate form of democratic decision-taking. It may be better to recognize that what we confront is a limitation upon democratic decision-taking which is a feature of any (however reformed) market system, and that what we face is a *choice* between a more extensive democracy and those qualities (efficiency, consumer sovereignty, individuality or whatever), which it is claimed the market is best able to guarantee.

Market socialism and the state

A second set of difficulties surrounds the treatment of the state under market socialism. It is one of the aspirations of market socialism to rid socialism of its pejorative association with the state. Of course, market socialists do not argue that, *left to itself*, the market will deliver the sort of society to which socialists aspire. Along with most neo-liberals and conventional economists, they acknowledge that there are significant areas of market failure and, as even many neo-liberals recognize, these market failures may create grounds for quite substantial 'corrective' intervention by the state. I have argued elsewhere that at least one form of contemporary market failure – the environmental externalities of untrammelled market growth – in fact justifies a quite extensive repoliticization of decisions which are now left to the market.[34] But as some of their neo-liberal critics have been quick to point out, market socialists see a role for the state and, indeed, for planning which goes well beyond this rectification of market failures. Nove, for example, concludes that under market socialism 'the role of the state will be very great, as owner, as planner, as enforcer of social and economic priorities'.[35]

It is quite wrong to see in this the 'old Adam' of the socialist, unable, despite declared intentions, to shuffle off his or her tutelage to the state. For the roots of this continuing commitment to the state lie much more in the theoretical indeterminacy of the market.[36] This is a very widespread problem and a commonplace of the feminist literature on the welfare state, which stresses the systematic incapacity of the market (and, indeed, of the state) to provide adequately for the most basic requirements of its constituent population.[37] As is quite clear in the writing of a number of market socialists, whether or not we judge the outcome of market transactions to be appropriate will depend on a number of other criteria in the context within which markets operate. Perhaps most important among these is the prior distribution of resources and opportunities. Markets will only operate in a way which is consonant with the ambitions of market socialism if these preconditions are significantly and repeatedly 'rigged'.

We can illustrate this problem by turning briefly to the perspective of a more traditional socialism. One of the central criticisms that traditional socialists have directed at the market is that its outcomes are inequitable. A part of the market socialist response is to insist that it is *capitalist* markets that are inequitable, not markets in themselves, and it is indeed the case that a part of the traditionalists' case would be met by the disappearance of private capital. But this would not entirely satisfy their claim. For there remain the arguments that, even without private capital, markets are insensitive to need and fail to reward merit.

Both of these issues are addressed by David Miller. On the first of these questions, Miller properly points out that there are very considerable difficulties in identifying what would count as 'basic human needs' (though it is surely clear that on a global scale basic human need does go unmet, while others satisfy their patently non-essential wants). He is also right to point out that creating a non-market institution which would allocate goods to satisfy these needs is itself extremely difficult. Yet this does not really meet the underlying intuitive core of the traditional socialist position. To put it in suitably lurid terms, the argument is that because the market responds to marketable assets (such as cash), rather than to needs, the millionaire may overwinter in the south of France, while the pensioner dies of hypothermia for want of the money to heat her flat.

Miller has an answer for this problem: under market socialism 'we must adopt a distributive policy which ensures that everyone has adequate resources to satisfy their needs, in advance of other resources being made available to meet non-basic desires'. This is not 'an argument for abandoning markets, but rather for framing the market in such a way that primary income is more equally distributed, with special supplements for those who are unable to earn an adequate income in the labour market . . . With market socialist institutions in place, people will be able to meet most of their needs through normal market purchases'. It will still be appropriate for certain needs, for example medical provision, to be met outside the marketplace.[38] This seems to me to be a substantial (and perfectly proper) 'concession' to the traditional socialist position. But it does put in doubt the distinctively 'market' quality of Miller's market socialism. Only the most enthusiastic proponents of the most centralized planning have ever called for non-market provision of what Miller calls 'mundane private goods – food, clothing, household items and so forth', and Miller's model might be thought to describe arrangements which look remarkably similar to existing (if radicalized) welfare states. While some welfare state provision is 'in kind' (notably in health and education), pensions and income maintenance provision, for example, redistribute cash to their beneficiaries to enable them to meet their needs through purchases in the market. What is an appropriate level for this redistribution, to what extent the needs of all are to be met in preference to satisfying the wants of existing asset-holders is a decision taken (more or less democratically) through the state. It is not a decision reached through the market. Miller insists that 'with market socialist institutions in place, people will be able to meet most of their needs through normal market purchases', but this rather begs the question of how socialists are *previously* to have attained a (re)distribution of income which is sufficiently equitable to allow of this happy outcome.[39] We must, I think, assume that any form of market society which is to be consistent with the aspirations of the market socialists will require a strong and interventionist state, indeed a state whose interventions would almost certainly be *more* extensive than those that we find in existing welfare states.

Given this, and in contrast to what has been written about the democratization of enterprises, it is not clear that market socialists have thought radically enough about the sorts of change in democratic arrangements that this requires *at the level of the state*. At times, the approach to democratic state reform is almost dismissively conservative. Thus, for Nove, 'a multiparty democracy, with periodic elections to a parliament' and a Schumpterian model of democracy as 'competition between elites' enters his account of 'feasible socialism' as a 'political assumption'.[40] Miller, by contrast, is quite radical in his aspiration that under market socialism the politics of *interest-aggregation* should increasingly yield to politics as *dialogue*.[41] But while he is properly reticent about proffering an institutional 'blueprint' for this dialogic politics, it remains unclear how even in the very broadest terms such a politics could be realized in a large-scale, pluralist society in which our interaction with most of our fellow citizens will still be through the competitive medium of the market. Of course, it may be something of an embarrassment to a strategy that promises to rid socialism of its association with the state to discover that its state institutions may need to be more extensive and more interventionist than those of classical social democracy. None the less, if, as seems inevitable, market socialism will require very extensive state intervention, it is clear that plans for the radical democratization of the state must be as important as plans to democratize individual economic enterprises.

Market socialism and internationalism

A third difficulty can be found in the market socialists' under-theorization of the *international* context of rivalrous nation-states and transnational markets, and their comparative neglect of the constitutional relationship between differing levels of democratic governance. Thus, little has been written about the international context of market socialist societies, about the relationship between national governments and the international order, the place of the nation-state under market socialism in both the realm of international supra-governmental institutions and, still more importantly, the international market. There is an irony here. The market socialist model is very much one for 'socialism in one nation-state'. Yet interest in market socialism was largely fuelled by the seeming impossibility of pursuing a national-based socialist or social democratic strategy (largely because of the disabling effect of international markets). It is precisely because incomes policies, full employment and a national consensus on citizenship (all of which we can find in the programmes of market socialists) were so difficult to sustain that socialists found themselves having 'to learn to love the market'. Similarly, little has been written about the potential clash between differing layers of democratic governance within a market socialist polity. Yet it is clear that there may well be clashes between a democratically elected government and democratically self-managed cooperatives and, as a number of commentators have recognized, this tension is likely to be most acute over the allocation of scarce capital. Since there is a suggestion that control over credit and capital allocation could be devolved from the immediate control of the government to quasi-independent banking organizations, the strains that may be placed upon the democratic structure should be clear.

A feasible socialism?

Finally, I come to the question of the *feasibility* of the market socialist model. One of the greatest claims of its advocates is that, if market socialism is perhaps less heroic than its traditional forerunners, it is at least 'a workable, feasible sort of socialism'.[42] It shares with social democracy an impatience with those more idealized visions of a future socialist society which, it argues, are incapable of realization. But market socialism can only be represented as a more 'feasible' socialist strategy where it is stripped of all its more radical connotations. Market socialism may appear to recommend itself to the 'practical' wing of social democracy, as a way of reversing the electoral consequences of a decline in the popularity of the traditional socialist agenda. But this can probably only be achieved by attaching the label 'market socialism' to what is more properly a 'social market economy' (in which vigorous capitalist economic growth is to be encouraged to permit some increment for the expansion of public services). But the proposal at the heart of the market socialist model we have considered here is the socialization of all but very small-scale capital. This is indeed a very radical intention. It is also quite essential to the defence of market socialism as a strategy for 'socialism with markets'. As we have seen, traditional socialist criticism of the market socialist project is repeatedly deflected by the insistence that its arguments are with capitalist markets, not 'markets under socialism'. However, if this more radical version of market socialism is to be defended, and this is essential to its defence as an *authentically* socialist model, it is not clear that it has the quality of enhanced feasibility that its advocates suggest. The crucial issue here is the question of transition. There is now a substantial classical and contemporary literature on the problems of a gradualist parliamentary democratic transition to socialism, culminating in the rather gloomy prognoses of Adam Przeworski.[43] It is difficult to see why market socialism should be any less vulnerable to these difficulties than other radical forms of social democracy. Indeed, in some senses, the prognoses for market socialism look *worse* than those that apply to other radical strategies, notably the model of the wage-earners' funds. However unsatisfactory has been the lived experience of 'wage-earners' fund' socialism, it does at least have a coherent account (on paper) of how a radical but *gradualist* strategy for socialization could be effected. Market socialism, by contrast, seems to require a fairly brief and wholesale transformation. This, interestingly, was Oskar Lange's view.[44] It seems also to be supported by Jon Elster's recent writings on the cooperative economy, which stress the difficulties of 'islands of co-operativism' in a greater capitalist sea.[45] It may be that the circumstances for a successful cooperative economy require that the great bulk of economic activity should be transferred into the cooperative sector within a comparatively short period. Under circumstances in which more traditional socialist strategies have had to be abandoned at least in part because of the difficulties of pursuing 'socialism in one national economy', it is difficult to see how the radical socialization which market socialists proffer is more readily realizable than, say, the very traditional policy of nationalizing the 'commanding heights' within an autarchic economy.

The contemporary advocacy of market socialism offers some very real theoretical gains in our thinking about the democratization of economic decision-taking. Its recognition of the (real but limited) strengths of markets, its desire to disentangle socialism from the bureaucratic state, its renewed interest in democracy *within* the workplace are all to be welcomed. However, it is (as yet) quite incomplete. Much more needs to be said about the (many) areas of market failure, about the ways in which the parameters for market exchanges are to be set and sustained, about the (equally important) democratization of the state and, finally, about how a model of market socialism can be married to political practice without suppressing everything that makes it radical and distinctive.

Conclusion: The Economic Limits of Democracy

Finally, what is the salience of our discussion of market socialism to the more general debate on the limitations of economic democracy? Certainly, it is testimony to the acute difficulties, both theoretical and practical, of defending a more traditional account of the socialist project. A belief in the omnicompetence of centralized planning, the unproblematic accountability of the sovereign state or the authenticity of a unitary socialist morality is increasingly difficult to sustain.[46] At the same time, and despite market socialism's own theoretical and practical limitations, it also shows that we are not obliged to accept the neo-liberal recommendation that 'actually existing liberal democracy' is the only viable form that democracy may take in large-scale and economically developed societies. The traditional socialist insistence that democracy is a principle that should be applied to economic life (as the area in which people's most fundamental interests are constituted) still seems to me to be compelling. Market socialists attempt to redeem this claim (while endorsing social plurality and checking the power of the state) by confining themselves to a largely '*micro*-economic' form of democracy, based upon democracy *within* individual enterprises. But as influential theorists such as Nove and Miller at least tacitly recognize, even this limited form of economic democracy is impossible without a powerful and interventionist state. As we have seen, objections to the democratic credentials of traditional forms of state intervention in both east and west (and, we might add, under both socialist and non-socialist regimes) are well founded. But 'circumventing the state' is not an option (as even practising neo-liberals have discovered over the last decade) and this should encourage us to give still greater attention to the ways in which states' action (at local, national and supra-national levels) can be made more democratically accountable. For all the difficulties that face *this* project, there is certainly no reason to believe that we have exhausted the constitutional and institutional reforms which might improve the democratic credentials of existing state formations. Overall, the conclusion we may draw is straightforward. There may indeed be some economic limits to democracy; but we are still very far from reaching them.

NOTES

1   See, for example, H. Arendt, *The Human Condition* (Chicago, University of Chicago Press, 1958); F. A. Hayek, *Law, Legislation and Liberty* (London, Routledge and Kegan Paul, 1982).
2   See C. Pierson, *Marxist Theory and Democratic Politics* (Berkeley, CA, University of California Press, 1987), pp. 7–83.
3   See M. Friedman, *Capitalism and Freedom* (Chicago, University of Chicago Press, 1962).
4   See C. Pierson, *Beyond the Welfare State?* (Cambridge, Polity Press, 1991), pp. 40–8 and 149–52.
5   See Pierson, *Beyond the Welfare State?*, pp. 45–7.
6   F. A. Hayek, *Law, Legislation and Liberty* (London, Routledge and Kegan Paul, 1982).
7   Hayek, *Law, Legislation and Liberty*, Vol. III, pp. 1–3.
8   Hayek, *Law, Legislation and Liberty*, Vol. II, p. 109.
9   Hayek, *Law, Legislation and Liberty*, Vol. I, p. 55.
10 Hayek, *Law, Legislation and Liberty*, Vol. II, p. 102.
11 Hayek, *Law, Legislation and Liberty*, Vol. III, p. 3.
12 Hayek, *Law, Legislation and Liberty*, Vol. I, p. 1.
13 Hayek, *Law, Legislation and Liberty*, Vol. II, p. 86.
14 Hayek, *Law, Legislation and Liberty*, Vol. III, pp. 105–27 and 151.
15 Hayek, *The Road to Serfdom* (London, Routledge and Kegan Paul, 1944), p. 52.
16 See M. Ellman, *Socialist Planning* (Cambridge, Cambridge University Press, 2nd edn, 1989). There is some suspicion that the Soviet celebration of the centrally planned command economy was, at least in part, an *ex post* rationalization of a system that developed for quite other reasons under Stalin.
17 See Ellman, *Socialist Planning*.
18 J. Habermas, 'The new obscurity: the crisis of the welfare state and the exhaustion of utopian energies', in J. Habermas (ed.), *The New Conservatism* (Cambridge, MA, MIT Press, 1989), pp. 48–70; J. Keane, *Democracy and Civil Society* (London, Verso, 1988).
19 See, for example, S. Lash and J. Urry, *The End of Organised Capitalism* (Cambridge, Polity Press, 1987); D. Harvey, *The Condition of Postmodernity* (Oxford, Blackwell, 1989).
20 Lash and Urry, *The End of Organised Capitalism*; Harvey, *The Condition of Postmodernity*; C. Offe, *Disorganized Capitalism* (Cambridge, Polity Press, 1985); C. Offe, 'Democracy against the welfare state?', *Political Theory*, 15:4 (1987), 501–37.
21 H. Radice, 'The national economy: a Keynesian myth?', *Capital and Class*, 22 (Spring 1984), 111–40; D. Held, 'Democracy, the nation-state and the global system', in D. Held (ed.), *Political Theory Today* (Cambridge, Polity Press, 1991), pp. 197–235. Not everyone accepts that the capacities of national government have been so transformed by changes in the global economic order: see, for example, D. Gordon, 'The global economy: new edifice or crumbling foundations?', *New Left Review*, 168 (1988), 24–64.
22 E. Mandel, 'In defence of socialist planning', *New Left Review*, 159 (1986), 5–37; A. Callinicos, *The Revenge of History* (Cambridge, Polity Press, 1991).

23 R. Meidner, *Employee Investment Funds* (London, Allen and Unwin, 1978); G. Esping-Andersen, *Politics Against Markets* (Princeton, NJ, Princeton University Press, 1985).

24 D. Miller, *Market, State and Community: theoretical foundations of market socialism* (Oxford, Clarendon Press, 1989), p. 10.

25 See O. Lange, 'On the economic theory of socialism', in O. Lange and F. M. Taylor (eds), *On the Economic Theory of Socialism* (Minnesota, University of Minnesota Press, 1938).

26 Although the discussion here focuses primarily upon West European formulations of market socialism, it is worth noting that the same concern with both economic efficiency *and* economic (and political) democratization is also to be found in the more recent advocacy of market socialism in Eastern Europe. For a review of the Eastern European experience, see J. Kornai, *Vision and Reality, Market and State: contradictions and dilemmas revisited* (London, Harvester Wheatsheaf, 1990).

27 Z. W. Xian, 'On the socialist market system and its model', *International Journal of Social Economics*, 16:2 (1989), 54–8; A. Nove, *The Economics of Feasible Socialism* (London, Allen and Unwin, 1983); L. G. Stauber, *A New Program for Democratic Socialism: lessons from the market-planning experience of Austria* (Carbondale, IL, Four Willows, 1987); D. J. Gayle, 'Singaporean market socialism: some implications for development theory', *International Journal of Social Economics*, 15:7 (1989), 53–75.

28 Nove, *Feasible Socialism*, pp. 227–8.

29 See, for example, J. H. Carens, *Equality, Moral Incentives and the Market: an essay in utopian politico-economic theory* (London, Chicago University Press, 1981); S. Estrin and J. Le Grand, 'Market socialism', in S. Estrin and J. Le Grand (eds), *Market Socialism* (Oxford, Clarendon Press, 1990), pp. 1–24; Miller, *Market, State and Community*; J. A. Yunker, 'A new perspective on market socialism', *Comparative Economic Studies*, 30:2 (1988) 69–116; J. A. Yunker, 'Ludwig von Mises on the "artificial market"', *Comparative Economic Studies*, 32:1 (1988), 108–40; Stauber, *A New Program for Democratic Socialism*.

30 See, for example, C. Lindblom, *Politics and Markets* (New York, Basic Books, 1977), pp. 172–84; R. Dahl, *A Preface to Economic Democracy* (Berkeley, CA, University of California Press, 1985), p. 111.

31 Mandel, 'Socialist planning'; M. Dobb, *On Economic Theory and Socialism: collected papers* (London, Routledge and Kegan Paul, 1955).

32 Miller, *Market, State and Community*, p. 207.

33 Miller, *Market, State and Community*, pp. 220–3.

34 Pierson, *Beyond the Welfare State?*, pp. 193–4 and 217–18; see also F. Hirsch, *Social Limits to Growth* (London, Routledge and Kegan Paul, 1977).

35 Nove, *Feasible Socialism*, p. 229; A. De Jasay, *Market Socialism: a scrutiny* (London, Institute for Economic Affairs, 1990); A. Schuller, *Does Market Socialism Work?* (London, The Centre for Research Into Communist Economies, 1988).

36 See A. Sen, 'The moral standing of the market', *Social Philosophy and Policy*, 2:2 (1985), p. 19.

37 Pierson, *Beyond the Welfare State?*, pp. 69–79.

38 Miller, *Market, State and Community*, pp. 148–9.

39 Miller, *Market, State and Community*, p. 128.

40 Nove, *Feasible Socialism*, pp. 197–8.

41 Miller, *Market, State and Community*, pp. 252–75; see also Miller's chapter in this volume.

42 Nove, *Feasible Socialism*, p. ix.
43 A. Przeworski, *Capitalism and Social Democracy* (Cambridge, Cambridge University Press, 1985).
44 Lange, 'On the economic theory of socialism', pp. 124–5.
45 J. Elster, 'From here to there: or, if cooperative ownership is so desirable, why are there so few cooperatives?', *Social Philosophy and Policy*, 62:2 (1988), 93–111.
46 For an interesting attempt to defend the latter, see M. Luntley, *The Meaning of Socialism* (London, Duckworth, 1989).

9

SOCIALISM AND DEMOCRACY

Alex Callinicos

As the twentieth century draws to a close, the prosperous liberal democracies preside triumphant over the world. Not only has the coalition of states which opposed them collapsed, but its claim to represent a rival and superior social system is thoroughly discredited. In a third world which now seems likely to be swelled by the successor states of the former Soviet Union and its clients, neo-liberal economic remedies have become the norm: under the slogan of 'structural adjustment' governments are persuaded to dismantle their public sectors, abolish consumer subsidies, and integrate their economies into the world market. Some of the casualties of such measures then join the throng of 'economic migrants' seeking a share of the advanced countries' success. The few who penetrate the ever more elaborate barriers designed to deny them access to the wealthy north discover strange societies. Perhaps in a historical perspective the most striking peculiarity of the advanced capitalist societies is their privatization: individuals are encouraged to make the focus of their lives the discovery of meaning in and the surrounding with material comforts of certain very narrowly defined personal relationships. Zygmunt Bauman has highlighted the importance of 'seduction' – the development of ever-growing dependency on needs which can only be fulfilled through the market – as 'the paramount tool of integration ... in a consumer society'; indeed, he argues that 'seduction', and its indispensable accompaniment repression, 'make "legitimation" redundant'.[1] Certainly politics in the privatized societies of late capitalism is symptomatic of a shrivelled public sphere: electoral competition increasingly follows the American model, as a premium is placed on the relative capacities of media manipulation possessed by parties differing little in programme or principle. It is hardly surprising that, with the organized left traumatized by the revival of *laissez-faire* and the collapse of 'existing socialism', the pain that lies beneath the surface of these apparently pacified liberal democracies should find expression in a revival of the extreme right.

The global triumph of liberal democracy must thus be set alongside its inner discontents. One response to the latter is to seek to remedy them from within a framework consistent with the basic presuppositions of liberal democracy, perhaps the most important of which is the separation of state and civil society, and therefore the exclusion from the domain of matters governed by the sovereign electorate of most decisions about the production and distribution of goods and services. Another, however, is to seek to devise a form of democracy which does not respect this separation. Such is the course pursued by classical Marxism. Its objective, as defined in such texts as Marx's *The Civil War in France* and Lenin's *The State and Revolution*, is at once the overthrow of the capitalist mode of production and an *extension* of democracy. This proposal is, of course, now very widely discredited. Nevertheless, I defend it in what follows. My reasons for doing so will, I hope, become clear.

I wish, however, to draw what is perhaps an artificial distinction among the causes of Marxism's general discredit. It is, above all, the fate of the Russian Revolution which has encouraged the conclusion that (as Leszek Kolakowski put it) socialist democracy is like 'fried snowballs', a contradiction in terms. Now I have argued that the Stalinist system – the social domination of the *Nomenklatura* – as it took shape at the turn of the 1920s represented not the realization of the Marxist project, or even a necessary consequence of the methods used by the Bolsheviks to gain and retain power, but a counter-revolution, the suppression of the democratic potential contained in the revolutions of 1917 and the installation not of socialism, but of a particular variant of capitalism, bureaucratic state capitalism. There is, consequently, a profound historical and political *discontinuity* between classical Marxism, defended in the Stalin era by Trotsky and his followers, and (no longer) 'existing socialism'.[2] Rather than rehearse this argument, which necessarily turns on questions of historical interpretation of the October Revolution and its aftermath, once again, I wish here to concentrate on the theoretical case for and against a distinctively socialist form of democracy.

One way into these arguments is to consider some recent remarks by a writer generally regarded as one of the chief contemporary defenders of Marxism, G. A. Cohen. Cohen lists 'the four principal criticisms of the market in the socialist tradition', namely that it is '(1) inefficient, (2) anarchic, (3) unjust in its results, and (4) mean in its motivational presuppositions'. Cohen considers the first two criticisms 'misplaced'. (1) accuses the market of allocative inefficiency on the grounds of the waste caused by its unplanned character. But, Cohen argues, Mises and Hayek were right to claim that the market organizes information better than any central planner could, and it has 'prove[d] possible to correct for market deficiencies through external regulation which falls far short of comprehensive planning'. (2) finds another reason for condemning the unplanned nature of the market, namely that it 'means that society is not in control of its own destiny'. 'Individual self-direction,' Cohen objects, 'a person's determining the course of his own life, may have value per se, but collective self-determination does not.' (3) and (4) stand, however, as criticisms of the market. '[T]he market distributes in unjustly unequal amounts', and '[t]he immediate motive to productive activity in a market society is usually some mixture of greed and fear'. Therefore, although market socialism 'preserves the income injustice caused by differential ownership of endowments of personal capacity', it is to be preferred, *faute de mieux*, to existing capitalism since it at least addresses the defects identified by (3) and (4).[3]

Cohen is, I believe, wrong to abandon two of the classic socialist criticisms of capitalism; exploring why this is the case may help clarify the reasons for continuing to seek a democratic alternative to liberal democracy. For it should be clear that it is a pretty liberal kind of socialism which Cohen now advocates. Socialism seems primarily a matter of adjusting market transactions to eliminate unjust outcomes and alter motivations: thus he seems to look to tax reforms as the chief way of realizing the principle of justice ('From each according to his ability, to each according to his needs') which Marx proposed should govern the higher stage of communism.[4] It seems to me that this preoccupation with distributional and motivational considerations leads Cohen to under-estimate the force of criticisms (1) and (2), which represent Marx's deepest and most distinctive objections to capitalism. The question of allocative efficiency cannot be adequately addressed without confronting the issue of socialist planning, which I touch on below. It is still worth saying at this stage that those attracted to some variant of market socialism tend greatly to overestimate the extent to which 'existing capitalism' has overcome what Cohen calls its 'deficiencies'. It is not simply a matter of the plight of that large majority of humankind for whom the market still offers very little, or even of the persisting and indeed recently growing inequalities of wealth and income in the advanced economies (which it has too often been left to conservative commentators such as Kevin Phillips to highlight).[5] More fundamentally, the tendency to relatively regular, protracted and profound economic crises, which Marx held to be an intrinsic feature of the capitalist mode of production, shows no real sign of abating. The world economy has experienced three major recessions in the past twenty years – those of 1974–5 and 1979–82, and the one which began in 1990 and as I write continues. In the same period, as the widespread disarray of social democracy indicates, the ability of states to control the business cycle by 'external regulation' has been seriously undermined, fundamentally by the internationalization of capital. Marx's contention that economic crises were symptoms of the structural limits of the capitalist mode of production, not the contingent consequences of faulty policies or institutions, has yet to be refuted.[6]

The question of collective autonomy takes us closer to the issue of democracy itself. Cohen accepts that 'social decision-making' is sometimes justified, but 'for instrumental reasons, such as, sometimes, to promote individual freedom'.[7] I take it that Cohen is not here identifying individual freedom with negative liberty, the absence of external constraint, but is rather arguing that individual self-determination has primacy over collective self-determination. One issue here is whether individual and collective autonomy may be more closely related than this way of putting it suggests. It might be that my ability to plan my own life is bound up with capacities whose development is contingent on my participation in collective decision-making as a citizen. This seems to be a strand of thought present in Rousseau's writings and the classical republican tradition more generally. A second consideration is that the reasons we have for valuing collective autonomy instrumentally give it greater importance than Cohen's presentation would suggest. The already disastrous, potentially catastrophic consequences of the uncontrolled competition of states and firms on the natural environment draw attention to a respect in which humankind gaining collective control over their world is a matter of some urgency. We should prize collective autonomy if only on instrumental grounds. But, thirdly, unless we recognize that it is also an intrinsic good we cannot make sense of important aspects of human experience. The most obvious case is the transformation undergone by individuals through their participation in popular revolutions. Both historical record and observation (albeit largely mediated by the ability modern communications have given us to witness great events) suggest that at the height of mass upheavals those taking part are filled with a sense of achieving collective control over their own lives. This feeling of shared destiny and power was strongly conveyed by the East European revolutions of 1989 – an impression made no less moving by the fact that this brief euphoric moment of self-determination was preceded and followed by mass apathy, induced in one case by a

Stalinist police state, in the other by the discovery of the market's reality at first hand. However fleeting such episodes, they suggest that political participation may be valued not just for the other goods to which it is a means, but for itself.

Now one of the chief claims sometimes made for socialist democracy is precisely that it realizes this good of collective self-determination more fully than liberal democracy can.[8] It does so by abolishing the separation of economy and polity characteristic of market capitalism. The principle of democratic self-government is thus extended to economic life; correlatively, politics is brought down to earth by being systematically related to the problems of everyday life, and is thus infused with a direct relevance to citizens' practical concerns very different from the electoral facade concealing the higgling of bureaucracies and interest groups which represents the real conduct of affairs in liberal democracy. This fusion of economics and politics takes, in the classical Marxist tradition, the institutional form of a producers' democracy, a hierarchy of workers' councils ascending from the individual workplace to national (and indeed international) congresses of delegates. Unlike the case in the Stalinist command economy, where the *Nomenklatura* formed the apex of power, decisions in this system flow initially upwards, as delegates are selected (subject to immediate recall) to the higher levels of representation, from which a reciprocal flow of decisions percolates down.

There are, of course, many objections which can, and have been directed at this conception of socialist democracy.[9] I concentrate here on arguments denying that it is *feasible*. My reason for doing so is that such arguments often form the background of other criticisms – for example, those directed at socialist democracy's *desirability*. For example, one might argue that socialist democracy threatens individual freedoms, not so much because it abolishes the separation of state and civil society, but because, as a system of decision-making it is intrinsically liable to break down; attempts to correct for its dysfunctions will tend to produce a concentration of power which, in the absence of the defence mechanisms provided by an autonomous civil society, will soon produce a full-blooded totalitarianism.[10] Much, then, turns on whether or not socialist democracy is practicable as a system for managing complex and increasingly globally interconnected industrial societies.

Let us first consider the economic feasibility of socialist democracy – an issue put top of the agenda first by the impact of Alec Nove's polemic *The Economics of Feasible Socialism* (1983) and then by what Mikhail Gorbachev used to call 'life itself'. Nove's arguments represented a particularly powerful restatement, illustrated with a wealth of detail provided by the bureaucratic command economies of what was still then the Eastern bloc, of the classic liberal claim, developed particularly by Mises and Hayek, that a market economy is inherently superior at handling information to any form of planning.[11] It is in this context that the idea of market socialism – that is, of combining the market's allocative efficiency with forms of distribution more in accord with socialist conceptions of justice – has attracted some attention. Two recent versions – Roberto Unger's 'empowered democracy' and David Miller's 'pure model of market socialism' – outline fairly similar sets of institutional arrangements: workers' cooperatives (Unger calls them 'teams of workers, technicians, and entrepreneurs') produce for the market on a competitive basis, while capital is allocated from a publicly owned fund by a plurality of investment agencies.[12]

Now the question is whether market socialism of this kind can remedy the defects identified by the traditional socialist critique of capitalism. Cohen provides reasons for thinking that it offers no answer to criticisms (3) (injustice) and (4) (appeal to greed and fear).[13] What about criticisms (1) and (2), which I believe should not be as readily abandoned as Cohen proposes? Notice that these criticisms are closely connected. (1) condemns capitalism for its anarchy: the economy, constituted as it is by competing capitals, prevents people from exercising collective control over their lives. But competition is also central to the charge of inefficiency: it is the competitive accumulation of capital which, Marx believes, underlies the tendency of the rate of profit to fall that is chiefly responsible for capitalism's chronic liability to economic crisis.[14] There seems to be no reason to believe that market socialism as outlined by Unger and Miller would avoid either of these ills. Inasmuch as the workers' cooperatives compete with one another, the producers respond to social forces outside their control. Why should not one outcome of this competition be generalized market failure of the kind that has once again become a familiar feature of economic life since the early 1970s? Neither Unger nor Miller directly addresses this question, though the former implicitly concedes the possibility of involuntary unemployment:

> The individual worker does not even have an absolute or permanent right to job tenure within his enterprise or team, and the enterprise or team has no absolute or permanent right to the resources temporarily put at its disposal or to the wealth it accumulates through their use. But every citizen does have an unconditional right to the satisfaction of his legally defined minimal welfare needs.[15]

Unger and Miller seem to think that market socialism will continue to require what the latter calls 'politically determined intervention in the

market', certainly to meet 'minimal welfare needs',[16] probably to control
the business cycle which unregulated competition would otherwise
generate. The difficulty which they must then confront is the apparent
impasse which policies designed politically to control market economies
have faced since the onset of stagflation in the second half of the 1960s;
this is one of the two practical experiences – the other is the failure of
attempts to marry market mechanisms to Stalinist command economies
in Yugoslavia and Hungary – which have led some former market
socialists to opt for the market *tout court*.[17] Market socialism thus seems
to be an ineffectual attempt to avoid the real choice, namely that between
sticking with full-blooded market capitalism and replacing the market
with an economy controlled by what Marx called the 'associated
producers'.

It is, of course, incumbent on those advocating the latter alternative to
offer a plausible account of how a planned economy could be devised
which would avoid both the political evils (absence of even the most
elementary forms of democracy, structural inequalities) and the
economic dysfunctions (information overload, overaccumulation, built-in
scarcities) endemic in the now disintegrating command economies of the
east. Pat Devine makes an interesting attempt to give such an account in
Democracy and Economic Planning (1988). His model of 'negotiated coordination' is intended as a response to what Devine calls 'Nove's
challenge ... : "There are horizontal links (market), there are vertical
links (hierarchy). What other dimension is there?"' Devine answers:
'There is no other dimension – but vertical links do not have to be
hierarchical, in any authoritarian sense, and horizontal links do not have
to be market-based, in the sense of being co-ordinated *ex post* by the
invisible hand of market forces. Both can be based on negotiated coordination.'[18] Devine conceives of negotiated co-ordination as the form of
planning appropriate to what he calls a 'self-governing society'; that is, a
society acting 'on the principle that decisions and their implementation
are the responsibility of and should be undertaken by those affected by
them'. Realization of this principle requires both the supplementation of
representative with direct democracy and the abolition not of 'the
functional division of labour between people who are experts in different
things' but of 'the social division of labour between experts and non-
experts'. Changes of this nature would not, however, lead to the
emergence of a conception of the social good so unitary as to render
decisions over the allocation of resources uncontroversial. Devine thus
rejects the view often (mistakenly in my opinion) attributed to the
classical Marxist tradition that abolition of capitalism will lead to an 'end
of politics' in the sense of contested decision-making; a multi-party

system, accompanied by a wealth of other forms of voluntary association, is thus a necessary feature of a self-governing society.[19]

Political and social changes in a broadly democratic and egalitarian direction underpin the introduction of an economic model 'in which the necessary information for effective centralized and decentralized decision-making in the social interest is generated without recourse to market forces'. Self-managing production units would operate within parameters laid down by a system of planning – that is, a system of *ex ante* economic coordination. Broadly speaking, three levels of decision-making would exist. At the national level, '[b]road social priorities and changes in strategic direction' would be determined by the representative assembly, choosing between plan variants drawn up by a national planning commission. Changes in production capacity within the framework established by the national plan would be decided by negotiated coordination bodies for particular industries: represented on each such body would be 'those who work in the production units concerned, and in interdependent production units, those who live in the communities affected, customers, and usually also the concerns of some interest and cause groups'. Finally, the use of existing capacity would be up to the individual production units (on whose governing bodies would be represented not only the producers themselves but also relevant outside interests); in particular, the production units would set the prices of goods and services, whose distribution would be effected by market exchange. This would not, Devine insists, 'imply the operation of market forces, in which production and investment decisions are made atomistically *ex post*'.[20]

It is the idea that a wide range of economic decisions should be left to horizontal but non-market oriented negotiations between affected producers and consumers that is the most distinctive feature of Devine's version of economic planning. He argues that

> the model of negotiated co-ordinations differs from co-ordination by centralized command in that decisions about investment within a branch of production are decentralized to the negotiated co-ordination body for that branch, which involves all the production units for that branch and is able to make full use of all available information. It differs from co-ordination by market forces in that all investment decisions with a branch of production are co-ordinated *ex ante*, on the basis of all the available information, not *ex post*, through attempts to correct wrong decisions that were made on the basis of only part of the available information. It differs from both the other models in that the people affected by investment decisions are the people who make the decisions, consciously, in the light of an awareness of their mutual interdependence.[21]

This is not the place for a detailed discussion of the strengths and weaknesses of Devine's attempt to rehabilitate the idea of a planned economy.

To my mind one of its main difficulties is less economic than political. Devine envisages the forms of economic democracy he proposes as being simply tacked on to existing parliamentary institutions: thus he proposes, in Britain, the replacement of the House of Lords with a 'House of Interests'. Little thought is given to the incoherences likely to be caused by the coexistence, not so much of direct and representative democracy, but of two forms of representative democracy, one based on geographical constituencies, the other on self-governing production units. This blind spot is perhaps related to Devine's association with Eurocommunism, now largely defunct in Britain but in the 1980s associated with *Marxism Today*, which in many ways represented a return, in Gramscian garb, to the old social-democratic tradition. There is perhaps a contradiction between the radical imagination Devine shows about the possibilities of economic transformation and the timid political strategy in which he seeks to contain it.[22]

Robin Blackburn raises a more strictly economic objection to Devine's model: 'While the multimillion-product complexity of a modern economy can be monitored, requiring it to be positively "negotiated" is asking a very great deal.'[23] Blackburn's thought seems to be that the scale of the task required of the negotiated coordination would overload the system, perhaps generating its own distinctive irrationalities. Devine addresses a related objection, namely that so much time would be taken up in negotiated co-ordination as to impose serious economic costs on any society seeking to apply such a model. Devine points out that '[i]n modern societies, a large and possibly increasing proportion of overall social time is already spent on administration, on negotiation, on organizing and running systems', both for quasi-technical reasons (for example, 'the growing complexity of economic and social life') and for reasons reflecting the nature of 'existing societies' – 'commercial rivalry and the management of the social conflict and consequences of alienation that stem from exploitation, oppression, inequality, and subalternity'. Devine contends that 'there is no *a priori* reason to suppose that the aggregate time devoted to running a self-governing society based on negotiated co-ordination would be any greater than the time devoted to the administration of people and things in existing society. However, aggregate time would be differently composed, differently focused and, of course, differently distributed among people.'[24]

Devine's point can be generalized into an important defence of socialist democracy. Blackburn's objection is in fact a particular version of a more general criticism of socialist democracy, namely that it involves a hopelessly cumbersome system of decision-making (I remember a well-known playwright saying that his doubts about Marxism began when he tried to envisage workers' councils running the whole of Europe). It is now more or less a cliché that one of the most salient features of our times is the growth of what David Held calls 'global interconnectedness' – the development especially of transnational economic relationships which have significantly undermined the power of nation-states and encouraged the devising of various forms of *ad hoc* international coordination (for example, those which have evolved around the meetings of the Group of Seven top industrial powers). These changes, Held rightly suggests, represent a 'challenge to the idea and coherence of democracy': even the limited degree to which citizens have control over political decisions in the liberal democracies is compromised by the emergence of centres of power transcending national boundaries.[25]

The problem has several dimensions. The existing forms of international coordination are, in general, not subject to any form of democratic accountability. Most involve either market transactions between autonomous capitals or the kind of essentially bureaucratic procedures through which decisions are taken inside multinational corporations. Even where liberal democracies have sought to cooperate, notably in the G7, matters follow the norms of traditional diplomacy, which are notoriously unamenable to any form of parliamentary control; and even if this were not the case, the vast majority of the planet's population would be unrepresented at these meetings. The effectiveness of such forms of political cooperation is in any case open to question, given the growing intensity of conflicts of interest between the major western powers which has proved such a marked feature of the new epoch opened by the 1989 revolutions. However, it is not just that existing forms of international coordination are unaccountable and often inefficient, but that their scope is much too limited. This is in part a consequence of the continued vitality of the system of nation-states: the power of individual states (even the greatest) may have declined, but national rivalries show no sign of abating, and indeed are if anything likely to intensify as a result of the disintegration of the Soviet Union and its empire. At the same time, international economic life is largely unregulated, and trends emerge from the atomistic decisions of competing capitals, with disastrous consequences – the cycle of boom and slump, the depletion of the ozone layer, the vast inequality in the distribution of resources between north and south.

What is to be done? Held proposes the gradual democratization of international life, based on what he calls the 'federal model of democratic autonomy'. Even conceived as a primarily political process this is a mammoth task, as is shown by the efforts at European union, which have thus far resulted in a set of Heath Robinson structures largely outside any form of direct democratic control. Held is aware that this process of democratization must embrace global 'civil society', but is very vague about what this might involve, talking about 'a civil society that is neither simply planned nor merely market-orientated, but, rather, that is open to organizations, associations, and agencies pursuing their own projects, subject to the constraints of a common structure of action and democratic processes'.[26] Here the merits of the kind of socialist planning envisaged by Devine stand out by comparison. Devine seeks to build the coordination of decision-making by producers and those affected by these decisions into the very structure of economic life. One of the most obvious advantages of such a model is the requirement it imposes that consideration of the broader consequences of particular investment choices be an inherent part of the procedures through which these choices are made. A market-based form of decision-making of course treats such consequences as externalities not directly relevant to the expectations of profitability on which investment decisions are based. Proposals somehow to integrate say, environmental considerations into the pricing process implicitly concede the point made by socialist critics, namely that, left to its own devices, the market generates globally irrational outcomes.

So, just as Devine suggests that the complexity of modern societies forces us to devote an increasing proportion of time to coordination tasks, so one might argue that the development of global inter-connectedness leaves us with no choice other than that between different forms of coordination. Do we settle for the existing forms of international cooperation, limited, inefficient and undemocratic as they are, or seek to replace them with forms based on the extension of democratic control, not merely to the evolving global polity, but to the economic sphere as well? It is not clear to me that the claim that decision-making under socialist democracy would be in certain respects slower and more cumbersome than that involved in market-based transactions, even if true, is necessarily a decisive objection. For is speed necessarily a virtue? Is the ability to move billions of dollars across the world in micro-seconds, thanks to technological innovation and the globalization of financial markets, really conducive to rational economic decision-making, on any but the most narrowly profit-orientated definition of rationality? To say this is not to advocate the Luddite rejection of advanced communications technology: on the contrary, such technology could, in different circumstances, promote democratic discussion and control. The trouble is with the social relations making for an intensification of global competition, with potentially appalling consequences.

The point of these arguments is to urge that it is worth persisting with the idea of socialist democracy. It does not follow that any particular formulation of this idea – for example, Devine's model of negotiated coordination – is likely to be wholly satisfactory. But continued discussion of socialist democracy, attempts theoretically to elaborate it and practically to realize it – all this seems to me an even more urgent task than it was before what one might call the double revolutions of 1989 and 1991. I have criticized Roberto Unger's version of market socialism above, but I completely endorse his observation, written 'before the revolution', that 'the stigma and shame of our time' is 'a sense of social life combining an awareness that nothing has to be the way it is with a conviction that nothing can be changed by deliberate collective action'.[27] These attitudes, which evidently inform the postmodernist craze, have been reinforced by what was for many the final disillusionment caused by the fall of 'existing socialism'. It is strange that 1989/91, so dramatic a demonstration that 'nothing has to be the way it is', should have instead reinforced a restriction of the political imagination to the confines imposed by the market. To me it seems rather to be a time to think big.

NOTES

1   Z. Baumann, 'Is there a postmodern sociology?', *Theory, Culture and Society*, 5:2–3 (1988), 217–37, pp. 221–2.
2   A. Callinicos, *The Revenge of History* (Cambridge, Polity Press, 1991).
3   G. A. Cohen, 'The future of a disillusion', *New Left Review*, 190 (1991), 5–20, pp. 16–18.
4   Cohen, 'Future', pp. 18–19.
5   K. Phillips, *The Politics of Rich and Poor* (New York, HarperCollins, 1991).
6   See especially C. Harman, *Explaining the Crisis* (London, Bookmarks, 1984).
7   Cohen, 'Future', p. 18.
8   C. B. Macpherson, *Democratic Theory* (Oxford, Oxford University Press, 1973).
9   Among the most important which I do not consider here in any detail is the charge of 'productivism' – namely, that, by making the workplace the primary unit of representation, socialist democracy disenfranchises those groups relatively excluded from work: women are often cited as the main case of such a group. A response to this objection could be made at two levels: (1) its proponents ignore the very pronounced tendency toward the incorporation of the bulk of the adult population in both the advanced economies and the industrializing portions of the third world into wage-labour, of which the growing involvement of women in formal employment is perhaps the most striking example (these issues are discussed at some length in A. Callinicos and C. Harman, *The Changing Working Class* [London, Bookmarks, 1987], and L. German, *Sex, Class and Socialism* [London, Bookmarks, 1990]); (2) adjustments could be made in the system of workplace representation to incorporate those disadvantaged by it without compromising this system's chief virtue, namely, the connection it establishes between democratic decision-making and people's everyday lives.

10 Elements of such an argument are advanced by, for example, Tim Wolforth: see, for example, Wolforth, 'Transition to the transition', *New Left Review*, 130 (1981), 67–81, and Wolforth, 'In the grip of Leninism', *Against the Current*, 36 (1992), 41–5.
11 See especially F. A. von Hayek (ed.), *Collectivist Economic Planning* (London, Macmillan, 1935).
12 R. M. Unger, *False Necessity* (Cambridge, Cambridge University Press, 1987), for example, pp. 225–6, and D. Miller, *Market, State, and Community* (Oxford, Clarendon Press, 1989): the 'pure model' is outlined on p. 10, while the requirement of 'a plurality of investment agencies' is introduced on p. 310.
13 Cohen, 'Future', pp. 14–19.
14 K. Marx, *Capital*, Vol. III (Moscow, Progress, 1971), part III. For recent restatements of Marx's theory of crises which provide rebuttals of the standard criticisms directed against it, see Harman, *Explaining*, ch. 1, and J. Weeks, *Capital and Exploitation* (Princeton, NJ, Princeton University Press, 1981), ch. VIII.
15 Unger, *False Necessity*, p. 498.
16 See Miller, *Market*, pp. 95 ff.
17 See, for example, W. Brus and K. Laski, *From Marx to the Market* (Oxford, Clarendon Press, 1989).
18 P. Devine, *Democracy and Economic Planning* (Cambridge, Polity Press, 1988), pp. 109–10.
19 Devine, *Democracy*, pp. 141, 180, 210 and 153. See also Callinicos, *Revenge*, pp. 115–16 and 127–31.
20 Devine, *Democracy*, pp. 190–1 and 236. See also pp. 22–3 on the distinction between market forces and market exchange.
21 Devine, *Democracy*, pp. 237–8.
22 Devine, *Democracy*, pp. 148–9, and, generally on political strategy, ch. 11. See my critique of British Eurocommunism in 'The politics of *Marxism Today*', *International Socialism*, 29 (1985), 128–68.
23 R. Blackburn, '*Fin de siècle*: socialism after the crash', *New Left Review*, 185 (1991), 5–66, p. 48, n. 72.
24 Devine, *Democracy*, pp. 265–6.
25 D. Held, 'Democracy, the nation state and the global system', in D. Held (ed.), *Political Theory Today* (Cambridge, Polity Press, 1991), pp. 197–235, p. 225. See also Held's chapter in this volume.
26 Held, 'Democracy', p. 234.
27 R. M. Unger, *Social Theory* (Cambridge, Cambridge University Press, 1987), p. 2.

10

MILITARY POLICIES AND THE STATE SYSTEM AS IMPEDIMENTS TO DEMOCRACY

Robert C. Johansen

The universal acclaim that democracy enjoys at this historical moment does not mean that all is well for democracies. Even where democratic systems enjoy a long tradition, they now struggle, often with only limited success, to deliver basic services such as national security which people expect their governments to provide. Indeed, providing these services constitutes the reason for which governments exist. Yet evidence mounts that the growth of complexity in decision-making, the increase in governmental disdain for public participation in national security decisions, and the rise of societal interdependency and interpenetration are draining the democratic content from even well-established national democratic institutions. This challenge to democratic *content* occurs even though the political *forms* within countries like the UK or the US remain similar to those that, in an earlier era, produced political outcomes that could properly wear the label 'democratic'.

Contemporary challenges to democracy even in well-established democratic societies are perhaps most pronounced in the military sphere. Despite the era of good feeling that follows the end of the Cold War, current military policies impose severe limits on democracy. They will not be eliminated without radical changes in the state system. After careful examination of US political processes, one of the foremost students of democratic systems, Robert Dahl, has concluded: 'no

I thank David Held and Debra DeLaet for helpful comments on the preparation of this paper. I also thank the Kroc Institute for International Peace Studies at the University of Notre Dame and its supportive Director, John J. Gilligan, and the John D. and Catherine T. MacArthur Foundation, for their support of the research and writing of this chapter.

decisions can be more fateful for Americans, and for the world, than decisions about nuclear weapons. Yet these decisions have largely escaped the control of the democratic process.'[1]

The growing challenges to democracy and the liberal democratic state have arisen without fanfare, indeed without most people being aware of the fateful process underway. This analysis seeks to redress the lack of awareness by examining the ways in which military policies encroach upon democratic processes and values. The discussion focuses primarily on the US, but the findings are applicable to other democracies as well, especially to those that also emphasize military power in their security policies. Democracies without nuclear weapons may not face the extreme violations of democratic values demonstrated in the US, but the fundamental national security problems posed by nuclear weapons exist in less extreme form in non-nuclear security policies as well. Moreover, even weak states which are not enamoured by military power find it increasingly difficult, if not simply impossible, within the traditional nation-state system to provide both security and democratic control over security policies for their citizens. These problems are a result of living in an age of technologically advanced military instruments, ecological fragility and economic interdependence. They are not a product of unique US, British, French, Indian, Japanese or other experience.

These problems are rooted in an increasingly dysfunctional connection between national military power and liberal democratic societies. A cluster of assumptions about the nature of international relations and an associated set of military values commonly underlie contemporary military policies and impose limits on the practice of democracy. To be sure, different supporters of a particular military policy may hold a variety of rationales for the policy. None the less, this variety exists within an underpinning cluster of assumptions that can be described as a 'military mind' which informs most thinking about the 'requirements' of security policy. Civilians who consider themselves democratic may display the military mind as much as or more than professional military people. The relevant qualities are summarized below, with a recognition that the extent to which one subscribes to them may vary from person to person.

Military Mentality as a Threat to Democracy

The military mind emphasizes the weakness and selfishness of the individual. Compensation for these individual failings is found in organization, leadership and discipline, and in the subordination of the individual to the group.[2] Within the military mind Samuel Huntington reports a tendency to believe that the '"weak, mediocre, transient individual" can only achieve emotional satisfaction and moral fulfillment by participating in "the power, the greatness, the permanence, and the splendor" of a continuing organic body'. Indeed, the military ethic is 'basically corporative in spirit. It is fundamentally anti-individualistic.'[3]

At this fundamental point of origin, conflicts arise between military and democratic values. Military organizations emphasize group conformity and discipline; democratic organizations value non-conformity and people who think for themselves. The military world-view, in a dogmatic form, celebrates the loyalty of a citizen to 'my country right or wrong'. In practice this dogma has been accepted unreflectively by many liberal democrats as one of the limits military necessity imposes on the practice of democracy. In contrast, a more sensitive democrat makes support for his or her government always somewhat tentative and conditioned upon governmental respect for life, because democratic thinking at its best extols respect for all people and the belief that life is sacred, or at least highly valued. A military mentality assumes that any war declared by a competent authority is justifiable; more sensitive democrats, most of whom are not pacifists but who do subscribe to just war thinking, acknowledge that many wars may fail to meet the moral standards required to make them justifiable.

Military thinking, perhaps too easily accepted by liberal democrats in practice, also emphasizes the security and preservation of the state because the state constitutes the source of the military's existence and legitimacy. Yet democratic values stress the security and preservation of people, not of any particular institutions nor, especially in this age of interdependence, of state sovereignty as traditionally understood.

The military world view of international relations can be summed up within the time-honoured maxim: 'If you want peace, prepare for war'. Even though people with a military mentality may desire to avoid war, they are professionally required to prepare for war and to be prepared for the worst possible contingency. The enlightened democrat understands that such preparations in the long run encourage the likelihood of war and that preparations for peace, which are often impeded by preparations for war, are more prudent and valuable.[4]

The military mind constructs organizations that are hierarchical and anti-democratic. Command structures emphasize obedience and immediate, unquestioned response, whereas democracy requires constant questioning of authority and mindfulness of what one does and why one does it. Military culture discourages reflection, discussion of issues, and consideration of policy options that are non-violent and respectful of the lives of others. Yet these qualities are *essential* ingredients for government based on the consent of the governed.

At best, military organizations may buy time, through the threat or use of force against predatory actions by another country, to protect a democratic society and enable it to bolster its democratic qualities after peace is restored. It is widely recognized that during war many of democracy's liberal values, such as free speech, open discussion of national security questions, freedom of association and movement, and the absence of conscription will be compromised in the short run with the hope that the society will return to more liberal values in the long run. But there is little recognition of the need to question the widespread belief that the 'military virtues' – discipline, patriotism and willingness to fight for one's country – are intrinsically healthy for democracies. Yet any decision to wage war, no matter how justifiable it may seem from the standpoint of a single society, is an extreme denial of democratic values, because making war means willingness to take the lives of other people who have not been consulted about, let alone given their consent to, the decision to target them for destruction.

In sum, to the extent that the military mind pervades society, authoritarianism is promoted and democracy is undermined. In addition to the fundamental conflict between democratic and military world-views, there are several other reasons why the presumed 'requirements' of national security have impeded the fulfilment of the democratic principle. The technical complexity of weapons and strategies, the secrecy in policy planning and execution, the deception used to confound other countries and domestic political opponents, the speed of response required in time of crisis, the extreme concentration of power in the hands of a few decision-makers, and the unavailability, disuse, or undemocratic nature of global governance to manage reliably the needs for security enhancement – all these, to which we now turn, undermine democracy.

The Complexity of Modern War and Weaponry as a Threat to Democracy

This second problem arises because democratic processes are 'not well equipped to deal with questions of exceptional complexity'.[5] The complexities of military security are technical, political and moral. Understanding technical strategic issues often requires knowledge of scientific and technical information that ordinary citizens can hardly be expected to master. The jargon used by strategists adds to the problem. Decision-making elites often refuse to take seriously anyone who has not mastered the acronyms and technical language. Those initiated into the nuclear priesthood often 'consciously think they do indeed know best'. As a result, they do not attempt to explain policy options and often 'find it useful to cloak many of their actions in a veil of secrecy, sometimes in violation of the legalities of democratic procedure'.[6]

Politically, the adversarial process between political parties, which is considered a hallmark of democracy on domestic questions, simply has not worked on military issues. Dahl's study of US political processes demonstrates that US nuclear policies 'were made for the better part of thirty-five years with hardly a trace of an adversarial process except occasionally among a minuscule policy elite'.[7] Throughout the nuclear age, strategic choices 'were not even subjected to political debate . . . For all practical purposes, on these matters *no public opinion existed and the democratic process was inoperable*'.[8] More broadly, Bruce Russett has concluded that in modern representative democracies decisions on national security have been 'insulated from popular control and knowledge'.[9]

On the most far-reaching decisions over life and death and the future of civilization itself, people have been alienated from authority; they have not delegated it. The public has not debated the merits of fundamental policy options and sent clear signals or representatives to Washington, London or Paris to honour their preferences. Crucial decisions have been shaped by a nuclear priesthood, most of whom were not elected. Even if elected officials had decided every question, the decisions cannot be considered democratic if they were made in the absence of public debate and of a rudimentary understanding of where various policy paths might lead. A free press and elected legislatures are important accomplishments, but they do not constitute democracy. The point is not that the decisions were unwise, or that the public might have decided differently, or even that the public could not have thrown out the politicians if they had wanted to. It is that without knowledge of issues and options the public cannot be said to have participated in, and given consent to, decisions that profoundly affect them.

Where opinion polling did reveal clear public positions on strategic questions, US officials frequently ignored those preferences. For example, a majority of the US public has always opposed a strategy of using nuclear weapons first in combat, but officials have maintained their 'right' to employ nuclear weapons first if they considered it useful to do so. This difference over whether to initiate the use of nuclear weapons is highly significant because the public has also believed, occasionally by a margin as wide as 83 to 13 per cent, that even a limited nuclear war involving both the US and the former Soviet Union would have turned into an all-out nuclear war. By an even greater margin, the public has believed that 'there can be no winner in an all-out nuclear war',[10] so a first-use policy against the Soviet Union would not, in the public's eyes, have been prudent.

The public also strongly favoured halting US nuclear tests in response to the Soviet testing moratorium of the late 1980s,[11] but Washington repeatedly refused to do so. At other times the public has wanted much deeper arms reductions than Washington would contemplate.[12] In addition, when public polling and numerous referenda showed that a strong majority of the public supported a freeze on the testing and deployment of nuclear weapons, the government subverted these preferences by launching a campaign for the Strategic Defense Initiative with the false claim that this programme held promise for making nuclear weapons 'impotent and obsolete'.[13] Despite Washington's disinclination to seek public debate on security policy, US citizens have believed that 'the issue of nuclear war is too important to leave only to the President and the experts'. They reject the notion that nuclear policy 'is too complex for people like me to think about'.[14]

Even worse, when a prime minister or president faces embarrassing questions from legislators who do not share the executive's perception of threat, he or she is sorely tempted to resort to secret procedures, sometimes illegal, to protect his or her definition of the national interest or to advance a partisan interest. This happened, for example, during the Reagan administration's secret selling of arms to Iran and channelling of funds to the contras' war against Nicaragua.

Morally, security policy has denigrated democracy because of the likelihood that those who have technical knowledge used in decision-making may not also possess any special moral knowledge. Experts by their nature specialize in some fields and pay scant attention to others. Edward Teller may be widely acclaimed as the father of the H-bomb, but there would be far less agreement that he is the father of a new ethic for survival. Even if experts with technical knowledge are also moral philosophers, they have no right to make basic moral decisions for the masses of people.

On the other hand, the citizens who are entitled to decide their own fate cannot be expected to have some of the technical knowledge that would be useful in shaping strategic doctrine or arms control policies. Moreover, because means have a way of determining ends, it is simply not possible to say that the public should decide policy ends and the technicians will find the appropriate means. Ends and means as well as moral issues and technical knowledge are inextricably related. Add to these dilemmas the stark reality that on key issues no one has knowledge sufficient for seemingly necessary decisions. For example, even persons who advocate nuclear deterrence and limited nuclear war acknowledge that it would be foolish to retaliate with nuclear weapons against a missile attack if there were a high probability of triggering a nuclear winter that would destroy their own society. Yet we do not know the precise threshold of destructive power or the weather conditions under which such an event might occur.

Of course structural pressures of interstate competition in the existing international system provide the rationale for, and seem to legitimate, undemocratic decision-making and state-centric solutions to security problems. Yet those pressures can be mitigated in a wide variety of ways if governments truly seek to implement democratic values. International regimes, comprised of norms, rules and institutions, could be more vigorously constructed to increase incentives for international cooperation in the security field in the short run, and to create a transformed international system in the long run. Much more could be done to honour the democratic preferences of the public even with the existing international structures.[15] Only because Washington, London and Paris have placed higher priority on power for their elites than on democratic values could they have refused the opportunities, for example, to establish a total ban on nuclear weapons testing or an international organization to govern space and keep it free of weaponry.

Arms control policies, which could be the heart of efforts to reduce the role of military power and expand the influence of democratic institutions, further illustrate the negative impact that military policies have had on democracy. Until the advent of Mikhail Gorbachev's one-sided concessions to western governments in the late 1980s, four decades of arms control negotiations had yielded little more than a fine tuning and even a legitimation of the arms build-up. For several reasons, prolonged and largely fruitless negotiations often subverted the public's interest in arms control. First, prolonged arms control negotiations were used by advocates of more armaments to engage liberal supporters of arms control in support for expanded military spending. In order to 'bargain from a position of strength', more arms were needed for arms control, it seemed, than for security. When negotiations were in progress, executive officials asked Congress to support new weapons systems in order to strengthen the hand of negotiators with the Soviet Union.

Secondly, Washington always pressed for new weapons to be used as bargaining chips during negotiations. For example, the multiple independently targetable re-entry vehicle (MIRV) was developed in part for this reason. Because the Soviet Union was behind in guidance technology for MIRVs, it probably could have been induced to accept a MIRV ban. However, the US did not pursue this goal. When the ABM treaty limiting anti-missile missiles made multiple warheads unnecessary, the bargaining chip was deployed, not bargained away in negotiations with the Soviet Union.

Thirdly, because arms control negotiations are conducted in secret, the US public cannot play an effective role in ensuring that Washington itself offers reasonable proposals. Within secret negotiations it is only too easy for one side to place the blame for failure to agree on the other, meanwhile allowing all the new weapons systems that the military planners wanted anyway.

The purpose of arms control should be to limit the militaries of the US and its rivals, not legitimize their expansion. Yet the military's dominance of arms control illustrates the influence that military institutions have exerted over US diplomacy more generally. Because diplomacy is also conducted in secret, when there are enormously powerful political and economic influences acting behind the scenes, as is the case when the military–industrial complex flexes its muscles, diplomacy itself is less subject to public control and more likely to serve the influences of the military. As a result, US diplomacy has relied heavily on covert operations, the development of military and economic client states, and the threat or use of force, rather than on multilateral diplomacy or expanded use of arbitration and judicial settlement of disputes – instruments which are more congenial to democratic values.

The Speed of World Events and Warfare as a Threat to Democracy

Prior to the nuclear age, it was possible for countries to maintain relatively low levels of military preparedness during peacetime. Mobilization could begin after the threat of war appeared on the horizon. In contrast, modern warfare has required chronically high levels of military preparedness and the development of elaborate, highly classified war plans to enable immediate response in a time of crisis. These technological realities make it impossible to have parliamentary questions, let alone public debate, about whether and how to go to war in specific cases. In addition, in an age when changes occur rapidly, unforeseen issues usually arise between elections, as did the Iraqi occupation of Kuwait and the resulting war. As a result, even crude policy guidelines that the public may specify in an election are not likely to apply to unforeseen political choices.

Because the public may not have time to debate whether to declare war on an adversary, many observers conclude that the requirements for democratic decision-making must be reduced. Reduced requirements can be fulfilled, the argument goes, as long as the persons making the decision for war have been elected through democratic processes. But for the public merely to have elected the officials who decide to make war does not constitute democratic control over military policy unless the public has previously specified conditions under which war is to be preferred, the limits on how it is to be waged, and even how much collateral damage to people and the environment might be morally acceptable. Never have such deliberations taken place in any nuclear power.

Some observers claim that the conditions of democracy are satisfied by public choice of policy ends, such as defence of the state against external attack, even though the means to those ends are chosen without effective public debate and participation. But, as Dahl has pointed out, 'experts cannot be trusted to choose the means to broadly specified goals, for in choosing the means they would in effect determine the ends'.[16]

Secrecy and Deception as Threats to Democracy

Secrecy obstructs democracy by keeping the public ignorant of information that it needs to make wise policy choices. A decision about whether to support the war against Iraq's occupation of Kuwait in 1991, for example, may require knowledge of classified diplomatic exchanges that occurred before the Iraqi invasion, as well as confidential signals about the possibilities of a negotiated solution. Secrecy also limits the ability of people to find out whether their policy preferences, even when clearly articulated, are being followed. When a prolonged arms control negotiation ends without agreement, for example, the public may never know if their preferences for major arms reductions were being implemented by their own government. To take another example, only after Chile had been destabilized and President Salvador Allende died in a 1973 *coup d'état* did the US public learn how the US had secretly conspired to oust a democratically elected government.

The demands of the modern military are so pervasive and powerful that secrecy has undermined democratic political culture even when officials have used secrecy to prevent embarrassment to themselves rather than to enhance national security. To illustrate, in the late 1980s the Department of Energy reluctantly acknowledged to investigators that for thirty years it had been responsible, along with its predecessor, the Atomic Energy Commission, for hiding from the public a number of serious reactor accidents, including the melting of fuel and extensive radioactive contamination. They did not tell the public about releases of radiation, leaking radioactive wastes, severe health hazards to employees and the general public, and extensive radioactive contamination of the earth and atmosphere. In some cases they not only withheld vital information, they also deliberately deceived the public and members of Congress. For four decades the Energy Department has enjoyed complete control over whether to disclose information about its own misdeeds.[17]

The corrosive effect of military policies upon democracy can be illustrated further by the fundamental problems that arise in selecting bombing targets for destruction. Variations in targeting policy dramatically affect judgements about whether war can be considered morally justifiable. The US Catholic Bishops, for example, consider targeting population centres with nuclear weapons so inappropriate as to make such combat unjustifiable under any conditions. Even if during some crisis the public would decide to wage war, can it be expected to choose precise targets? This would be extremely difficult, if not simply impossible, yet the selection of targets could produce military and environmental consequences that might affect people's lives more profoundly than who 'wins' the war.

The use of covert operations, now widely accepted as a legitimate and essential part of the arsenal of democracies, strikes yet another blow at democracy. In a careful study of the Kennedy, Johnson, Nixon and Ford administrations, John Orman concluded that the four presidents 'were virtually *unaccountable* in the area of their covert foreign policy',[18] not only to the public, but also to Congress. For example, of thirty-three covert projects that the CIA undertook in Chile between 1963 and 1973, only eight were reported to Congress.[19] Following the overthrow of Allende, Congress conducted extensive hearings and passed legislation to prevent further executive branch irresponsibility and to guarantee that officials obeyed the law. Despite these efforts, there has been very little or no effective public control over CIA policies and operations. New illegalities subsequently occurred, most visibly in the Reagan administration. As congressional oversight committees have repeatedly noted, the power of the CIA has led to abuse because 'you can't really draw a distinction between the use of power by the CIA to protect sensitive information and the use of that same power to do almost anything they choose and then cover it up'.[20]

Not only have covert military practices flagrantly violated the democratic principle, they have also discouraged many people from believing that democracy *should* be honoured in the national security field, and from understanding what democratic integrity entails. The noxious effects of covert military deeds and military secrecy do not end with an assassination plot, the overthrow of an unwanted government, a contrived rationale for the use of force, or lies about radioactive hazards; they cumulatively erode mental and moral acuity about how far policies depart from democratic values. In short, even when deeds are undertaken far away in South East Asia or Central America, they undermine democracy at home. The extent to which a healthy democracy has been sedated by the Department of Defense and the CIA is illustrated in the recognition that it would be possible to end the violation of democratic principles by covert operations if Congress merely banned them completely, at least during peacetime, as Senator Harold Hughes and Representative Leo Ryan recommended after their hearings in 1974.[21] Instead, an ethic has grown up that intelligence agencies should be free to decide ethical issues on the basis of what they and their tiny handful of overseers believe is necessary to protect the US. An extreme expression of this view came from James Angelton during congressional hearings: 'It is inconceivable that a secret intelligence arm of the government has to comply with all the overt orders of the government'.[22]

Covert operations have contributed to a dangerous indifference by members of Congress and the public towards the vital functions of democracy, if not towards its superficial rituals. For example, when President Reagan and his closest aides 'sold weapons to a terrorist regime in Iran in order to finance a terrorist revolt in Nicaragua', their actions led them 'to make a mockery of the Constitution, dishonor their oaths of office, and seize for themselves the powers of despotism'. Subsequent congressional investigations 'absolved them of their crimes and confirmed them in their contempt for the law and the American people'.[23] The US national security state, whose managers have consistently excluded the public from life-and-death decisions, nurtures authoritarian tendencies throughout US political culture, but young people seem especially vulnerable. A recent survey of US citizens between the ages of 18 and 29 showed that this generation 'knows less, cares less, and is less critical of its leaders and institutions than young people in the past'.[24] Two-thirds of all eligible voters, or as many as 120 million Americans, do not bother to vote in some national elections.

The Military–Industrial Complex as a Threat to Democracy

Ever since the nuclear age began, government officials, usually with the acquiescence of poorly informed members of Congress and the public, have been adopting military appropriations and strategic doctrines that have seriously undermined the prospects for democracy within domestic society. This has occurred without anyone announcing an attack on democratic values, of course, but it would be dishonest to ignore the extent to which economic and political elites have tried, frequently with success, to pull the wool over the eyes of the public in order to advance their own economic interests and to obtain greater political and military power, both domestically and internationally. Although these highly respected people presumably have not been malicious, by their practices they have undermined democratic political culture.

Although President Eisenhower warned the US about the unwarranted influence of corporations with large military contracts and their political alliance with the armed forces and with members of Congress dependent upon them for continuation in office, no effective antidotes to this military–industrial complex have been employed throughout the more than three decades since he left office. The failure of either Republican or Democrat administrations to counter this unwarranted military influence may be evidence that the power of the complex is too great to oppose with impunity. Richard Falk, one of the few scholars to examine the impact of nuclear deterrence on democratic values, has concluded that, despite the reduced tensions between east and west, it probably remains true that 'the nuclear national security state has sufficiently immobilized the institutions and procedures of representative democracy to render them almost ineffectual when it comes to challenging the fundamental content and framework of official policy in the war/peace area'.[25]

Indeed, the strength of the military–industrial complex and its ability to skew political decisions in an undemocratic direction has increased since Eisenhower's farewell address. The main military contractors among the Fortune 500 companies have spent tens of millions of dollars every year to influence US military policies. Because large corporations charged some of these costs to the Department of Defense as part of administrative expenses,[26] a large share of military advocacy was paid for by members of the public. Citizens were financing their own victimization as they lost their rightful political power to military corporations. Because the pro-military elements of the US government directly or indirectly finance many of the lobbying and public relations activities that generate support for large-scale military spending, the military–industrial complex contains a self-perpetuating, self-aggrandizing dynamic. Favouritism is demonstrated in the government-sponsored profit margin of the ten largest military contractors, which the US Census Bureau reported to be a 25 per cent return on equity. This was more than twice the average return for other manufacturers in the mid-1980s.[27]

The military contracting industries also constitute the largest corporate political action committees in the US, contributing more money than any other interest group in an attempt to affect the outcome of elections. The strength of the political action committees, which *doubled* their financial contributions during the first four years of the Reagan administration, plus the tendency of contractors to spread production among manufacturers in virtually every congressional district, have made major weapons systems 'virtually impossible to eliminate'.[28]

In addition, every decade roughly 2,000 highly paid individuals move between the Department of Defense and the major contractors.[29] Because of military contractors' close access to the early definition of research and development policies, they play a key role in determining future weapons systems. These corporations also undertake grassroots lobbying efforts on behalf of military spending programmes. In the late 1970s, for example, Rockwell spent $1.35 million, of which a substantial portion was reimbursed by the Defense Department through contracts with Rockwell, to mobilize employees, stockholders, community groups and mass organizations on behalf of the B-1 bomber.[30] As a result, the 'powerful flow of people and money' between the military contractors, the executive branch and Congress has produced 'an "iron triangle" on defense policy and procurement that excludes outsiders and alternative perspectives'.[31]

The Concentration of Military Decision-making Power as a Threat to Democracy

A fundamental contradiction also exists between military strategy and democratic government because the high stakes associated with modern warfare seem to justify war plans and secret operations that are to be carried out by the executive branch acting alone, beyond democratic control. Furthermore, because any corner of the globe, no matter how remote the country or distant the ocean, could become either a launching point for US weapons and intelligence operations or a target for US weapons if it came under an adversary's control, secretive, interventionist foreign policies have been easily extended from basic east–west deterrence to any country or ocean where the president deems it 'necessary' to intervene.

As a result, four decades of US military policies have encouraged the growth of what has been called the imperial presidency.[32] This operating mode constitutes a grave threat to democracy because it combines an interventionist US foreign policy with a president not subject to meaningful controls by the public or Congress. With its origins in President Franklin Roosevelt's tendency to ignore Congress in prosecuting the

Second World War and in signing executive agreements, it grew enormously with the creation of the CIA and the execution of many covert operations. It received further impetus during the Korean and Vietnam wars. President Reagan expanded this tendency further in US operations to support anti-government insurgencies in southern Africa, Afghanistan and Central America. US marines were deployed in Lebanon in 1982 and kept there beyond the 60-day deadline provided for in the War Powers Resolution that Congress had previously passed to restrain the imperial presidency. Ronald Reagan and George Bush also treated this resolution in a cavalier manner in the invasions of Grenada and Panama. Similarly, in the bombing of Libya, Congress was 'excluded from any meaningful decision-making role'.[33] Indeed, even after alarms sounded over the excesses of the Vietnam War and Watergate, executive officials 'circumvented the authority of Congress and the courts, viewed themselves above the law, particularly in foreign policy matters, and used secrecy and distortion to deceive Congress and the public in order to accomplish their policy objectives'.[34]

Presidential consultation with Congress before using force in the war against Saddam Hussein in 1991 at first may seem to represent something of a departure from this trend. But the hasty resort to force before giving sanctions and diplomacy time to work, the political difficulties posed for any members of Congress who dared to oppose the president's war policies, the congressional and UN inability to establish constraints on US destructiveness, and congressional unwillingness to protect freedom of the press in reporting on this conflict reveal the extent of military influence in US political culture.

Even more distressing for the future of democracy is the extreme concentration of power over the decision to use nuclear weapons. For the decision to launch nuclear weapons to rest solely with the president, as is the case in the US, concentrates more power of life and death in the hands of a single individual than has ever before existed at any time in history, including the most authoritarian rulers of all time. This fact alone demonstrates the profound incompatibility of modern military policy and democracy. No individual, no matter how wise, no matter how righteous, no matter how popular, should ever be allowed to hold in his or her hands the power to make what are the most crucial and irretrievable decisions in the history of humanity. Such power cannot be considered legitimate in a democracy.

Equally unsettling, presidents Eisenhower, Kennedy and Johnson seem to have secretly delegated to military commanders their authority to launch nuclear weapons if the president himself became incapacitated. One might presume that other presidents have done the same.[35] Moreover, under conditions of nuclear combat, communications for command and control might be so interrupted that battlefield commanders would be given authority to make decisions about the use of nuclear weapons.

Despite the unacceptability of concentrating power over human civilization and the biosphere in the hands of one or several persons, we must recognize also that the more widely and democratically the powers of deliberation and decision-making are spread, the less effective the nuclear deterrent may become, because instantaneous response becomes difficult if not impossible. It does seem that either democracy or weapons of mass destruction must be given up. If war is not abolished, democracy will be.

Traditional National Sovereignty as a Threat to Democracy

Contemporary military policies reinforce and legitimate a concept of national sovereignty in which a national government recognizes no formal responsibility to any authority other than its own state. US leaders, civilian and military alike, claim that the US, and by implication other nations as well, has a right to decide when to go to war without answering to any higher authority. When disputes arise about whether a use of force is justified, the US will be the sole judge of its own rectitude.

In this age of interdependence, a militarily unqualified reinforcement of traditional national sovereignty inhibits the fulfilment of democratic principles. Traditional concepts of sovereignty have placed the locus for decision-making in national capitals, but today many of the decisions that affect the lives of people within country A are made in countries B, C and D. If the military, economic and environmental policies of country B affect the people in country A, but A's military policies perpetuate the legal fiction that A and B are not subject to any authority outside their borders, then those military policies undermine both security and democracy. Existing ideas about military security are too narrowly circumscribed by nationally defined territory. Real security for US citizens depends on trans-territorial factors: Russian nuclear policies, Japanese trade policies, the European Community's economic policies, Israel's immigration and settlement policies, and perhaps even Mexico's family planning policies. Military policies act as an anti-democratic force because they channel a society's energies into the maintenance of traditional sovereign boundaries at a time when 'the very process of governance is escaping the reach of the nation-state'.[36]

US military policies have attempted, feebly at best, to take account of the loss of a state's invulnerability in the nuclear age by forming alliance systems, such as NATO, which share the costs of military preparedness and expand the geographical domain of military preparation and combat. However, until the independent arms control initiatives of Mikhail Gorbachev, NATO's military policies generally did not take account of the need for security to be held in common with one's adversary. Even with the dismantling of the Soviet Union, NATO has been slow to seize opportunities to denuclearize and demilitarize parts of Europe which, if utilized when they first became a realistic possibility in the late 1980s, would have made the fragmentation of the Soviet Union in 1991 less dangerous and the prospect of independent military forces in the former Soviet republics in 1992 less problematic and fearsome. But the undemocratic patterns of policy-making and content of security policy impeded more prudent security policies in the US and most NATO governments. An important window of opportunity for European demilitarization and enhanced nuclear nonproliferation went unutilized.

The end of the Cold War and the dismantling of the Warsaw Pact and the Soviet Union have made the early 1990s an opportune time for introducing innovative policies. Whether future conflict is east–west, north–south, or some presently unforeseen configuration, the underlying point remains the same: contemporary security policies continue to reinforce adversarial military relations among national sovereignties, not serious diplomatic programmes to include the adversary within a system of universal rules and a form of transnational governance that would deliberately induce a nation-state to give up its own national war-making function of sovereignty in return for other governments throughout the world doing the same. Yet there can be little doubt that the human species must move soon in this direction if it is to survive, and to survive with dignity.

Equally important but more surprising, the species must also move in that direction if any state is to enjoy *democracy* in the future. In an age of interdependence, 'democracy can only be fully sustained', as David Held has pointed out, 'in and through the agencies . . . that form an element of and yet cut across the territorial boundaries of the nation-state'. He correctly notes that 'democracy will result from, and only from, a nucleus or federation of democratic states and agencies'.[37] Rule-making intergovernmental and transnational organizations are necessary for modern democracy even though they are antithetical to the world of militarily protected national sovereignty. Democratic values can be implemented domestically only if they are simultaneously implemented in boundary-transcending organizations. Thus contemporary military policies are self-defeating in so far as they cling to a unilateral 'right' to decide when to use military force.

A 'national democracy' is gradually becoming a contradiction in terms, just as 'national security' is a dubious concept because in an age of interdependence no *national* entity can secure itself by itself. To overstate only slightly, national democrats are like apartheid democrats: they want democracy for their own group, yet they want it achieved separately from other groups. However, by trying to nationalize democracy they segregate people artificially and without their consent, even though the different groups are functionally interdependent. They are thus forced to behave autocratically or imperialistically toward those people outside their own group. Conversely, they are themselves under-represented in neighbouring societies whose decisions affect them. Contemporary military policies thus obstruct the growth of what is described below as 'democratic security', characterized by a recognition that the inter-penetrations of the world's societies ultimately require that *each* of the world's national governments must be held accountable to *all* people affected by its major decisions, whether or not they live within that government's territorial borders.

As interdependence forces us to climb out of the box of national sovereignty and into the expansive atmosphere of openly shared, trans-national sovereignty over decisions for limiting violence and military arsenals, it becomes clear that *any* use of war or collective violence is a profoundly undemocratic act, because the people to be killed have not given their consent to be killed. There is usually no presumption of individual guilt against the common soldiers of another country, let alone any due process to determine guilt before they are put to death. War is an extreme and more deadly example of taxation without representation: those people who are most affected (by being targeted by another country) are the ones least represented in the strategic decisions that threaten their lives.

Conclusion: The Need to Transform National Security into Democratic Security

In conclusion, US military priorities have militarized modern political culture in the US. This military acculturation has proceeded more subtly but no less perniciously than did the growth of traditional militarism in the nineteenth and early twentieth centuries in some parts of Europe. Today there may not be overt glorification of war – although the trium-phalism that Americans felt after the bombardments of Iraq came close to it – or the presence of a Prussian military class. But for half a century in the US the pursuit of military strength and vast destructive power has come to dominate the federal budget, wield unwarranted influence within the economy, shape arms control policy even in a period of detente, warp diplomacy, exert decisive influence in election campaigns, skew the media of mass communications, and pervade the culture to such an extent that democracy, on every issue crucial to the military, is held at bay.

In short, the contemporary military policies of the US and presumably of all nuclear powers[38] severely limit the practice and threaten the lifeblood of democracy. These policies produce anti-democratic consequences in three domains. First, they discourage democracy *internally* within people's minds and psychological dispositions by requiring citizens to accept life-and-death policies flowing from their own government even though they exercise no genuine control over those policies; by asking citizens to be willing to shorten or extinguish the lives of millions of other people, whether through economic hardship unnecessarily exacerbated by military priorities or through war, without any determination as to whether the victims' fate at the hands of US military policies is justifiable; and by inhibiting people in other countries from enjoying democracy, in a transnational sense, because they have no reliable representation in the decision-making councils of the US or other external governments.

Secondly, contemporary military policies discourage democracy *domestically* by legitimizing military and political institutions that are hierarchical and authoritarian; by insisting on secrecy and practising deception in decision-making; by mounting covert operations; and by skewing political and economic resources away from equitable service of people's needs into the inequitable service of those with vested interests in the military–industrial complex.

Thirdly, contemporary military policies discourage democracy *internationally* by obstructing multilateral diplomacy; by impeding the growth of intergovernmental institutions and transnational reformulations of sovereignty; and by reinforcing the sovereign separation of states and thereby their irresponsibility toward people in neighbouring societies.

Policies governing high levels of military preparedness in general and weapons of mass destruction in particular have escaped democratic control over the past four decades, regardless of who has been in power. In Dahl's words, 'the democratic process has clearly failed to function in controlling what may well be the most important decisions that will ever be made on this earth'.[39]

The undemocratic, psychologically unhealthy conditions surrounding the conception, gestation and life of modern military policies have given birth to monstrous problems for democracies. Beyond their immediate effects, they have also introduced long-term malignant growths in the life of democracy more generally. Indeed, nuclear weapons 'by their very existence, forever obliterate the occasion of "peace", thereby . . . depriving a democratic polity of one of its most essential preconditions'. For the nuclear powers, 'democracy, as a political framework, seems to be a permanent casualty of the nuclear age, although democratic forms, as an increasingly empty shell, can persist . . .'.[40] Underneath the shell, US military policies have extinguished democracy over central aspects of US society and its future security.

If, as Dahl concludes, US nuclear policies 'have . . . been arrived at without even the ordinary constraints of the democratic process', and if the reasons for this undemocratic phenomenon operate in every democracy that possesses nuclear weapons,[41] must we reluctantly accept undemocratic political systems, at least for governing policies on nuclear weapons and other complex security issues? Or must we give up nuclear weapons and other comparably complicated military instruments in order to restore democracy?

The prevailing view in the US seems to be that democracy must be compromised to prepare continuously for war and to enable war to be fought if and when the need might arise. Yet an alternative view, which this author holds, is that military policies must be limited to enable democracy to survive. To restore democracy, in Falk's words, 'depends on the downgrading and eventual elimination of nuclear weapons as an element of international political life'.[42] This can be done safely because security needs can, in any case, no longer be met through preparation for nuclear warfare. They can only be addressed by gradually establishing national, transnational and intergovernmental democratic controls over the war-making function of sovereignty around the world. We should let democratic needs constrain military wants, rather than allow military wants to constrain democratic needs. This priority is necessary because without it democracy will be destroyed from within; this priority is possible because alternative means are becoming available for maintaining security.[43]

The preceding analysis sketches my conclusion that as long as the liberal democratic state attempts to function as a national security state, it will not be viable. Rather than achieve security *and* democracy, or security *at the expense of* democracy, it will achieve *neither* security *nor* democracy. Our goal should be to implement 'democratic security', a new imperative simply because national security is inviable.

Democratic security policies[44] can be built upon three fundamental values. First, all people are entitled, as a matter of their birthright, to participate in, and to determine together, those decisions that profoundly affect their lives, as do decisions about security policies. Security policies cannot be excluded from open debate over policy options and from participatory or representative decision-making without both destroying democracies in the long run and corrupting security policies in the short run. 'If power tends to corrupt, it corrupts most absolutely in the field of security where manipulative power, secrecy, psychological shadows, and violence grow profusely if left unchecked'.[45]

Secondly, the purpose of democratic security policies is to provide security for *people*, for all people, and not merely for abstractions like the state or for elites that represent only a small segment of one country's people or of world society's total population. Stated differently, the security interests of a majority of people should not be sacrificed by governing elites to protect a state, the contemporary state system and its obsolescent code of international conduct, or the interests of any elites.

Thirdly 'democracy' in this analysis signifies far more than a majority-rule procedure of participatory or representative decision-making. It also means a positive relationship among people that includes respect for the fundamental rights of others.

Future exponents of democratic security will recognize that demilitarization and democratization reinforce each other. We can democratize world society by demilitarizing security, and we can demilitarize security by democratizing world society. But we can do neither by following the current military policies of the great powers. The end of the cold war provides an unusual opportunity, which remains tragically unutilized, for all democrats to embark with new purpose and urgency upon a transformation of the code of international conduct and the establishment of transnational institutions that will move us closer to a warless world in which democracy can flourish.

NOTES

1 R. Dahl, *Controlling Nuclear Weapons: democracy versus guardianship* (Syracuse, Syracuse University Press, 1985), p. 3.
2 See V. Van Dyke, *International Politics* (New York, Appleton-Century-Crofts, 1972), pp. 148–50.
3 S. Huntington, *The Soldier and the State: the theory and politics of civil–military relations* (Cambridge, MA, Belknap Press of Harvard University Press, 1957), p. 109.
4 For discussion of 'preparations for peace' see R. Johansen, 'Do preparations for war increase or decrease international security?', in C. Kegley (ed.), *The Long Postwar Peace: contending explanations and projections* (New York, HarperCollins, 1991), pp. 224–44.
5 Dahl, *Controlling Nuclear Weapons*, p. 8.
6 B. Russett, *Controlling the Sword: the democratic governance of national security* (Cambridge, MA, Harvard University Press, 1990), p. 148.

7   Dahl, *Controlling Nuclear Weapons*, pp. 13 and 16.

8   Dahl, *Controlling Nuclear Weapons*, p. 34 (emphasis in original).

9   This is the conclusion of Russett, *Controlling the Sword*, p. 147.

10 T. Wicker, 'No to nuclear war', *New York Times* (7 Oct. 1984), p. IV:21.

11 'Public favors halting US A-tests if Soviet moratorium continues', *The Gallup Report*, 248 (May 1986), pp. 20–2.

12 'Americans favor agreement with Soviets going beyond nuclear weapons limitations; endorse destruction of existing warheads', *The Gallup Report*, 188 (May 1981), pp. 3–10; 'Kennan proposal to break nuclear arms race supported by overwhelming margin; international inspection plan favored', *The Gallup Report*, 196 (Jan. 1982), pp. 13–17.

13 R. Reagan, 'President's speech on military spending and a new defense', *New York Times* (24 March 1983), p. A 24.

14 Russet, *Controlling the Sword*, p. 158; Americans Talk Security, *Compendium of Poll Findings on the National Security Issue* (New York, Daniel Yankelovich Group, 1987), p. 306.

15 For example, US political leaders have failed to lead the way for strengthening the UN; at times a far larger portion of the public than of the leadership has considered enhancement of the UN to be an important goal. See J. E. Reilly (ed.), *American Public Opinion and US Foreign Policy* (Chicago, The Chicago Council on Foreign Relations, 1987), p. 37.

16 Dahl, *Controlling Nuclear Weapons*, p. 11.

17 K. Schneider, 'Energy Dept. says it kept secret mishaps at nuclear weapon plant', *New York Times* (4 Oct. 1988) pp. 1 and 12.

18 J. Orman, *Presidential Secrecy and Deception: beyond the power to persuade* (Westport, CT, Greenwood Press, 1980), p. 191.

19 Admiral S. Turner, *Secrecy and Democracy: the CIA in transition* (Boston, MA, Houghton Mifflin, 1985), p. 83; US Congress, Senate, Select Committee to Study Governmental Operations with Respect to Intelligence Activities, *Final Report*, Book 1, Chapter X (26 April 1976).

20 Senator Alan Cranston, interviewed in 'New law to guard national secrets?', *US News and World Report* (18 Aug. 1975), p. 37.

21 Turner, *Secrecy and Democracy*, p. 85.

22 Quoted by Turner, *Secrecy and Democracy*, p. 178. Although this admittedly reflects an extreme statement of the position described here, the idea that congressional efforts to restrain the CIA should be evaded if it is possible to do so without political embarrassment has been widespread among operatives of the Nixon and Reagan administrations. A report by former CIA official John Stockwell suggests that George Bush's attitude may not be much different. Stockwell reports that when Bush became Director of the CIA, his job was to investigate and discipline those who had clearly broken laws. Instead, he chose to ignore evidence and briefings by CIA officers, including Stockwell, about wrongdoing. According to Stockwell, Bush manipulated potential evidence in a criminal investigation of the CIA's actions in Angola. 'Bush assigned a young attorney from the General Counsel's office to go through [Stockwell's] files and purge them of any documents that would be incriminating in case the Congress or the Justice Department subpoenaed them'. See 'John Stockwell on CIA propaganda techniques', *Propaganda Review* (Winter 1990), p. 18; J. Sharkey, 'Back in control: the CIA's secret propaganda campaign puts the Agency exactly where it wants to be', *Common Cause Magazine* (Sept./Oct. 1986), p. 37.

23 L. H. Lapham, 'Democracy in America?' *Kettering Review* (Fall 1991), p. 12. After congressional investigations of covert activities by the White House and the Federal Bureau of Investigation, a Senate select committee report noted that such policies were 'unworthy of a democracy and occasionally reminiscent of the tactics of totalitarian regimes'. Quoted by K. E. Sharpe, 'The real cause of Iran-gate', *Foreign Policy*, 68 (Fall 1987), p. 19.

24 Quoted from the Times Mirror Centre for the People and Press by Lapham, 'Democracy in America?', p. 13.

25 R. Falk, *The Promise of World Order: essays in normative international relations* (Philadelphia, PA, Temple University Press, 1987), p. 113.

26 G. Adams, *The Iron Triangle: the politics of defense contracting* (New York, Council on Economic Priorities, 1981), p. 12

27 M. Renner, *National Security: the economic and environmental dimensions* (Washington, DC, Worldwatch Institute, Worldwatch Paper No. 89, 1989), p. 77, n. 108.

28 'Political concerns of lawmakers bring increases in the Pentagon's budget', *New York Times* (17 May 1985), p. D 22.

29 Adams, *Iron Triangle*, p. 13.

30 Adams, *Iron Triangle*, p. 14.

31 Adams, *Iron Triangle*, p. 15.

32 See A. Schlesinger, Jr, *The Imperial Presidency* (Boston, MA, Houghton Mifflin, 1973); T. G. Carpenter, 'Global interventionism and a new imperial presidency', *Cato Institute Policy Analysis*, 71 (16 May 1986), p. 15.

33 Carpenter, 'Global interventionism,' p. 15.

34 M. J. Blackman and K. E. Sharpe, 'De-democratizing American foreign policy: dismantling the post-Vietnam formula', *Third World Quarterly*, 8 (Oct. 1986), p. 1271.

35 See Dahl, *Controlling Nuclear Weapons*, p. 33; P. Bracken, *The Command and Control of Nuclear Forces* (New Haven, CT, Yale University Press, 1983), pp. 197–201.

36 For a brief but brilliant discussion of the issues raised in this section, see D. Held, 'Democracy and globalization', *Alternatives*, 16:2 (1991), 201–8. See also Held's chapter in this volume.

37 Held, 'Democracy and globalization', p. 208.

38 Dahl, for one, believes that the conditions which have put nuclear policies outside democratic processes in the US also operate with similar consequences in all nuclear weapons countries.

39 Dahl, *Controlling Nuclear Weapons*, p. 16.

40 Falk, *Promise of World Order*, pp. 81 and 88–9.

41 Dahl, *Controlling Nuclear Weapons*, pp. 5–6.

42 Falk, *Promise of World Order*, pp. 88–9.

43 These include enforceable arms reductions with intrusive inspection, an enhanced role for compulsory judicial settlement, the potential expansion of UN peacekeeping and a possibly expanded role for people's power.

44 These are discussed in R. C. Johansen, 'Real security is democratic security', *Alternatives*, 16:2 (1991), 209–42.

45 Johansen, 'Real security', p. 210.

11

DEMOCRACY AND THE MEDIA –
WITHOUT FOUNDATIONS

John Keane

Public Service Media

For more than a generation, the public service broadcasting model has been considered a pillar of parliamentary democracy. Especially in Western Europe, public service radio and television have been seen as devices for protecting citizens against the twin threats of totalitarian propaganda and the crass commercialism of market-driven programming and, thus, as devices essential to a system of representative government, in which reasonable, informed public opinion plays a central mediating role between citizens and their state institutions. Today, these same public service media are slipping and sliding into a profound identity crisis. Deeply uncertain about their sources of funding and the scope and nature of their contemporary political role, they are caught up in a wider problem, evident in all of the old democracies, in which trade unions, political parties and other older mechanisms of representation are weakened and Balkanized.[1]

Symptomatic of this malaise is the manner in which the current defenders of the public service model rest their case upon a self-paralysing tautology: public service media are viewed as synonymous with institutions like RAI, the BBC and the *Länder* broadcasters in Germany, whose reputation, size, diversity and privileged position enable them to attract talent, to innovate and to produce balanced, quality programming available at a nominal cost to the entire citizenry of the nation-state. No doubt, the important practical achievements of public service media in this sense should be recognized.[2] The twentieth-century attempt to provide a service of mixed programmes on national radio and television channels available to all, often in the face of technical problems and pressing commercial considerations, has arguably widened the horizons of public awareness of social life. For a time, the 'provision of basic services' (*Grundversorgung*, as the German Federal Constitutional Court puts it) helped to *decommodify* the media. It diminished the role of accounting and corporate greed as the principal qualities necessary to media management. It enforced specific national rules covering such matters as the amount and type of advertising, political access, balanced news coverage and quotas of foreign programming. It succeeded for a time in protecting employment levels in the national broadcasting industries of countries such as Canada, Australia, Britain and the Federal Republic of Germany. The public service model also legitimized the presence of ordinary citizens in programmes dealing with controversial issues and problems. It has helped to make idiomatic, conversational styles respectable. And, significantly, it has publicized the pleasures of ordinariness, creating entertainment out of citizens playing games, talking about their experiences or delighting themselves in events as disparate as football and tennis matches, religious ceremonies and dancing to the current top ten.

There are nevertheless difficulties in the argument that existing public service media are a bulwark of democratic freedom and equality. It underestimates the ways in which technological change – the advent of cable and satellite television and community radio – has slowly but surely destroyed the traditional argument that the scarcity of available spectrum frequencies blesses public service broadcasting with the status of a 'natural monopoly' within the boundaries of a given nation-state. Defenders of existing public service media also understate the ways in which the alleged 'balance', 'quality' standards and universalism of existing public service media are routinely perceived by certain audiences as 'unrepresentative'. The repertoire of programmes channelled through existing public service media cannot exhaust the multitude of opinions in a complex (if less than fully pluralist) society in motion. The public service claim to representativeness is a defence of *virtual* representation of a fictive whole, a resort to programming which *simulates* the actual opinions and tastes of *some* of those to whom it is directed.

Music is a pertinent example. Although, for obvious reasons, music has always occupied the bulk of radio time, it has proved impossible in the long term to provide programming with general appeal on public service radio because a shared national musical culture has never existed. Different music appeals to different publics, whose dislikes are often as strong as their likes, and that is why the twentieth-century history of radio has resulted in a gradual fragmentation of mass audiences into different taste publics.³ Public service media cosset audiences and violate their own principle of equality of access for all to entertainment, current affairs and cultural resources in a common public domain. For reasons of a commitment to 'balance', government pressures and threatened litigation, the public service representation of such topics as sexuality, politics and violence also tends to be timid. Certain things cannot be transmitted, or not in a particular way. When they are transmitted, their disturbing, troublesome or outrageous implications are often closed off. And public service media - here they are no different from their commercial competitors - distribute entitlements to speak and to be heard and seen unevenly. They too develop a cast of regulars - reporters, presenters, commentators, academic experts, businesspeople, politicians, trade unionists, cultural authorities - who appear as accredited representatives of public experience and taste by virtue of their regular appearance on the media.

All this is grist to the mill of those favouring 'deregulation', for whom market competition is the key condition of press and broadcasting freedom, understood as freedom from state interference. That is why defenders of the public service model who talk only about preserving the 'quality' and 'balance' of the existing system make a crucial strategic mistake. 'Save the public service model' is a self-defeating position in the fight against those who consider market-driven media as a necessary condition of democracy. It concedes too much. Market liberals are attempting to rewrite history. They aim to brand the public service model as paternalistic, as timocratic, as an assault on the old European heritage of liberty from state control. Their fight to rewrite history from above serves as an important reminder that those who control the production of traditions, who dominate the present and manipulate the past, are likely also to control the future. And it reminds us that the debate over who shall inherit the old European vocabulary of 'liberty of the press' is long overdue, and that gaining the upper hand in these controversies is imperative for the survival and development of a public service communications system which resolves the flaws of market liberalism, and which, consequently, is more genuinely open and pluralistic, and therefore accessible to citizens of all persuasions.

But what would a redefined, broadened, and more accessible and accountable public service model look like in practice? What would be its guiding principles? In *The Media and Democracy* I argued that public service media could build on the decommodifying achievements of the original public service model, all the while acknowledging that it has now slipped into a profound and irreversible crisis.⁴ A fundamentally revised public service model would aim to facilitate a genuine commonwealth of forms of life, tastes and opinions, to empower a plurality of citizens who are governed neither by despotic states nor by market forces. It would circulate to them a wide variety of opinions. It would enable them to live within the framework of multilayered constitutional states which are held accountable to their citizens who work and consume, live and love, quarrel and compromise within independent, self-organizing civil societies which underpin and transcend the narrow boundaries of state institutions.[5]

In practice, the redefinition of the public service model requires the development of a purality of *non-state* media of communication which both function as permanent thorns in the side of political power (helping thereby to minimize political censorship) and serve as the primary means of communication for citizens situated within a pluralistic civil society. It also requires the adoption of measures which protect civil society from the self-paralysing effects of market-based media. It necessitates the regulation and maximum feasible reduction of private corporate power over the means of communication. It is unlikely, of course, that market transactions could ever be eliminated from the heart of a complex, pluralistic civil society. Market transactions can function as useful accessories of social life, enhancing its productiveness, flexibility and efficiency.[6] Market-influenced media can also function as important countervailing forces in the process of producing and circulating opinions; they are not only economic phenomena but sites of significa-tion that often run counter to opinion-making monopolies operated by churches, states and professional bodies. But, contrary to the claims of market liberalism, that does not mean that civil society and its media must be ruled by 'market forces'. There is nothing 'natural' or 'necessary' about profit-seeking, privately owned and controlled communications media. There are in fact many different types of market, whose actual designs – contrary to the slogan, 'Leave it to the market' – do not crystallize spontaneously. A self-regulating market is utopian, Karl Polanyi pointed out,[7] in that it cannot exist for long without paralysing itself and annulling its *social* preconditions. The actual or optimal shape of a market transaction must therefore always be crafted by political and legal regulations. It never emerges spontaneously or grows without the benefits of *non-market* support mechanisms provided by other institutions of civil society and through the state itself. And it always exists in a condition of political uncertainty, either recovering from a reform, wriggling against or cuddling up to existing regulations, or awaiting the next round of regulation.

It is difficult to be precise about which market-regulating and market-suspending strategies can maximize freedom of communication, since their actual shape and effectiveness will vary from context to context, and from time to time. One thing is nevertheless clear: the maximum feasible *decommodification* and 're-embedding' of communications media in the social life of civil society is a vital condition of freedom from state and market censorship. The recent attempts to restrict advertising aimed at children (in Italy), to ban unsolicited faxed junk mail (in the US) and the widening concern everywhere about sexism and racism in the commercial media exemplify and foreshadow the general principle: communications media should not be at the whim of 'market forces' but rather placed within a political and legal framework which specifies and enforces tough minimum safeguards in matters of ownership structure, regional scheduling, programme content and decision-making procedures.

Such public intervention into the market-place must avoid slipping into the reductionist demonology of the evil press baron. The obsession with media magnates has little in common with a politics of maximizing freedom and equality of communication. It understates the complexity of issues in the field of media politics and whets old-fashioned appetites for 'nationalizing' the media and placing them under centralized state control. As far as possible, censorious and bureaucratic forms of regulation should be avoided. Public intervention in the market should be open, accountable and positively enabling. It must use publicity to fight against the lack of publicity. It should seek to rely upon the techniques of 'eyebrow lifting', informal and visible pressures which encourage the media to develop programming policies in support of decommodification. When that fails, or is likely to fail, public regulation should aim to entangle capitalist media in a carefully spun spider's web of financial and legal obligations and public accountability. Pubic intervention in the media market-place should always attempt to 'level up' rather than 'level down' citizens' non-market powers of communication. It should seek the creation of a genuine variety of media which enable little people in big societies to send and receive a variety of opinions in a variety of ways. It should aim to break down media monopolies, lift restrictions upon particular audience choices and popularize the view that the media of communication are a public good, not a privately appropriable commodity whose primary function is to produce and circulate corporate speech for profit.

In practical terms, the maximization of freedom and equality of communication requires efforts to 'de-concentrate' and publicly regulate privately owned media and to restrict the scope and intensity of corporate speech. The creation of politically accountable, supra-national regulatory bodies, skilled at dealing with such matters as ownership,

advertising, tariffs and network access conditions, is imperative.[8] Such
bodies must be backed by national initiatives which restrict the media
power of private capital by forcing such large corporations as News
Corporation, Axel Springer Verlag and Fininvest to submit to tough
legislation which specifies programme quotas and restrictions upon
advertising and cross-media ownership. Large media corporations should
be treated as *common carriers*. They should be forced by law to carry
various citizens' messages if indeed they agree to carry anyone's messages
(which they must do in order to survive financially). For example, legal
and financial encouragement could be given to efforts to guaranteeing
rights of access during certain hours on radio and television to individuals, groups and independent programme-makers. Such encouragement
would help to build the electronic equivalent of Speakers' Corner and
add a much-needed new element of spontaneous drama, fun and intellectual vitality to the media. The absolute powers of private media
corporations to construct reality for others could also be broken down by
the introduction of democratic decision-making procedures, including
experiments (such as those pioneered at *Le Monde*),[9] with worker
participation and the formation of 'management teams' (*équipes de direction*).

Freedom and equality of communication also require the drastic
loosening of libel laws in favour of small producers of opinion, which find
themselves unable to risk or to survive a libel claim against them by large
corporations and professional bodies. It further presupposes the establishment of media enterprise boards to fund alternative ownership of
divested media. Freedom of communication requires public support for
new enterprises, particularly in areas (such as videotex, interactive television and electronic mail facilities) where entry costs and risks to
potential investors are prohibitively high. Freedom of communication
undoubtedly requires the establishment of publicly owned printing and
broadcasting enterprises which utilize funds raised by an advertising
revenue tax or a spectrum usage fee to facilitate new and innovative start-
ups which test the market. Greater public support is needed for small
production companies which operate within a regulated market and
work to distinctive programming remits (as in the Channel 4 model in
Britain). And, especially in the transition towards a more democratic
order, freedom from state and market censorship necessitates prefer-
ential treatment of information publishers with a pluralistic cutting edge
– of iconoclastic, independent and rigorous media such as *El Pais*,
founded a few months after Franco's death, Radio Alice, Bologna's
former experimental radio station, which denied 'reality' and rejected the
idea of schedules, and the courageous Czechoslovak newspaper, *Lidové*

Noviny, all of which have played a critical role in the struggle for democratic procedures.

Inevitably, stricter limits upon the production and circulation of opinions by means of market transactions would imply greater state hectoring of civil society. This is why new mechanisms such as 'government in the sunshine' legislation, which ensure that political power is held permanently accountable to its citizens, are so important. It is also the reason why the undermining of both arcane state power and market power from below requires the development of a dense network or 'heterarchy' of communications media which are controlled neither by the state nor by commercial markets. Publicly funded, non-profit and legally guaranteed media institutions of civil society, some of them run voluntarily and held directly accountable to their audiences through democratic procedures, are an essential ingredient of a revised public service model.

Numerous examples come to mind. The BBC model of broadcasting institutions, funded by a licence fee, could remain a leading symbol of the non-market, non-state sector, but only at the price of the abolition of the present system of government appointment of its management, the acknowledgement that their original (Reithian) brief is not fully attainable, and their internal democratization (perhaps along the lines of the system adopted in the Federal Republic of Germany, where representatives of 'socially relevant groups', including political parties, exercised some measure of influence over such matters as programming schedules, personal budgets and organizational structure). Other examples of this sector include the development of local independent cinemas and recording studios and leased-back broadcasting facilities. Political newspapers could be publicly subsidized. A dense and user-friendly network of community libraries equipped with the latest information technologies could be strengthened. Cooperatively run publishers and distributors, community radio stations and other conventional non-profit media would continue to play an important role in strengthening the foundations of a pluralist civil society. More versatile interpersonal communication could be ensured through publicly funded and equitably distributed telefaxes, videotex systems and electronic mail facilities. The development of publicly funded teleshopping facilities, which are most useful to housebound and senior citizens, would also have priority. And support could be provided for the development of new types of equipment – interactive televisions, digital copiers, camcorders and music synthesizers – capable of supporting the communication of opinions among various groups of citizens.

As far as possible, these non-market, non-state media would feed upon the increased flexibility and power and reduced costs of information processing provided by the new microelectronic technologies. These technologies, as market liberals have been quick to point out, have profound implications for a revised public service model. They are revolutionary heartland technologies, whose cost-reducing effects, and ever-widening applicability throughout civil society and the state, enable citizens to communicate in previously unthinkable ways. They are potentially a species of 'democratic technics' (Mumford). Improvements in their performance are not yet complete. Optical fibre channel capacity, software quality, random access memory (RAM) capacity, chip density and processing speeds continue to undergo rapid improvement. Nevertheless, these technologies have several characteristics in common that are unique to them as a group. They treat all kinds of information (speech, text, video, graphics) in digital form, thus facilitating the transfer of the same data between different media. The new technologies decrease the relative cost of information processing; bulk operations that would previously have been unthinkable can now be carried out. The decreasing size of equipment and the speedier information-processing and error-checking capacities also enable smaller-scale, decentralized and user-friendly operations within a framework of greater coordination and strategic control which links operations over vast distances. And – this feature is crucial – the new information technologies rupture the traditional television and radio pattern of offering a continuous sequence of programmes to mass audiences. Instead, the new electronic services strengthen the hand of 'narrowcasting' against broadcasting. They offer information on a more individualized basis: at any given moment, the 'receiver' is required to choose or to process the specific information he or she wants.[10]

At the same time, paradoxically, the microelectronic technologies tend to 'socialize' certain means of communication.[11] They reinforce the principle, lampooned by market liberals but essential to a revised public service model, that the means of communication belong to the public at large. The new technologies no doubt encourage the misuse of their socializing potential – evidenced in the rising concern about personal eavesdropping devices and 'junk calls' using synthesized voices and automated dialling – but such examples of the 'invasion of privacy' by digital means are symptomatic of the broader tendency whereby the element of rights to dispose of property privately become obsolete in the communications field. It has always been difficult to define property rights in the broadcast media. Those holding rights to occupy a plot of land or to mine the gold or uranium beneath its surface can establish precisely the dimensions of their claims. By contrast, broadcast frequencies are intangibles ('ether') that become meaningful as property only in conjunction with the technical means of transmission and reception. A similar problem of definition is evident in the treatment of postal systems and telephone networks as common carriers of signals. This problem of defining property rights is exacerbated by microelectronic technologies. Producers of information are also finding it difficult to keep their 'products' scarce and exclusive. They invoke copyright laws, frustrate attempts to copy data, scramble signals and mount other rearguard actions. But information is widely reproduced, transmitted, sampled and reconfigured without permission. In the US, where 'theft' of satellite television signals was to be prevented by scrambling them with the allegedly foolproof VCII system, it is estimated that half of the descramblers are now used illegally, adjusted to bypass the transmitters' controls. Such practices challenge the principle of privately controlled means of communication. Communication comes to be seen as *flows* among publics rather than as an exchange among discrete commodities which can be owned and controlled privately as things. This trend is arguably strengthened by the high-capacity digital networks (such as ISDN) currently being planned and constructed in Japan, Europe, the US and elsewhere. These networks enable individuals and groups to transmit 'private' messages to others through a common network, subject only to covering the cost of the transmission, which in any case could be reduced by treating the networks as a public facility, rather than as a source of private profit.

And Democracy?

In practice, these priorities – a new constitutional settlement, state regulation and restriction of private media markets and the development of a plurality of non-market, non-state communications systems – would radically alter the prevailing definition of the public service model, without capitulating to the charms of market liberalism. Public service media would henceforth refer to the whole infrastructure of state-funded and state-protected and non-state institutions of communication which serve to circulate opinions among a wide plurality of citizens. Among the key advantages of the revised public service model sketched here is its theoretical and practical recognition of complexity. It recognizes that 'freedom of communication' comprises a bundle of (potentially) conflicting component freedoms. It acknowledges that in a complex society the original public service assumption that all the citizens of a nation-state can talk to each other like a family sitting and chatting around the domestic hearth is unworkable; that it is impossible for all citizens simultaneously to be full-time senders and receivers of information; that at any point in time and space some citizens will normally choose to remain silent and only certain other individuals and groups will choose to communicate with others; and that (as the famous Red Lion decision of the US Supreme Court affirmed)[12] this freedom publicly to express or receive opinions is not identical with the freedom to own and to control the means of communication.

In acknowledging the facts of complexity, diversity and difference, this revised public service model offers an additional advantage. It harbours doubts about whether any one person, group, committee, party or organization can ever be trusted to make superior choices on matters of concern to citizens. The new public service model embraces the insight of the Czech humorist, Jan Werich, who observed that the struggle against the stupidity of those who exercise power is the only human struggle that is always in vain, but can never be abandoned. In sum, the public service model is best seen as a vital requirement of an open, tolerant and lively society in which great big dogmas and smelly little orthodoxies of all kinds are held in check, and in which, thanks to the existence of a genuine plurality of media of communication, various individuals and groups could openly express their solidarity with (or their opposition to) other citizens' likes and dislikes, proposals, tastes and ideals.

Fundamental questions to do with democracy arise at this point. Would a revivified public service model serve to reinforce or to contradict conventional wisdom about democracy? Could it deepen our appreciation of its positive advantages – and its limitations? Clear-headed responses to such questions are important, both because the subject of the media is neglected by virtually all contemporary democratic theorists and because the concept of democracy itself is presently dogged by confusion masked by familiarity. Much recent writing on democracy seems unaware of this confusion, instead relying on the textbook technique of restating with great unoriginality themes and problems familiar to previous generations of political theorists. In several recent works I have attempted to break this habit and to stretch the limits of the democratic imagination by proposing a non-foundationalist understanding of democracy as a system of procedural rules with pluralist implications. These rules specify *who* is authorized to make collective decisions and through which *procedures* such decisions are to be made, regardless of the areas of life in which democracy is practised. In contrast to all forms of heteronomous government or 'monocracy' (Mastellone), democracy comprises procedures for arriving at collective decisions in a way which secures the fullest possible and qualitatively best participation of interested parties and their representatives. At a minimum – here the normative implications of my proceduralist definition of democracy become evident – democratic procedures include equal and universal adult suffrage in constituencies of various size; majority rule and guarantees of minority rights, which ensure that collective decisions are approved by a substantial number of those entitled to make them; the rule of law; constitutional guarantees of freedom of assembly and expression and other liberties, which help ensure that those expected to decide or to elect those who decide can choose among real alternatives; and various social policies (in fields such as health, education, child-care and basic income provision) which prevent market exchanges from becoming dominant and ensure that citizens can live as free equals and thereby enjoy their basic political and civil entitlements.

In large-scale, complex societies, regular assemblies of 'the people' as a whole are technically impossible. Direct democracy, the participation of citizens in the *agora*, is suited only to small states and organizations in which, according to Rousseau, 'the people find it easy to meet and in which every citizen can easily get to know all the others'. That is why modern democracy requires both mechanisms of representation and the institutional division of state and civil society; that is, the building of a pluralistic, self-organizing (international) civil society which is coordinated and guaranteed by multilayered (supranational) state institutions, which are in turn held permanently accountable to civil society by mechanisms – political parties, legislatures and communications media – which keep open the channels between state and social institutions. Expressed differently, a democracy is a multilayered political and social mosaic in which political decision-makers at the local, regional, national and supranational levels are assigned the job of serving and codefining the *res publica*, while, for their part, citizens living within civil society are obliged to exercise vigilance in preventing each other and their rulers from abusing their powers and violating the spirit of the commonwealth.[13]

A critic might ask: 'But what is so desirable about democracy, aside from the fact that most people today say it's a good thing? Isn't the term democracy polluted by its diverse and contradictory meanings, as Sartori has pointed out? And anyway, why sympathize with *your* particular understanding of democratic procedures? What is so special about it?' Such questions exploit democracy's lack of philosophical self-confidence. They need to be answered. In a famous aphorism, Novalis pointed out that philosophy *qua* philosophy is required to explain itself. This aphorism applies equally to contemporary democratic theory, which is slowly waking from an extended period of merrymaking. Despite their current popularity, democratic ideals nowadays resemble a homeless drunk staggering uncertainly in search of a lamppost for support, if not illumination. This was not always so. For the past two centuries virtually every democratic thinker in Europe and elsewhere has attempted, with some confidence, to justify democracy by referring back to a substantive grounding principle. There are many cases that can be cited: the belief of Mazzini that the growth of democracy is a Law of History; the argument of Georg Forster, Tom Paine and others that democracy is grounded in the natural rights of citizens; the Benthamite assumption that democracy is an implied condition of the principle of utility; the conviction of Theodor Parker that democracy is a form of government based on the principle of eternal, God-given justice; and the (Marxian) claim that the triumph of authentic democracy is dependent upon the world-historical struggle of the proletariat. Belief in these various first principles has today crumbled. The salient philosophical themes of our era are the insistence on the horizoned and biased character of human life, the emphasis on the cognitive intransparency of the world, and awareness of the impossibility of substituting certain knowledge of the 'independent' structures of the 'real world' for uncertain and tentative theoretical interpretations and revisable practical judgements. Democratic theory cannot ignore this trend, and that is why, in my view, democracy is no longer understandable as a self-evidently desirable norm. Democracy is now suffering a deep (if less than visible) crisis of authority which cannot be cured by concocting such ersatz imaginary foundations as rational argumentation, principles of autonomy or knowledge of a 'good which we can know in common' (Sandel).

Can democratic theory live without such foundationalist assumptions? Can democracy come to be seen by those who enjoy or envy it as a system guided by a 'higher amorality' (Luhmann) that discourages moralizing politics and refuses to judge opponents as 'enemies'? In *Public Life and Late Capitalism* I first argued (against Habermas and others) that democracy should not be treated as a form of life founded upon substantive normative principles. Following a clue provided in Hans Kelsen's *Vom Wesen und Wert der Demokratie*,[14] I proposed that the sense of common purpose of pre-modern societies cannot democratically be recreated under modern conditions, and I suggested that the philosophy of democracy cannot become a universal language game, capable of knowing everything, refuting all its opponents and pointing to the practical synthesis of all differences. I further proposed that democracy is best understood as an implied condition and practical consequence of philosophical and political pluralism, which is not itself a philosophical first principle but instead understandable through the logic of occasion, as practised among the pre-Socratics. And I concluded that the separation of civil society from the state, as well as the democratization of each – a post-capitalist civil society guarded by a democratic political system – are among the necessary conditions for enabling a genuine plurality of individuals and groups openly to express their solidarity with (or opposition to) others' ideals and forms of life.

This understanding of democracy takes care of the objection that the very term 'democracy' is polluted by its diverse and contradictory meanings. Paradoxically, it insists, against Sartori and others, that what is viewed as 'democratic' at any given time and place can be maintained and/or contested as such only through *these* democratic procedures. These normatively inclined procedures are the *conditio sine qua non* of post-foundationalism; whoever rejects them falls back either into the trap of foundationalism and its pompous belief in truth and ethics or into a cynical and self-defeating relativism which insists that there are no certain or preferable guidelines in life, thereupon displaying the same logical incoherence as the Cretan Epimenides, who truthfully declared that all Cretans were liars.

When seen in this new way, the concept of democratization not only escapes the twin traps of relativism and foundationalism. It also joins hands with the revised model of public service media sketched above. Each requires the other, if only to underscore its abandonment of the futile search for transhistorical ideals, definite truths and safe highroads of human existence. Each is driven by a profound scepticism and mistrust of power and ideals and the devils they produce. Together, they make it more possible for us to live without the indefensible ideological claims – progress, truth, history, humanity, nature, socialism, individualism, utility, nation, the public good and sovereignty of the people – upon which the early modern advocates of democracy and 'liberty of the press' based their claims for greater equality and freedom.

Risks and Reversals

The non-foundationalist understanding of democracy and public service media sketched here undoubtedly requires elaboration. New and undogmatic arguments for the compatibility and superiority of the democratic method and public service communications are needed. Consider just one randomly chosen example from the field of environmental policy.

Anxiety about the effects of environmental waste and degradation on human life in the next century has grown considerably in recent years. There are justified fears that certain key resources will be depleted, that toxic wastes will affect our health, and that climatic changes may occur. Indeed, both the scale and complexity of these ecological problems and the difficult task of shifting to sustainable patterns of growth confront us with massive *risks*, in the sense of probable hazards to human life resulting from our exposure to certain substances and eco-systemic changes.[15] The production and distribution of environmental risks is now for the first time becoming problematic on a global scale, and their probable growth suggests that we are in the midst of a massive, long-term experiment with ourselves and our biospheric environment. The harmful risks generated by water pollution, radiation and the greenhouse effect have levelling effects upon us. They are neither geographically nor sociologically limited. They criss-cross national boundaries and boomerang on rich and poor, the powerful and the less powerful alike. They tend to devalue the economic and aesthetic value of property (as the death of forests shows). And many of the new environmental risks – from poisonous additives in foodstuffs to nuclear and chemical contaminants – are 'invisible'. They elude human perception and, in certain cases, their effects are detectable only in the offspring of those who are currently affected.

In the face of these unprecedented environmental risks, democratic procedures – backed up by public service media which serve as early warning devices that circulate new and controversial opinions about such risks – have a renewed and wholly novel pertinence at the end of the twentieth century. The key point – still poorly recognized in democratic theory and media studies – is that both democratic procedures and public service media facilitate the *disapproval* and *revision* of established agreements, and that for this reason they are uniquely suited to complex societies beset with ecological problems. A plurality of uncensored media could break down the present pattern of simplified and prejudiced media reporting of risks. Current media coverage of risks often apes the point of view of governments, corporations and professional information czars. Insufficient attention is given to the opinions of dissenting scientists and to events not prepackaged for audience consumption. General assignment and local-beat reporters and their editors are often ill informed about the complexity of risk situations. Risks tend to be treated as isolated and sensational novelties. They are neither situated in wider sociotechnical contexts nor placed in the perspective of alternative or competing risks. They are reduced to the status of 'accidents' and 'calamities', along with tornadoes, mid-air collisions, chemical-plant fires and gas explosions.

A public service system of communications would be likely to transform these patterns of risk definition. It would reduce the quantity of prejudiced and sensationalist media reporting of hazards, the premature disclosure of poorly analysed information and the oversimplifications and distortions in interpreting technical risk information. It could help to expose the hidden socioeconomic and political powers working self-interestedly to manage the public definition of risks. It could heighten awareness of the deep uncertainties in risk estimation and management. Public service media could thereby stimulate the public acceptance of level-headed strategies for reducing or eliminating serious risks.

In these tasks, public service media would undoubtedly be aided by more and better democracy in the institutions of civil society and the state. Democratic procedures are superior to all other types of decision-making, not because they guarantee both a consensus and 'good' decisions, but because they provide citizens who are affected by certain decisions with the possibility of reconsidering their judgements about the quality and unintended consequences of these decisions. Democratic procedures sometimes allow the majority to decide things about which they are blissfully ignorant. But they also enable minorities to challenge blissfully or stubbornly ignorant majorities, to bring them to their senses. Democratic procedures enable citizens to think twice and to say 'no'. They are for this reason best suited to the task of publicly monitoring and controlling (and sometimes shutting down) complex and tightly coupled 'high-risk' organizations, whose failure (as in Bhopal, Three Mile Island, Chernobyl and Ust-Kamenogorsk) can have catastrophic ecological and social consequences. Max Weber once defined democracy for General Ludendorff's benefit (and with his approval) as a system in which 'the people choose a leader who then says, "Now shut up and obey me"'. Such impatience with disagreement and the clash of opinions misses the key advantage of democracy. Democratic procedures increase the level of flexibility and reversibility - or 'biodegradability' - of decision-making. They invite dispute. They create dissatisfaction with conditions as they are, and even stir citizens to anger. And they recognize the inescapable need in social and political life to resort to Solomonic judgements (Elster). In the face of uncertainty about how to cope with our own ignorance, democratic procedures encourage incremental learning and trial-and-error modification or 'muddling through'. Decisions are based on revocable preferences which are, in turn, the resultant of deliberate and considered confrontations among at least several competing points of view.

Only democratic procedures, reinforced by a plurality of communications media, can openly and fairly select certain kinds of danger for public attention, and carefully monitor and bring to heel those responsible for managing risky organizations, thereby minimizing the possibility of error and reducing the chances of the big mistake. Democratic procedures and public service media are in this respect essential correctives to the wishful (Hayekian) belief in the decentralized anonymity of the market as a superior, self-correcting mechanism in a world of complex pressures and interconnections. They are also important correctives to the mistaken trust in the therapeutic powers of unbridled technical expertise, for they raise the level and quality of 'risk communication' by guaranteeing the open flow of opinions and risk evaluations and controversies back and forth among citizens, academic experts, administrators, interest groups and social movements. Democratic procedures combined with public service media can open up and render accountable the process in which citizens, experts and policy-makers comprehend, estimate, evaluate and deal with the probabilities and consequences of risks. They are an indispensable means of rendering accountable those politicians and entrepreneurs who turn a blind eye to the environmental damage and 'normal accidents' (Perrow) which plague high-risk projects. They are vital means of breaking down unwarranted confidence in 'the facts'. They help ensure that risk data are expressed in publicly understandable terms, that the profound uncertainties surrounding risk estimates are widely appreciated, and that the intuitive sense of risk among citizens is acknowledged and respected, not dismissed as 'irrational nonsense'. Public service media and democratic procedures are also vital methods of controlling professional experts who seek to define acceptable levels of risk by means of technical analyses of probability – or simply by falling back on the childish solipsism that whatever is not believed could not possibly be harmful. Democracy and public service media are reflexive means of controlling the exercise of power. They are unsurpassed methods of checking the unending arrogance and foolishness of those who wield it. Contrary to the view of conservatives, who blindly trust in the unadventurous prudence of the anointed few, they are the best friends of practical wisdom. Democracy and public service media are unrivalled early warning devices. They help to define and publicize risks that are not worth taking. They dampen the reckless impulse to sail uncharted oceans, to risk getting lost or shipwrecked. They ensure that a known good is not lightly surrendered for an unknown better. They navigate the rough seas of uncertainty with caution and prudence.

This does not mean that mature democracies tend to produce social and political equilibrium. Under enduring dictatorships (Franco's Spain or Husák's Czechoslovakia are examples) time appears to stand still. Even though individuals continue to be born, to grow up, fall in love, quarrel, to have children and to die, everything around them becomes motionless, petrified and repetitious. Life is utterly boring. Potential scandals are systematically hushed up. Individuals are required to nod off into a 'permanent siesta' (Bastos). In fully democratic systems, by contrast, everything is in perpetual motion. Citizens are not only caught up in the turbulence produced by the self-paralysing tendencies of democracy,[16] they are also catapulted by their liberty into a state of permanent unease. There is difference, openness and constant competition among power groups to produce and to control the definition of reality. Hence, there is always an abundance of information flows. And there are public scandals which unfold when publics learn about events which had been kept secret because, if made public in advance, they could not have been carried out.

All this is unavoidable and proper. For the chief and unsurpassed advantage of democracy is not that it guarantees peace and quiet and good decisions, but that it offers citizens the right to judge (and to reconsider their judgements about) the quality of those decisions. Democracy is rule by publics who make and remake judgements in public. That is why the public service model outlined here is not a recipe for creating a heaven of communication on earth. It would in practice not put a stop to public controversies about the meaning and scope of either democracy or 'freedom of expression'. Freedom of communication is not something which can be realized in a definitive or perfect sense. It is an ongoing project without an ultimate solution. It is a project which constantly generates new constellations of dilemmas and contradictions. Dworkin has pointed out, correctly, that freedom of communication is therefore jeopardized by cost – benefit analyses and the forlorn search for general and substantive rules for deciding particular disputes about the scope and meaning of 'freedom of communication'.[17] A more fully democratic society guaranteed by public service media will surely suffer from ongoing 'jurisdictional conflicts',[18] such as whether broadcasting should be controlled locally or defined territorially or based upon relatively homogeneous ethnic, cultural, economic or political identities. There will be endless debates about pornography and obscenity or about what constitutes seditious or libellous speech. To what extent should corporate speech and advertising-funded media be permitted? Is a statutory right of reply of citizens against their media representatives a good thing? Should freedom of expression across nation-state frontiers be constitutionally guaranteed? Is the grip of television loosening? Are there occasions – the *lustrace* policies of the post-communist countries might be an example – when freedom of expression serves to reduce freedom of expression?

To imagine a world free of questions of this kind and unencumbered by debates over what may or may not be published, transmitted, read, seen or heard is like imagining a society without politics: all the people in it would have to be dead. In democratic societies, the scope and meaning of freedom of communication and the process of representation will always be contentious, whereas a society that is drugged on either money or political authority, and which contains no controversies over freedom of expression and representation, is a society that is surely dying, or dead.

NOTES

1 See Pierre Rosanvallon, 'Malaise dans la représentation', in François Furet et al., *La République du Centre* (Paris, Calmann-Lévy, 1988).
2 The most sophisticated defence of the public service broadcasting model is Paddy Scannell, 'Public service broadcasting: history of a concept', in A. Goodwin and G. Whannel (eds), *Understanding Television* (London, Methuen, 1989), and 'Public service broadcasting and modern public life', *Media, Culture and Society*, 11 (1989), 135–66.
3 Paddy Scannell, 'Music for the multitude?: the dilemmas of the BBC's music policy, 1923–1946', *Media, Culture and Society*, 3 (1981), 243–60. The decline of the paternalist tradition in British radio is also well examined in Richard Barbrook, 'Melodies or rhythms?: the competition for the Greater London FM radio licence', *Popular Music*, 9:2 (1990), 203–19.
4 John Keane, *The Media and Democracy* (Cambridge, Polity Press, 1991).
5 See the sketches provided in Graham Murdock and Peter Golding, 'Information poverty and political inequality: citizenship in the age of privatized communications', *Journal of Communication*, 39:3 (1989), 180–95, and Jeffrey B. Abramson et al., *The Electronic Commonwealth: the impact of new media technologies on democratic politics* (Princeton, NJ, Princeton University Press, 1988).
6 Alec Nove, *The Economics of Feasible Socialism* (London, Allen and Unwin, 1983).
7 Karl Polanyi, *The Origins of Our Time* (London, Victor Gollancz, 1945).
8 See Nicholas Garnham, *European Communications Policy* (London, CCIS, Oct. 1988).
9 See J. W. Freiberg, *The French Press: class, state, and ideology*, (New York, Praeger, 1981), ch. 3.
10 Ian Miles, *Information Technology and Information Society: options for the future* (Brighton, Sussex University, 1988).
11 G. J. Mulgan, *Rethinking Freedom in the Age of Digital Networks* (London, CCIS, Oct. 1988).
12 *Red Lion Broadcasting* v. *FCC*, 395 US 367, 23 L. ed. 2d 371, 89 S. Ct. 1794 (1969).
13 This theme is developed in J. Keane, *Public Life and Late Capitalism* (Cambridge and New York, Cambridge University Press, 1984), and J. Keane, *Democracy and Civil Society* (London and New York, Verso, 1988).
14 Hans Kelson, *Vom Wesen und Wert der Demokratie* (Tübingen, Vandenhoeck and Ruprecht, 1981, first published 1929), pp. 98–104, and his 'Foundations of democracy', *Ethics*, 66 (Oct. 1955), 1–101.
15 Ulrich Beck, *Risikogesellschaft: Auf den Weg in eine andere Moderne* (Frankfurt am Main, Suhrkamp, 1986), and Beck, *Gegengifte: Die organisierte Unverantwortlichkeit* (Frankfurt am Main, Suhrkamp, 1989).
16 The self-paralysing tendencies of democratic regimes are discussed in J. Keane,

'O mõci in nemõči demokracije', in John Keane, *Despotizem in demokracije* (Ljubljana, KRT, 1990), pp. 209–47 – an interview conducted by Tomaž Mastnak and published in Slovene, and forthcoming in English in my *Twentieth Century Political Thought.*

17 Ronald Dworkin, 'Devaluing liberty', *Index on Censorship*, 17:8 (Sept. 1988), pp. 7–8.

18 On jurisdictional conflicts see Robert A. Dahl, *Dilemmas of Pluralist Democracy: autonomy vs. control* (New Haven, CT, and London, Yale University Press, 1982), p. 85.

12

DEMOCRATIC CITIZENSHIP IN A POST-COMMUNIST ERA

Danilo Zolo

Which Citizenship?

In the era of post-communism the concept of 'citizenship' is likely to become a fully legitimate component of the European political lexicon. For decades this concept has been strictly pertinent to British and American political thought, and even in this area it has not played a very significant role. Today a number of authors, especially in Italy and England, agree on the importance of the notion of citizenship for a conception of democracy that is both non-formalistic and faithful to the principles of western liberal tradition. The idea of citizenship seems to be able to fill the theoretical and political void – the 'democratic melancholy'[1] – which many authors see as the distressing consequence of the fall of the communist utopia. However, these authors give the concept of citizenship very different meanings, and therefore attach divergent political values to it.[2]

In this chapter I would like to contribute to a more rigorous conceptual delimitation of the term, and at the same time to propose a specific theoretical and political conception of citizenship. Of course it is not my ambition to elaborate a definition which is empirically rigorous or even claims explanatory capability. My aim is rather to work out an interpretation which is simple and coherent from a theoretical point of view and can be plausibly referred to the political, social and cultural events which in modern Europe originated this notion.

From a theoretical and epistemological point of view I will mainly refer

Translated from the Italian by Francesco P. Vertova.

to systems theory, though in a very liberalized form with respect to the approach of its founding fathers, from Bertalanffy to Luhmann.[3] Moving from the classical theses of T. H. Marshall, I will discuss the more recent contributions by Anthony Giddens, J. M. Barbalet and David Held. Finally I shall set out my own point of view.

Marshall: Citizenship and Social Equality

According to Marshall, the distinctive feature of modern citizenship that opposes it to feudal status is its tendency towards equality.[4] An 'image of ideal citizenship' always emerges where the institutions of citizenship develop. This 'ideal citizenship' operates as a standard for measuring actual political achievements and as a target of increasing social expectations.[5] Citizenship rights, however, in spite of their pressure towards equality, cannot be separated from the rise and development of capitalism, and capitalism 'is a system not of equality, but of inequality'.[6] On this paradox Marshall's entire reflection is centred. How can western political systems become stable and develop, Marshall asks, if they are based on such a radical conflict between 'opposing principles'?

As is well known, Marshall held that in the early development of the market economy the attribution of civil rights to individuals was a functional necessity. At this stage the (civil) logic of status did not conflict with the (market) logic of contract. For civil citizenship enabled each individual to engage him- or herself as 'an independent unit' in economic competition, and legitimized the denial of social protection on the grounds that all citizens were presumed to be equipped with the legal means to affirm and protect themselves.[7] As to political citizenship, Marshall maintained that it was 'full of potential dangers to the capitalist system'[8] because it provided the working class with a means – the peaceful use of political and trade union power as an alternative to violent revolution – which was the road to the reforms of the 'egalitarian policies' of the twentieth century and the establishment of social rights.

Marshall acknowledged that social citizenship cannot undermine the non-egalitarian logic of the market. The extension of social benefits is not and cannot be directed towards equality of income. Rather, it can achieve a 'general enrichment of the concrete substance of civilized life' through the reduction of risks and insecurity and the equalization of less fortunate citizens with respect to health, employment, age and family conditions.

Social citizenship implies a sort of invasion of the logic of contract by the logic of status because it tends to subordinate market prices to social justice and to replace free exchange with the declaration of rights. These rights have become so deeply embedded in the system of contract that they can no longer be said to be foreign to the practice of the market. It can be said, therefore, that while social citizenship cannot remove inequalities, it can 'alter the pattern of social inequality'.[9] What remains is no longer inequality of status but simple inequality of income within some limited sectors of private consumption. And this kind of inequality is much more socially acceptable. The tension between the opposing principles of citizenship and the market, thanks to the social compromises it makes possible, is therefore an essential factor in the stability and development of industrial societies.[10]

Giddens, Barbalet and Held: Criticism of Marshall's Evolutionary Optimism

It can hardly be denied that Marshall's account of citizenship is optimistic in nature. Remarkably optimistic is the idea that citizenship naturally tends towards equality, thanks to a kind of evolutionary continuity among the different stages of its development. Equally optimistic are Marshall's evaluations concerning the targets that the welfare state has reached, or could reach.

On these aspects of Marshall's thought has developed, as is well known, a theoretical debate in which Anthony Giddens, J. M. Barbalet and more recently David Held have taken part. Giddens was the first to blame Marshall for presenting the development of citizenship rights as a gradual process, emerging spontaneously from the 'enlightened' development of market institutions through the benevolent protection of the state, rather than as a product of the political struggles of subordinate classes.[11]

J. M. Barbalet, for his part, claims that Marshall's analysis sees citizenship rights as substantially homogeneous, and that this is the reason why their development is described by him as a steady and gradual passage from the civil to the political and the social stage. According to Barbalet, this approach prevents the analysis of the internal tensions of citizenship rights, particularly the tension between civil rights, whose exercise increases the political and economic power of their holders, and social rights, which are simply consumers' rights and therefore do not provide people with any power.[12] In any event, the provision of 'social rights' to citizens, Barbalet maintains, should not be confused with the social policies of the welfare state. They are quite different things. The social provisions of the welfare state cannot be understood simply as the outcome of the political struggles of subordinate classes, as the legal sanction of their interests imposed upon the dominant classes. Social and welfare policies also play an important role in social integration, political security and economic development, and are constantly subordinated to the fulfilment of these functional requirements. It cannot be maintained, therefore, that while civil citizenship was perfectly compatible with capitalist development, political and social citizenship challenge the system of inequality of the market economy.[13] In fact, Barbalet claims, the so-called social rights do not alter power relations within the productive sphere, because they affect the mechanisms of the distribution of resources rather than those of their production.

In a brilliant and polemical essay, David Held[14] has recently claimed that 'the entire scheme through which Marshall and Giddens examine the relationship between class and citizenship is partial and limited'.[15] Both Marshall and Giddens, Held maintains, underestimate the complexity of modern citizenship in that they rigidly connect it with the issue of class and the capitalist mode of production.

According to Held, this leads to a 'restricted conception' of citizenship, since citizenship is to be conceived as full participation of individuals in the community they belong to.[16] In western history this participation has been faced with obstacles of various kinds, including gender, race and age. Any discussion of citizenship must therefore account for the different struggles that groups, movements and classes have waged against specific forms of discrimination, social stratification and political oppression. Crucial political issues such as the reproductive freedom claimed by the feminist movement, or the problems raised by black movements, the ecologists, the defenders of children's rights or the advocates of the moral status of animals and nature, cannot be ignored, as they are by both Marshall and his Marxist critics.[17] On the other hand, in spite of the many criticisms that can be made of the market economy, one cannot overlook the close historical link between capitalist development, the differentiation of the economic system from the political system, and the extension of civil and political rights in the framework of western political pluralism.

Secondly, Held claims that today no discussion of citizenship can be limited to a consideration of the situation of individual rights within the nation-state. The process of globalization has widened the gap between citizenship, which bestows rights upon individuals within a single national community, and the development of international legislation, which imposes new regulations on individuals as well as on governmental and non-governmental organizations. In spite of this gap, the area of possible conflict between the rights and duties established by national authorities and those provided by international agencies is growing wider.

The Dimension of Modern Citizenship

In my view, Held's criticism of the 'restricted conception' of citizenship is justified in some important respects. What seems to me completely acceptable is his proposal to abandon the Marxist outlook and his insistence on individual 'autonomy' as the key idea for a non-restricted conception of citizenship rights.[18] Marxist thinkers, following the young Marx of *The Jewish Question* have always been suspicious of democratic citizenship. They have opposed to it an organic conception of democracy and an economic and class-centred analysis of the bourgeois state. This has led to a tendency, which seems partly to affect even Giddens's and Barbalet's approach, to underestimate the whole universe of the rights of liberty, of pluralism and of the rule of law, often criticized as a piece of pure formalism and a *deceptive* illusion. Within Marxist revisionism, the issue of citizenship rights has also been perceived instrumentally, as a gradual and peaceful alternative to socialist revolution, rather than as a strategic goal in itself. Hints of this position can be found even in Marshall's theory of citizenship.

Today, the theoretical crisis of Marxism and the collapse of the experience of 'actually existing' socialism allow no room for an instrumental conception of democratic citizenship. In the post-communist era the dispute over the anti-capitalist potential of political and social rights has lost any theoretical or practical interest, even within the welfare state. The crucial problem is quite different. What can be taken for granted is not the future triumph of an actually existing or imaginary socialism, but in its place the absolute supremacy of capitalism and market economy. Given the necessity of conciliating rights with the market, the problem of democratic citizenship is that of whether, in post-industrial societies, there is room for an experience of democracy and the rule of law which is not totally subordinated to the market model and its competitive logic. In this respect it seems difficult not to agree with David Held's theses.

However, I remain unconvinced by the tendency, which can be found in Held and in many other authors,[19] to broaden the scope of citizenship so as to include in it all of the normative claims that have emerged in this century in the west: civil and political liberties, social, economic and industrial rights,[20] 'reproductive rights' (including both the right to abortion and the right to a free motherhood),[21] children's rights, ecological rights, rights to genetic integrity, not to mention the rights of future generations, of non-human beings and of inanimate objects.[22]

It is doubtful whether, from the standpoint of a coherent theory of citizenship, this concept can usefully include any new category of interests which may become publicly acknowledged. In my view this normative inflation of the concept of citizenship runs the risk of diluting its historical and functional significance, of ignoring the formal and substantive differences which distinguish the various kinds of rights and, above all, of ignoring the tensions existing among them. From both a practical and a theoretical point of view this may blur the relationship between citizenship and democracy and prevent the elaboration of a realistic strategy for establishing the rights of 'democratic citizenship'.[23]

Citizenship and Social Differentiation

Against the tendency to broaden the concept of citizenship and to underestimate its internal tensions, I propose what I consider a useful and coherent notion of citizenship, which takes the following points into account:

1   Modern citizenship is closely related to the process of functional differentiation which leads to the emergence of 'formal' legal and political institutions. Legal and political formalism is the result of the two major processes of differentiation accompanying the rise of the modern state: the separation of the political subsystem from the ethical and religious one, and the autonomization of the economic subsystem from the political one.[24] The attribution of citizenship 'formalizes' individual agents precisely because it abstracts from the (economic, social, religious and so on) determinations which characterize them within other primary subsystems.

2   The problem of citizenship as the legal and formal attribution of the status of citizen – that is, the status of an individual entitled to rights within the political system – is a *modern* problem which emerges against the background of the great bourgeois revolutions and parallels the development of industrial capitalism. In this sense the notion of citizenship is primarily to be opposed to that of 'subjection', according to which individuals are not entitled to any rights as regards political authority, but are simply subjected to duties and commands.

3   From both the 'quantitative' point of view of the designation of the members of citizenship and the 'qualitative' point of view of the definition of its normative contents, the notion of citizenship rests on the individualist assumptions of classical liberal theory. It is the individual, rather than the family, the clan, the city, the nation or humankind, that is the 'legal subject'. The status of citizen stems from

bourgeois claims to individual freedom against the state and, as a consequence, from the 'limited' character of the political system, from its being a constitutional state bound by mechanisms of division and checks on power. Thus modern citizenship counters the classical and Christian idea, from Aristotle to Thomas Aquinas to Rousseau, of organic membership of the city. Political organicism sees individuals as part of a stratified system of social relations, resting on grounds that are both ethical and natural. On the contrary, modern citizenship sanctions individuals' selective membership of the partial and artificial dimension of politics.

4   Citizenship operates within the sovereign sphere of the modern state; that is, of a national, territorial and bureaucratic political organization. Natural law theory sees citizenship rights as natural and universal rights to which any human being is entitled as a member of a political community. In practice, however, the provision of the formal legal protection and the positive benefits associated with citizenship is regulated by the modern political code, which is a functional code hinged on the requirements of 'security' and 'regulation of fear'. This qualifies universal rights through both rules of exclusion and rules of subordination.[25] In principle only the members of a national political community are citizens, in opposition to the 'foreigners'.

It is clear from this historical and theoretical framework that the only plausible meaning of citizenship is the 'republican' one, at least in the (broad) definition Jürgen Habermas has recently proposed: 'The republican component of citizenship is completely seperated from membership of a pre-political community in which integration is achieved through descendance, tradition and a common language. The identity of a nation made up of citizens is not constituted by ethnic or cultural affinities, but by the practice of the citizens themselves, actively exercising their rights of participation and communication'.[26] As a consequence, it is evident that some meanings of citizenship are neither interesting nor pertinent and, besides, that some normative attributions to citizens cannot easily be included in the stock of citizenship rights.

In particular, those meanings of citizenship are not pertinent which presuppose an Aristotelian (Aristotelian and Thomist, Aristotelian and Rousseauian, and so on) understanding of the political system seen as the general social system; that is, as a functionally undifferentiated system. According to this view citizens' rights and duties are grounded on the ethical and metaphysical ideas of the common good and the 'good life', and the values associated with those ideas can be secured through politics. Today, after the collapse of Leninist Jacobinism and the failure of 'actually existing socialism', this pre-modern version of citizenship is put forward by English and American communitarians and, in Europe, by the advocates of the *Rehabilitierung der praktischen Philosophie*.[27] Both of them oppose ethical relativism, formalism and scientism, which they see as the distinctive features of modernity. Instead they take an intrinsically normative view of political citizenship, designed to be the moral premise of a fully human experience of order and participation. They oppose a 'communitarian' and non-competitive (cooperative) conception of citizenship to the individualistic and competitive one.

In my view this conception of politics, taking on the experience of scarcely differentiated social groups, conflicts with the fundamental features of modern industrial societies. These features are a high degree of differentiation of social functions, a wide ethical and cognitive pluralism, an increasing autonomization of individuals from the normative pressure of tradition and collective beliefs, and the decline of the centrality of the political system with respect to other primary social subsystems. In contemporary industrial and post-industrial societies the political system is no longer the universal social system theorized by Aristotle. It is a functional subsystem among others (such as the subsystems of economy, science and technology, religion, family, leisure and so on). Any attempt to make the political system as central and universal as it was in ancient societies is bound to superimpose the model of brotherly love, friendship and (paternalistic and patriarchal) family relationships on the conditions of increasing functional abstractness of complex societies.

I think that, contrary to the tendency to merge and contaminate differentiated functional codes, it will be more and more necessary in the future to distinguish between values that can be pursued by political means and values that cannot and that should be entrusted to other functional subsystems. The realist conception of politics I personally propose leads to the conclusion that the political system cannot, without serious drawbacks, perform any function other than that of 'reducing insecurity' through the management of 'social risks'. It follows that the political system is an 'exclusive' rather than a universally inclusive system and that it is not egalitarian, for it inevitably involves a degree of subordination of the ruled to the rulers.

The Internal Tensions of Democratic Citizenship

My elaboration of a notion of citizenship that David Held (along with others) is likely to consider 'restricted' is not meant to be an academic exercise. In my view its theoretical utility, if any, is that it can suggest a ranking of priorities from the standpoint of a democratic strategy of 'struggle for rights'.[28] Most importantly, it enables one to account for the functional tensions threatening democratic citizenship in the post-industrial countries.

A realist consideration of the history of European constitutionalism can hardly warrant Marshall's, Bobbio's and probably Held's opinion that the emergence of rights is the major mark of historical progress in the modern world.[29] The claim to 'human rights' and their enactment in the constitutions of modern states and in the declarations of international agencies are the core of the Enlightenment project of modernity and its individualist, rationalist and secular idea of emancipation.[30] Even those who are ready to endorse this project without reserve and to consider modernization as 'historical progress' cannot but grant that this project has met with overwhelming obstacles and is still largely uncompleted. Today a vast literature – the literature of crisis and 'post-modernism' – polemically points out that the project has not been accomplished, or has simply failed.[31]

Both the idea of a linear development of rights – from the civil to the political and the social sphere – and the idea that this development is the product of successful struggles, rather than self-moving evolution or benevolent concession, express an emphatic and rhetorical view of modernity. A realist account of the theory and history of rights shows that the declaration and enforcement of rights does not simply correspond to the victory of individual values over economic and political oppression. Rather it points to the emerging awareness that rights are increasingly endangered in complex societies. Here we are faced with a disquieting paradox: the process of social differentiation leads to the advent of civil and political citizenship, which is a body of individual rights of liberty and participation. But in societies governed by sophistic-ated and ever-faster technical development, those very rights are threatened by the steady increase in the power of humans over humans and of humans over nature, and this is mostly an unbalanced and destructive power.[32]

Not only does a realist analysis show that citizenship rights are 'groundless' because of their empirical origin, depending on different historical contingencies, though usually characterized by civil conflict or war.[33] Most importantly, it shows that rights present internal functional inconsistencies which risk depriving them of any practical significance, as authors of chiefly Marxist inspiration have suggested. But Marxist accounts are flawed in that they fail to grasp the variety of functional domains from which the internal tensions of citizenship in differentiated and complex societies emerge. I will give a sketch of three general aspects of this phenomenon, which it is worth discussing in greater detail.

In the early 1950s, T. H. Marshall could maintain, as we have seen, that citizenship rights involve a pressure towards equality. Today such a claim could seem a theoretical blunder or a provocative political remark. Actually quite the opposite seems true: citizenship rights involve a pressure towards inequality. Only the Olympian irenism of such an academic moralist as John Rawls can ignore the moral of the defeat of communism and the crisis of democratic socialism, namely that liberty and equality are largely conflicting values. This conflict, which is conspicuous in the opposition between the rights of liberty and social rights, as Norberto Bobbio has lucidly acknowledged,[34] is internal to civil citizenship itself and is not balanced by universal franchise and the other components of political citizenship.

A number of rights falling under the normative catalogue of citizenship amount merely to the protection of 'negative freedom', which means that they simply limit state interference in individual lives. Among these are the rights of personal freedom, freedom of opinion, privacy and, most typically, the procedural guarantees of habeas corpus. But in addition to these there are rights, such as the liberties of contract, of association, of the press and of economic enterprise, which have a remarkable capacity for acquisition, for under certain conditions their exercise provides their holders with political and economic power. Since in a free-market society only a minority of people command enough political, economic and organizational resources to benefit from the acquisitive capacities of the latter kind of rights, it follows that citizenship produces inequality and freedom in exactly the same manner as the market produces inequality and wealth.

It must be added that the circuits of political and social transactions among the stronger agents of corporate citizenship – parties, trade unions, economic and financial corporations, State bureaucracies, secret organizations, professions and so on – operate a systematic discrimination between the interests of those groups which possess great organizational and bargaining powers, the interests of associations having no strategic positions in the system of the technological division of labour, and, finally, the great majority of citizens. The latter are simple economic and political 'consumers' who possess no powers of organization and bargaining and to whom no affiliations (not even those of a clandestine or criminal kind) can offer the slightest opportunity to foster their 'diffuse interests'.[35] Thus not only the fulfilment of social expectations but the very protection of each citizen's fundamental liberties risks being dependent less on his or her entitlement to citizenship rights than on his

or her potential for corporate affiliation. The more powerful the organization of which a citizen is a member and the higher the rank he or she
has in it, the more effective is the fulfilment of his or her expectations of
protection. Conversely, lack of capacity for affiliation – the example of
third world immigrants in the countries of the European Community is
quite typical – means *de facto* (and sometimes *de jure*) exclusion from
citizenship. If the notion of citizenship implies individual entitlement to
civil and political rights and equality before the law, then the formal
dimension of citizenship is itself threatened, for the real actors of civil and
political life are no longer individuals as such but, at most, affiliated
individuals.

It might be objected, appealing to a thesis of Marshall's, that within the
welfare state the egalitarian logic of social rights harmonizes well with
the anti-egalitarian logic of acquisitive rights, for the former tends to
balance and even undermine the latter. Actually Barbalet's argument that
the so-called social rights do not belong to citizenship and, more
radically, are not rights at all seems to me to be very strong.[36] Within the
welfare state it is indeed the 'social services' that are compatible with the
logic of acquisitive rights and the market, though even this thesis is now
being questioned by neo-liberal critics.

If the rights to employment, education and health-care could be
claimed as rights in the strict sense of the word – that is, if they could be
legally formalized and enforced by the courts – they would surely conflict
with the logic of freedom and the market. Instead, the social services do
not seem to have any influence on the mechanisms of political and
economic transaction, which in advanced industrial societies multiply
inequalities and spread them over an increasingly wide range of spheres
of experience.

Now that the socialist alternative has fallen without glory and, in the
west, democratic citizenship is universally recognized as essential, no
strategies come into sight which can reconcile the status of citizen with
however modest an egalitarian political demand. It might even be denied
that the political subsystem is the structure best suited for promoting
equality within citizenship. In recent years this seems to have been
proved by the battle for women's emancipation, which has mainly been
fought by non-political means. Perhaps in the future other functional subsystems will be able to produce that 'tendency towards equality' which for
two centuries European progressism has in vain entrusted to political
Jacobinism.

A second functional inconsistency concerns the relationship between
the exercise of citizenship rights and individual autonomy. By autonomy I
mean an individual's ability to know and somehow to control the pro-

cesses affecting his or her own cognitive and volitional acts. My use of this concept is meant to be free, as far as possible, from those ethical and ontological assumptions which assimilate autonomy to such notions as integrity, responsibility, moral dignity or the absolute value of the person.[37] I want to make the point that, in post-industrial societies dominated by multimedia communication, there is an increasing tension between the oligopolistic exercise of 'negative liberties' in the domains of culture, information, entertainment and leisure on the one hand, and on the other hand the capacity for orientation and self-identity by individuals exposed to the symbolic pressure of the mass media.

Recent developments in communication research have shed light on the asymmetry which exists between the communicative roles of those agents who put out information and those who receive it. The first class of agents consists of professional groups formally organized as capitalist business concerns or as bureaucratic structures, as well as of non-professional groups – parties, lobbies, firms, religious organizations, etc. – having a privileged access to the use of mass media. The second class consists of agents who have no form of social cohesion and make use of – to varying degrees and selectively, but still without possessing any capacity for communicative interaction – a symbolic universe already reduced through the selections of the information-producing class.[38] Thus it comes about that the selective and distorting procedures of mass communication not only convey to the recipients the contents of a selected and distorted piece of information, but also transmit to them the mental framework through which selection and distortion take place. In the long run this framework establishes itself in the psychology of the audience – it is the so-called 'agenda-setting effect' – until it turns into subjective criteria for the selective organization of the recipients' attention, awareness and motivation.

This form of dependence is worsened by the tendency of the recipients of mass communication, once they become accustomed to a purely symbolic perception of the social environment, to economize on direct experience. This tendency results in social torpor and operational inertia, particularly in connection with the traditional forms of collective participation in political life. According to some authors this could help to account for the decline of citizenship and of the sense of political membership which characterizes societies deeply influenced by the information revolution, such as the US.

A third potential inconsistency is that between citizenship rights and the so-called 'cosmopolitan rights'. As David Held has pointed out, this functional antinomy chiefly concerns the conflict between each particular citizenships and the universal drift of international regulations interfering with the legal systems of states. This antinomy yields a tension which might turn out to be 'expansive' and 'inclusive', in that it might extend and give practical significance to citizens' ability to have some negative liberties respected by national jurisdictions, through resorting to higher international authorities. Moreover, it might result in citizenship including some 'ecological rights' capable of being formalized as individual rights. But there is another and probably more relevant aspect which goes in the opposite direction; that is, it tends to produce reductive and exclusive effects. This is the struggle for the attainment of 'prized' citizenships by an enormous mass of people coming from underdeveloped continental areas with high demographic rates. This struggle takes the form of a mass migration of individuals who are economically and politically very weak. They have no citizenship and no rights but they exert, through their pervasive penetration into the chinks of western citizenship, an irresistible pressure for equality. The reaction of citizenships threatened by this 'cosmopolitan' pressure – in terms both of violent exclusion of immigrants and of practical denial of their legal and social status – seems bound to write in the next decades some of the most tragic pages in the civil and political history of western countries.

In my view, only a full awareness of the historical and functional irreversibility as well as of the limitations and tensions of citizenship can allow for a satisfactory theoretical elaboration of it in the framework of a more general reconstruction of democratic theory. A coherent theory of democratic citizenship could inspire, in the era of post-communism, a 'struggle for rights' which does not amount to a generic rhetorical slogan. Above all, this 'struggle for rights' should not end up in a paradoxical appeal to the loyalty, the sense of responsibility and the moral duties of citizens, things which strengthen their subordination to democratic authorities.

Notes

1 Cf. P. Bruckner, *La mélancolie démocratique* (Paris: Éditions du Seuil, 1990).
2 Some Italian authors favour a revival of citizenship as an antidote against postmodern poisons. Others, such as Giovanna Zincone, find the notion of 'citizenship' useful as a standard, from the standpoint of the people, of the actual democratic character of a political system. See G. E. Rusconi, 'Se l'identità nazionale non è più motivo di solidarismo', *il Mulino*, 40:1 (1991), 37–46; P. Scoppola, 'Una incerta cittadinanza italiana', *il Mulino*, 40:1 (1991), 47–53; A. Panebianco, '"Representation without taxation": l'idea di cittadinanza in Italia', *il Mulino*, 40:1 (1991), 54–60; G. E. Rusconi, 'Patriottismo della Costituzione', *il Mulino*, 40:2 (1991), 321–7; P. G. Pasquino, 'Ex voto: gli strumenti della

cittadinanza politica', *il Mulino*, 40:2 (1991), 328–38; P. Pombeni, 'Una certa idea di cittadinanza', *il Mulino*, 40:3 (1991), 456–61; G. Zincone, 'Due vie alla cittadinanza: il modello societario e il modello statalista', *Rivista italiana di scienza politica*, 19:2 (1989), 223–65; G. Zincone, *Da sudditi a cittadini* (Bologna, Il Mulino, 1991); S. Veca, *Cittadinanza* (Milano, Feltrinelli, 1990). For the English debate see in particular these recent works: J. M. Barbalet, *Citizenship* (Milton Keynes, Open University Press, 1988); D. Held, 'Citizenship and autonomy', in D. Held, *Political Theory and the Modern State* (Stanford, Stanford University Press, 1989). See also D. Held, *Models of Democracy* (Cambridge, Polity Press, 1987).

3   See on this subject the first chapter of D. Zolo, *Democracy and Complexity* (Cambridge, Polity Press, 1992).

4   T. H. Marshall, 'Citizenship and social class', in T. H. Marshall, *Class, Citizenship, and Social Development* (Chicago, University of Chicago Press, 1964), pp. 78–9.

5   Marshall, 'Citizenship', pp. 92–3.

6   Marshall, 'Citizenship', p. 92.

7   Marshall, 'Citizenship', pp. 95–6.

8   Marshall, 'Citizenship', p. 102.

9   Marshall, 'Citizenship', p. 127.

10 Marshall, 'Citizenship', pp. 133–4.

11 A. Giddens, 'Class division, class conflict and citizenship rights', in Giddens, *Profiles and Critiques in Social Theory* (London, Macmillan, 1982), pp. 171–3 and 176; see also A. Giddens, *A Contemporary Critique of Historical Materialism* (London, Macmillan, 1981), pp. 226–9; A. Giddens, *The Nation State and Violence*, vol. II of *A Contemporary Critique of Historical Materialism* (London, Macmillan, 1985), pp. 204–9.

12 Barbalet, *Citizenship*, pp. 19–20.

13 Barbalet, *Citizenship*, pp. 43 and 64–7.

14 D. Held, 'Citizenship and autonomy', pp. 189–213.

15 Held, 'Citizenship and autonomy', p. 189.

16 Held, 'Citizenship and autonomy', pp. 202–3.

17 Held, 'Citizenship and autonomy', p. 199.

18 Held, 'Citizenship and autonomy', pp. 200–3; see also D. Held, *Models of Democracy* (Cambridge, Polity Press, 1987).

19 See the abundant bibliography quoted by Norberto Bobbio in his introduction to *L'età dei diritti* (Turin, Einaudi, 1990), pp. xi–xxi.

20 Cf. Marshall, 'Citizenship', pp. 103–4 and 122; Held, 'Citizenship and autonomy', p. 201.

21 Held, 'Citizenship and autonomy', pp. 201–2.

22 Cf. Bobbio, *L'età dei diritti*, especially pp. xiv–xv.

23 A plausible account would distinguish at least three great families of normative claims: civil and political rights (citizenship rights); the so-called 'social rights' characterizing the welfare state; and cosmopolitan and ecological rights. Normative claims falling under the tendency to 'specify' human rights, such as children's rights, the abolition of discriminations against women, the rights of mentally disabled people, the rights of elders, rights to biological integrity and so on, could be variously distributed among these three basic categories.

24 Against Anthony Giddens, David Held maintains that the differentiation between the political and the economic spheres is the condition not only of capitalist development but also of the rise of civil and political liberties. See Held, 'Citizenship and autonomy', p. 205.

25 On the notion of 'regulation of fear' and the principles of exclusion and sub-ordination as functional rules of the political code, see the concluding pages of the second chapter of Zolo, *Democracy and Complexity*.

26 J. Habermas, 'Cittadinanza e identità nazionale', *Micromega*, 6:5 (1991), p. 127.

27 See on this subject F. Volpi, 'La riabilitazione della filosofia pratica e il suo senso nella crisi della modernità', *il Mulino*, 35:6 (1986). See also the two classic volumes edited by M. Riedel, *Rehabilitierung der praktischen Philosophie* (Freiburgh, Rombach, 1972-74).

28 On the 'struggle for rights' see the insightful concluding pages of Luigi Ferrajoli, *Diritto e ragione* (Roma-Bari, Laterza, 1989), pp. 987-93.

29 Cf. Bobbio, *L'età dei diritti*, p. viii.

30 See A. Cassese, *I diritti umani nel mondo contemporaneo* (Roma-Bari, Laterza, 1988).

31 See, for instance, C. Galli (ed.), *Logiche e crisi della modernità* (Bologna, Il Mulino, 1991).

32 This is granted by Bobbio himself in *L'età dei diritti*, p. xv.

33 Bobbio, *L'età dei diritti*, pp. viii–xv.

34 Bobbio, *L'età dei diritti*, pp. 40–1.

35 On this subject see the fourth chapter of Zolo, *Democracy and Complexity*; see also V. Mura, 'Democrazia ideale e democrazia reale', *Teoria politica*, 6:1 (1990).

36 Barbalet presents three arguments: (1) social rights are not in themselves rights of participation in a 'common national community', but are 'conditional opportunities' which make possible such participation; (2) while civil and political rights are necesarily universal and formal, the so-called social rights are meaningful only when conceived of as claims to substantive benefits, and these can never be universal but are particular and selective; (3) to an unparalleled degree with respect to political and civil rights, social rights are conditional on the existence of a developed' economy, an administrative and professional structure and an effective fiscal basis.

37 Cf. E. Santoro, 'Per una concezione non individualistica dell'autonomia individuale', *Rassegna italiana di sociologia*, 32:3 (1991), 268-311.

38 See: K. Lang and G. E. Lang, 'The mass media and voting', in W. Schramm and D. Roberts (eds), *The Process and Effects of Mass Communication* (Chicago, University of Illinois Press, 1972); M. E. McCombs, 'The agenda setting approach', in D. D. Nimmo and K. R. Sanders (eds), *Handbook of Political Communication* (Beverly Hills, CA, Sage, 1981); M. E. McCombs and D. L. Shaw, 'The agenda-setting function of the mass media', *Public Opinion Quarterly*, 36:2 (1972), 176-87.

Part IV

The Dynamics of Democratization: Risks and Possibilities

13

CONSOLIDATIONS OF DEMOCRACY

John A. Hall

The extraordinary events of the last years have encouraged optimism about the prospects for democracy. Sometimes such optimism can be naive and excessive. That spirit led Francis Fukuyama to declare famously that we are witnessing an 'end of history' in which liberalism, capitalism and democracy – the exact relations between which were not explained – have finally triumphed over all rivals.[1] This dangerously equates the mere breakdown of authoritarian regimes with the successful transition to consolidated democracies. This will not do. After all, there have been great waves of democracy in the past which have been followed by renewed bursts of authoritarian rule: thus the age of democratic revolutions was followed by Metternich's system of order, the birth of new national democracies after the Treaty of Versailles by the spread of fascism, and the confident belief of the first two decades of the Pax Americana that economic growth would ensure democracy by an insistence, at the time most convincing, that growth in developing countries depended upon 'bureaucratic-authoritarian' rule.[2] It would, however, be a mistake to replace an optimistic evolutionary view with a cynical and pessimistic cyclical alternative. For the last two centuries *have* witnessed an increase, often interrupted and certainly slow, in the number of stable democracies.[3] Accordingly, this chapter entertains a careful and limited optimism, basing itself less on vague generalities than on historical specificities.

Some light can best be cast on what is a huge subject by beginning with three of the initial attempts, two successful and one failed, at consolidating democracy: this both allows clarification of what we characteristically mean by democracy and encourages understanding of the support given to it by different social classes. This is followed by the listing of a set of abstract factors that enable democratic rule to be consolidated; it is important to note immediately that such factors (and the constellations between them) so vary in salience over historical time as to rule out any simple model for consolidations of democracy. What will be offered instead is a set of feasible possibilities for selected areas of the contemporary world.

A 'Loyal Opposition' and Its Impact on Social Class

That we characteristically take democracy to mean more than rule by the people is easily demonstrated. No one can doubt but that it was the French Revolution that placed democracy on the agenda of modern history. None the less, the bitter, no-holds-barred struggle for power among the revolutionaries points to the fact that democracy is normally held to depend upon the workings of settled institutions. What matters above all is the creation of a loyal opposition; that is, an opposition which refuses to entertain plans to change the system and to exterminate its rivals – thereby of course ensuring its own safety.[4] Let me first describe the creation of this institution in Britain between 1675 and 1725 and in the US between 1780 and 1840. Once that has been done, it will then be possible to see why this institution matters so very much.

During the reign of Charles II, most English people had memories of civil war, regicide, treason, the political division of families, foreign interference and religious persecution. It is accordingly remarkable that within half a century a form of political stability had been achieved within which opposing views and parties were tolerated. Most striking of all was the creation of the concept of a loyal opposition – a concept which in time led to state salaries for those who opposed what the party in power was trying to achieve![5] How was this transformation possible?[6]

Broadly speaking, the growth of a legitimate opposition went hand in hand with a diminution of popular control. Differently put, the political nation found peace because it could accept contestation without having to embrace democracy. A myriad of policies and institutional changes supports this claim. The rage of party was severely curtailed both by raising the costs of elections and by the passing of the Septennial Act, making elections far less frequent than before; equally, the growth of a landed oligarchy meant that election expenses became bearable only by the very rich. Remarkably, participation in elections and levels of literacy fell in the century after the Restoration.[7]

The political nation also became more united. The extreme Jacobites were excluded by use of treason acts. More importantly, a common identity of economic, political and social power was established by a marriage of interest: the land tax that hurt the Tories was diminished (not least because the Whigs became less belligerent), and they in turn accepted the entry of the City into the British power structure – with frequent nuptials acting as a cement to the union. What is noticeable is that every section of the political elite gained, especially since these were years of social development and economic growth in which politics was by no means the sole avenue to fame and fortune. Further, the effectiveness of the political system was enhanced by an increase in the power of the executive over the legislature, not least by the use of placemen, whose numbers rose dramatically in this period. Britain in this period, for all the acceptance of (non-Jacobite) opposition, came to be ruled by a single party – making it resemble, say, post-1945 Japan rather than modern Britain.

Consideration of the creation of a party system in the early US depended quite as much upon an extraordinarily favourable set of circumstances.[8] The early American leaders had sought, not least in *The Federalist Papers*, to create a world in which social harmony would reign: parties were seen as mere irresponsible factions. None the less, between 1794 and 1801 a peaceful transfer of power from Federalists to Jeffersonians took place, and it was not long until fully developed justifications for political parties were being produced. Again, several factors stand at the back of this moderate course of political development. First, property was widely diffused, and levels of literacy were extremely high. One important corollary of this was again that politics was not all-important: there were other avenues of social mobility, and anyone deprived of office was accordingly still able to prosper. Secondly, the elite had considerable training in politics. It had drawn up two constitutions, and was accordingly deeply versed in the languages of law and of rights. These were conservative men, not prone to sudden moves which would put the commonweal at risk; in effect, they felt themselves to be members of a single family. Thirdly, the revolutionary process had not seen violence of the sort that characterized the French Revolution, and the resort to violence thereafter was not deemed natural. Moreover, the fact that the revolution had been made against the state meant that no standing army was available to suppress political rivals; and this course of action was anyway ruled out for the Federalists given that their opponents had a geographically cohesive power base in Virginia. The implicit self-denying ordinance here was much reinforced by the behaviour of the Founding Fathers. Most obviously, Washington chose to model himself after Cincinnatus – that is, he did not seek to capitalize on his military reputation, even though Hamilton had made him distrust Jefferson. But it was Hamilton who understood Jefferson's character. He was no radical: in power he effectively abandoned his own programme and adopted that of Hamilton, and took care not to persecute any of his political rivals. In a nutshell, the founding moment of the new regime was one which set a powerful and beneficent precedent for subsequent politics. Finally, one should note that in the key years in which power was transferred the US was faced with no issue of any great import. Most obviously, no geopolitical pressure affected the US, given that Europe was embroiled in the Napoleonic Wars.

What has been described to this point is the creation of political trust within a political class. Contest was to be within bounds, and nothing was to be done that would disrupt a settled set of expectations. Opposition was allowed largely because those in power felt that it would not threaten their interests. It is important to emphasize again that the confidence of the powerful in this matter was enhanced by the fact that popular pressures did not present them with much problem – indeed, the British case sees a growth in political stability in part because of the exclusion of the people. What had been achieved was the liberalization of politics. This seems to me an historical achievement in its own right. What matters more generally, however, is the impact that institutionalizing a loyal opposition had on later democratization: of especial import in this connection is the manner in which early liberalism affects the character of social classes.

The US tells us little about this because democratization followed so closely upon the acceptance of opposition. The fact that the people had fought for independence created a measure of trust between political elite and people, as well as ruling out any consolidation of oligarchy. Jackson placed popular politics firmly at the centre of the stage, and by the end of his presidency virtually all adult white males had the vote. In contrast, the entry of the people on to the political stage in Britain was slow and tortured. The spread of civil society that went hand in hand with the creation of a unique commercial society in eighteenth-century Britain served as a backdrop to the re-emergence of popular politics.[9] Popular pressures combined with divisions within the political elite to allow 'economical reform' within the state in the wake of the loss of the first empire. Those pressures were sufficiently strong and autonomous to rule out any permanent move to reaction in response to the French Revolution. Instead a long process of franchise reform was instituted – albeit that process left Britain in 1914 less democratic in formal terms than Germany, its main geopolitical and economic rival. But this consideration should not hide the fact that German votes were of limited value: whereas Britain had full parliamentary control of expenditure, Germany most certainly did not, remaining at once politically authoritarian and socially mobilized. Much hangs upon this contrast.

The difference between the two cases can be understood in terms of the sequence of political development.[10] Where liberalism precedes democracy, democratization is likely to present no threat; in contrast, the entry of the people on to the political stage before the establishment of basic liberalism is likely to undermine the chances for successful consolidation of democratic regimes. The straightforward reason for this can be seen by considering the rise of labour, although the same principle applies quite generally to popular movements. Where a working class was faced by a liberal state, it tended to organize at the industrial level; in contrast, illiberal states with anti-socialist and anti-union laws forced workers into becoming politically conscious. This principle helps us understand why there was no socialism in the US and why Czarist Russia produced a working class which was not just politically conscious, as was that of Imperial Germany, but genuinely revolutionary: in the former case citizenship had been achieved prior to industrialization, while in the latter the despotic and erratic policies of autocracy ruled out reformism.[11] The nature of the political regime affects the character of social movements in such a way as to produce vicious and beneficent cycles of political development. In Britain, a liberal state habitually encouraged a moderate and reformist working-class movement; and in any case, the British middle classes never felt very threatened precisely because the franchise was not widespread. In Germany, an illiberal state produced a labour movement that sounded very threatening – a fact that was of great consequence given that there were few restrictions on male suffrage. Accordingly, the German middle classes were driven to support reaction, first in the Wilhelmine period and then in Weimar, rather than, as with key sections of their British equivalents, to support reform.

These observations about the sequence of political developments are of such importance that they deserve emphasis. This can best be given by offering three reflections upon Barrington Moore's famous statement that there can be no democracy without a bourgeoisie.[12]

In so far as the bourgeoisie was opposed to the state, there is great plausibility to Moore's equation: for democracy rests ultimately upon pluralism, that is, upon a wide spread of negative resisting power. Certainly the popular pressures that helped make Britain liberal evolved naturally from commercial society. In this context, it is worth noting that it makes little sense to speak of a unitary bourgeoisie. The popular pressures that came to a head in the campaign for 'Wilkes and Liberty' were derived from the petty bourgeoisie, a class fragment which deserves a better press, certainly in contrast to large capitalists, than it has habitually received.[13] It is also important to be exact about the character of British liberalism. John Stuart Mill – to whose views about the 'rules of the game' we return later – typified liberal ideology: workers were to be given the vote provided that they became literate and sober, and accepted the laws of political economy. Further, if a liberal state offered workers the carrot of the right to organize, it also wielded a considerable stick against those who challenged the system radically: many of the leading Chartists were deported.[14] None the less, the fact remains that this liberalism had a tremendous social impact. Workers who could organize struggled against their bosses rather than against the state; differently put, liberal society proved to be essentially stable since conflicts were diffused through civil society rather than concentrated against the regime.

But the critics of Moore's position are of course quite correct to say that the bourgeoisie has not always been the friend of liberty, as the behaviour of the German bourgeoisie in both Wilhelmine and Weimar Germany very clearly illustrates.[15] This bourgeoisie owed much of its existence to the state: the state had created the nation and aided industrialization, and it thereafter served as the bulwark against genuinely radical pressures from below. This class was perfectly happy to live in an authoritarian *Rechtstaat*, in which nation and order had greater importance than political liberty. It would be mistaken, however, to argue that the German middle class was inevitably illiberal. The regime played an active role in destroying liberalism through a policy of 'divide and rule'. The state's creation of distrust between Catholic and Protestant middle-class parties weakened liberalism not just in the Wilhelmine period but in Weimar as well. In summary, the absence of liberalism owes a great deal to interest but at least something to the strategy of the ruling elite.

Finally, critics of Moore are correct to point out that the consolidation of democracy owes a good deal to a class that plays no significant role in his great *Social Origins of Dictatorship and Democracy*.[16] *A priori* considerations suggest that the working class stands to benefit from democracy; comparative historical evidence demonstrates that working-class parties sought both to extend the franchise and to institutionalize social rights. None the less, this positive thesis cannot be accepted absolutely without qualification. If classes have interests, they also have, as we have seen, characteristic styles. When working-class parties adopted revolutionary rhetoric, they played some part in hindering the consolidation of democracy. In so far as such rhetoric was, so to speak, thrust upon them by the way in which ruling elites treated them, it is clearly unfair to blame working-class parties for this. But there were degrees of freedom at work in this whole area, and some blame can be attached to popular parties. Certainly, the worst possible combination was the presence of a rhetoric which was not at all real – that is, the striking of revolutionary attitudes by a party which was essentially reformist. The German Social Democrats exemplified this position, with catastrophic consequences in the Weimar years.

Enabling Factors, Past and Present

To turn from historical examples to a listing of analytic points is not as great a change as it might seem: just as analytic points were sought from history, so too must the analytic points be historically contextualized. This whole strategy of enquiry is, of course, heavily indebted to the pioneering work of Robert Dahl.[17] For one thing, these enabling factors are interlinked and mutually supporting, while not every case of successful consolidation has satisfied all of the enabling conditions. For another, the 'openness' of this set of factors leaves a great deal of room for the exercise of political skill and judgement. None the less, not all the factors taken to be important here are mentioned by Dahl; equally the logic of justification is often not the same for those factors which he did consider.

Sequence

This factor has already been elucidated at length, and in more detailed terms than those used by Dahl himself. Briefly, if one virtue of having liberalism prior to democratization is that it encourages moderation on behalf of those entering the political stage, another is that it ensures that the powerful are not unduly threatened: and such reassurance is absolutely necessary if political modernization is to take place at all.

There are cases in the contemporary world which have benefited from this sequence. Hungary allowed a considerable measure of opposition before the introduction of open political competition, while Brazil's whole pattern of development distinguishes it from Argentina at this point.[18] None the less, so much attention was given to this factor for a negative reason: this beneficent sequence is not now generally available. Plans to curtail the franchise are now inadmissible. This means that contemporary consolidations of democracy are different from and much harder than those in the past. The pessimism generated by this consideration is, however, offset by other factors which happily gain in power in contemporary circumstances.

Property

The greater the concentration of property, the less likely is it that democratic rule will be consolidated. Fundamental land reform and attacks on
excessive concentration of industry are necessary conditions for democracy.

In agrarian circumstances, free farmers – in the west of the nineteenth-
century US, New Zealand and Australia – have formed the underpinnings
of democratic regimes. Much the same is true of the Swedish peasantry,
habitually a fourth estate and possessed of considerable independence. In
contrast, concentration of landholding, whether in pre-socialist Eastern
Europe or in Latin America, is – with one exception – inimical to democracy. The single exception in question is the commercially-minded
landed aristocracy of eighteenth-century Britain. Where most landed
elites needed the state to repress labour, the British elite, partly because
of an initial concentration in agricultural products not requiring large
inputs of labour, was content to survive in the market-place, relatively
free from and occasionally resistant to the state.[19]

In industrial circumstances, a wide spread of property-holding is likely
to provide support for democracy, with concentration in property equally
being hostile to it. We have seen that whereas popular pressures for
reform in eighteenth-century England arose naturally from a civil society
strengthened by the spread of commerce, forced and state-led economic
development in Wilhelmine Germany created an important elite of large
capitalists opposed to democracy. In the contemporary world, one fears
that the increasing concentration of industrial power in South Korea is
such as to limit the chances for democratization: the leaders of the
chaebols seem prone not to accept new union rights, not surprisingly given
that they prospered so strikingly when labour was controlled by the state.
In contrast, the diversification of economic activities within Taiwan is a
positive factor that may allow further democratization.[20]

We cannot leave this factor at this point. For what is property? For
much of history, property is indeed something material and physical. But
this may no longer be so. Late industrial society seems ever more to
depend upon the skills of educated labour. This class fragment often
depends upon freedom of information and movement, and tends to place
technicism above integrating ideologies.[21] It is thus a resource for
democratization – as social movements from Rio to Seoul and from
Peking to Prague so clearly show. The pressures applied by educated
labour are likely to be greatest, it should be noted, where it feels that its
way of life is limited or blocked by the regime it faces, as was true for

many socialist societies in Eastern European, most notably Czechoslovakia. But even the economic success of South Korea is not such as to control anger on the part of educated labour, particularly towards restrictions in civil rights, education and housing. But pressure from below is only one side of the equation: elites at times seek to placate educated labour in the hope that ensuing economic growth will help them in the struggle for power. In summary, a third stage in the industrial era is identifiable which is less favourable to state planning and the concentration of property than was the second stage, whether conducted under capitalist or socialist aegis. Accordingly, the logic of late industrial society may favour democracy, so that there may again be something to Adam Smith's equation of 'commerce and liberty'.[22]

State

Dahl is percipient on this factor, and my comments merely echo his. Two points are especially important.

Most obviously, a transition from authoritarian rule will be extremely difficult if a state has at its command powerful forces for repression capable of destroying dissent – as seems to be the case with Saddam Hussein since the Gulf War. Very few regimes have fallen when backed up by a bureaucratized army, something which merely sultanistic rulers like Somoza and Ceauşescu learned to their cost.[23] As important, however, is the situation of the armed forces within the political elite. When their position is central, democratization can only proceed if sufficient guarantees are given to ensure that they will stay in their barracks. Latin Americans know that when the tiger is in the cage it remains important to remember that he has his own key. Further, where repressive atrocities have been committed by the armed forces, democratization is less likely because the requisite social patience is very unlikely to be present in sufficient quantities.

International

The impact of international forces has not traditionally received sufficient attention from those concerned with problems of transition.[24] This is strange given the conspicuous importance of this factor. Germany and Japan became secure democracies in very large part at the hands of the Allies, while the defeat of the Axis powers allowed for the restoration of democracies throughout Europe. As manifestly obvious, surely, is the fact that it was the withdrawal of the Russian card that made political change possible in Eastern Europe. Czechoslovakia was probably as ready to make a transition to democracy in 1948 as it is today: its fate has depended entirely upon the wishes of its neighbour.

Several facets of the contemporary international order favour consolidations of democracy. Perhaps most important is the historic defeat of the two great revolutions of the twentieth century: communism and fascism are no longer transnational movements capable of serving as models of development. Both were beaten in war, one dramatically and the other in a long-drawn-out but finally decisive conflict. A key point about these models is that they no longer offer much in times of peace: their emphasis on autarchy and protectionism, so characteristic of the second industrial era, reduces the living standards of their citizens. It is important to note too that there has been something of an historic change on the part of international lending agencies. Such institutions were once prone to believe that authoritarianism was a necessary price to be paid for economic growth. The evidence of many decades, demonstrating quite clearly that authoritarian regimes are often utterly feckless, has been absorbed: dictatorships are no longer automatically supported, while far greater understanding is now being shown to nascent democracies.[25]

If much of this says there is no obvious alternative, it remains important to point to factors that make contemporary consolidations of democracy extremely difficult. Most obviously, economic liberalization – the removal of subsidies, increasing privatization and ending protectionism – imposes pain and social strain. The earliest consolidations of democracy benefited from a vibrant economy, capable of offering avenues of social mobility alternate to the political; if in the long run democratization does not bring at least some measure of economic success, it may well be doomed. Furthermore, it is worth remembering that the international economic order is still dominated by the US. That predatory hegemon places, largely for internal reasons, the well-being of its greedy consumers above even its own geopolitical interests, let alone the welfare of other states. Latin American democratization depends upon its ability to pay its debts, and this in turn depends upon access to open markets. Similarly, the fate of East and Central Europe may depend upon access to capital. Unfortunately, it is possible that the US may institute protectionist policies, while it is probable that it will continue to absorb, largely as a form of military rent, the world's excess capital.[26]

Attitudes

The necessary attitudes for a successful transition to democracy have already been identified, above all the determination not to take conflict too far and to live within a set of rules of the game. By and large, these attitudes need to be present early, so as to encourage the powerful to allow a transition to democracy to be initiated. This explains the importance of pacts which guarantee in advance that key interests will not be overthrown by political reform. This is a good moment at which to digress, so as to give an example of the openness inherent in democratization. In democratization, there is everything to be said for the maxim that one should not offend one's enemies when they have power, but be ruthless to them when they are weak. Pacts have a price attached to them – they tend to alienate the people who are well aware that agreements are being made among the political elite behind their back – and are best avoided when possible. If marked social inequalities make it, by and large, impossible to avoid pact-making in Latin America, the absolute defeat of Communist Parties in state socialist societies make it possible and wise to cleanse the bureaucratic and state apparatus of potential enemies – albeit, care must be taken not to harm newly founded legality by arbitrary and personalized vendettas.

There are two reasons for believing that contemporary attitudes favour consolidations of democracy, both unfortunately of a rather negative character. First, no alternative models of political economy are available, as noted, to help mobilize those who suffer either from expropriation or from structural economic change. Secondly, the decisive failure of statist economic models, whether capitalist or socialist in character, together with the obvious wealth of liberal democracies has encouraged a general belief that democracy will allow and encourage economic growth. Obviously some economic growth is necessary within a measurable time-frame if such attitudes are to be maintained.

Civil society

There is no more important topic in contemporary politics than the character and chances of civil society. But the concept itself is rather vague, albeit negatively it is easy to recognize societies which do not have it. Two elements of a definition can be offered – the presence of each of which helps towards the consolidation of democracy.

First and foremost is the presence of strong and autonomous social groups, able to balance excessive concentrations of power. In this context, a distinction can be drawn between the independent unions of North-West Europe and the clientelistically controlled unions of the Southern Cone of Latin America.[27] What matters still more is the creation of strong political parties able to represent the people and to ensure the adoption of better policies, and thereby to mediate political conflict.[28] Secondly, the notion of civil society does and should retain connotations of civility – a point which is linked to what has already been said about attitudes. One way of expressing the matter firmly is to insist that there is no link between the notions of 'civic virtue' and that of civil society. The former tradition surfaced in Rousseau and fed through to the French Revolution: it distrusted secondary organizations, and sought to make human beings unitary. Civil society represents the exact opposite: it endorses social diversity, together with a different view of the self.[29]

Single culture

This factor is so obvious that it needs no commentary. One is tempted to say: *remember* Yugoslavia! More particularly, one can predict that newly independent Slovenia, blessed with an homogeneous population, is more likely to consolidate its democracy than are newly independent Croatia or Bosnia-Hercegovina. This principle is all too easy to apply to other cases, especially to many of the former republics of the Soviet Union.

Memory

The importance of this factor is especially obvious in contemporary Eastern Europe. Existentialists have made a good case to the effect that it is impossible to live in a void, bereft of identity, with everything always open to question. The collapse of socialist ideas and institutions means that memories of the past are of the greatest importance. Where some are blessed, others are cursed. Czechoslovakia has memories of industry and of the beginnings of a functioning liberal democracy; in addition, the situation of Bohemia within Austro-Hungary represents a long tradition of constitutional politics. Romanians, Bulgarians and Albanians have nothing like this to remember; the absence of a model may well prove to be of the greatest importance.

Other memories can be as important, not least because they help create attitudes that favour consolidations of democracy. Memories of disasters – a Revolt of the Asturias, an invasion by Russian tanks in 1956 or 1968, a Kwangju Incident or a Tiananmen Square – can both fundamentally delegitimize a regime and so discipline the people as to make them able to find a different way. Founding moments are equally important. When 'history is on the move' one has the sensation of events speeding up, and of key decisions coming to the fore. The decisions taken in such open moments become codified, and pattern later events. One example of this – the beneficial consequences of Washington's decision not to make use of his military reputation – has already been noted.

The Chances for Consolidating Democracy

The pay-off for the discussion so far is simple and to the point. What are the differential chances for consolidating democracy within key areas in which it is now being attempted? It would be idle to pretend that this author knows every region – let alone all countries within them – equally well. None the less, some points do seem clear, and an attempt at general explanation may concentrate attention more generally.

A genuinely consolidated democracy is perhaps best judged to be one in which the alternation of parties in power is regular and accepted.[30] By this standard, the consolidation of democracy in Southern Europe is complete. Let me concentrate on the Spanish case.[31] Here there was a mass of favourable factors: the desire to enter the European Community, self-discipline going back to memories of the Revolt of the Asturias, the slow withdrawal of the military from political life, the presence of dense civil society networks, superlative political skill during the founding moments, and unity among the elite – not least the socialist leaders, determined to establish democracy rather than to engage in any social experiments that would create resistance. Spain benefited, moreover, from having a notably courageous monarch who played a key role in helping crush one attempted *coup d'état*. But not everything in the Spanish situation was favourable: the presence of regional nationalisms highly resistant to the centre presented considerable problems. The difficulties of dealing with Basques and, to a lesser degree, Catalans were severe – even including the assassination of one prime minister at a key point in the transition to democracy. That these difficulties were overcome is testimony to the force of the positive enabling factors.

The situation of most Latin American countries is by no means so rosy. Let me begin by noting that classic patterns of social formation, well illustrated by Argentina and Brazil, have always seemed likely to lead to differential chances for consolidation of democracy within the region. Early democracy in Argentina made it much harder for any process of liberalization to be controlled in such a way that the powerful were not so threatened as to strike back; equally, populism encouraged economic policies which were so catastrophic that they took Argentina out of the list of the top economic powers.[32] Additional negative factors include the presence of the military, an international situation hurting the economy through debt repayment, and the lack of genuine autonomy in the organization of key civil society groups. Brazilian liberalization is, in contrast, a more top-down affair, and to that extent has slightly larger hopes for success.[33] Against that must be set, however, the fact that Brazilian civil society is even less developed than that of Argentina, being largely confined to the coastal strip which is tied to the world economy.

We can gain some understanding of the most recent developments in Latin America by turning to Mexico, whose move away from protected import-substitution-industrialization is of great moment.[34] The state's retreat from the complete control and management of its economy seems, however, not to have been followed by political reorganization. On the contrary, between 1988 and 1991 the governing party improved its position in regional elections; Mexico looks set, in other words, to remain a single-party state. Furthermore, the opening to the world market and the selling of state industries was made possible only by the use of pork-barrel politics routed through traditional clientelistic networks. Traditional levers of power seem as present in contemporary Argentina and Brazil, both of which seek to imitate Mexico's new developmental model. Such developmental changes as there have been in those countries, notably the emergence of regional caudillos in Brazil, do not augur well for democracy. What continues to be sadly lacking throughout Latin America is a civil society – armed with its own developed political parties – that is truly independent of the state. All three countries touched on here currently suffer from falling living standards, very great and continuing inequality and the absence of fundamental land reform. One can hope that a swing back to authoritarian rule will not again take place in Latin America; but this hope is not at all well grounded in beneficent social trends.

East Asian development is now well enough known for it to be contrasted graphically with that attempted in Latin America.[35] The political economy of this region has benefited from fundamental land reform, and this gave the state considerable autonomy, as did an abundance of 'geopolitical capital', to plan economic development; that autonomy was, in addition, used extremely intelligently – protection to infant industries was not long lasting, the emphasis being on export-led development rather than on mere import substitution.[36] Such development occurred in regimes which were highly repressive, and bereft of traditions of civil society. None the less, the chances that political developments in this region will be sustained seems to me better than they are in Latin America. Here liberalization can precede democratization, with the latter taking place in conditions of relative economic success – rather than, as in Latin America and post-communist societies, in the midst of massive unemployment caused by total structural adjustment.

Korean chances of further political development are improving rapidly. There has been long-term pressure from educated labour, but that has been markedly offset by extreme concentration of property in the *chaebol*. International politics occasioned and underwrote military repression, but it is the possibility of reunification that is the key development that may have positive consequences. In a united country it will become impossible to label a reforming party as disloyal, and thereby to ignore it. What seems most likely in the short run is a move towards a Japanese situation in which opposition is allowed, but in which a single party always wins elections: despite the presence of elections, I consider this a grand liberalization rather than a full consolidation of democracy. The creation of such a system seems to be the ambition of the current president. In order for it to be achieved, greater inclusion of political opponents will prove necessary, as well as the creation of a new system of labour relations. In contrast, Taiwan's move towards democracy, which seemed so secure, based as it was on a much more diversified society, is beginning to face problems. The nationalist party which seeks to break the connection with the mainland is coming to be classified as a disloyal opposition. As democracy can only work in the absence of visceral conflict – that is, the disagreements which it can handle must be manageable within shared understandings – the political future in Taiwan is no longer bright.

Former communist societies are attempting an extraordinary double – and simultaneous – transition, to democracy and to capitalism. All countries have the difficulty that elite actions are constrained by instant democratic pressures: it is hard to see how economic liberalization can be achieved without the defeat of some large-scale strikes in the heartlands of heavy industry due to be destroyed by the introduction of the market. It is with this factor in mind that many authors have come to suggest that the east will come to resemble the south – by which they mean that it is likely to follow the Latin American pattern (which was in the inter-war period, by and large, its own) – of dependent capitalism in combination with polities oscillating between democracy and authoritarianism.[37] The fact that there are similarities should not obscure key differences. Post-communist societies have no equivalent of Latin America's intact and powerful landed elite. Revolution destroyed the landed elite, while the

Nomenklatura are now very clearly defeated. All in all, the amount of resistance from within the elite to radical change is in historical terms rather low. Furthermore, it is simply not possible to exaggerate the degree of disenchantment with communism. A window of opportunity exists because there is no desire to return to the past. In addition, at least at present, democracy is associated with wealth: the dislike of state intervention of any sort among leading sectors of public opinion is startling, at times disconcerting. Most important of all, however, is geography. Many East and Central European states are extremely happy to have policies directed by experts associated with the European Community. The desire to return to Europe means that there is considerable resistance to the reintroduction of authoritarianism. If these factors lend advantage, two others do precisely the opposite. Most obviously, the absence of faith in the regime led to trust in one's ethnic group – a situation especially likely to block moves to democracy in most of the former Soviet Union given the large number of ethnic Russians resident in the former peripheral republics. Secondly, it remains the case that no complete privatization has yet taken place. Until it does so, the state will dominate civil society, and thereby prevent any secure consolidations of democracy.

Beyond these general considerations is great diversity. Some countries are likely to succeed, others to fail. Hungary benefited from a degree of liberalization before democratization, and its party cadres apparently chose to abandon political power some time ago, aware that their economy offered them better chances of social mobility.[38] Several of the enabling factors favour Czechoslovakia, particularly its legacy of industry and democracy. Even Slovak secession may not be as destructive a force as is widely believed. The Slovaks, faced with possible claims by Hungary for the large population of Magyars within Slovakia, may well not totally wish to be independent of the protection of Bohemia – however much many Czechs would like to be rid of them! The splitting of Civic Forum is a potentially positive sign: party expression of different interests is a gain – but only on the condition that the members of these parties still feel themselves part of a single enterprise, as is probably no longer the case in Poland, and accordingly continue to socialize together. In contrast to all this, the Rumanian situation seems desperate. It has few historic legacies to help it consolidate democracy, and remains a Latin island in a Slav sea – as much at the mercy of Russia as before. The political vacuum caused by the collapse of the communist regime in the Soviet Union has been filled, as noted, by nationalism rather than by a strengthened civil society.

Much is being made in early 1992 of democratization spreading in other areas of the world, and a few comments are in order. China's attempt to fuse authoritarianism with the market is unlikely to prove successful in the long run, although it is important to note that most businesspeople currently depend upon the state, rather than upon autonomous civil society, not just for their existence but also for their profits.[39] General reasoning would suggest that democratization has the best chance of success after greater development and an increased softening or liberalizing of the regime. But change in China is some way away, and any guess at its form is unlikely to be high-powered. Harsher views are suggested by experience elsewhere. Indian democracy seems threatened by the revival of regional and religious sectarianism – which is not to say that a turn towards authoritarianism would in fact help its economic development. The revolt against authoritarian rule in Africa is of course profoundly to be welcomed. But there remains a world of difference between the breakdown of authoritarian rule and the consolidation of democracy. The structural problems that most African societies still face – tribalism, underdevelopment and overmighty armed forces – are such that one must doubt whether any of the transitions from authoritarian rule will be successfully completed. Finally, it is vital to note that the current wave of enthusiasm for democracy has not swept over every part of the world. Islam's puritanical style, so decisively in the ascendant in the contemporary world, does represent a societal model in its own right, and it is one that is clearly opposed to democracy. That an opposition must be loyal for democracy to work was powerfully apparent in the recent Algerian elections: had the Islamic party come to power, democracy would have been destroyed – just as it has been in any case.

Conclusion

The starting point of this chapter was Fukuyama's claim that the triumph of liberalism, capitalism and democracy has ended history. The arguments advanced here can usefully be seen, to begin with, as specifying – as Fukuyama did not – some of the relations between liberalism, capitalism and democracy. Liberalism is certainly part of what we customarily mean by democracy, and its early advent massively helped consolidate democracy by domesticating demands that came from below. Early liberalism was itself largely the product of the first commercial society, and to that extent capitalism played some part in the consolidation of democracy. Equally, the fact that late industrial capitalist society bases itself less on state central planning than on information may favour consolidations of democracy – especially if political leaders understand and act upon the 'logic' of industrial development. More generally, however, it is worth noting that every contemporary democratic society is capitalist. There is something to Weber's view that capitalism, by at least distinguishing economic from political power, is a base condition for democracy.[40] All this underlies the claim made here that the acceptance of capitalism is one of the 'rules of the game' that allow democracy to function.

But it is important in conclusion to draw some distinctions about this point. During the period of transition from authoritarian to democratic rule, there is a great deal to be said for the making of pacts that so reassure the propertied that they need not and should not oppose political development. None the less, in the long run democracy must involve some uncertainty about outcomes. If the rules of the game include acceptance of the market principle, they do not – in the long run – necessitate acceptance of any particular division of property. A fuller consideration of John Stuart Mill lends support to this point. Mill was entirely consistent in seeking to have conflict and change within certain accepted rules of the game: if the laws of political economy had to be accepted, there remained much room for schemes of improvement which would raise the condition of workers so dramatically that the distribution of property and income would be revolutionized. What is at issue can be put in different terms: capital should not be allowed to rest on some putative absolute rights; it needs instead constantly to justify its existence by efficient performance. As it happens, there seem to this author to be good reasons for believing that social democracy is both a just and an efficient option for a nation-state within capitalist society. To note that we have options, that others would dispute the preference noted, is of course to refute Fukuyama. Just as the ending of the Cold War has unfrozen history, so too do consolidations of democracy open up rather than close down historical possibilities.

NOTES

1　F. Fukuyama, 'The end of history', *The National Interest*, 16 (1989), 3–17.
2　Classic works on these oscillating moments include: R. R. Palmer, *The Age of the Democratic Revolution* (Princeton, NJ, Princeton University Press, 1959 and 1964), and H. A. Kissinger, *A World Restored* (Boston, MA, Houghton Mifflin, 1957); C. Maier, *Recasting Bourgeois Europe* (Princeton, NJ, Princeton University Press, 1975), and J. J. Linz and A. Stepan (eds), *The Breakdown of Authoritarian Regimes* (Baltimore, MD, Johns Hopkins University Press, 1978); and S. M. Lipset, *Political Man* (New York, Doubleday, 1960), and G. O'Donnell, *Modernisation and Bureaucratic-Authoritarianism* (Berkeley, CA, Institute of International Studies, 1973). For the most recent wave of democracy, see G. O'Donnell, P. Schmitter and L. Whitehead (eds), *Transitions from Authoritarian Rule* (Baltimore, MD, Johns Hopkins University Press, 1986), and D. Ethier, *Democratic Transition and Con-*

solidation in Southern Europe, Latin America and Southeast Asia (London, Macmillan, 1990).

3 Figures on the matter are contained in R. Dahl, *Democracy and its Critics* (New Haven, CT, Yale University Press, 1989), ch. 17.

4 I am influenced here by Barrington Moore, not least by an unpublished paper, 'Notes and queries on the theory and practice of legitimate opposition'.

5 A. S. Foord, *His Majesty's Opposition 1714–1830* (Oxford, Oxford University Press, 1964); G. Ionescu and S. de Madariaga, *Opposition* (London, Penguin, 1968).

6 I rely heavily in the following paragraphs on J. H. Plumb, *The Growth of Political Stability in England 1675–1725* (London, Penguin, 1969).

7 L. Stone, 'Literacy and education in England, 1640–1900', *Past and Present*, 42 (1969), 69–139.

8 M. Wallace, 'Changing concepts of party in the United States: New York, 1815–1828', *American Historical Review*, 74 (1968), 453–91; R. Hofstader, *The Idea of a Party System: the rise of legitimate opposition in the United States, 1780–1840* (Berkeley, CA, University of California Press, 1969).

9 G. Rudé, *Wilkes and Liberty* (Oxford, Oxford University Press, 1964); J. Brewer, *Party Ideology and Popular Politics at the Accession of George III* (Cambridge, Cambridge University Press, 1976); E. A. Wrigley, *Continuity, Chance and Change* (Cambridge, Cambridge University Press, 1988).

10 R. Dahl, *Polyarchy* (New Haven, CT, Yale University Press, 1971), first noted that early liberalization helped later democratization, and I am indebted to his work. None the less, the particular manner in which a liberal state determines the character of working-class movements is not something that features in his account.

11 There is now a large literature on this point. See, among others: D. Geary, *European Labour Protest 1848–1945* (London, Methuen, 1984); R. McKibbin, *The Ideologies of Class* (Oxford, Oxford University Press, 1990); M. Mann, 'Ruling class strategies and citizenship', *Sociology*, 21 (1987), 339–54; I. Katznelson and A. Zolberg (eds), *Working Class Formation* (Princeton, NJ, Princeton University Press, 1987); and T. McDaniel, *Capitalism, Autocracy and Revolution in Russia* (Berkeley, CA, University of California Press, 1988).

12 B. Moore, *Social Origins of Dictatorship and Democracy* (Boston, MA, Beacon Press, 1966), ch. 7 and *passim*

13 R. Hamilton, *Restraining Myths* (Beverley Hills, CA, Sage, 1975); L. Weiss, *Creating Capitalists* (Oxford, Blackwell, 1988).

14 M. Mann, *Sources of Social Power. Vol. 2: The Rise of Classes and Nations, 1760–1914* (Cambridge, Cambridge University Press, 1993), ch. 15.

15 The most sustained criticism has been offered by D. Rueschemeyer, E. Stephens and J. Stephens in *Capitalist Development and Democracy* (Cambridge, Polity Press, 1992). For a particularly striking study on Germany, see D. Blackbourn and G. Eley, *The Peculiarities of German History* (Oxford, Oxford University Press, 1984).

16 Rueschemeyer, Stephens and Stephens, *Capitalist Development and Democracy*, *passim*.

17 Dahl, *Polyarchy*. His views are slightly revised and much extended in *Democracy and its critics*.

18 J. Merquior, 'Patterns of state-building in Brazil and Argentina', in J. A. Hall (ed.), *States in History* (Oxford, Blackwell, 1986), pp. 264–88.

19 The importance of commercial agriculture is at the centre of Moore, *Social*

Origins of Dictatorship and Democracy; the points about small farmers are taken from Dahl, *Polyarchy*, and Rueschmeyer, Stephens and Stephens, *Capitalist Development and Democracy*.

20   A. Amsden, *Asia's Next Giant* (New York, Oxford University Press, 1990); R. Wade, *Governing the Market* (Princeton, NJ, Princeton University Press, 1991).

21   E. A. Gellner, 'Plaidoyer pur une liberalisation manquée', in Gellner, *Spectacles and Predicaments* (Cambridge, Cambridge University Press, 1979), pp. 334–40.

22   Cf. S. Rytina, 'Under what circumstances did a plutocratic elite support civil liberties', lecture at McGill University (1991).

23   J. Goodwin, *States and revolution in the Third World*, Harvard University Ph.D. thesis (1988).

24   L. Whitehead, 'International aspects of democratisation', in O'Donnell et al., *Transitions from Authoritarian Rule*, pp. 3–46. A forthcoming book by Diane Ethier will concentrate on the international factor.

25   K. Remmer, 'Democracy and economic crisis', *World Politics*, 13 (1990), 315–35.

26   J. A. Hall, 'Will the United States decline as did Britain?', in M. Mann (ed.), *The Rise and Fall of the Nation State* (Oxford, Blackwell, 1990), pp. 114–45.

27   N. Mouzelis, *Politics in the Semi-Periphery* (London, Macmillan, 1986).

28   F. Hagopian, 'Post-authoritarian Latin America: state retreat and political reorganisation', lecture at McGill University (1991).

29   J. A. Hall, 'Sincerity and politics', *Sociological Review*, 25 (1977), 535–50.

30   R. Dahrendorf, *Reflections on the Revolution in Europe* (New York, Times Books, 1990).

31   J. Maravall, *The Transition to Democracy in Spain* (New York, St Martin's Press, 1982).

32   C. Waisman, *Reversal of Development in Argentina* (Princeton, NJ, Princeton University Press, 1987).

33   This point has been challenged by F. Hagopian, 'Democracy by undemocratic means?', *Comparative Political Studies*, 23 (1990), 147–70. Some pacts have been so cosy and exclusionary, in Hagopian's view, that they have diminished trust, thereby hindering the consolidation of democracy. I take her argument as a criticism of the abuse of pacts, rather than a dismissal of them. Pacts may make sense, in other words, only when there are several parties to them.

34   Hagopian, 'Post-authoritarian Latin America'.

35   P. Evans, 'Class, state and dependence in East Asia: lessons for Latin Americanists', in F. C. Deyo (ed.), *The Political Economy of the New Asian Industrialism* (Ithaca, NY, Cornell University Press, 1987), pp. 203–26; B. Cumings, 'The abortive abertura: South Korea in the light of Latin American experience', *New Left Review*, 173 (1989), 5–33.

36   Deyo, *The Political Economy of the New Asian Industrialism*.

37   A. Przeworski, 'The "east" becomes the "south"?', *Political Science and Politics*, 24 (1991), 20–4, and Przeworski, *Democracy and the Market: political and economic reforms in Eastern Europe and Latin America* (Cambridge, Cambridge University Press, 1991). Cf. B. Misztal, 'Must Eastern Europe follow the Latin American way?', *European Journal of Sociology*, 33 (1992), pp. 151–79.

38   E. Hankiss, *East European Alternatives* (Oxford, Oxford University Press, 1990).

39   D. Wank, *Entrepreneurship, social structure and politics in post-Mao China*, Harvard University Ph.D. thesis (1992).

40   M. Weber, 'Socialism', in *Weber: Selections in Translation*, ed. W. G. Runciman (Cambridge, Cambridge University Press, 1978), pp. 251–62.

14

DEMOCRACY AND ITS FUTURE IN EASTERN EUROPE

Paul G. Lewis

Any attempt to predict the course of events in contemporary Eastern Europe is hazardous in the extreme and highly likely to be somewhat off-course before the results are published. Apart from the instabilities of the contemporary situation, the categories of analysis are themselves fluid and subject to change. Few may now remember the Union of Sovereign States that overlaid the terminal months of the Union of Soviet Socialist Republics. The fate of its successor, the Commonwealth of Independent States, will quite probably be equally insecure. The contours of the Balkans have changed with the progressive dissolution of Yugoslavia and the formation of new states in that area. Czechoslovakia (or, since March 1990, Czecho-Slovakia in the Slovak variant) threatens to go beyond the stage of hyphenation and split into two separate parts. The notion of 'Eastern Europe' in the contemporary context, therefore, requires some clarification.

For several decades after the Second World War, Eastern Europe was that region between the countries of the North Atlantic Treaty Organization and the European Community on the one hand, and those of the Soviet Union on the other. From the perspectives of the early 1990s and with the collapse of communist rule in Europe, though, the countries to the east of a unified Germany may now be grouped into three categories. First, there is East-Central Europe, which comprises Czechoslovakia, Hungary and Poland and consists of countries that have made a decisive break with their communist past, taken concerted steps towards the establishment of a democratic political system, embarked on privatization and the construction of a market economy – processes that have, however, not progressed without serious problems and setbacks.

Secondly, there are the Balkan countries of Albania, Bulgaria, Romania and Yugoslavia, which have experienced greater problems in confronting the tasks of democratic transition and economic transformation and, in the case of Yugoslavia, avoiding civil conflict and maintaining the established state structure. Thirdly, there are the countries that make up what now might be called Eastern Europe in that more conventional sense which accords with the view taken of the region before the westward extension of Soviet power after 1945. Eastern Europe, in this view consists mainly of Bielorussia, the Ukraine and Russia itself – to the extent that a meaningful distinction can be drawn between the parts of Russia which may be regarded as part of Europe (those to the west of the Ural mountains) and others which extend through Siberia to the Pacific Ocean.

Here, however, we shall draw on the experience of Eastern Europe in the more general post-war sense of the parts of Europe under communist rule, and consider the prospects for democracy facing such countries. The contrasts between the different parts of the region are striking and bear on their prospects of democratization. The more clearly European parts of the area – the countries of East-Central Europe, Slovenian and Croatian parts of the former Yugoslavia, and the Baltic states – have seen higher levels of economic development and the emergence of more modern societies. They are countries that, broadly speaking, mark the historic borders of Catholic influence in distinction to the Ottoman domination of the Balkans and the lands of long-established Russian control – itself subject to the Mongol yoke and cut off for a considerable period from decisive European influences. Some writers, however, place greater emphasis on a division which emerged in the first millennium and ran along the Rivers Elbe and Saale (slightly to the east of the border of the former German Democratic Republic), separating the lands where the steady development of a coherent European civilization could be observed from those where its influence and authority fluctuated over the centuries.[1] This division has played a part in forming the distinctive political cultures of the region and should also be taken account of in warning against the assumption of too close an identity between the traditions and inclinations of East-Central European society with those of the West European nations.

Nevertheless, the countries of East-Central Europe in the broader sense have led the way in terms of post-communist development, showing a greater commitment to the development of democratic processes and more success in the establishment of democratic structures. The greater development of what might be broadly termed civil society in those areas has been associated with a more sophisticated political culture and a constellation of social forces which bear positively on further prospects of democratic development.[2] Consider, for example, the course of the miners' demonstrations that took place in both Romania and Poland during 1991. In the first case, parts of Bucharest were laid to waste, deaths caused and part of the parliament building destroyed; in the second, demonstrations were held and organized opposition mounted to exert pressure on legislators. In Poland conflict was institutionalized and political participation contained within organized channels, a contrast that points both to existing levels of political development and to further prospects for democracy in the different countries of Eastern Europe.

Not all the contrasting developments and changes in the region, moreover, have grown out of processes of post-communist change. The aggressive Serbian role in Yugoslavian hostilities and the escalation of ethnic conflict there derived from the strategy of communist leader Slobodan Milosevic and his determination to use national tensions to enhance his political position (although post-communist forces in Croatia on more than one occasion showed themselves not unwilling to enter the fray). This was closely associated with the determination of the Yugoslav National Army, one of the last bastions of communist orthodoxy in the region, to retain the power it had for decades exercised over the whole country. Developments since the withdrawal of Soviet influence from the former Eastern Europe have thus tended to highlight the social diversity apparent within the region and its contrasting implications for the democratization process. More recent changes, associated with the evolving post-communist situation and the relics of communist power in the area, further suggest the fluidity of state borders as well as those of geographical categories that only recently seemed relatively fixed.

Neither is the situation particularly clear-cut in terms of the idea of democracy and conceptions of the basis for its development in the area. In terms of formal ideology the communist countries of Eastern Europe had, indeed, always espoused principles of socialist democracy and claimed, despite rather convincing evidence to the contrary, to be practising them. Parts of the official argument, moreover, met with considerable sympathy and at least partial agreement from some western scholars, and – particularly before the effects of the Khrushchev period were expunged by the years of Brezhnevite stagnation – significant areas of similarity with western democratic institutions and processes were identified. Political participation in the Soviet Union was in some cases judged to be no less extensive or significant than in the US and was by no means dismissed as being coerced or politically meaningless;[3] the role of interest groups was investigated and their share in political power argued for;[4] monolithic conceptions of communist society were rejected and in their stead ideas of 'institutional pluralism' proposed.[5]

The arguments based on Marxist-Leninist ideology were not wholly specious and reflected different conceptions of democratic thought that had some validity. The contrast between the modern conceptions of democracy that were articulated, if frequently in crude and somewhat distorted form, during the years of the Cold War is one with a lengthy history that extends back to the eighteenth century and the debates that crystallized at the time of the American and French revolutions.[6] In the discussions that accompanied the preparation of the American Constitution, Alexander Hamilton expounded the ideas of representative democracy that have come to prevail in modern liberal democracy, while the principles of direct democracy elaborated by Jean-Jacques Rousseau underlay the notions of popular power that gained momentum during the French Revolution and came to occupy a central place in the socialist tradition, taking on one of its less distinguished forms in the necrophiliac politics of the late Brezhnev era.

Now, superseding this bifurcation of the democratic tradition and with the degeneration of the socialist project in Eastern Europe, as well as the increasing global dominance of the alternative model, it is clearly western ideas of liberal democracy that have become dominant in contemporary conceptions of democratic transition in post-communist Europe. They may be most succinctly summed up in the features of polyarchy defined by Robert Dahl and characterized by the two broad characteristics of the situation in which they are operative: that in which effective citizenship is extended to a relatively high proportion of adults, and where the rights of citizenship include the opportunity to oppose and vote out the highest officials of government.[7] Such features are certainly sufficient to distinguish liberal democracy from the typical pattern of communist rule, where formal civic rights were not effective, society was governed by the privileged few and high officials could not be voted out of office.

But traces of alternative conceptions of democracy have by no means disappeared from Eastern Europe. Neither are all the implications of this new openness to western democratic values and the broader context in which 'actually existing democracy' is situated fully recognized or endorsed by the formally liberated citizens of the East European states. The collapse of communist rule and the emergence of new patterns of political behaviour have not necessarily marked a sharp break with the practices of state socialism and the values associated with it. The role of social movements in East-Central Europe like those of Solidarity in Poland and Civic Forum in Czechoslovakia has suggested the continuing validity of forms of direct democracy, in terms of the unmediated mass participation in political life and the part it played in securing the end of communist power.

Such movements, indeed, proved to be effective vehicles of opposition to communist dictatorship and met the needs of the moment in a number of ways. Developing outside and in opposition to the bureaucratized power structures which spread throughout the communist system, they provided a focus for the aspirations of society and its resentment against the agencies of the state, clearly subject to the dictates of the party and its specialized apparatus of power. They served to integrate those who shared the widespread disillusion with and antipathy against communist authority, and provided a distinctive vehicle for the expression of opposition whose form as well as content was quite antithetic to that of the existing establishment and incumbent power-holders. They were effective in conveying the distaste increasingly felt for the objectives and methods employed in the exercise of communist power, and embodied the spirit of 'anti-politics' that encapsulated the revulsion felt against Soviet-backed dictatorship.[8]

These movements were, further, often seen as the most suitable institutional basis for the transition to democracy. They promised avoidance of the divisiveness and cynical machine politics characteritic of western democracy, and seemed to guarantee the social cohesion and unity that would be necessary in the transition to democracy, and during the problematic economic transformation that also faced the countries of failed communism. Their commitment to developing complex programmes of social welfare and avoiding unemployment, despite hopes for a rapid transition to the market economy, built on the strong egalitarian tradition that had long existed in the region.[9] But many of these hopes proved to be short-lived. *Neues Forum*, in the view of the disenchanted German activist Jens Reich, was 'swept aside in the stampede towards unification' and a range of parties was soon established, each of which was firmly linked with a western counterpart that then oversaw a 'merciless electoral campaign' in East Germany.[10]

This was soon followed by the dissolution of Solidarity and Civic Forum in Czechoslovakia, which came as an equivalent source of frustration and disappointment to many of those involved. But it by no means opened the way to a smooth transition to liberal democracy or the acceptance of all the values that made its operation possible in the west. Signs like the strong showing of the reformed communist groupings in the Polish election of October 1991, and growing distaste in Russia for the 'democracy' that accompanied the progressive disorder of the gradually collapsing Soviet system, showed that commitment to liberal democracy was by no means universal or unqualified and that all the values embodied by the former system had by no means been abandoned.[11] The march towards liberal democracy and parliamentary rule was accompanied by alternative, and often unacknowledged, ideas of democratic practice which made their own contribution to the course of post-communist political development.

For many East Europeans democracy remains an ill-defined objective with diverse associations. In Poland, people's conception of democracy appeared to have shifted considerably over the years and by 1989, understandably if somewhat unrealistically in terms of immediate prospects, they had become largely synonymous with material wealth rather than being identified with political values or any system of political institutions.[12] The 'anti-politics' outlook put down strong roots and, in reaction to the ritualized public life of the Ceaușescu years, during their revolution in 1989 Romanians called for 'democracy, not politics'.[13] Almost universal throughout the region was the conviction that the withdrawal of the Soviets and the disappearance of the Iron Curtain meant that the East was 'returning to Europe', and this too was often what democracy meant for the former communist subjects. For 80 per cent of the majority of Poles who shared the idea of a 'return to Europe', the term for them meant the observance of human rights, freedom and civil liberty, free elections and the democratic exercise of power.[14] Not many, however, realized at the time that 'Europe' was more of an economic and political concept than a geographical one, and that it was not just the physical barriers to democracy that needed to be removed.

While the precise form that post-communist democracy might take was not certain, it also remained unclear what domestic forces existed to sustain East European democratization. As dictatorial communist rule began collapsing in 1989 the fact of its demise was easily, indeed far too easily, identified with the introduction of democracy – regardless of the meaning attached to it. Democracy, however, in whichever conception, certainly means more than just the absence of dictatorship, and the process of post-communist political transition is one of considerable complexity. This was without doubt not fully grasped at the outset by many people within and beyond Eastern Europe: the relatively speedy and fairly painless establishment of democracy was assumed to be on the cards, building on the evident success and popularity of movements like Solidarity and apparent guarantees of a smooth political transition like those achieved at round-table negotiations in Hungary and Poland. Even less were the traumatic effects of economic stabilization and reconstruction programmes foreseen, not just in the poorer countries of the Balkans but in more affluent and highly developed countries like Czechoslovakia and East Germany.

Economic dislocation, deprivation and material hardship have had a considerable impact on social processes in the region and, particularly as prospects of economic recovery rapidly receded, a major effect on the establishment of democratic processes. Polish national income fell drastically in 1990, the first year of the economic stabilization programme, and then by a further 15 per cent in 1991. A more cautious approach had been adopted in Czechoslovakia but there, too, national income fell by 13 per cent in 1991. Soviet gross national product fell by 12 per cent in the first nine months of 1991, and a 20 per cent drop in industrial output in Russia was anticipated for the first quarter of 1992 as Boris Yeltsin's reforms came into operation. Combined with the legacy of the communist period in terms of expectations and values as well as the influence of deeper-rooted regional traditions, the rigours of economic transformation exert further pressures on the process of democratization.

The extensive optimism and expectations of reasonably unproblematic political change were not restricted to the east. It was, of course, realized from the outset in western capitals that some form of western assistance would be needed – but it was generally argued that this should be provided as blueprints and professional advice, along the lines of the British Know-How Fund, rather than in the form of concrete aid. It seemed to many that there was little alternative to this general line of policy in any case. In the late 1980s, the population of the formerly communist East European countries together with that of the old Soviet Union totalled some 427 million; it takes only a little reflection on what the integration of the 16.6 million population of East Germany with the leading economy of Western Europe did to the enlarged Federal Republic (East Germany itself, of course, having been regarded for some years as the economic jewel in the communist crown) to realize the level of material support that might be needed.

However, the adoption of the Know-How approach, even if possibly the only realistic option for the western powers (let alone for the UK, one of the least dynamic economies of the European Community), also had other aspects and consequences that went beyond the sphere of government policy. For one thing, it tended to reflect the view that democratic transition and economic transformation were largely technical issues which were little affected by the social and cultural context in which they occurred. It was hardly surprising in this context that economic modernizers like Leszek Balcerowicz and Václav Klaus were the prime East European referents for western governments and the major guarantors of post-communist economic rectitude for organizations like the International Monetary Fund. This, it may be surmised, was because of rather than despite the fact that they were pushing programmes 'on a technocratic basis, without reference to the political conditions on which they can be sustained'.[15]

It was a perspective, moreover, that had a counterpart in intellectual circles with the 'end of history' thesis, to which considerable attention was paid around this time.[16] Although extensively criticized by many mainstream academics it was, clearly, also a source of fascination, not just for the subject it raised and its evident pedagogical benefits but because it did in fact reflect many of the views prevalent in 1989 at the time of the fall of the communist regimes. There just did not seem to be anywhere else for those countries to go but towards western-style democracy, and it was widely felt that the post-communist regimes would soon be on that path of development. This response tended to be reinforced by the absence of alternative frameworks within which the East European developments could be grasped. There was a paucity of alternative conceptions of post-communist development and East European democratization, apart from the depleted ranks of the stout (though largely unconvincing) defenders of Marxism and orthodox socialism, who claimed that the collapse of East European communism was merely the last gasp of Stalinism.

For most people, however, a more significant change was at issue – and one, moreover, on which existing scholarship provided few perspectives or theoretical guidance. Certainly, the idea of communism or 'actually existing socialism' as a distinct path of social development lost its credibility. Moore's thesis that communist revolution was one of the primary 'routes to the modern world' began to look highly doubtful.[17] That line was no longer seen as one taken (to return to Fukuyama's terminology) by the locomotive of history, and increasingly had the appearance of a siding now filled with engines which had run out of steam, and with rusting rolling-stock good for little else than the breaker's yard. Ideas of communist evolution, the maturing of its system and modernization within established structures, suddenly looked very threadbare. Like the evaluations of communist democracy and efforts to establish the comparability of eastern communism and western pluralism, they had been particularly popular during the 1960s and 1970s in the wake of the Khrushchev period. The view that 'pluralization and the reinstitutionalization that follows from it' constituted one of the 'irreversible trends' of European communism[18] had, indeed, virtually died with the expunging of the reform movement and the invasion of Czechoslovakia in 1968.

But mainstream political science also offered relatively little by way of guidance. Existing work on democratization processes and the conditions that influence the emergence of democracy shed little light on the development of post-communist societies.[19] The emphasis on endogenous factors and the role of capitalism found in much of the democratization literature does not favour its application to Eastern Europe.[20] Comparison with other cases of democratization are instructive but can hardly be conclusive, not least because of the concurrent processes of economic transformation and the efforts being made to construct market economies which really have no historical parallel. The context of democratization in Eastern Europe is also different from the other cases that have received significant levels of scholarly attention. The economic background to the changes which occurred after Franco's death in Spain was one of growth and steady preparation before the process of democratization began, while the regional and global conditions for further development then were considerably more favourable than they are for Eastern Europe in the 1990s. Spain, observes Adam Przeworski, 'is a miracle'[21] – and even a devout nation like that of the Poles should not count on replicating that experience.

Nevertheless, hindsight has also tended to diminish the obstacles that faced successful democratizing countries like post-Franco Spain: 'the South European transitions were rather more complicated than is sometimes remembered by Eastern European leaders'.[22] Regionalism threatened major instabilities and the military posed a serious challenge to the political leadership for a considerable number of years. The level of Spain's economic preparedness for the post-Franco transition did not mean that it was painless; unemployment rose to 21.5 per cent in 1985 before beginning to decline in time for the following year's election. The flow of EC funds and regional support schemes were a major bonus – but integration with the European Community also took its toll: German capital goods flowed in as import quotas were abolished and industrial tariffs reduced; production quotas were set on wine and olive oil to accommodate French and Italian interests, while full access for the Spanish fruit and vegetable sector was set ten years ahead.[23] The problems of democratization and concurrent integration with the EC were therefore considerable and the effort needed to achieve the miracle should not be ignored. That does not mean, however, that Spain was not better placed to make that effort than much of contemporary Eastern Europe.

On the other hand, more historical works on the emergence of democracy stress, naturally enough, the length of the period during which it has developed and the close association it has had with entrepreneurial capitalism.[24] The association of democracy with the rise and development of capitalism thus points to processes whose origins reach back several centuries, which hardly seems to offer much guidance to the rapidly changing world of the late twentieth century. Western democracy, moreover, did not develop because former regimes just collapsed and it became possible to install democratic institutions in their place. It was, rather, the outcome of a lengthy process of social struggle and group conflict which itself created conditions for the consolidation and persistence of democracy.[25] Finally, modern democracy has been in many ways one of the products of capitalist development and an outcome of capitalism, formed by the conflicts it throws up, rather than an accompaniment of its growth. Democracy certainly did not provide a *basis* for capitalist development – which is the programme foreseen for Eastern Europe.

Thus none of these general views seems to offer much direct help in grasping the nature and prospect of East European democratization: the socio-technical transfer and 'end of history' approach ignores the preconditions of contemporary political change in Eastern Europe and the cultural legacy with which democratization has to contend, simply positing the generalization of western experience; the body of mainstream political science literature does not connect at all well with the question of post-communist democratization; and historical studies, apart from the lengthy time span they take into consideration, suggest rather the priority of capitalist development over democratization. From these perspectives, it must be concluded, the prospects for democracy in Eastern Europe are very unclear – while the object of view itself, the condition of democracy, is also pretty blurred for many of those concerned.

Nevertheless, some of the general insights afforded into processes of democratization are by no means irrelevant to the prospects of democracy in Eastern Europe. This is particularly so if they are supplemented by an awareness of the historical legacy that bears on the contemporary situation, and the dynamics both of the immediate transition from communist to non-communist rule and of the experiences of the early post-communist period. These factors may be linked with the mass dimension of political change and the social context of political behaviour that influences the process of democratic transition.

Historical experience of democratic practices and the operation of democratic institutions in Eastern Europe has certainly been limited. Even in the countries of East-Central Europe, where the level of political development has generally been higher than in other areas, it was only Czechoslovakia that had a record of sustained democratic practice before the Second World War, and that, in the eyes of the Slovaks, was by no means unqualified. The influence of such traditional patterns of politics should not be exaggerated, particularly in view of the lengthy experience of communist rule (and the shorter, though traumatic, experience of wartime hostilities and Nazi occupation) and the major changes in the spheres of culture and social structure that took place under it. The effect of communism and the forms of political organization and behaviour it promoted probably tended, in any case, to reinforce existing perceptions of politics as a relatively elitist affair and to discourage spontaneous participation. There was little in these successive periods to encourage the development of the practices of a modern participatory democracy in Eastern Europe. Lengthy experience of authoritarian rule gives little hope of full democratization from this point of view.

The uncertain prospect of democracy is also linked with the problematic development of civil society and the role of social forces in Eastern Europe. With reference to Eastern Europe during the 1980s, 'civil society' became more of a slogan than an analytical concept. Its role in undermining the foundations of communist power and even its very existence in any meaningful sense have by no means been fully established.[26] Yet civil society, Ralph Dahrendorf has argued, is the key to the effective constitutional and economic development that alone can provide the social foundations for a free society and the growth of a firmly based democracy; 'it pulls the divergent time scales and dimensions of political and economic reform together. It is the ground in which both have to be anchored in order not to be blown away'. To lay these foundations, however, 'sixty years [or two generations] are barely enough'.[27]

From this perspective, the development and consolidation of stable democracies is a very long-term process – although one that, in comparison with the lengthy period over which democracy developed in Britain or France, is by no means unrealistic or unduly pessimistic. At issue here, though, is the existence of a developed and firmly rooted civil society that has the capacity to nurture and promote liberty – and this is by no means the situation in Eastern Europe, even as reflected in the views of those who have argued for the development of an effective civil society during the slow decline of communist rule. One immediate problem has resided in the fact that the apparent victory of civil society over communist dictatorship might be construed as leading less to political democracy than to populism, referring to the direct political dominance of 'the people' with little regard to constitutional arrangements, the institutional mediation of power relations or any protection of minority rights. It is an outcome seen in societies not dissimilar to those of Eastern Europe where political processes have been, at least initially, relatively unconstrained and where political transformation has been accelerated by rapid socio-economic change. The desires and aspirations of a greater fraction of society might indeed be better satisfied by the arrangements of such a political order – but this is not the same thing as the establishment of political democracy.

The problems of post-communist rule in Eastern Europe are in this sense not so different from the dilemmas and problems faced by western nations during analogous stages of their political development. Civil society, as John Keane has pointed out with clear echoes of Thomas Hobbes, 'can also degenerate into a battlefield',[28] and sovereign state power may for that reason be considered an indispensable condition for the democratization of civil society.[29] In this context it is the constitutional character of state power that becomes the prime issue. The question of minority rights is certainly firmly on the political agenda of a country like Poland, where the civil society that did emerge was significantly sustained by religious faith and supported organizationally by a strong Catholic Church. It was a situation in which a Polish liberal was driven to argue that 'a state in which morality forms the law is a totalitarian state'.[30] Neither were such tensions restricted to contexts of particularly strong clerical influence, and the negative implications for democracy of 'civil society in power' have also been highlighted in Slovenia.[31]

The question of civil society has been closely linked with the central role of the social movements that proved to be such a powerful vehicle for political opposition in the closing phase of communism in some areas of Eastern Europe. They, nevertheless, also reflected some of the characteristics of the power structures their activity and spirit were so set against. These were often not conducive either to general processes of democratization or to the development of the multi-party systems that are the prime institutional expression of modern representative democracy. They were, to varying degrees, inclusive and relatively undifferentiated forms of organization whose near-universal opposition to communist power mirrored the general Marxist-Leninist claims to overall leadership and inclusive authority. Their attachment to anti-politics, embodying religious, ethical and national sentiment, was also in practice not so far removed from the opposition of communist officials and Marxist resistance to pluralism.

The implicit values underlying East European movements in terms of their rejection of formal politics and doubts about the nature of state authority also stemmed from the ready identification of communist power with that of the state in general. At the outset such values were rarely contrasted with the normative underpinnings of western pluralism and the conditions for operating the modern democracies they also sought to establish. But tensions soon became evident and exerted an influence on the institutional development of post-communist systems as conflict developed within the inclusive social movements, and processes of decision-making, policy-implementation and the course of government itself became difficult to follow through. The context of the social movement was not one appropriate to cope with the degree of differentiation and complexity required if a diversity of views on strategy and tactics was to emerge, imaginative policy options were to be defined and a range of organized groups formed to confront the diverse demands of a pluralist, post-communist society, which alone offered the prospect of effective democratization.

The movements were also not well suited to one of the core processes of modern democracy and the forms of government it sustains – that of representation. Their tendency to adopt a general form and develop an inclusive form of organization had been linked with the objective, and often effective capacity, of expressing the hopes and feelings of society as a whole against party-state power. But this impressive aim and, on occasion, achievement of representing society as a whole against communist power reflected as much a process of transcending the forms of society, its actual structures and forms of division, as of articulating the movement's specific interests and of trying to achieve concrete objectives. It was often more a form of symbolic expression of national and religious sentiment (most notably in the archetypal emergence of Solidarity in 1980) than a process of representation in any way related to the articulation and pursuit of social interests observed in developed western democracies. Yet representation may be regarded as the critical innovation of the modern age that has made democracy a practicable form of rule and effective as a basis for government under contemporary conditions. Its emergence in symbolic form within the framework of the social movement rather than as a more pragmatic articulation of group interest was a further factor distancing the East European oppositions from the practice of western democracy.

Once the umbrella social movements started to fragment, moreover, the process of group differentiation took on extensive proportions. It became evident that the process of political party formation and organization would often be a matter of some difficulty – not just because of lingering anti-party sentiment and the problems attributable to the early stages of post-communist democratic development, but also due to the increasing social flux, uncertainty and frustration that surfaced as policies of economic transformation tightened the screw on an already hard-pressed population, while failing to provide any promise of improvement in the near future. It was in this sense unfortunate that Poland, for example, having launched its staunchly liberal policies early on, was the last of the East-Central European countries to hold a free general election. The outcome, with a turnout of only 43 per cent, was the representation in parliament of 29 separate groupings – and major difficulties in forming a government with any hope of stability or effectiveness. But even in Czechoslovakia, where Civic Forum had won a major victory in the election in June 1990, the subsequent break-up of the movement and splits in other political groups, often as much on grounds of personality as on policy, spelt such a degree of fragmentation that only a small minority of the new spectrum of parties would gain subsequent parliamentary representation if the same electoral threshold was applied as in 1990. Only in Hungary did the six-party system that had emerged from the 1990 elections seem to hold relatively steady, though even here there were grave doubts about the authenticity of the new parliamentary democracy.[32]

The holding of free elections is nevertheless an important step in the transition to democracy in Eastern Europe. Apart from the representation of public opinion and the articulation of social interests, the stability and effectiveness of governments and the nature of ruling elites are all critically influenced in liberal democracies by elections and the operation of parties. Even the partially free Polish elections of June 1989 were responsible for an extremely high level of renewal among parliamentary deputies, with 422 members (92 per cent) entering parliament for the first time.[33] According to one analysis it suggested that a 'great departure has been made from the previous system of leadership recruitment. It is undoubtedly an important step towards the democratisation of social relations.'[34] Focus on the changing composition of governing bodies and the formation of new elites is central to the process of East European democratization. For in the democratic transition literature it is elites, rather than masses or movements of popular protest, that emerge as the principal actors.[35] 'Almost always', states Samuel Huntington, 'democracy has come as much from the top down as from the bottom up.'[36] In the work of analysts like Moore and Rustow, as well as in more recent accounts of the post-Franco democratization in Spain,[37] it is the role of elites that is assigned the greatest weight.

While the mass dimension of political change and the social context of democratization have certainly not been irrelevant to East European developments and the prospects for democracy there, the role of elites has been no less important – and, in the light of previous comparative analysis and theoretical discussion, may turn out to be the critical factor. Elites supportive of the communist regime as well as those against it

certainly played a central part in the East European transition to democracy (and, particularly, the pre-transition phase that occurred as authoritarian regimes underwent initial liberalization). While broad social
movements were often the characteristic mode in Eastern Europe for the
mobilization and expression of discontent and the articulation of opposition, the critical junctures of regime transition and mechanisms of power
transfer lay very much within the domain of elite politics – but their role
and activities have become more problematic as the process of transition
has developed.

If some East European countries increasingly took on the political
form of fractured systems during the 1980s – showing clear signs of
immobilism and instability – the opening of round-table negotiations,
first in Poland and then in Hungary, reflected the classic features, outlined by Arend Lijphart, of 'overarching cooperation at the elite level'
identified as the essential characteristic of consociational democracy.[38]
Numerically depleted and organizationally weakened by martial law and
Jaruzelski's militarized rule, Solidarity leaders decided to enter negotiations with reformist figures in Poland's ruling communist circles following
two further outbreaks of industrial unrest during 1988, developments
which led directly to the more far-reaching events of 1989. Strong ties
were maintained in Hungary between members of the original Democratic Opposition, which was later the basis for the Alliance of Free
Democrats, and reformist circles in the ruling party, which also led to
decisive negotiations and the declaration of a joint commitment to
reform in September 1989.

While, obviously, these developments were marked by the specifics of
the East European context during this period, they did reflect features of
historical democratization processes and elements of the interactions
that had formed established western democracies. In Britain, for example,
democracy was established through processes of gradual change and
piecemeal elite accommodation – introduced first for the upper layers of
the bourgeoisie and commercialized landowners and then extended to
other sections of the bourgeoisie. It occurred, as Göran Therborn points
out, within a framework combining unity and division – sections of the
working class benefiting from the drive of the bourgeoisie for greater
political representation and forming part of an alliance in the move
towards greater democratization. While working-class agitation was
often an indispensable part of the bourgeois movement towards democracy, the political advance of the working class was dependent on the
patronage of the bourgeoisie and was 'nowhere capable of achieving
democracy by its own unaided resources'.[39]

This trajectory points to features very different from the beginnings of democratization in Eastern Europe – but there are also some similarities. The processes of elite accommodation and the enhanced political status of previously disenfranchised and marginalized groups are to some extent common ones. It could also be argued that the Solidarity elite in Poland and its equivalents in Hungary acted the historical role of the western bourgeoisie in opening the way to regime change and mass political participation – although they lacked the material base of the western bourgeoisie and the economic resources and skills that could be used as a source of consistent political influence. There were further paradoxes in the East European situation and discrepancies with the historical model. The period of elite accommodation was soon superseded by the overwhelming dominance of non-communist, or more accurately anti-communist, forces and the rapid eclipse of the former communist elites. Representatives of so-called 'under-classes' were not assimilated and awarded a share in power – given the withdrawal of the Soviet underpinnings of the East European power-structure, they simply stepped in and took it over.

This sequence of events weakened the association and linkage between different social forces that had opened the way to effective democracy in the west. In particular, existing elites were not so much modified in their outlook and orientation by the assimilation of new forces – and thus strengthened in terms of their capacity to deal with the increasing pressure of contemporary demands – but replaced by others with quite different backgrounds and ranges of experience.[40] The elites transformed in the original processes of modern democratization, moreover, were those already associated with and accompanied by processes of early capitalist development. This has not been the case in Eastern Europe, where new elites – of uncertain or mixed provenance – have generally assumed or been charged with the task of creating market economies and, ultimately, the social structures and groups that have historically been associated with processes of democratic development.

The role of elites in the East European democratic transition thus emerges as a particularly critical one, not just because of the negotiated character of the early cases of regime change, but also because of the political flux and institutional vacuum left with the collapse of communist power. This, further, was followed by the fragmentation of the broad social forces that formed during the period of communist decline and oversaw the early months of democratic transition. In this situation, not surprisingly, the role of leadership has been a particularly important one.[41] The outlook and actions of Mikhail Gorbachev can hardly be underestimated in determining the new course on which Eastern Europe has been set, but great influence has also been exerted by individuals like

Helmut Kohl, Lech Wałęsa, Václav Havel and Boris Yeltsin. Nevertheless, despite the importance of personal judgement at critical moments of historical change, it is not individuals that govern the momentum and stability of democratic development (although many may harbour the illusion that they do) but broader structures or, at least, groups that cohere around the political leader.

Institutions like parliaments and parties are in the early stages of development, however, and their consolidation and growth are also likely to be dependent on the prior emergence of elites and integrated groups of politically influential individuals sharing some common vision of the region's future. It is, indeed, institutions that provide solutions to the problems of democratization,[42] and it is in this area that the prospects for democracy in much of Eastern Europe look particularly bleak. The emphasis on personality and the deep-rooted mistrust of the state and its agencies throughout the region have, as George Schöpflin points out, militated against the post-communist development of democracy and left new institutions 'locked in a cycle of relative weakness'.[43] But the problem is not restricted to institutions and directs attention back to the character of the post-communist elites, whose background does little to inspire confidence in their capacity to form an effective government *équipe*; this was an experience 'formative of the new political elites as resisters. It in no way equiped them for power.'[44]

In the absence of established elites or effectively operating institutions, the political situation remains an unstable one and the process of democratization threatens to stall. The problem in Poland has recently been summed up as one where society is in search of appropriate leaders while a variety of putatative leaders are looking for a social constituency.[45] In this context it is not surprising that there have been fiery debates and controversies throughout Eastern Europe about the status and continuing influence of the former elites and the adoption of policies of more thorough-going 'decommunization'. Despite the collapse of the communist system and the crumbling of its official structures, many communist functionaries were still very much around and well connected with centres of power and influence.

But domestic influences, and the role of national elites and discrete social groupings, by no means exhaust the range of factors that bear on contemporary prospects for democracy in Eastern Europe. The democratization of the post-communist countries, as well as the processes of economic recovery and development which are intended to accompany it, are critically dependent on international support and processes of regional and global integration. Democratization may proceed in several ways within this overall context, and the further prospects of democracy differ according to the range and level of factors involved. By no means the least important aspect is the legitimating role of the democratization process within international relations.[46] It provides critical support for programmes of economic recovery and a framework for the further transformation of economic structures and processes, although it has already become apparent that there is significant variation in the international impact on democratic transition in Eastern Europe.[47]

The granting of associate EC status to Czechoslovakia, Hungary and Poland in December 1991 represented a significant change in their international status which, as in the case of Spain, should eventually help consolidate the progress already made towards democracy and improve prospects of economic development. If Eastern Europe is likely overall to face the same politics and economics of poor capitalism as countries in Latin America, characterized by political instability and uneven economic growth, it at least has the benefits of geography which give it some chance of participating in the advantages of Western Europe.[48] Nevertheless, contemporary conditions of economic transformation and the growing integration of Eastern Europe economies with the global economy already recall specific problems that have faced Latin American democracy and the consolidation of its political structures under economic conditions of 'dominated incorporation': dominated because the Latin American countries were enmeshed in relations of capitalist dependence and occupied a subordinate position within its international system; incorporation because they were linked with and dependent on the international system without being effectively integrated within it or possessing the capacity to use its energies for the purposes of national society.[49]

This form of incorporation, Göran Therborn has argued, imposed powerful obstacles to the unification of the Latin American states and the consolidation of their structures of rule – the position of key officials, for example, resting to a large extent on external sources of power and leaving them with highly selective relations in respect to national or local groups. If replicated in Eastern Europe, such a pattern might lead to the furthering weakening of national elites, continuing problems in establishing relations with suitable social constituencies, and a relatively weak position from which to spearhead the thrust towards democracy. The critical role of finance minister Leszek Balcerowicz in sustaining international (and notably IMF) support for Poland, and the substantial resentment he provoked in domestic political circles, already provide an instructive example of this tendency in Eastern Europe. As attacks on the role of the IMF in contributing to the loss of Polish sovereignty and the continuing destruction of the Polish economy emerge, and views on the growing colonial status of the country are expressed, it becomes clear that critical lines of political division are drawn across national society and often integrate East European politicians more successfully with international institutions than with domestic constituencies.[50]

Yet, in comparison with other areas of Eastern Europe, the more developed countries – which, despite its problems, still include Poland – enjoy considerably better prospects for democracy than the Balkans and most areas of the former Soviet Union. As well as facing, in all probability, problems surrounding the efficiency of the state apparatus and its adequacy for a range of new tasks, they also – already in Yugoslavia and quite possibly in the former Soviet Union within the foreseeable future – confront the more fundamental problems of state formation and territorial realignment. These have already, in some cases, erupted into civil or cross-border wars and the escalation of ethnic conflict. The basic issues of modern statehood are raised in true Weberian form by questions both of territoriality and of the contested control over armed forces and the means of violence in the former Soviet Union. Rather than modern processes of pluralization and democratization, such situations direct attention further back to the pre-democratic, pre-modern conflicts that gave rise to the practical deliberations and classic theoretical works of Bodin and Hobbes. This in itself suggests the distant prospects of modern democracy in at least some of the countries of Eastern Europe.

NOTES

1   I. T. Berend, 'The historical evolution of Eastern Europe as a region', *International Organization*, 40 (1986), 329–346; J. Szücs, 'Three historical regions of Europe', in J. Keane (ed.), *Civil Society and the State* (London, Verso, 1988).

2   For a range of views on this issue, see Keane, *Civil Society and the State*, and P. G. Lewis (ed.), *Democracy and Civil Society in Eastern Europe* (London, Macmillan, 1992).

3   D. R. Little, 'Mass political participation in the US and USSR', *Comparative Political Studies*, 8 (1976), 437–60; J. F. Hough, 'Political participation in the Soviet Union', *Soviet Studies*, 28 (1976), 3–20.

4   H. G. Skilling and F. Griffiths (eds), *Interest Groups in Soviet Politics* (Princeton, NJ, Princeton University Press, 1971).

5   J. F. Hough, 'The Soviet system: petrification or pluralism?', *Problems of Communism*, 21 (1972), 25–45.

6   P. G. Lewis, 'Democracy in modern societies', in J. Allen, P. Braham and P. Lewis (eds), *The Political and Economic Forms of Modernity* (Cambridge, Polity Press, 1992).

7   R. Dahl, *Democracy and Its Critics* (New Haven, CT, Yale University Press, 1989), p. 221.

8   Expressed by writers like G. Konrad, *Antipolitics* (London, Quartet, 1984), and V. Havel, 'Anti-political politics', in Keane, *Civil Society and the State*.

9   M. Glenny, *The Rebirth of History: Eastern Europe in the age of democracy* (Harmondsworth, Penguin, 1990), p. 201.

10 J. Reich, 'Reflections on becoming an East German dissident', in G. Prins (ed.), *Spring in Winter: the 1989 revolutions* (Manchester, Manchester University Press, 1990), p. 92.

11 P. Lewis, B. Lomax and G. Wightman, 'The emergence of multi-party systems in East-Central Europe', in H. Klingemann, G. Pridham and T. Vanhanen (eds), *Rooting Fragile Democracies: regime transition in Eastern Europe* (Cambridge, MA, Harvard University Press, 1993); S. Hakamada and G. Rozman, 'Coping with modernity', in G. Rozman (ed.), *Dismantling Communism* (Baltimore, MD, Johns Hopkins University Press, 1992).

12 'The human face of democracy', *The Warsaw Voice* (24 Sept. 1989).

13 K. E. Jorgensen, 'The end of anti-politics in Central Europe', in Lewis, *Democracy and Civil Society in Eastern Europe*.

14 *Rzeczpospolita* (Warsaw, 13 Sept. 1990).

15 P. Hirst, 'The state, civil society and the collapse of Soviet communism', *Economy and Society*, 20 (1991), p. 232.

16 F. Fukuyama, 'The end of history', *The National Interest*, 16 (1989), 3–17.

17 B. Moore, *Social Origins of Dictatorship and Democracy* (London, Allen Lane, 1967).

18 G. Ionescu, *The Politics of the European Communist States* (New York, Praeger, 1967), p. 271.

19 P. G. Lewis, 'Democratization in Eastern Europe', *Coexistence*, 27 (1990), 248–54.

20 D. McSweeney and C. Tempest, 'The political science of democratic transition', paper presented at the annual conference of the Political Studies Association (1991).

21 A. Przeworski, *Democracy and the Market: political and economic reforms in Eastern Europe and Latin America* (Cambridge, Cambridge University Press, 1991).

22 G. Pridham, 'Comparative approaches to democratic transition: Southern European experience, system change in Eastern Europe and the role of political parties', paper presented at the annual conference of the Political Studies Association (1991), p. 16.

23 J. Story, 'Spain and Europe', in Story (ed.), *The New Europe* (Oxford, Blackwell, 1992).

24 Moore, *Social Origins*; G. Therborn, 'The rule of capital and the rise of democracy', *New Left Review*, 103 (1977), 3–41.

25 D. Rustow, 'Transitions to democracy: towards a dynamic model', *Comparative Politics*, 2 (1970), 337–63.

26 Lewis, *Democracy and Civil Society in Eastern Europe*, especially pp. 6–8.

27 R. Dahrendorf, *Reflections on the Revolution in Europe* (London, Chatto and Windus, 1990), p. 93.

28 J. Keane, *Democracy and Civil Society* (London, Verso, 1988), p. 22.

29 Hirst, 'State, civil society and the collapse of Soviet communism', p. 222.

30 *Polityka* (29 Sept. 1990).

31 T. Mastnak, 'Civil society in Slovenia: from opposition to power', in Lewis, *Democracy and Civil Society in Eastern Europe*, pp. 147–8.

32 Lewis, Lomax and Wightman, 'The emergence of multi-party systems'.

33 P. G. Lewis, 'Non-competitive elections and regime change: Poland 1989', *Parliamentary Affairs*, 43 (1990), p. 100.

34 J. Wasilewski, 'Dilemmas and controversies concerning leadership recruitment in Eastern Europe', in Lewis, *Democracy and Civil Society in Eastern Europe*, p. 124.

35   McSweeney and Tempest, 'Political science', p. 8.
36   S. Huntington, 'Will more countries become democratic?', *Political Science Quarterly*, 99 (1984), p. 212.
37   Pridham, 'Comparative approaches', p. 12.
38   A. Lijphart, 'Typologies of democratic system', *Comparative Political Studies*, 1 (1968), p. 22.
39   Therborn, 'Rule of capital', p. 34.
40   Samuel Huntington suggests that cases like Poland and Czechoslovakia were examples of elite transplacement rather than replacement, where democracy was the joint product of government and opposition groups. This might have been true of the early stages of transition – but Huntington could not have foreseen the rapidity of the communist withdrawal; see Huntington, 'Democratization and security in Eastern Europe', in P. Volten (ed.), *Uncertain Futures: Eastern Europe and democracy* (New York, Institute for East–West Security Studies, 1990), p. 41.
41   G. Stokes, 'Lessons of the East European revolutions of 1989', *Problems of Communism*, 40 (1991), p. 21.
42   Przeworski, *Democracy and the Market*, p. 39.
43   G. Schöpflin, 'Post-communism: constructing new democracies in Central Europe', *International Affairs*, 67 (1991), p. 239.
44   Hirst, 'State, civil society and the collapse of Soviet communism', p. 231.
45   M. Marody, 'Silni i madrzy', *Polityka* (8 Feb. 1992).
46   Lewis, 'Democratization in Eastern Europe', p. 258.
47   G. Pridham, 'Democratic transition and the international environment: a research agenda', Occasional Paper of the Centre for Mediterranean Studies, University of Bristol (1991).
48   Przeworski, *Democracy and the Market*, p. 190.
49   'The travail of Latin American democracy', *New Left Review*, 113–14 (1979), 99–101.
50   *Polityka* (18 Jan. 1992).

15

THE ALTERNATIVES TO 'LIBERAL DEMOCRACY': A LATIN AMERICAN PERSPECTIVE

Laurence Whitehead

There is one good reason for using Latin American evidence to document general arguments in comparative politics, and one bad reason. The *good* reason is that the subcontinent offers a sufficiently wide array of well-elaborated political structures and experiments to provide fertile ground for systematic comparative analysis. (For example, there is at least one long-standing 'model' liberal democracy – Costa Rica; one 'model' communist state – Cuba; one neocolonial democracy – Puerto Rico; one counter-insurgency regime – Guatemala; and a large range of intermediate political forms, many of them insecure and contested.) The *bad* reason is that observers from other regions have sometimes invoked stylized or even stereotypical images of Latin American politics to illustrate – or dramatize – arguments that would not be regarded as solid if applied to better-known (more 'serious') political processes.

With regard to liberal democracy and its alternatives, Latin American experience can be particularly rich and rewarding for comparativists, but only if they guard against the danger just mentioned. The subcontinent contains twenty republics, nearly all with a century or more of independent political existence. (Moreover, it is becoming increasingly fruitful to add the various newer island states of the Caribbean, and to make select extra-regional comparisons with, for example, Spain, Portugal and the Philippines.) These twenty republics are all in a sense 'children of the French revolution' and their political history is impregnated with references to European and North American influences and parallels. They were in the vanguard of international liberalism when they repudiated monarchism, aristocracy and slavery in the past century, and at least in theory their governments have long rested on the principle of popular sovereignty.[1] However, these early experiments with an oligarchic[2] form of liberal democracy (often closely associated with efforts to reassure foreign investors and to strengthen market economies) produced very varied results. The region offers every kind of example: slow but steady progress; rapid advance followed by abrupt reversal; gradual disintegration; spectacular downfall; and equally spectacular emergence out of apparently overwhelming adversity. It is a central and ongoing question of political debate in nearly all of these countries which of these characterizations applies to which periods, and why. These debates are so intense and heartfelt because they express an almost permanent sense of insecurity and uncertainty about the solidity and relative performance of the various regimes in question.

These Latin American debates about the nature of democracy in what many would call peripheral and dependent societies, about the erratic history of liberalism and constitutionalism in the region, and about the limited advantages and uncertain prospects of this type of political regime all raise questions that are of far more than purely regional interest. Indeed it may be a salutary corrective to some of the more static and complacent versions of democratic theory (for example, in the Anglo-Saxon contractarian tradition) to re-examine implicit assumptions concerning the natural or inevitably superior nature of liberal democracy within a setting where such claims also require persuasive demonstration. It is not possible in this brief chapter to do justice to the complex and controversial Latin-American-based discussions on these themes,[3] and indeed what non-regionalists initially require are some brief unhedged judgements that may teeter on the brink of stereotyping, despite the disclaimer above. The obvious (oversimplified) questions include: why has there been such a sustained swing towards democratic forms of governance in the region over the past twenty years? Are the old alternatives to liberal democracy really finished, or just in abeyance? What *kind* of democracy is emerging – how consolidated, how participatory, how efficient, and so on? For example is the real alternative to stable liberal democracy unstable populist democracy? How restrictive are the conditions under which the latter can evolve toward the former? Answers to these regional questions should provide evidence helping to address, and perhaps to reformulate, some of the general ideas about liberal democracy elaborated elsewhere in this volume.

First, why has the region seen such a strong move to democratic forms of government since the mid-1970s? What follows are broad-brush tendency statements, without all the necessary qualifications and exceptions. The 1980s witnessed the latest in a succession of democratizing 'waves' that punctuate the history of the region (as indeed they also punctuate European history). The periods 1944–8 and 1955–62 were also powerful movements – the first cut short by the Cold War and the second by the aftershocks of the Cuban Revolution. Neither had the breadth or momentum of the past decade. Any explanation must be multi-causal and here there is only space to list the factors without properly weighting them. For one thing, neither the Cold War nor the Cuban Revolution intervened to cut short the process. (The Nicaraguan revolution may arguably have produced some such effect in Central America, but not more generally.) For another, the business interests and foreign investors that had rallied to authoritarian military regimes in the 1960s began to see these overly statist and apparently unaccountable governments as a source of danger rather than of protection, so they withdrew their support. (There were several sources of danger here: uncontrollable military expenditure and disrespect for private enterprise; counter-productive and indiscriminate use of repression and censorship; inability to institutionalize a smooth succession, and so on.) On the economic front, unrestricted sovereign lending surged and then went into reverse, leaving overconfident authoritarian regimes suddenly responsible for unmanageable fiscal crises. But perhaps a more sophisticated political explanation is required here. In most countries authoritarian rule was sufficiently durable and successful to 'sober up' or 'deradicalize' the opposition. A return to democracy no longer seemed so dangerous, because the opponents of military rule had learnt a severe lesson. The same idea can be expressed in different terms by saying that democratiza-tion was the product of a stalemate. Reformist, populist or socialist projects had been attempted and had failed; reactionary authoritarian projects had also been attempted and had also failed. All the main contenders for power were therefore forced to conclude that they would do better by settling for a 'second-best' outcome – a framework of rules within which they could compete without facing persecution, although without much hope of implementing their full programmes. In such circumstances, of course, many political contenders will have some non-democratic antecedents, and so risk the suspicion (which may initially be justified) that their new-found espousal of democracy is merely instru-mental and insincere. Provisional democratic credentials have to be fairly readily available, if broad-based democratization is to proceed, although final judgements can only be made *post mortem*. The current catchphrase for this idea is 'democracy by default' and it is said to apply almost throughout South America. Note that it implies a lowering of popular expectations of what can be achieved through political action, and there-fore favours neo-liberal (or at least low participation) forms of electoral politics. Note also that it applies best to South America, rather than to Mexico, or the Caribbean. The Central American cases are also more complex, because there the alternative to accepting some democratic forms was the continuation of a possibly regional civil war, with the associated risks of external intervention.[4] In addition to the lessons learnt from these experiences of internal political statements, in the past decade there has also been a powerful international 'contagion' effect at work, which has reinforced the movement towards at least formal observance of democratic processes throughout the subcontinent. Another contributory factor has been the support provided increasingly from outside Latin America – by the party internationals, the Catholic church, the European Community and such US-funded agencies as the National Endowment for Democracy. In general the literature analysing democratization in contemporary Latin America has rated such international factors as of secondary importance, but the transformation of Eastern Europe and developments in Nicaragua and Panama (and prospectively in Cuba) indicate the need for some reconsideration of this view.[5]

Notwithstanding the force of the current democratizing wave, a doubt remains. Are the old alternatives to liberal democracy really vanquished, or just in abeyance? Here we shall try to tackle this question *before* examining the durability, effectiveness and so on of the new democratic regimes. This procedure may seem odd, particularly given the stress on 'democracy by default' in the previous section. The default could end, new totalizing projects with a capacity for mobilizing and transforming society may rally support, and if so these fragile democracies would seem poorly placed to resist the challenge. However, the procedure adopted here makes sense if one distinguishes between two types of alternative to fully consolidated an effective liberal democracy.

The first type is of explicitly anti-democratic alternatives. They rest on explicit critiques of the inadequacies (either universal or local) of liberal democracy, and they offer more or less coherent and comprehensive alternative images of the social and political order. Communism was certainly of this kind. One variant survives in Cuba, and another continues to display considerable military strength in much of Peru. But even so it is pretty apparent that the Cuban model has been ideologically vanquished, delegitimized as well as materially crippled by the evaporation of communism in the Soviet Union. The liquidation of Cuban influence in Africa and Central America confirms the eclipse of this explicit alternative to liberal democracy, which is becoming increasingly anachronistic and unviable. This alternative is no longer real in Latin America, and it is doubtful whether it can ever be resurrected in any central role. The other well-elaborated regional alternative might be loosely called 'fascism',[6] and has more recently been known in the guise of 'national security ideology'. Here too there is only space for a sweeping generalization on a subject that merits more care. In the absence of a credible communist threat, and in view of the lamentable record of these movements when in power, it is plausible to assert that their day has passed. (Even at their strongest the national security regimes were not quite the systematic alternatives to liberal democracy that they appeared – they were mostly 'regimes of *exception*',[7] meaning that they envisaged an eventual return to more normal forms of politics, once the circumstances precipitating their installation had been overcome.) Does this exhaust the range of explicitly anti-democratic possibilities? Not entirely – there was clerical corporatism for a while, and some of the simpler forms of personal and military rule (Stroessner's patrimonial regime in Paraguay, 1954–89, for example) were almost explicit about their repudiation of liberal values. My assessment, however, is that in future the regional democratic consensus will probably be robust enough to discourage the re-emergence of new movements of this type. The apparent failure of current attempts to salvage a 'duvalieriste' form of government in Haiti lends some support to this view. More ambitiously, a case could also be argued that this applies not only to Latin America but also to much of the rest of the world, where other forms of illiberal legitimation such as white minority rule, and perhaps Islamic fundamentalism, are potentially available. Certainly in Latin America, instead of rallying to explicitly anti-democratic alternatives, I would expect those threatened by liberal values to react (as the Mexican authorities have done so successfully) by paying them lip-service while seeking to resist their full implementation.

This, then, is the second type of alternative to fully consolidated liberal democracy, which is clearly more insidious, and also more ambiguous in sign. The Latin American literature on 'facade' democracies[8] (compare with the Portuguese phrase *para os ingleses ver*, which refers to the old habit of holding elections 'for the English to look at') should be taken seriously, but there is also force to the counter-argument that once a governing elite accepts the theoretical hegemony of liberal institutions, once it pays lip-service to popular sovereignty expressed through open elections, a process of habituation is set in motion which tends over time to turn the 'facades' into more real structures. The question of civilian control over the military provides a pertinent illustration. Although the jury is still out on this, there is an accumulation of evidence that many fragile new democracies which initially just *pretended* to subordinate the armed forces to the rule of law are gradually progressing towards a more genuine supremacy of constitutional norms.

So what kind(s) of democratic regime can we expect to survive in Latin

America (and perhaps also in other parts of the third world and the ex-communist world) – how consolidated, how liberal, how effective at governing, how capable of democratizing society at large? The references to my comments 'democracy by default' and 'facade democracy' already indicate some reasons for doubting that the general outcome will be fully consolidated, liberal and effective democracy. But before elaborating on the less prepossessing outcomes that may seem more probable, one should warn against undifferentiated pessimism (what Hirschman calls 'fracasomania')[9] Costa Rica and the islands of the Commonwealth Caribbean are remarkably solid liberal democracies which have survived some impressive historical and geographical adversities. In a more qualified way, Venezuela and Puerto Rico also have strong claims to success. A reasonable 'tendency statement' would be that both in Latin America and in Eastern Europe there will be further such success stories in the next few years – not necessarily the ones that seem most obvious today. However, since it may reasonably be doubted that these will be the norm, the rest of this chapter will concentrate on a range of intermediate possibilities: impotent, bankrupt and socially explosive democracies, 'unstable populism'; neo-liberal 'depoliticized democracies'; and internationally dependent or insecure democracies.

It is very difficult to outline briefly the main characteristics of 'unstable populist democracy' or to indicate the reasons for its likely prevalence, without falling into the negative stereotyping mentioned at the outset.[10] These can easily be perceived as 'unserious' democracies, frivolous imitations of political arrangements that properly developed elsewhere, closer to home. My objection to this perspective is two-fold. It fails to do justice to the historical traditions and social forces that tend to generate Latin America's distinctive forms of political expression, and it reinforces a sense of complacency about the nature of democratic institutions in Western Europe and North America that is usually unjustified by the comparative record, and that in any case hinders genuinely detached understanding.

That said, there is a growing body of opinion within Latin America which argues that many of the emerging new democracies are showing little tendency to 'consolidate' or to 'institutionalize' according to the (supposedly) classical pattern. Instead, what we may find is highly presidentialist forms of government, in which some flamboyant individual leader emerges almost from nowhere, captures the majority vote on the basis of the vaguest of slogans and the loosest of commitments, and then proceeds to govern arbitrarily without restraint from party structures, parliamentary processes of legal or bureaucratic norms, until popular support is exhausted and another equally ill-prepared and erratic individual takes his or her place. Several terms have been proposed to analyse these recurrent patterns – 'plebiscitary democracy' and '*movimentismo*' are among the most current. In my opinion none is as evocative as the term coined by the Venezuelan writer Valenilla Lanz over sixty years ago – '*Cesarismo democrático*'.[11] In any case, identifying such a political morphology is only the beginning of an analysis. We then need an explanation of the reasons why it reproduces itself so effectively, and whether over the longer term it is likely to break down, to stabilize, or to evolve into a more institutionalized structure.

These are the central issues in debate among Latin American political scientists today. In different countries the emphasis shifts from one aspect of the problem to another but the central cluster of issues remains the same. (For example, in some countries the party structures are quite strong and the question becomes how to overcome their rigidity; in others the central problem may seem to be administrative corruption, or the failure of the legal system rather than erratic political leadership; in still others the fiscal crisis and the consequent collapse of state patronage may take centre stage. But in fact these are all interrelated, and when progress is made on one front another item from the same cluster typically comes to the fore.) One influential current of opinion, not shared by this author, regards presidentialism as the heart of the problem and recommends parliamentarism as the indispensable solution. Others argue, by contrast, that a switch to parliamentarism could well result in a policy paralysis that might only be overcome by extra-constitutional means.[12]

Another current of interpretation stresses the acute social inequality, insecurity and loss of welfare that has accompanied democratization, arguing that in these conditions popular frustration or desperation can be expected to destabilize any institutional order. Of course the masses vote for demagogic saviours, since responsible politicians offer them no hope. Although this argument has been bolstered by the outcome of several recent elections, in which outsiders with no real party support or political track record have been swept to victory in anti-political campaigns (such as Fujimori in Peru), it rests on various dubious assumptions, such as that the public attributes social distress to democracy, when in fact they may understand that the two are separate; and it denigrates the activities of political bargaining and persuasion that characterize the democratic process. A third, neo-liberal, line of thought will be discussed in the next section.

In summary, then, my own position is that while *some* of these fragile and unstable regimes may gradually develop into consolidated, liberal and well-institutionalized regimes of the West European kind, and a *few* may visibly break down (through armed conflict, extreme social unrest, followed by new 'regimes of exception'), the range of conditions just enumerated is sufficiently widespread and entrenched to make probable a more or less indefinite continuation of the present political forms in more than a few countries. Even where progress towards consolidation is most notable, the prospects of relapse into 'unstable populism' remain very real. Even where 'regimes of exception' are once again attempted they are likely to prove temporary interruptions.

The strongest challenge to this position comes from what may loosely be labelled the 'neo-liberal' school of thought. Curiously, this vigorously anti-Marxist body of analysis is often characterized by a crude economic determinism of the type we used to associate with vulgar Marxism (a point I have elaborated in relation to the most influential statement of the neo-liberal case, Hernando de Soto's *The Other Path*).[13] However, the more sophisticated versions of this argument require careful considera-tion, particularly since, rightly or wrongly, neo-liberal ideas are being used to shape strategies of democratization in an increasing number of countries.

Their central claim is that what may be called 'populist democracies' are economically irrational: they violate property rights and therefore essential human freedoms; for that reason they are not only inefficient but also in a profounder sense undemocratic; and that by extending the scope of 'market' systems of allocation and by rolling back the state the social underpinnings of this 'politicized' or 'rent-seeking' economy can be dismantled.[14] Their preferred economic reforms – monetary stabilization, privatization, the enhancement of private property rights and 'openness' – will also in due course provide the social foundations for consolidated liberal democracy. If they are right then Latin America is in the process of escaping from an unstable, poorly institutionalized and economically and socially unsuccessful present, and can within a decade or so construct fairly well-consolidated, conventional, liberal capitalist democracies – as Chile has already done.

There is only space here for very brief and inadequate comments on this line of argument. First, it must be conceded that in certain cases something like this is likely to happen, although it is far from clear that this will be the *general* outcome; even when neo-liberal success seems most complete (as in contemporary Chile), detailed observation can expect to find substantial and potentially destabilizing counter-currents. Secondly, the neo-liberal strategy holds up the offer of a fully con-solidated liberal democratic end-state, but in order to reach that condi-tion it typically condones a considerable amount of interim illiberalism. Trade unionists, public employees, pensioners, the unemployed and so on may be tempted to use their democratic rights to oppose neo-liberal policy prescriptions. If so the theory will represent their actions as illegitimate ('rent-seeking' and so on) and so may justify repression. 'Depoliticization' of the economy may only be achievable if economic policy-makers are insulated from social feedback, if media criticism is restrained, and if resistance to the new patterns of property ownership is met with the full force of bourgeois (not necessarily democratic) law. Of course, once neo-liberal theorists have condoned such *means* to achieve their allegedly democratic *ends*, the old, old question arises as to how, if at all, they are eventually to free themselves from the instruments they have used. The ideological and intolerant *style* of neo-liberal policy-making is well illustrated by the fact that whenever the observable results fall short of what was promised by the theory, the typical response has not been to reconsider the doctrine but to prescribe a stronger dose of the same medicine. Thirdly, then, we must enquire what *kind* of a democracy would in due course be stabilized and consolidated if the neo-liberal programme met with complete success – in what sense would it be democratic at all?[15] Certainly *participatory* democracy tends to clash with the ideal of a 'depoliticized' market system, and far from advancing such causes as women's rights, racial equality or a social rights conception of citizenship, the neo-liberal model tends to dismantle whatever protections may previously have existed.[16]

There is nevertheless a major weakness in all these criticisms of the neo-liberal route to democracy. At least it offers the possibility of eventually arriving at a stable, viable, liberal regime. The alternative of permanent crisis and insecurity under 'unstable populism' seems unable to offer any such prospect. In fact it is the poorest, the most vulnerable, the racially subordinate and so forth who suffer most under erratic populism, despite intermittent rhetoric in their favour. Paulo Sergio Pinheiro, for example, has shown that the return to democracy in Brazil has been accompanied by a marked deterioration in that country's human rights performance.[17] True, the police no longer torture articulate middle-class dissidents, but instead the residential areas of the main cities bribe the police to murder street children. Examples like this can be multiplied, particularly with reference to the countryside.[18] Most of the now quite abundant literature criticizing Latin America's democratization as elitist and unconnected with the lived experience of the mass of the population (the 'social movements' perspective) fails to distinguish adequately between neo-liberal and paternalist (or clientelist) strategies of democratization. Both may be opposed to autonomous participation from below, but only the neo-liberal strategy (extending the role of the market) seems capable of leading to regime consolidation. Here there is a paradox. Current Latin American experience can be invoked to argue that the only path to democratic 'consolidation' (a stable, durable and effective regime) is through sustained implementation of drastic 'neo-liberal' market reforms. In the absence of such reforms fragile 'populist' democracies will remain unstable, ineffective and indeed incoherent, lacking all the 'credibility' needed for responsible governance. The paradox is that what can be consolidated by these means would seem to exclude many of the features commonly associated with full liberal democracy (high participation, authentic political choice, extensive citizenship rights). Where a more ambitious – authentic – vision of democratization is attempted it would seem that nothing can be con-solidated. The choice would be between a stunted version of liberal democracy that works, or a generous vision of social democracy that remains a mirage (the Chilean Constitution of 1980 versus the Brazilian Constitution of 1988).

Like most dichotomies this contrast, though real, is too stark. It can be softened by separating out the effect of fiscal crisis, and by viewing regime consolidation as a long-term and non-linear process. Democratization and fiscal crisis broadly coincided during the 1980s (although a good case can be made that these were quite separate processes that just happened to interact, and were not necessarily connected). When fiscal crisis reaches the point of catharsis (as in Bolivia in 1985, Argentina in 1989, Brazil perhaps in the near future), the government – whether democratic or otherwise – faces a choice between accepting paralysis and impotence in virtually all spheres of public activity, or cutting back/discontinuing large areas of previous responsibility in order to achieve a minimum degree of efficacy in high-priority areas. What recent experience of fiscal crisis seem to be demonstrating is that the political costs of abandoning unrealistic promises of state assistance and interventionism are less prohibitive than they seem, because public expectations of government are violently lowered by the spectre of hyper-inflation. Thus, after a certain 'threshold of crisis' has been passed it is possible for democratic politicians to achieve surprisingly dramatic gains in authority, credibility and even electoral support by promising and attempting much less than before. The secret of success is to demonstrate that the limited tasks remaining on the public agenda really are achievable ('neo-liberal effectiveness'), and also perhaps to keep open the hope of some future prospect of re-enlarging the agenda. The second element is more debat-able than the first, and in its absence fiscal crisis would simply inaugurate the new era of immutable neo-liberal democracies desired by the right. But the survival of so many fragile democracies in Latin America is not merely due to the absence of explicit alternatives; it also derives from the hope that in the end these regimes will start fulfilling some of their promises. Democratic procedures must be analytically distinguished from substantive outcomes, but there is always a link between the two. It is provided by the fact that under democratic rules the electorate's future options are not foreclosed. In the short run the experience of fiscal crisis may have reduced popular expectations of public policy so low that the right's paradise of *laissez-faire* seems within reach, but if the consolidation of democracy takes a generation or more, by the time the process is complete the electorate will have overcome that trauma, and the choice between 'neo-liberal' and 'social democratic' alternatives can be taken at least partly on its merits.

In consequence there is scope for further work focusing on the conditions that would have to be met in order to reconcile political democratization with economic efficiency and social participation. As social democratic theorists have long argued (for example, Schumpeter), such conditions are highly restrictive. In theory it may be possible to devise paths to consolidated social democracy that bypass the inequities of neo-liberalism and the irresponsibility of populism, but no one in contemporary Latin America has yet discovered how to do it in practice (despite the efforts of many very talented advisers). Reasons for pursuing this enquiry may be partly ethical but can also be grounded in some arguments from 'realism'. The consolidation of any type of democratic regime takes a generation or more, so the neo-liberals are at least right not to despair at the first setbacks. The key requirement seems to me a mutually reinforcing process by which both economic and political expectations are stabilized and brought into line with underlying material and institutional possibilities.[19] Market discipline provides one variant of this process that must to some extent be accepted, but in contrast to the neo-liberal perspective others see considerable need and some scope for democratic *political* processes of persuasion, organization, education and compensation. Lest this sound like the illusion of the 'socialist third way' recently condemned by Ralf Dahrendorf,[20] one could comment that (1) the neo-liberal model may also be an illusion, in which case we are all floundering; (2) such attempts should be viewed not as a blueprint, but as a political method – the policy contents must emerge from a process of democratic consultation; and (3) Dahrendorf's strongest criticism of social democracy was that it entered into crisis as a result of its own success. In Latin America (and other new democracies) this kind of objection lies far in the future. In present social conditions a *viable* programme of social democracy could potentially attract a large popular majority.

Of course it must be acknowledged that even in the prosperous and stable democracies of Western Europe there are powerful constraints on the extent to which 'viable' forms of social democracy can stray, if not from dogmatic neo-liberal models, then at least from the broader confines of liberal capitalist democracy. One major source of constraint arises from the differentiation of identities and the conflicts of interest that come to divide the beneficiaries of the European welfare state as it ages. Similarly in Latin America, even though welfare provision has never been anything like universal, the system has aged badly and its support coalition (partly providers of welfare, partly beneficiaries and partly aspirants to membership) has become very fragmented. In addition, most Latin American societies are characterized by extremes of heterogeneity (regional, ethnic, linguistic and gender as well as class based), which gravely weaken the constituency in favour of universalistic welfare policies even when the resources for this are available. The second major source of constraint on European social democracy, the requirements of capital accumulation in a market economy, are of course far more acute in post-debt-crisis Latin America. In consequence, loosely 'social democratic' alternatives to neo-liberalism in Latin America will face simultaneous fire from two fronts. On the one hand they will be criticized as hopelessly over-optimistic given the weak productive base, and on the other they will be faulted as far too cautious and gradual given the rawness of existing social inequalities. Thus the potential popular majority for a viable form of social democracy is likely to prove large but volatile. This will not entirely preclude the development of more participatory and welfare-orientated alternatives to *laissez-faire*, but it means that any such process will probably be slow, troubled, and vulnerable to clientelistic distortions.

Such constraints are reinforced by the growing internationalization of economic processes. Social democracy is associated with Keynesian demand management in a single, partially insulated nation-state. Inflation and the fiscal crisis has eliminated whatever scope there was for Keynesianism, and the ultra-protected and inward-looking economies of individual Latin American countries are now destined for integration in the world market under regimes of greatly increased economic openness. This argument has considerable force but should not be applied mechanistically. The internationalization of the Mexican economy is a very different process from that of the Bolivian; the geopolitical context often counts for a great deal (for example, Costa Rica's pivotal role in stabilizing liberal principles in Central America); and when a degree of economic success is achieved, the scope for autonomous policy choice tends to expand once more. In any case, 'internationalization' is more complex and ambiguous in sign than is often recognized. Perhaps during the 1980s its main manifestation was the uncontrolled movement of private capital between nations, which reduced the policy autonomy of all governments and strengthened the political bargaining power of capitalists. But during the 1990s the uncontrolled international migration of labour may well prove equally relentless, with consequences for economic management (and for the stability of democratic institutions) that are quite distinct. Despite these imponderables, both theory and evidence still suggest to me that in the longer run, even in a very liberal international economic order (which is by no means assured), there ought to remain a substantial area of political discretion open to the governments of well-consolidated democracies.[21]

One very significant fact about Latin America, which may differentiate the subcontinent from most of the other new democracies currently under construction, is that it has a very long history of more or less stable frontiers. By international standards it has long been a 'zone of peace', and within nearly all republics the process of national integration has advanced to such a point that secession, partition or annexation of territory are unlikely. Many other states are attempting to democratize at the same time as they establish new national identities – a far more conflict-ridden enterprise.[22]

Another important feature of Latin American democratizations is that for the most part they proceeded by negotiation ('pact') rather than rupture. Consequently they were slow to unfold, taking years or even decades, whereas the post-Berlin democratizations are occurring overnight and sweeping away many of the institutional structures which went before.

A third generalization is that Latin American democratizations occurred in long-established but poorly functioning market economies. By contrast, many of the most recent regime changes are occurring in countries where market principles of allocation have to be established from scratch, rather than merely reformed. There are pluses and minuses to this contrast. It may be helpful to draw on a stock of expertise in commercial law, accountancy, international commerce and so on, but since market institutions have for so long worked so badly in Latin America it may be hard to eradicate their entrenched vices. The East Europeans have both less experience and fewer preconceptions. It could therefore be argued that it will be easier to promote modern capitalism in that setting than in a subcontinent where the elites have learnt the attractions of a primitive variant. On the other hand, Burke's flowery phrases about the legacy of failed revolutionary experiments acquire a chilling new resonance as the situation in parts of Eastern Europe continues to degenerate.[23]

Finally, Latin America is notorious for the extravagance of its social inequalities, perhaps more extreme than anywhere else in the world. It has been argued that this provides the key to the region's instability and lack of institutionalization. More egalitarian societies (for example, those accustomed to universal education and health-care) might provide a more promising setting for social democratic consolidation. However, the counter-argument would be that in many ex-communist countries the explosion of inequalities likely to accompany marketization will generate more unrest and resistance than the mere continuance of long-lived injustices in a climate of greater freedom. This chapter has stressed 'democracy by default' as the central feature of the Latin American experience, and has commented on the way social expectations have been (and must be) lowered if these fragile democracies are to consolidate. Both these points would tend to lend credence to the counter-argument just stated.

Overall, then, it is difficult to find good arguments that the prospects for consolidated and participatory democracy are better in Eastern Europe than in the Latin subcontinent. Within Latin America quite a variety of political regimes may continue to be found. Explicitly anti-democratic ideologies and systems of government are in headlong retreat and seem unlikely to return. A few fully consolidated, reasonably autonomous and conventionally 'liberal' democracies may well emerge. But at least for the near future the norm will be a more provisional and unsatisfactory form of constitutional rule – 'democracy by default'. The limitations on these democracies will vary from country to country: restrictions on national sovereignty; curtailment of political choice by market mechanisms; 'facade' arrangements intended to project an external image of pluralism without disturbing traditional power relations; the persistence of undemocratic structures in rural areas; policy paralysis derived from fiscal crisis; misguided design of institutional arrangements; a fragmented civil society incapable of generating legitimacy or social consensus (and the list could be extended further). Thus most Latin American democracies are likely to remain provisional, incomplete and unconsolidated, at least for the next few years. This should not be considered particularly surprising or shocking, however. The consolidation of democracy is a process that must take at least a generation, or longer. So long as the framework of representative institutions is kept intact the prospect remains open that a future government, under pressure from the citizenry, will rectify omissions, correct errors or enlarge rights as required to complete democratization. Whether the outcome of such a process should be called a 'liberal democracy' will be an enduring source of controversy, since rival projects are likely to compete for the same label. Given the liberal and republican traditions of Latin America, and the influence of the US and Europe, the label is likely to be viewed

positively (in contrast to, say, the Islamic world), even if the contents
prove idiosyncratic.

NOTES

1 François-Xavier Guerra is currently disinterring much neglected evidence on the
  nature and importance of the formal systems of political representation that
  operated during the nineteenth century. See his 'Les Avatars de la représentation
  en Amérique Latine au 19eme siécle', paper presented to the conference Voter
  en Amérique Latine at the Fondation Nationale des Sciences Politiques, Paris
  (Jan. 1991). For an alternative view see G. Dealy, 'The tradition of monistic
  democracy in Latin America', *Journal of the History of Ideas*, 35 (Oct.–Dec. 1974).
2 'Oligarchic' forms of electoral representation were widespread in Latin America
  in the late nineteenth and early twentieth centuries. Export-led growth
  encouraged the establishment of constitutional regimes which could be relied
  on to honour contracts with foreign traders and investors. Local power was
  highly concentrated in the hands of a property-owning elite (usually of
  exporters) and a very restricted franchise ensured that such 'oligarchs' were
  well represented in national assemblies. For an illuminating case study of this
  oligarchic electoral system, which also includes a comparative discussion, see
  M. J. Gonzales, 'Planters and politics in Peru', *Journal of Latin American Studies*,
  23:3 (Oct. 1991).
3 Major reference points include G. O'Donnell, P. Schmitter and L. Whitehead
  (eds), *Transitions from Authoritarian Rule: prospects for democracy* (Baltimore, MD,
  Johns Hopkins University Press, 1986); L. Diamond, J. Linz and S. M. Lipset
  (eds), *Democracy in Developing Countries: Latin America* (London, Adamantine
  Press, 1989); B. Stallings and R. Kaufman (eds), *Debt and Democracy in Latin
  America* (London, Westview Press, 1989); R. Pastor (ed.), *Democracy in the
  Americas: stopping the pendulum* (New York, Homes and Meier, 1989); G. di Palma,
  To Craft Democracies (Berkeley, CA, California University Press, 1990); A. F.
  Lowenthal (ed.), *Exporting Democracy: the United States and Latin America* (Balti-
  more, MD, Johns Hopkins University Press, 1991). In addition to these widely
  disseminated publications there is an explosion of literature with more restricted
  circulation, some of it very worthwhile. Illustrative examples include *Quel Avenir
  Pour la Démocratie en Amérique Latine?* (Paris, Editions du CNRS, 1989); F. W. Reis
  and G. O'Donnell (eds), *A democracia no Brasil: dilemas e perspectivas* (Sao Paulo,
  Vértice, 1988); Carlos Strasser, *Para Una Teoria de la Democracia Posible* (Buenos
  Aires, Grupo Editor, Latinoamericano, 2 vols, 1990, 1991); and some of the 40 or
  so *cuadernos de CAPEL* published since 1985 by the Comite de Asesoria y
  Promoción Electoral of the Inter-American Institute of Human Rights, San José,
  Costa Rica, such as No. 23, *La Constitución Norteamericana y su Influencia en Latino
  América*, and No. 24, *La Constitución de Cádiz y su Influencia en América*.
4 This argument was developed in G. di Palma and L. Whitehead (eds), *The Central
  American Impasse* (London, Croom Helm, 1986). See also Lowenthal, *Exporting
  Democracy*.
5 For example, see L. Whitehead, 'The international dimension of democratisation: a survey of the alternatives' paper presented at the XVth World Congress of
  the International Political Science Association in Buenos Aires (July 1991).

6   See in particular H. Trindade, 'La question du fascisme en Amérique latine', *Revue Française de Sciences Politique*, 2 (1983) and H. Trindade, *La Tentation Fasciste au Brésil* (Paris, Editions de la Maison des Sciences de l'Homme, 1988).

7   See A. Rouquié, 'Demilitarization and the institutionalization of military-dominated politics in Latin America', in G. O'Donnel, P. Schmitter and L. Whitehead (eds), *Transitions from Authoritarian Rule* (Baltimore, MD, Johns Hopkins University Press, 1986).

8   See, for example, L. Maira in di Palma and Whitehead, *The Central American Impasse*. See also Edward Herman and Frank Brodhead (eds), *Demonstration Elections: US staged elections in the Dominican Republic, Vietnam and El Salvador* (Boston, MA, South End Press, 1984).

9   A. Hirschman, 'The search for paradigms as a hindrance to understanding', in A. Hirschman, *A Bias for Hope: essays on development and Latin America* (New Haven, CT, Yale University Press, 1971).

10 For a political analysis of Brazilian democracy which is consistent with this label, but which is not easily dismissed as an instance of negative stereotyping, see Bolívar Lamounier (ed.), *De Geisel a Collor: o Balanço da Transiçao* (Sao Paulo, IDESP, 1990). For an economic interpretation focusing on the spectacular cases of Chile and Peru, see R. Dornbusch and S. Edwards, 'Macro-economic populism', *Journal of Development Economics*, 32 (1990).

11 Guillermo O'Donnell and Giorgio Alberti are refining these terms for a forthcoming conference at the European Centre for the Study of Democratisation in Forlí. See also L. V. Lanz, *Césarismo Democrático: estudio sobre las bases sociológicas de la constitución efectiva de Venezuela* (Caracas, Tipografia Garrido, 4th edn, 1961).

12 Juan Linz is the most influential advocate of parliamentarism: see J. Linz, 'The perils of presidentialism', *The Journal of Democracy*, I:1 (Winter 1990). His ideas have been taken up in quite a few South American republics: see, for example, the Argentine Consejo para la Consolidación de la Democracia, *Presidencialismo vs Parlamentarismo* (Buenos Aires, Editorial Universitaria de Buenos Aires, 1988). The same articles by Linz and Lijphart also appear in B. Lamounier (ed.), *A Opçao Parlamentarista* (Sao Paulo, IDESP, 1991), although, in clear contradiction to the Linz thesis, Brazilian self-declared parliamentarists accept the inevitability of a directly elected presidency. For a healthy corrective to this Brazilian academic consensus see R. Lessa, 'Constrangimentos a toda reforma institucional futura' paper presented at the XVth Annual Conference of ANPOCS, Caxambú, Mina Gerais (Oct. 1991).

13 H. de Soto, *The Other Path: the invisible revolution in the third world* (London, I. B. Tauris, 1989). First published in Lima, the title explicitly contrasts neo-liberalism to the 'Shining Path' pursued by Peru's Maoist insurgents. In 'Algunas reflexiones sobre "el Estado" y el sector informal', *Revista Mexicana de Sociologia* (1990), I argue that de Soto's analysis borrows from vulgar Marxism, merely substituting the informal sector for the proletariat, and 'the state' for 'the bourgeoisie'.

14 See, for example, A. Krueger, 'The political economy of the rent-seeking society', *American Economic Review*, 64:3 (1974); R. Findlay and J. D. Wilson, 'The political economy of leviathan', in A. Razin and E. Sadka (eds), *Economic Policy in Theory and Practice* (New York, Macmillan, 1987); D. Lal, 'The political economy of economic liberalization', *World Bank Economic Review* (Jan. 1987).

15 'Unfortunately, liberal democracy can mean either . . . freedom of the stronger to do down the weaker by following market rules; or it can mean equal effective freedom of all to use and develop their capacities. The latter freedom is in-

consistent with the former.' C. B. Macpherson, *The Life and Times of Liberal Democracy* (Oxford University Press, 1979), p. 1.

16 Although Paul Cammack overstates his case, he has a point in arguing that 'the accepted principles of liberal democracy and current practice of liberal economic doctrines stand in flagrant contradiction to the two central strategies – co-optation and repression – upon which Latin American democracy generally continues to depend'; see P. Cammack 'Democracy and development in Latin America', *The Journal of International Development*, 3:5 (1991) p. 550.

17 P. S. Pinheiro, 'The legacy of authoritarianism in democratic Brazil', paper presented at the XVth World Congress of the International Political Science Association in Buenos Aires (July 1991).

18 J. Fox (ed.), *The Challenge of Rural Democratization: perspectives from Latin America and the Philippines* (London, Frank Cass, 1990).

19 L. Whitehead, 'Democratization and disinflation: a comparative approach', in J. Nelson (ed.) *Fragile Coalitions: the politics of economic adjustment* (Washington, DC, Overseas Development Institute, 1989).

20 R. Dahrendorf, *Reflections on the Revolution in Europe* (London, Chatto and Windus, 1990).

21 D. Held, 'Democracy, the nation-state and the global system', *Economy and Society*, 20:2 (May 1991). Held's chapter in this volume raises broader theoretical issues about the impact of 'globalization' (understood to mean much more than just the intensification of international economic exchanges) and such central concepts of democratic theory as 'constituency', 'accountability' and 'participation'. Such issues acquire a sharp focus in contemporary Latin America where, for example, a Panamanian citizen's right to choose his or her own president is likely to seem a poor substitute for participation in US politics, where the key decisions affecting Panama are really taken. The Puerto Ricans have taken this reasoning to its logical conclusion: 'What US efforts at democracy promotion in the Caribbean basin seem to assume is that democratisation can be a *substitute* for what Washington regards as unacceptable or impractical assertions of national sovereignty'. See. L. Whitehead, 'The imposition of democracy', in A. F. Lowenthal (ed.) *Exporting Democracy: the United States and Latin America* (Baltimore, MD, Johns Hopkins University Press, 1991), p. 257. Even Mexican politicians may now devote as much attention to wooing US opinion as that of their home electorate: see L. Whitehead, 'Mexico and the "hegemony" of the United States', in R. Roett (ed.), *Mexico's External Relations in the 1990s* (New York, Lynne Riener, 1991). Nevertheless, Held's general point holds true for Latin America, that 'the degree to which the modern state enjoys "autonomy" under various conditions is under-explored' and requires careful specification before one rules out the possibility of national democracies within a global liberal system.

22 A. Przeworski, *Democracy and the Market: political and economic reforms in Eastern Europe and Latin America* (Cambridge, Cambridge University Press, 1991), p. 190, identified 'geography' as Eastern Europe's main hope of escaping the fate of the Latin American democracies ('the politics, the economics, and the culture of poor capitalism'). But he does not rate that hope very highly, nor does he specify with any precision the dynamics of the contrast, nor consider the possibility that Latin America's 'geography' could save that region from the fate of the East European democracies.

23 'If commerce and the arts should be lost in an experiment to try how well a state

may stand without these old fundamental principles, what sort of a thing must be a nation of gross, stupid, ferocious, and at the same time poor and sordid barbarians'; see Edmund Burke, *Reflections on the Revolution in France* (Harmondsworth, Pelican, 1973 edn), p. 174. Compare A. C. Copetas, *Bear Hunting with the Politburo* (New York, Simon and Schuster, 1991).

16

SUB-SAHARAN AFRICA

Geoffrey Hawthorn

The authors of a recent World Bank essay on the state are probably right to say that 'the conventional wisdom' of those whose first interest is in the development of poor societies 'has been that things ought to be done "one at at a time": first, economic growth; second, social equity; third, civil and political liberties'.[1] These people have extrapolated from what they have taken to be the experience of Gerschenkron's 'late developers' in Europe at the end of the nineteenth century and the beginning of the twentieth, the parallel experience of Japan, and the more recent economic and political history of the 'newly industrializing countries' (NICs) in East and South-East Asia. Economic growth, they have argued, demands a high rate of capital formation, structural changes, consistent decisions and stability; these require a strong and continuous authority, incompatible with the short-term electoral competition and frequent changes of direction in 'democracy'.[2] Their more general assumption – one could call it 'utilitarian' – has been that development consists in that outcome which maximizes the total or aggregate welfare of a population, understood as an increase in the national product and individual income. If this requires intervention, so be it, and if not, not. The question of means is secondary, and purely practical.

This view is now out of fashion. At the beginning of the 1980s, the difficulties that many third world governments had been having in financing their deficits became a crisis. Debts were increasing, interest

I am grateful to Eric Acheampong, Mark Chingono, David Held, Mette Jacobsgaard, John A. Thompson and several participants at a conference on 'governance' in Africa, arranged by the World Bank and Queen Elizabeth House at Oxford in May 1991, for comments on the first version of this chapter.

rates were rising, a recession in Europe and North America was reducing the income from exports, and in part because of their own poor performance, in part because of the US' decision to run a deficit itself, they found it impossible to raise further external finance. They had no choice but to seek assistance from the International Monetary Fund. As a condition of its loans, the IMF insisted on financial stabilization and 'structural adjustment'. Public enterprises would have to be reduced, trade barriers removed, and public expenditures cut. (The World Bank imposed similar conditions, although they were fewer and more selective, and on the whole less severe.) At first, the issues were seen to be purely economic. To the IMF, they remain so. To others, however, including the World Bank and the bilateral donors, difficulties in reducing the scope of the state, the effects of adjustment on other interests, and evidence of how markets can fail, especially for the poor, make it clear that they are also political.

The new wisdom is accordingly more pragmatic. The Bank now points to the experience of the Scandinavian countries. These, it argues, 'have successfully combined private ownership and market competition with government actions to ensure an egalitarian income distribution, provide insurance against loss of income caused by disabilities, and address market failures'.[3] There can also be a principled case. This – call it 'contractarian' and 'pluralist' – assumes that states exist to maximize the benefits of social cooperation; they have therefore to concern themselves with the standard of living. But this is not defined by outcomes. We have no warrant for saying what these should be, and we cannot rely on people's own expressed preferences, which may have been formed in circumstances we would not want to accept.[4] The utilitarian emphasis on total welfare is certainly mistaken; ends in a society will be plural and incommensurable, and cannot be aggregated – even if, like some rights, they can be traded. We should reject conceptions of the good and concentrate on the right. Governments exist to provide those entitlements and empowerments through which people can themselves best decide and effectively act.[5] Means do matter; democracy, after all, is desirable.

But what might it consist in? Minimally, a regular competition for power, the rules of which are agreed in advance and the outcome of which is at least formally decided by those over whom the power is to be exercised. This is less than contractarians would require. For that, there would have also to be non-political rights and means with which to exercise such rights. But the hope is that this, which would mark a more truly liberal democracy, would follow from the competition. (A liberal democracy certainly cannot be said to be that kind of democracy in which individuals, as individuals, are political agents. There is no such kind. In the politics of democracy, it is numbers – the organization of numbers into parties that in part form and express individual interests as they also subsume them and claim to represent them – which matter.)

Students of politics have suggested one or other of two conditions for a minimal democracy. The political class will agree on the rules of competition if its members can agree on the general shape and direction of the society.[6] Or its factions will make sure that if they do not win, they do not thereby lose the chance of competing altogether.[7] For the first of these, Dahl has argued, a society must not exhibit extreme inequalities of economic power or material desert, wide differences of culture, or an unresolved dispute about who should bear arms.[8] For the second, Przeworski suggests, the agreement cannot be substantive; that could too easily be broken by those in power. It must be procedural. 'Democracy', he argues, 'can only be established if there exist institutions that would make it unlikely that the competitive political process would result in outcomes highly adverse to anyone's interests given the distribution of economic, ideological, organisational and other relevant resources.'[9]

The second condition is the more convincing. It fits important cases, like India, which the first does not. It acknowledges that political competition is a competition for power. It can also account for that extension of the rules of rule by which the outcome of the competition is decided by those over whom the power is to be exercised, and account also for the extension of rights: members of the political class will be willing to concede when they are institutionally secure.

In practice, however, at least in the newer states, the picture is not so clear. Before they had agreed on who they were, and had institutions within which they could securely compete, the political classes in these states had often extended the vote to deploy electors in its unsettled disputes about the rules of rule themselves. Hence the common oscillation between extravagant populisms and reactive authoritarianisms. In that region – often called 'sub-Saharan Africa' – which lies in the area bounded by the southern Sahara, Lake Turkana, the Limpopo and the Atlantic, there is not even the first condition for a minimal democracy: the state itself has not been secure.

Several parts of several countries – areas of Angola, Mozambique, Chad and Uganda, for instance, northern Cameroon, north-eastern Kenya, south-western Senegal, the eastern Central African Republic and eastern Zaïre – have intermittently been beyond the effective jurisdiction, in two or three cases even the effective military control, of their capitals. The authority of many states in the region has been reduced by their failure to deliver the elementary securities and thus – from Burundi, for example, Equatorial Guinea, Mozambique, Rwanda, Uganda, Zaïre and countries in the Sahel – by extensive migrations. No political class in any sub-Saharan country has complete sovereignty – what Gramscians would describe as an effective 'hegemony' – over it.[10] If we accept that the democratization of a domestic politics cannot begin to be an issue until the pre-existing political class has control of the relevant territory and the people in it – or until those who have made a revolution against this class are themselves sufficiently secure to concede a competition – it would be surprising if any state in sub-Saharan Africa were minimally democratic.

There is almost nowhere an established habit, pre-dating the colonization from Europe, of exercising central authority or of submitting to it. Over the *longue durée*, Lonsdale suggests, 'Africa's most distinctive contribution to the history of humanity has been the art of living in a reasonably peaceful way without the state.'[11] With the small exceptions of Rwanda and Burundi, no modern state in sub-Saharan Africa corresponds to the boundaries of any that existed before colonization. None of the thirty-four modern states, therefore, has the precondition for a *res publica*; each, except Liberia, has only its colonial past. The colonial states, however, were 'alien in derivation, functionally conceived, bureaucratically designed, authoritarian in nature, and primarily concerned with issues of domination rather than legitimacy'.[12] Africans were simply their subjects. In the 1940s and early 1950s, they were also increasingly exploitative. To the politicians who inherited them from the Europeans, they were, *faute de mieux*, a more or less conscious model. To the citizens, the states these men made have more often than not increased the incentive to refine the art of living without a state at all.[13]

The economic and social circumstances of sub-Saharan Africa have also been distinctive. The ecology is generally unfavourable – soils are poor, pests are plenty – and people have usually been too few. As a result, agriculture in the savannahs and forests has not generated a surplus that anyone would wish to appropriate and convert. No doubt connected to this, rights to land have often remained collective, or vague. Wealth has accordingly been generated less by production than by trade, and power has in the past come not in the control of non-human assets – the control of land, for example, or of some other non-human capital – but in the control of people. Elsewhere, there have long been economic and social classes; in sub-Saharan Africa, there have been lineages.[14]

Where Africans have found it hard, as they often have, to extend political loyalty, their strategy – characteristic, as Hirschman has remarked, of acephalous states and, one might add, of those in which fixed material assets are less important – has been not to use 'voice', the precursor in Europe and elsewhere of 'democracy', but to make an 'exit'.[15] The wise man, the Amhara peasants in Ethiopia used to say, 'bows low to the great lord and silently farts'; 'la bouche qui mange', as they say in Cameroon, 'ne parle pas'.[16] And if this mouth cannot eat, it moves; the discontented segment and migrate. This is why there is a long tradition, sharpened by the attractions of trade over production, and a continuing expectation, sharpened by the expectation of foreign aid, of help from outside. It seems reasonably certain that even if sub-Saharan Africa had not been colonized in the nineteenth century, its economic circumstances and social character would have made it unlikely to generate states of the kind that emerged in early modern Europe and Asia.[17] There, even now, such states are – to a greater extent than anywhere else – an alien form.

But they exist. There are nine or ten with populations of less than two million, eight or nine with populations of between two and four million, thirteen or fourteen with populations of between five and eleven million, and seven – Ghana, Kenya, Mozambique, Nigeria, Tanzania, Uganda and Zaïre – with populations larger than that. As modern states in the modern world order – the order prefigured seventy years ago in the dismembering of the German and Ottoman empires at Versailles and at the start of concerted decolonization after the Second World War, made explicit for ex-colonial territories in the United Nations' *Declaration on the Granting of Independence to Colonial Countries and Peoples* in 1960 – they have juridical sovereignty. This is marked by formal constitutions, executives and legislative assemblies, one or more – in some countries now, even many – political parties, elections, capital cities, armies, public administrations, currencies, banks, national accounts, ambassadors and advisers from other states; and there is, as elsewhere, a political theatre with which to celebrate these attributes and impress their authority on the people.[18]

The leaders of these states have also, if often rather fitfully, tried to establish a more practical sovereignty through economic and social 'development'. This has been financed by grants and loans to the states themselves, to a lesser extent by direct overseas investment in private enterprises, to a small extent by local capital. It has depended, however, on primary exports – minerals from Guinea, Nigeria, Zaïre and Zambia, more commonly agricultural products from large estates in Côte d'Ivoire, Malawi and Zimbabwe, from smaller farmers in countries like Ghana, Senegal and Uganda – which have usually been collected and marketed by the state. The measures of growth are not very reliable. In the boom in commodity prices to the late 1960s, however, all agree that the rates were considerable, and that they have deteriorated since. In nine countries between the later 1960s and the late 1980s, the average rate of growth of GNP per head each year was actually negative, and above 1 per cent only in Burundi. It fell drastically in the 1980s. There were by then very large deficits and difficult debts – by the end of the 1980s, scheduled debt-service payments in the region were seventy per cent of the value of exports. In the first half of the decade, exports fell by thirty per cent and imports by more than twice as much. In the eight years from 1980 to 1987, in the course of which there was a change from a net inflow to a net outflow of funds, not least to the IMF itself, the rate of growth was –2.8 per cent a year for the region as a whole. More than half its people, it is now thought, because of this, and because of the long neglect of food producers, live in absolute poverty. Infant mortality, it is true, has fallen slightly; but in all but a few societies – Zimbabwe, Sao Tomé and Príncipe, Burundi, Zambia, Kenya – it hovers still at around 10 per cent of all births, in six at around 15 per cent, and in Sierra Leone it may be higher than anywhere else in the world. Where information is available, it seems that between a third and half of all the children who do survive are stunted. Educational enrolments have risen, but in only a few places – Zimbabwe, Zambia, Kenya, Togo, Cameroon, Cape Verde – are almost all those in the relevant age group reported to be in primary school.[19]

There are the elements of civil society. There are large farmers and many smaller ones. (Landless rural proletariats, however, are rare.) There are independent businesses and the kinds of formal institution and less formal association pursuing the kinds of interest which are elsewhere characteristic of the middle classes. There are many small traders. There are white-collar employees. There is even, in some societies, a sizeable working class. But occupational categories do not reflect actual relations. These and the identities which mark them are usually more local, always more complex, and change with perceived advantage. Because so much economic life is so dependent on the state – through state contracts, the granting of licences and the collection of duties and taxes, agricultural marketing boards, and state and parastatal enterprises themselves – they are also more connected than is usual elsewhere with the politics of office. There is everywhere what Bayart calls a social and political *hybridation*.

Terray has characterized it as an alliance between the worlds of the air-conditioner and the veranda. There are, as he describes it, two 'co-existing forms of government' in which the state 'appears as a conglomerate of positions of power the occupants of which are at the same time in a position to assure themselves of substantial revenues and to spread around situations, prebends, bonuses and services'.[20] Politicians and administrators enjoy the prebends, as well as the opportunities for more open predation, that regulation offers.²¹ (The connections are not merely local or intranational. There are also close international ties. Beyond the state as well as within it, there is a 'reciprocal assimilation of elites'.)²² But the object is not just to accumulate for accumulation's sake. Authority itself lies in being able to parade resources – who would respect a leader, Kenyatta once asked, who went around on a bicycle? – and allocate them to others. Those in power have had both to take and to distribute portions of the state, and for this reason, to enlarge it.²³

This coupling of worlds, however, the dialectic, it has been called, of order and disorder, the running-together of what to a liberal mind are the public and the private, is not stable. If the powerful are to retain their power, they must have clients, and the clients themselves must have something. The consequent distribution of resources, however, can scarcely be said to be a redistribution. Because of the scarcity – and the expectation everywhere of scarcity – that pervades daily life in Africa, the reciprocal assimilation of elites through the activities of the state has been an engine for generating a disproportionate share of resources for the political classes themselves. It is perhaps true that the political relations of what has been described as a 'patrimonialism' can be said to be what it is for otherwise powerless Africans to be 'represented', to have governors who are 'accountable', even to enjoy a degree of 'transparency'.²⁴ But the clients are rarely content with these relations. Now and again, there are popular outbursts – and where there is a common language, a sufficient literacy, and a free press, as in Cameroon, for instance, Nigeria, and Senegal, a continuous satire – against those who violate the norms of acceptable allocation and enrich themselves too much. More generally now, there is the more or less active resistance of the many religious groups, which have spread in the 1970s and 1980s, the informal economy, banditry, a retreat into self-provisioning in the villages, and at the limit, migration.²⁵

The political classes in sub-Saharan Africa are in origin distinctively political classes, at most two generations old.²⁶ They have had little or no economic base outside the state. Their position within it has also been precarious. They have not been economically or politically secure enough to allow competition among themselves, have resisted electoral decision, and have usually been unwilling to extend rights. In more or less directly personal ways, they have deployed their positions within what remain the directive and authoritarian frames of post-colonial states. In some respects, at some moments, their rule might have been 'representative', accountable', and 'transparent'. In two or three instances – in Taubman's Liberia, for example, Kenyatta's Kenya, and Houphouët-Boigny's Côte d'Ivoire – it has even been skilled; these three men took care – as Taubman's and Kenyatta's successors have not – to listen to different interests and incorporate them into their governing councils.[27] But the rule has not usually been responsive in ways that would be recognised by anyone outside Africa, or by many within it, as acceptably 'democratic'.[28]

In the 1980s and 1990s, 'the African continent', as Bayart puts it, and the IMF agrees, has been in danger of 'disappearing from the map of world capitalism'.[29] To try to stop this happening, the IMF and the World Bank have been imposing their now familiar – although by no means identical, in some respects indeed openly opposed – programmes for financial stabilization and structural adjustment. At the least, one might suppose, these will have required those in the state to trim their operations; at most, they could undercut state power altogether. This is not so. In two places in the first half of the 1980s, Rawlings's Ghana and Sankara's Burkina Faso, the pressure for reform was enthusiastically used as an excuse for redemption. (Burkina Faso, 'the land of honest men', was the reforming colonels' own new name for Upper Volta.)[30] Elsewhere also, if nowhere quite so dramatically – in Moi's Kenya, for instance, Houphouët-Boigny's Côte d'Ivoire, Babangida's Nigeria, Diouf's Senegal, the previously Marxist-Leninist Benin and even the still nominally Marxist-Leninist People's Republic of the Congo – leaders have welcomed the new programmes.[31] (This is not peculiar to Africa. In Britain in 1976, Callaghan and Healey were similarly ready to accept help from the IMF and its conditions; Chun seized the opportunity for stabilization and structural reform in an economic crisis in South Korea in the early 1980s; and Salinas in Mexico, Andres Pérez in Venezuela, Menem in Argentina, and Sarney and Collor in Brazil have all done so more recently.) This is not just because these men have had no alternative. It is also because they have been presented with a means – for which they could blame outsiders – of reducing the power of those who had become dangerously independent patrons in their extended states.

The leaders of states of this kind, in which economic patronage has been an important part of political power, have always had to guard against those, individuals as well as associations, who might weaken their control. In sub-Saharan Africa, they have also had to insure against the possibility that some might escape from their jurisdiction altogether. (Mobutu insisted against all the technical and economic advice that electricity should be run from the hydroelectric plant below Kinshasa to Shaba, so that he could shut it off if there were more rumblings there of rebellion, or incursions from Zambia.) To those in the presidential palaces, therefore, the political opportunities presented by the international financial institutions are generally welcome. And they are not merely opportunities to attack other patrons. Sankara and Rawlings, and Museveni in Uganda, have used them also to seek support in the country-side. And in Burkina and Ghana, as well as in Mozambique, Angola, Nigeria, Senegal and elsewhere, governments have used the pretext of protest at the rises in the prices of wage-goods in the cities to uproot the politically troublesome urban poor – a move that in Dakar is called 'déguerpissement' – in the name of 'improvement' or the 'fight against juvenile delinquency'. Only in Zambia did the government balk at urban riots at the price of food, and reject the IMF's programme. Some leaders have even derived a more personal advantage from reform; Houphouët-Boigny persuaded the World Bank to agree to attach the Côte d'Ivoire's 'Direction des grands travaux' to his own office.

In themselves, therefore, the measures being imposed by both multi-lateral and bilateral donors in sub-Saharan Africa will not directly serve democracy. In reducing the power of the opposition, they reduce the opportunity for competition within the political classes themselves. Technocrats, who have few political connections with the rest of the society and are in many cases dependent on their ties with the IMF and foreign donors, are replacing political bosses in the ministries. (They may nevertheless do something to improve the states' administrations, and to reduce their costs. In 1986, Guinea's civil service was accounting for 50 per cent of current public expenditure, the Central African Republic's for 63 per cent. In the Gambia, the civil service doubled in size between 1974 and 1984; in Ghana during much the same period, it was increasing five times more quickly than the labour force.)[32] The poorer farmers, who do not stand to gain from the improved internal terms of trade for agri-culture that the economic adjustments require, and urban workers and the urban poor, who suffer from the reduction in services and rises in the price of food and other wage-goods, are discontented. But there is nothing in the adjustment programmes themselves to give them a voice.

The reforming regimes, as observers have remarked, are accordingly suspended. A political space has opened up beneath them. The ruling Parti Socialiste in Senegal has said that as part of what it proposes as a 'renewal', it wants to see this filled with a less patrimonial, less corrupt, more 'modern', 'multi-party' politics. But the results so far are equivocal. The PS continues to manage elections; the province of Casamance in the southwest of the country is actually rebelling; many smaller areas are retreating into self-help, which includes more smuggling; and the voices of Islam are increasing in number and strength, although there is no sign that they wish to assume state power – merely to put pressure on those who have it.[33] There is no reason to expect anything very different anywhere else. And no other sub-Saharan state has been as used to open and steady political competition as Senegal. In detaching themselves from their old political roots, and in many cases being no nearer to 'capturing' all of their populations, the political leaders who have already acceded to the new economic disciplines may have solved one problem only to lay themselves open to one or both of two others: to a *coup d'état* in the presidential palace itself and to resistance – or, like Traoré in Mali in the spring of 1991, even rebellion – in the cities and perhaps even from those in the countryside who are not benefiting from the rise in agricultural prices. The temptation to repress – already evident in Kenya and Nigeria, where Babangida even forbade debate on structural adjustment – is plain.[34]

But there are contrary indications. The end of the Cold War has made the US more willing to act against politically closed regimes of the right. The collapse of state socialism in Eastern Europe has deprived the African left of its models and of political and material support. Western donors are pressing for a greater openness. African intellectuals are less inclined to blame the north for their countries' problems, more willing to blame their own leaders. For one or more of these reasons, the leaders of at least fifteen countries in sub-Saharan African have, however unwillingly, made at least a formal move to some sort of democracy. Competition within the political class, this might suggest, could increase.[35]

In the eighteenth century, at least in England, such competition meant 'factions', and factions, it was thought, were a threat to the dignity and integrity, even perhaps the stability, of the realm. Since then, the political classes in the more established states have had the confidence to turn them into parties; in time, with the extension of the vote, 'mass' parties. Citizens have been more or less successfully persuaded that their concerns – which parties themselves have helped to fashion – can be met by one or another of these organizations, and that there is no need to press claims outside them. This is not to say that Rousseau's mockery of the English in the 1750s and Schumpeter's cynicism about the system more generally by the 1940s – that in elections, voters were able merely to choose between sections of the oligarchy, and asked to be quiet in between – have lost their force. The political directions of modern mass parties and the balance of power within them usually owe little to popular pressure; special interests outside the parties continue to have influence; and it is now often suggested that many popular concerns are more effectively pressed outside parties altogether. It is therefore too simple to assume that for the purposes of influence, or for holding politicians to account, the kind of competitive electoral democracy now practised in Europe, North America and Australasia is an unequivocally desirable form, and too simple to suppose that it is settled. None the less, something like it is the most practicable means yet devised with which to ensure that there is some competition within the political class and that citizens have a say in its outcome. In the established democratic states, however, unlike most of those in the Third World, there are institutions to guard against outcomes that are too adverse.[36]

Like all ruling groups, those in sub-Saharan Africa have many factions – as Houphouët-Boigny has nicely said, they are riddled with 'sénégalité' – and they all have formal political parties. But the factions – those within the Parti Socialiste in Senegal itself and the numerous *groupuscules* to the left of it are a good example – are constantly shifting and usually ephemeral. They do not turn on ideology or principle or an enduring difference of opinion about policy, certainly not on anything that could be seen as a 'structural' division within the society or even the political class. They revolve around individuals. Heads of state and of ruling parties have been careful to distance or destroy them when they can, and to incorporate or rotate them when they cannot. Indeed one or two of the longer-lasting heads of state in sub-Saharan Africa – Houphouët-Boigny, for example, and Mobutu – have been masters of this art. Such factions have not been proto-parties.

Now, however, for external rather than internal reasons, opposition parties exist in many states. It is too soon to say whether these will be able effectively to fight competitive elections. Multi-party states have existed intermittently in the past, and there have been elections. But these have in all but one or two instances been rigged by the ruling group, which has had the resources of the state, including its own patronage, to deploy. And the contending parties have owed more to factional disputes within the intersecting elites, and to personal squabbles, than to any wider or deeper or more enduring difference of identity and interest. If such differences do exist – leaving aside the principled but fitful hostility of secondary school children and students, especially in the Francophone countries – they have yet to settle into clear, enduring and effective forces.

The political differences that there are turn still on the sense of being deprived of what Nigerians, in their old British image, call a slice of 'the national cake', of the resources that since independence have been the gift of the state. Even if there were not, as there has been, a hostility to the language and divisions of class in politics in sub-Saharan Africa, the richer middle classes are too small in number to form a party, and have hitherto been implicated in the status auo. In the pre-existing economic order, urban workers and trade unions are dependent on the state and the ruling party. *Les petits*, the *petit bourgeoisie* itself and the peasants, even where they have a common interest, which is unusual, and a common awareness of that interest, tend not to be well organized. (As I have suggested, African 'peasants' have usually protested by smuggling cash-crops out of the country, or by withdrawing from their production alto-gether to grow food for themselves or for local trade, or by moving away.) The identities and interests of 'ethnicity' – a product of the colonial administrations' attempts to make some sense of the social divisions – are less steady than they have seemed.[37] If the new opposition parties are not simply deterred from their purpose, they too may collapse into 'sénégal-ité'. (The American pressure on Mobutu to allow competition is an instance of how ambiguous the evidence still can be. Mobutu has tried to ride the tiger, as he has done in the past, by encouraging difference him-self. By the beginning of 1992, this 'multi-Mobutuism', as Zaïrians were calling it, had produced more than 200 opposition parties. On the other hand, three of these are large, and his tactic may rebound.)[38]

Against this, liberal optimists will argue – as they have for the past forty years – that a more enduring and politically steady division of interests, and a more concentrated electoral competition between them, will come with 'economic development'. The potential rewards of the modern state have enlarged the arena within which power is pursued. It has also increased the resources – including those from outside – that there are to fight for. So far, this has changed little else. A balanced growth, however, will increase the number of people with a stake in the system, reduce their risks, and strengthen the institutions necessary to sustain a political competition.

This is indeed optimistic. For many economies, growth is still in question, even if in Ghana, since 1983 the darling of the international institutions, it has recently been averaging about 5 per cent a year. Also, what there is may not be balanced. And even if it is, it will almost certainly not be sufficient. Political interests are not only defined by economics. They are also defined by politics itself. This was so in Gers-chenkron's 'later developers' in Europe, in which the old ruling groups were slow to see that they had politically to accommodate the peasants and the increasing numbers of urban and industrial workers, and as a result found themselves in fights they could have avoided. It has more recently been so in the third world. Sometimes, as in Nicaragua under Somoza in the 1970s, the political exclusion has been so blatant and com-plete that it has overridden all other differences and led all the excluded to favour a radical change. Sometimes, as in India under the Congress governments of the early 1970s and 1980s, it has been less direct, a mat-ter more of neglect than rejection, has not elided other differences – it may even have exacerbated them – and has led to a more energetic protest at the polls.[39] In the face of the increasingly centralized states in sub-Saharan Africa, one could just suppose that the 'democracy movement' there might have a similar effect. But even if a radical socialism or a radical nationalism are still live options there – and in the early 1990s, the current is running in the opposite direction – the institutions to insure against its likely excesses are not yet firm.[40]

In the parlous economic condition in which most sub-Saharan states now find themselves, as much hangs on the policies of the donors, the international institutions and the western states that continue to exercise so much influence in Africa as it does on politicians and citizens in the states themselves. But if the donors' aid and loans continue, as they have in the past, to flow directly to the state – and this is true whether growth then follows or not – and if structural adjustment continues, it is far from clear that a popular enthusiasm for democracy will be sufficient to resist the resultant concentration of power in the presidential palaces and ministries of finance.

Could the donors help to avoid such an outcome? Principled objections to trying to influence a country's internal politics – objections which have been made against donors in the past – are now weakening. In the later 1950s and through the 1960s and 1970s, even into the 1980s, the post-colonial enthusiasm – and guilt – that was reflected in the United Nations' *Declaration* seemed definitively to have quashed the old presumption of 'positive sovereignty' – that 'a people' had to be civilized before it could be given self-rule – in favour of a new, more 'negative' assumption, that a people had a right to self-determination whatever the perceived 'inadequacy', as the *Declaration* put it, 'of political, economic, social or educational preparedness'. In the 1990s, however, it is coming increasingly if still quietly to be argued that the sovereignty of what Jackson has recently described as the 'quasi-states' of the third world – which in sub-Saharan Africa include more than just the seventeen or so with populations of less than four million – is no longer sacred. Considerations of human rights may override it. And now that the intoxication of political independence in the countries themselves – and the anger at economic and political 'dependence' – is wearing off, the threat of persistent underdevelopment may make both leaders and their critics more willing, in some respects, to relinquish it.[41]

But it is not, at first sight, clear what outsiders could do to advance democracy in Africa. The temptation for donors to try to bypass not only politics but also the states' own administrations – in so far as that distinction, even now, can be made in sub-Saharan Africa – will only postpone the political uncertainty. Diplomats will insist, and rightly, that it could also rebound. A more practical alternative to attending almost exclusively to the central state – canvassed recently by the US, and supported by the example of the more democratic of late-late developers – would be to lend directly to indigenous private enterprises. But it would not be easy to find a sufficient number of any size in most African states. It would probably be more useful, socially, politically, and in the longer run perhaps economically too, even if it would be practically more difficult, to encourage smaller concerns. The best option may be either to try to persuade the leaders to pay more attention to their connections at the base, or, if they resist, which is not unlikely, to address those at the base directly, not only by supporting smaller enterprises and what the World Bank has called 'intermediary institutions' – it points to the National Christian Council in Kenya – but also by insisting, as the multilateral – but not most bilateral – donors still rarely do, on tighter criteria of local implementation.[42] This could serve to revive the local initiatives which were more or less directly quashed by the colonial administrations – in Lugard's policy, for example, of 'indirect rule' through local chiefs – and which have since been ignored, or suppressed, by post-colonial regimes. (Examples might include the peasants' associations which have come together to repair the old state irrigation schemes in Senegal, women's marketing cooperatives in Zimbabwe, and the rotating credit groups that are organized through Christian churches in southern Nigeria.)[43] It could serve to express an interest in some of the social preconditions of the representativeness, accountability and transparency that many Africans want. On the most optimistic view, it could start to generate the kind of trust in politics and public action more generally that they need. In the longer run, it might even do something to induce those crucial institutional guarantees which before and after independence the regimes, as well as many foreign donors and investors, have done much to pre-empt.

This, if it is plausible at all, is for the future. But could a 'minimal democracy' produce it? Lonsdale makes a case.

> High-political competition can well encourage claims to deep responsibility. It may also give supporters some, if rarely much, scope to keep their leaders to their word by threats of defection. The stratagems of power can thus become the conventions of freedom. A culture of political accountability can emerge. Its calculated moralities can create a community, with a competitive interest in its shared history.[44]

This goes to the heart of an important part of democratic theory. Does electoral competition entail political inclusion? Or is inclusion a separate matter? The record of the now-established democracies is equivocal. On one reading, political inclusion was granted by the political class in these countries only when it at last felt secure. On another reading, inclusion had to be fought for. The truth, if there is a truth to be had, no doubt lies in between. True or not, however, it is not relevant to sub-Saharan Africa. For it is the conclusion to an argument which presumes that the question is how a competitive democracy can emerge from absolutism.[45]

Absolutist states were, in their absolutism, states. They controlled their territories and the population within them. And even if they did not emerge from an already existing political community, they almost always served to create one. Those who came later to contest them, whether in France in the later 1780s, or in Chile, South Korea or South Africa in the later 1980s, could take that community for granted, or at least could take it that there was a community to be fought for. There have been absolutisms too in independent Africa. But they have not been constructive. Nguema's Equatorial Guinea, Amin's Uganda, Bokassa's Central African Empire, even Mobutu's Zaïre, are all instances of more or less deliberate political division and social devastation, little different, in the end, from King Leopold's Congo Free State. They may have even been worse. Leopold's domination, as the Bakongo used to say, was 'Bula Matari'; it did at least 'break rocks'. More recent tyrants have just broken heads.

Lonsdale's hope for sub-Saharan Africa is that instead of building on an already existing 'competitive interest in a shared history', which does not there exist, a competitive high politics – what I have been calling a minimal democracy – can create it, and create it, moreover, not only in the Equatorial Guineas and Ugandas and Zaïres but in most of the other states also, *against* what is for the majority of citizens the *un*shared history of the past thirty years. It is not, he agrees, a high hope. Indeed, there is no precedent for it anywhere.

But as I indicated at the end of the previous section, this is not to say that there is no hope at all. If there have been 'cultures of accountability' in Africa, they have been provincial, in local associations of those who have lived and worked together and shared a vernacular. These associations were feared by the few early modern African kings, ignored by the colonialists, and suppressed by the first post-colonial regimes. But it is the inefficiencies of these regimes – and the symbolically unappealing identities they have offered – which have kept many local associations alive, and there is now a powerful coalition in their favour. The international institutions, the bilateral donors and many younger African intellectuals, as well as the people themselves, are all arguing for them.[46] Only the regimes, even – so far – those like Rawlings's and Museveni's which claim to support a devolution, still resist them.

The conclusion must be paradoxical. Hope for even a minimal democracy in sub-Saharan Africa cannot lie in encouraging a united but unresponsive political class to compete. There is a political class, but it is not of this kind, and the political community it might have created does not exist. Nor can it lie, as one kind of modern liberal might propose, in creating a population of sovereign individual citizens who will rationally combine across the space of the state peacefully to negotiate their interests. This also would require a sense of community in existing states. (But it is not to say that there should not and cannot be the usual protections against personal violation.) If the hope for a democracy lies anywhere, it is in those associations which the successive architects of 'the modern state' in Africa, pre-colonial, colonial and post-colonial, have all dismissed as primordial, parochial and divisive.

The shape of such a democracy is obscure. All that can perhaps be said of it is that if it too turns out to be minimal, it will be minimal in a different sense. One can agree with Amilcar Cabral that, in the colonial period, all Africans were forced to live someone else's history, and might add that most have been asked to do so since independence. The irony – one hopes that it will not be yet another African tragedy – is that they may in this respect find their own voice and a political place at the moment at which – because there are new views of the limits of sovereignty, or even, perhaps, because their economies are put into effective receivership – the sovereign nation-state ceases to be the frame in which they can do so.

NOTES

1   World Bank, *World Development Report 1991* (New York, Oxford University Press, 1991), p. 136.
2   A. Gerschenkron, *Economic Backwardness in Historical Perspective* (Cambridge, MA, Harvard University Press, 1946), the argument summarized at pp. 343–4. The contrast is with an idealized picture of the sequence in the early developers – for example, T. H. Marshall, *Citizenship and Social Class* (Cambridge, Cambridge University Press, 1950) – in which civil rights were extended before industrialisation, political rights were conceded with it, and social rights followed. The best account of the relations between the economic growth and politics of a model NIC is now J. -E. Woo, *Race to the Swift: state and finance in Korean industrialisation* (New York, Columbia University Press, 1991). The crucial issue, Woo argues, is the way in which industrialization has been financed. It is tempting to generalize her argument to suggest that where the state itself is responsible for raising and managing funds for investment, as in the capitalist NICs and an internationally isolated socialism, it will not be enthusiastic about political competition; but that where it does not have this responsibility, either because internal markets can provide the funds, or because they are coming directly to private enterprises

from outside, it will care less. The first of these two paths roughly corresponds to what Gerschenkron desribed; the second to what A. O. Hirschman described as 'late-late development' in Latin America ('the political economy of import-substituting industrialisation', *Quarterly Journal of Economics*, 82 [1968], 1–32). There are, however, exceptions: for instance, Singapore – G. Rodan, *The Political Economy of Singapore's Industrialisation: national state and international capital* (New York, St Martin's Press, 1989).

3 World Bank, *World Development Report 1991*, p. 36.

4 The distinction between utilitarian conceptions of 'welfare' as income, commodities or actual choices and 'the standard of living' as an entitlement to what he calls 'capabilities' has been pressed by A. Sen, *The Standard of Living* (Cambridge, Cambridge University Press, 1987); in the same volume, B. Williams argues that this is to have to think of rights. Expressed preferences are affected by existing entitlements; they are 'shifting and endogenous rather than exogenous, and as a result are a function of current information, consumption patterns, legal rules, and general social pressures': C. Sunstein, 'Preferences and politics', *Philosophy and Public Affairs*, 20 (1991), 3–34, especially p. 10.

5 P. Dasgupta gives a clear summary of the theoretical and empirical reasons for making this move in 'Well-being and the extent of its realisation in poor countries', *Economic Journal*, 100 (Conference 1990), 1–32. It is an important and attractive part of Dasgupta's argument that some rights can be seen as means as well as ends; not all are inviolable, and there can be trade-offs between them. For the purposes of public policy, one might say that the standard of living 'consists of those components . . . the enhancement of which would be the appropriate subject of a social contract between individuals wishing to share the benefits of social cooperation': P. Seabright, 'Pluralism and the standard of living', ms, pp. 9, 13.

6 Classically, J. Schumpeter, *Capitalism, Socialism and Democracy* (New York, Harper, 1942). In the 1950s and 1960s, this was blandly restated to say that there should be agreement on 'common values'; this argument was nicely exposed by B. Barry, *Sociologists, Economists and Democracy* (London, Collier-Macmillan, 1970).

7 Classically, D. A. Rustow, 'Transitions to democracy', *Comparative Politics*, 2 (1969–70), 337–64; more recently, A. Przeworski, 'Democracy as a contingent outcome of conflicts', in J. Elster and R. Slagstad (eds), *Constitutionalism and Democracy* (Cambridge, Cambridge University Press, 1988), pp. 59–80.

8 For example, R. A. Dahl, *Polyarchy* (New Haven, CT, Yale University Press, 1971), summary at p. 4.

9 Przeworski, 'Democracy as a contingent outcome of conflicts', p. 66. If we assume that the pre-existing regime is inclined to the right, and that the protagonists in the putative democracy are of both right and left, this will mean that the right will want to have institutions that are acceptable to both parties and which guarantee that its privileges are not threatened, and that the left, to meet the second of these conditions and so be acceptable to the right, will want to demobilize any extra-institutional forces that may have called for more radical change. But as Przeworski points out, if the members of the pre-existing regime – soldiers, say, or conservative communists – cannot persuade any party to defend their privileges in a democratic competition, and cannot thus be sure that these privileges will not be overridden, they may not concede.

10 The absence of effective sovereignty is emphasized by R. H. Jackson and C. G. Rosberg, 'Why Africa's weak states persist: the empirical and the juridical in

statehood', *World Politics*, 27 (1982–3), 1–27, who observe that many states in sub-Saharan Africa are recognized more by other states than by many of their own citizens. This is one reason why standing armies are politically important, and why calls for the abolition or even the substantial reduction of these armies are not likely to be heeded. J. D. Y. Peel defends the description 'political class' for sub-Saharan Africa on the reasonable ground that it 'points to the fact that social power was overwhelmingly the product of political or state bureaucratic office rather than of any material resource held independently of it': 'Social and cultural change', in M. Crowder (ed.), *The Cambridge History of Africa. Vol. 8: From c.1940 to c.1975* (Cambridge, Cambridge University Press, 1984), pp. 142–191, especially p. 184. There are of course exceptions to almost all the generalizations I offer here; I have space to mention only the more important.

11   J. Lonsdale, 'States and social processes in Africa: a historiographical survey', *African Studies Review*, 24 (1981), 139–225, especially p. 139, my emphasis.

12   N. Chazan, R. Mortimer, J. Ravenhill and D. Rothchild, *Politics and Society in Contemporary Africa* (London, Macmillan, 1988), p. 41.

13   The most comprehensive recent interpretation of modern African politics is J.-F. Bayart, *L'Etat en Afrique: la politique du ventre* (Paris, Fayard, 1989; London, Longman, 1992). Attractive in its insistence that one has to understand the *longue durée* of African history in order to understand the present, this is, however, very much an essay on the politics, says little about the colonial period, discusses economic issues only in passing, and is sceptical – in places even dismissive – of the new civilizing mission of 'development'. Also J. Lonsdale, 'Le passé de l'Afrique au secours de son avenir', *Politique Africaine*, 39 (1990), 135–54.

14   G. Hyden has recently restated the point: 'The conditions of governance in Africa are determined by three fundamental factors: (1) a legacy of land abundance, (2) the absence of a ruling class, and (3) the predominance of social over territorial types of organisation' ('Local governance and economic-demographic transition in rural Africa', in G. McNicoll and M. Cain (eds), *Rural Development and Population: institutions and policy* (New York, Oxford University Press for the Population Council, 1990 [supplement to *Population and Development Review* 15 (1989)], pp. 193–211, especially p. 195). This generalization does not apply to the one or two areas in which an intensive and profitable agriculture has produced a class with a vested interest in the resultant surplus: in Zimbabwe, for instance, in northern Nigeria, and in the Kenya highlands. There is an interesting discussion of some consequences of 'the predominance of social over territorial forms of organisation' in J. R. Goody, *Production and Reproduction* (Cambridge, Cambridge University Press, 1976).

15   A. O. Hirschman, 'Exit, voice and the state', *World Politics*, 31 (1978), p. 94. On two modern instances and their generalizability, see V. Azarya and N. Chazan, 'Disengagement from the state in Africa: reflections on the experience of Ghana and Guinea', *Comparative Studies in Society and History*, 29 (1987), 106–31.

16   A. Hoben, 'Social stratification in traditional Amhara society', in A. Tuden and L. Plotnicov (eds), *Social Stratification in Africa* (New York, Free Press, 1970), p. 212, quoted by J. Lonsdale, 'Political accountability in African history', in P. Chabal (ed.), *Political Domination in Africa: reflections on the limits of power* (Cambridge, Cambridge University Press, 1986), p. 130. On Cameroon, see Bayart, *L'Etat en Afrique*, p. 236.

17   There is a brief and balanced summary of present thinking about Africa's political economy to the present in Chazan et al., *Politics and Society*, pp. 219–60.

18   The theatre is not infrequently spiced with local devices. The ways in which
     some modern African leaders have used the symbols of chiefdom, for instance, is
     familiar. There are also more exotic examples. President Eyadéma of Togo once
     survived a plane crash in which the two – white – pilots were killed. He had what
     remained of the DC-3 moved to Lomé, where it now sits, nose-down but suitably
     embellished, a sign of his quasi-divine powers over nature and the once superior
     race. C. M. Tulabor, *Le Togo sous Eyadéma* (Paris, Karthala, 1986), is a revealing
     account of this aspect of his regime.

19   For the rates of growth for 1965–89, World Bank, *World Development Report 1991*,
     Table 1, p. 204; for 1980–7, World Bank, *Sub-Saharan Africa: from crisis to sustain-
     able growth* (New York, The World Bank, 1989), Table 1, p. 221. (For the latter
     survey, the Bank includes ten countries – Botswana, Comoros, Djibouti, Ethiopia,
     Lesotho, Madagascar, Mauritius, Seychelles, Sudan and Swaziland – which fall
     outside what I define as sub-Saharan Africa. But these do not significantly affect
     the average of –2.8 per cent. The range of rates of growth in the remaining 34
     countries in 1980–7 was from 4.5 per cent in Cameroon – one of only three to
     exhibit a rate of more than 1 per cent – to –5.6 in Zambia (and –8.2 in
     Mozambique, but that has partly been due to internal war). The decreasing
     importance of foreign direct investment in Africa in the 1980s is described in
     United Nations Centre on Transnational Corporations, *The Triad in Foreign Direct
     Investment* (New York, UNCTC, 1991). On poverty, see United Nations Develop-
     ment Programme, *Human Development Report 1990* (New York, United Nations,
     1990), p. 18, and World Bank, *World Development Report 1990* (New York, Oxford
     University Press, 1990), for example at p. 42, where it is suggested that real rural
     living standards in Tanzania declined at an average of 2.5 per cent a year from
     1969 to 1983, that the decline in urban standards was even greater, and that even
     in Nigeria, which had profited from the rise in oil prices in 1973 and 1979,
     consumption in the 1980s fell by 7 per cent a year, reducing living standards at
     the end of this decade to the level of the mid-1950s. On other social indicators,
     United Nations Development Programme, *Human Development Report 1991* (New
     York, United Nations, 1991); *World Bank, World Development Report 1991*, Tables
     28 and 29, pp. 258 and 260; and World Bank, *Sub-Saharan Africa*, Tables 31 and
     32, pp. 272 and 274.

20   E. Terray, 'Le climatiseur et la véranda', in *Afrique plurielle, Afrique actuelle: hommage
     à Georges Balandier* (Paris, Karthala, 1986), pp. 37–44, especially pp. 38–9.

21   One commentator has gone so far as to suggest that prebends are the stuff of
     politics in an African state: R. A. Joseph, *Democracy and Prebendal Politics in Nigeria:
     the rise and fall of the Second Republic* (Cambridge, Cambridge University Press,
     1987). Politics there, as Joseph describes it, is 'an unremitting and unconstrained
     struggle for possession and access to state offices, with the chief aim of procuring
     direct material benefits to oneself and one's acknowledged communal or other
     sectional group' (p. 75). In wha is perhaps an extreme case, for it is a sensitive
     province, the regional commissioner of Shaba in southern Zaïre had a nominal
     salary in 1974 of $2,000 a month, and was estimated to receive a further $100,000
     a month in prebends: C. Young and T. Turner, *The Rise and Decline of the Zaïrian
     State* (Madison, University of Wisconsin Press, 1985), p. 245. The historical roots
     of this pattern can be seen to lie in the need to exercise force to get people to
     work for accumulation: A. Mbembe, 'Pouvoir, violence et accumulation', *Politique
     Africaine*, 39 (1990), 7–24.

22   The phrase is Bayart's, *L'Etat en Afrique*, pp. 193–226. Governments in sub-

Saharan Africa frequently assist each other, sending police and soldiers, for instance, to put down each other's disturbances, and they have cooperated in ostracizing the puritanical populists – Okello in Zanzibar in 1964, Rawlings in Ghana in 1979, Doe in Liberia in 1980, Sankara in Burkina in 1983 – who might seem to threaten their established practices. Some of the most lucrative economic opportunities outside the state – certainly for trade – lie in those parts of those countries – in Angola, Sierra Leone, Uganda and northern and eastern Zaïre, for instance – over which the state itself has no effective control: for the last, there is a revealing account in J. McGaffey, *Entrepreneurs and Parasites: the struggle for indigenous capitalism in Zaire* (Cambridge, Cambridge University Press, 1987).

23 African states have been said – not just in the international development community in the 1980s – to be 'overdeveloped', but this is ambiguous and misleading: C. Leys, 'The "overdeveloped" post-colonial state: a re-evaluation', *Review of African Political Economy*, 5 (1976), 39–48.

24 J.-F. Médard, 'La régulation socio-politique', in Y.-A. Fauré and J.-F. Médard (eds), *Etat et bourgeoisie en Côte d'Ivoire* (Paris, Karthala, 1982), pp. 75ff.; for general discussion see C. Clapham, *Third World Politics: an introduction* (London, Croom Helm, 1985), which concentrates on Africa. Lonsdale's 'Political accountability in African history' is a wide-ranging, reflective and penetrating account of previous arrangements. A clear local endorsement of the importance of patrimonialism for representation is quoted by Joseph, *Democracy and Prebendal Politics*, p. 67.

25 Azarya and Chazan, 'Disengagement from the state in Africa'. The relative readiness to move has been given as a reason for the relatively few popular calls for secession. The two calls that have led to civil war were from what were then Katanga in Congo-Kinshasa and Biafra in Nigeria; in each case, however, they were calls from local elites – and their international backers – who wanted to take advantage of the minerals in these regions. At present, popular pressure for secession in sub-Saharan Africa may be strongest in the province of Casamance in south-western Senegal. But moves to secede presuppose a commitment to the idea of the state, if not to the state one actually inhabits, and that commitment, as I have said, is still in question. Where such moves have been made, they have hitherto been resisted by neighbouring states and by the Organization of African Unity. The 'informal economy' characteristic of many third world cities was first described and defined for the slums of Accra: J. K. Hart, 'Informal income opportunities and urban employment in Ghana', *Journal of Modern African Studies*, 11 (1973), 61–89. At one point, it was even favoured as the site of possible 'development': International Labour Office, *Employment, Incomes and Equality: a strategy for increasing productive employment in Kenya* (Geneva, ILO, 1972). See also McGaffey, *Entrepreneurs and Parasites*.

26 Pre-colonial kingdoms often recruited slaves, who had no local social ties, and so did some early colonial armies. Many of the first converts to the faith of the influential Christian missionaries, who were therefore the first to learn the colonizer's language, had also been slaves, or were outcasts of other kinds: Lonsdale, 'Political accountability in African history', p. 140. Many of these people were in a good position to inherit the colonial states.

27 A. R. Zolberg, *One-Party Government in the Ivory Coast* (Princeton, NJ, Princeton University Press, 1964), p. 283. R. H. Jackson, 'Planning, politics and administration', in G. Hyden, R. H. Jackson and J. Okumu (eds), *Development Administration: the Kenya experience* (Nairobi, Oxford University Press, 1970), pp. 177–8.

28 It is too simple to see almost all patrimonial government in sub-Saharan Africa as instances of purely personal rule, as, in sixteen cases, do R. H. Jackson and C. G. Rosberg, *Personal Rule in Black Africa: prince, autocrat, prophet, tyrant* (Berkeley CA, University of California Press, 1982). At the same time, sharp typologies of structural difference (of the kind suggested, for instance, by Chazan et al., *Politics and Society*, pp. 133–45) seem exaggerated. Perhaps the most striking exception to the generalization about democracy has been Senegal. There is a long tradition there, pre-dating the French but reinforced by the pattern of the colonial economy, of sophisticated local self-government, both within the Moslem brotherhoods and without, and Léopold Senghor and his Union Progressiste Sénégalaise acknowledged this in trying to rule by discussion and consensus. Only in the general election in February 1988 did the ruling party – now the Parti Socialiste, led by Abdou Diouf – lose its nerve and, before the results were announced, arrest the leader of the opposition, unreasonably accusing him of inciting violence. (Observers agree that the results of this election may have been rigged, but also agree that the PS would have won.) On Senghor in Senegal, see J. G. Vaillant, *Black, French and African: a life of Léopold Senghor* (Cambridge, MA, Harvard University Press, 1990); on the election in 1988, see C. Coulon and D. B. Cruise O'Brien, 'Senegal', in D. B. Cruise O'Brien, J. M. Dunn and R. Rathbone (eds), *Contemporary West African States* (Cambridge, Cambridge University Press, 1989), pp. 148–9. See also note 39 below.

29 Bayart, *L'Etat en Afrique*, p. 258. The IMF expressed the same fear in 1990.

30 There are interesting accounts by R. Jeffries, 'Ghana: the political economy of personal rule', and R. Otayek, 'Burkina Faso: between feeble state and total state, the swing continues', in O'Brien et al., *Contemporary West African States*, pp. 13–30 and 75–98. Rawlings continues in power, but Sankara was deposed in 1987.

31 At least thirty states in sub-Saharan Africa are at present formally committed to implementing 'structural adjustment' programmes. But often – for example, after the boom in cocoa and coffee prices in the Côte d'Ivoire between 1975 and 1978, which prompted an increase in public spending and an associated explosion of political patronage – the implementation has been understandably delayed: Y.-A. Fauré, 'Côte d'Ivoire: analysing the crisis', in O'Brien et al., *Contemporary West African States*, pp. 59–73. In Zaïre, the moment of truth has been more directly political, and more recent. For geopolitical reasons that have only recently ceased to obtain, the US insisted through the 1980s that the IMF continue to extend its facilities to Zaïre even though it had long since become clear, as the most informed of European commentators on the country put it, that it had 'ceased to exist as a macro-economic entity': J.-C. Willame, 'Political succession in Zaïre, or back to Machiavelli', *Journal of Modern African Studies*, 26 (1988), 37–49, especially p. 48.

32 World Bank, *Sub-Saharan Africa*, p. 57. Civil service reform has been taken more seriously in Ghana than anywhere else in sub-Saharan Africa, but the Rawlings government has still to institute effective measures for controlling recruitment to the service.

33 Coulon and O'Brien, 'Senegal', pp. 154ff.

34 Jeffries, 'Ghana'; also Coulon and O'Brien, 'Senegal', and C. Clapham, 'Liberia', in O'Brien et al., *Contemporary West African States*, pp. 145–63 and 99–111 and J. Herbst, 'The structural adjustment of politics in Africa', *World Development*, 18 (1990), 949–58. Clapham suggests a decline in 'representativeness' and 'accountability' in Liberia from Taubman's 'True Whig' regime to Doe's. The leaders'

vulnerability has always been acute. 'Like that of an elder in a lineage, or the head of a network in an urban *quartier*, the preeminence of a president [in Africa] is always circumstantial, and depends on his own individual performance. It increases' – or not – 'week by week, in the hard world of intrigue and "court politics"': Bayart, *L'Etat en Afrique*, p. 276. In all but a few countries, this vulnerability was increased at the moment of independence by the fragility of state power: Lonsdale, 'Political accountability in African history', p. 156. The idea of an 'uncaptured' population is G. Hyden's, *Beyond Ujamaa in Tanzania: underdevelopment and an uncaptured peasantry* (Berkeley, CA, University of California Press, 1980). B. Kagarlitsky has described the authoritarian response to adjustment in Africa as 'market Stalinism': quoted by M. Watts, 'Visions of excess: African development in an age of market idolatry', *Transition*, 51 (1991), p. 134. In regimes elsewhere in the third world where there has been a centralization of state power, the rulers have been able to put down resistance by increasing expenditure on the police – this was Indira Gandhi's tactic in India after her deliberate concentration of power in the early 1970s – or – as with the SNI in Brazil, SAVAK in Iran, the KCIA in South Korea, and analogous agencies elsewhere – to pre-empt it altogether by instituting extensive and effective means of 'internal security', often established with advice from the US in the wake of the Nixon Doctrine. An instance of recent increases in expenditure on the police is Nigeria since 1986. An instance of an effective domestic intelligence agency in Africa, again established with American but here also Israeli help, is the Centre National de Documentation in Zaïre, a country in which many other agencies of the state have atrophied. Many regimes make use of modern technologies of control and of those older devices – the destruction of settlements and forced internal migration, compulsory labour, imprisonment without trial, torture, and so on – which they recall from colonial days; see for instance Mbembe, 'Pouvoir, violence et accumulation'. And in many African countries, of course, there are separate, regularly paid and well equipped corps of – more often than not foreign – palace guards. In learning to live as abandoned clients with even fewer state services – 'vivre sénégalisement', as they now say in Senegal – the poor have fewer guarantees, and are more exposed to the whims of the centre.

35   This class might also devolve its responsibility to non-political bodies. If rates of economic growth in the subcontinent remain low, leaders and those who might challenge them from within the political class will have even fewer opportunities to gain legitimacy and sustain it by distributing resources. They might therefore see an advantage in passing responsibility – and if need be, blame – for the decline in the standard of living to those who cannot, at least directly, be connected with them. They would certainly be wise to do so if the citizens believe, as they are reported by some to do, that the consequences of the programmes of stabilization and adjustment have broken the 'post-colonial social contract' for the distribution of welfare and other goods. The first of these suggestions, at the conference at which this chapter was first given as a paper, is Laurence Whitehead's; it fits with the policies of several Latin American governments in the later 1980s (and also with that in Britain after 1979). The second is Adebayo Olukoshi's.

36   On reservations about the nature and benefits of electoral competition between mass parties in the established democracies, see C. S. Maier, 'Introduction', and A. Pizzorno, 'Politics unbound', in Meier (ed.), *Changing Boundaries of the Political: essays on the evolving balance between the state and society, public and private in Europe*

(Cambridge, Cambridge University Press, 1987), pp. 1–24 and 27–62; also
A. Panebianco, *Political Parties: organisation and power* (Cambridge, Cambridge
University Press, 1988), especially the conclusion. In some of these democracies,
what might have seemed to be firm guarantees have proved not to be. And from
a British point of view – in a state in which the distribution of representatives
does not nearly match the distribution of votes, in which the power of Parliament
is minimal, in which a right-wing government since 1979 has steadily reduced
the powers of local authorities, which control some services, and in which the
same government has tightened the legislation on 'official secrecy' – it is not self-
evident that whatever it may ensure by way of security and welfare, a nominally
more 'advanced' democracy is strikingly more representative, accountable or
transparent than ones which are less so.

37   'Ethnicity' or 'tribalism' was once much vaunted as a basis of political alliances in
Africa, and said to be an obstacle to a common citizenship. In Africa, however, as
everywhere, such identities are entirely situational or contextual. There are real
differences of locality, language, culture and occupation, but these do not explain
why one rather than another is picked out to mark a difference in dispute, or why
a difference is given the name that it is. ('The evidence we have ... is that in
certain situations Africans ignore either class differences or tribal differences [or
both], and that in other situations these differences become significant ... in
their opposition to the Europeans, Africans ignore both their "class" and tribal
differences. Inside a tribal association such as those found in Southern Rhodesia I
would expect oppositions to be phrased in terms of "class" differences. I would
expect the discussion within a teachers' or clerks' association to be phrased in
terms of tribalism. The same people who stand together in one situation may be
bitterly opposed in another': J. C. Mitchell, *The Kalela Dance: aspects of social
relations among urban Africans in Northern Rhodesia*, Rhodes-Livingstone Institute
Paper No. 27 [Manchester, Manchester University Press, 1956], p. 43. I have
been encouraged in my thoughts on this by Federico Varese.) Ethnicity has been
activated in politics – in Sekou Touré's Guinea, for instance, in Stevens's Sierra
Leone, repeatedly in Nigeria, most recently in the election in Benin, which may
turn out to have reversed the division of spoils between the north and south of
the country – when the leaders of the state, or other groups with a control over
resources, openly divert these resources to their own group. And it is ethnicity
which has been activated because of the weakness of other identifications and
frames of collective pressure. (On the political importance still of locality, see
J. M. Dunn, 'The politics of representation and good government in post-colonial
Africa', in Chabal, *Political Domination in Africa*, p. 168.) For the argument that
ethnic consciousness in Africa – like the consciousness of caste in India – was
exacerbated and brought into politics by the decisions of colonial administrators,
see, for instance, R. H. Bates, 'Some conventional orthodoxies in the study of
agrarian change', *World Politics*, 36 (1983–4), 234–54. In the manner of the
current economic theory of institutions, Bates has elsewhere argued ('Modernisation, ethnic competition and the rationality of politics in contemporary Africa', in
D. Rothchild and V. A. Olorunsola [eds], *State versus Ethnic Claims: African policy
dilemmas* [Boulder, CO, Westview Press, 1983], pp. 152 and 164–5) that ethnic
groups are sufficiently large to win in the struggle for resources and sufficiently
small to benefit from having done so. A difficulty with this argument is that in sub-
Saharan Africa, such groups have varied greatly in size.

38   The figure of 200 is Jean-Claude Willame's. The outcome of the political opening

in South Korea, however, is unlikely to be repeated in any African country. (In the summer of 1987, the US took advantage of a political crisis in Seoul to persuade President Roh Tae-woo to reduce the constraints on political contest. Two existing opposition parties were strengthened and a new one formed. But in January 1990, Roh persuaded two of the three to combine with his ruling Democratic Justice Party to form a new one which would have the two-thirds majority required in the National Assembly to change the constitution. The idea was to introduce cabinet government by parliamentary majority in the Japanese manner. Japan's Liberal Democratic Party has ruled without interruption for forty years. It is no coincidence – everyone believes – that the new ruling party in Korea call themselves the Democratic Liberals.) In Korea, unlike sub-Saharan Africa, there is a long tradition of central, conciliar rule, and a deep suspicion – in some quarters, even an incomprehension – of the desirability of open contest. There is a full account in M. Lee, *The Odyssey of Korean Democracy: Korean politics, 1987–1990* (New York, Praeger, 1990).

39 This has been stimulated by the decline of Congress and the concomitant rise of other contenders for state and union power. In some states, like West Bengal, the transition has been relatively steady, and new institutions of political access and control have emerged; in others, like Bihar, it has not, and there has been an increase in violence. The changes are described and explained by A. Kohli, *Democracy and Discontent: India's growing crisis of governability* (Cambridge, Cambridge University Press, 1990).

40 One such institution, of course, is a reasonably neutral rule of law. And this can also affect development itself. In Guinea, for instance, the implementation of agricultural reforms is at present stalled over the question of who has the rights to the vacant cultivable land and who will enforce those rights. While the serious but poor and politically impotent cultivators wait for this question to be answered, those closer to events in Conakry are taking advantage of the delay by themselves acquiring the use of – and perhaps eventually a title to – land which was confiscated from the Touré family and their associates after Sekou Touré died in 1984. (I owe this fact to Gerard Peart, a research student from Cambridge working on the effects of structural adjustment in rural Guinea.) This again is not, however, peculiar to Africa. In Bolivia the government acknowledges that although it has done much to stabilize the currency and reform the economy, it cannot attract the investment it needs because it is seen still to be too vulnerable to interests which may in one way or another subvert such investment. It is a further mark of Senegal's success in sustaining democracy to the early 1980s, if not to the present – in this respect a truly liberal democracy, and not just a minimal one – that in 1981, Amnesty International praised its record on the recognition and extension of civil rights.

41 R. H. Jackson, *Quasi-States: sovereignty, international relations and the third world* (Cambridge, Cambridge University Press, 1990). In the 1980s, the US was less tolerant of its clients' refusals to democratize than it had been in the preceding three decades, and on several – South Korea in 1987, for example, and Chile in 1988 – it put pressure. Other members of the Security Council, it has been said, may be reluctant to allow any precedent for intervention on grounds of 'human rights'; they are themselves vulnerable, aware that since irredentist and secessionist claims – which they may make or suffer – have proved largely fruitless, the discontents that fire such claims are now being restated in the more acceptable rhetoric of 'human rights'. It is true that the insistence of the new

European Bank for Reconstruction and Development – that the countries it might help in Eastern Europe first show their 'democratic' credentials – might be taken as a precedent; but it might equally be taken as an exception for a not-to-be repeated case. A more cautious view of the prospects for claims against national sovereignty is taken by J. Mayall, *Nationalism and International Society* (Cambridge, Cambridge University Press, 1990), although as his title indicates, Mayall is thinking more of the possibility of a truly 'international society' than of selective and piecemeal interventions.

42　The recommendation of the Task Force on the World Bank and Public Administration in Developing Countries in 1980, that the Bank should take time to inform itself about the political and administrative idiosyncracies of each country, was obviously sound. The emphasis on implementation, about which the World Bank has in the past been curiously casual, is consistent with the Bank's more recent recommendations for attention to be paid to small farmers and so on in formulating, implementing and monitoring adjustment programmes in Africa. See World Bank, *The Social Dimensions of Structural Adjustment in Sub-Saharan Africa*, SDA Project Unit Africa Region (Washington, DC World Bank, 1989). The Bank's suggestion about intermediary institutions and its example of the NCC in Kenya is in World Bank, *Sub-Saharan Africa*, p. 61.

43　The British administrations' 'native chiefs' were often remote from the organizations of cultivators and traders; indeed, they often saw them as political opponents, and colluded with the British in trying to reduce or even eliminate their influence. Rawlings's PNDC in Ghana has instituted District Assemblies to encourage what it calls 'participation' at the local level. But one-third of the members of these assemblies are appointed by the PNDC itself, and not elected, and there is no competition between parties. The examples of the associations in Senegal, Zimbabwe and Nigeria are given by Watts, 'Visions of excess', p. 139.

44　Lonsdale, 'Political accountability in African history', p. 138.

45　Consider, for instance, B. Moore, *Social Origins of Dictatorship and Democracy*, Rustow, 'Transitions to democracy', and the essays on Iberia and Latin America in the 1970s and 1980s in G. O'Donnell, P. C. Schmitter and L. Whitehead (eds), *Transitions from Authoritarian Rule: tentative conclusions about uncertain democracies* (Baltimore, MD, Johns Hopkins University Press, 3 vols, 1986).

46　It is an older generation of self-consciously cosmopolitan intellectuals who have argued, like Chinua Achebe, that 'tribalism' disenfranchises because it deprives voters 'of the power to hold the politician truly accountable through common action with other voters across the land': see Achebe, *The Trouble with Nigeria* (London, Heinemann, 1984), pp. 52ff., quoted by Lonsdale, 'Political accountability in African history', p. 141. My sense of the mood of the younger intellectuals comes largely from private conversations.

17

DEMOCRATIZATION IN ASIA

David Potter

Despite the Asian political terrain being so vast, volatile and variegated, there is value in trying to consider democratization trends generally in that part of the world. Comparative evidence from all Asian polities is briefly referred to in what follows although I give a little more attention to Indonesia, South Korea and India for reasons indicated later. I also consider briefly the democratic prospects of Asia's Communist Party mobilization regimes.

Theory

There are at least two broad types of theory of democratization resting in part on comparative Asian evidence. The first, agency-led and structural-functional, singles out a range of variables like political leadership, political culture, ethnic cleavage, political parties and so on that purport to provide an explanation of why democratization has or has not occurred. The work of Diamond, Linz and Lipset, and their colleagues, is an example.[1] In my view, such explanations usually resemble a shopping list which does not, as an ensemble, explain democratization very well, although such variables can provide a useful checklist of factors to be borne in mind when trying to grapple with detailed questions about democracy at different levels within Asian countries and elsewhere. The

From Kathleen Gough, I first heard intelligently argued the case for socialist democracy. During most of her distinguished career she worked on Indian questions, but her last book was on Vietnam, to which I refer briefly below. She died in September 1990, and I offer this chapter as a tribute to her, a former colleague of mine and very dear friend.

other broad type of theory centres on historical structures of class, state and transnational power which have been more or less favourable to democratization. Examples are Barrington Moore[2] and his successors – most recently Rueschemeyer, Stephens and Stephens.[3] Their work, in my view, provides a stronger basis for analysing democratic trends and prospects.

Moore's book created a sensation when it first appeared because it was out of sorts with nearly everything else being said at the time in the dominant paradigm of behavioural political science. The analysis was distinctive in being comparative-historical, rooted in the varying natures of capitalist transformation, or the lack of it, and concerned centrally with changing structures of class and state power which shaped the political trajectories that took place in the countries he examined. His successors have built on his work while struggling with the numerous problems it raised.[4] Moore had little to say about the role of the urban working class or transnational power structures, and Therborn,[5] Skocpol,[6] O'Donnell[7] and others helped to build these and other considerations into the general approach. *Capitalist Development and Democracy* by Rueschemeyer, Stephens and Stephens pushed these ideas further. Their work was based on comparative historical evidence from Europe, Latin America and elsewhere, and the authors suggested that their theoretical propositions and findings provided insights into processes of democratization in Asia too, referring, for example, to South Korean and Taiwanese experiences. Major features of their theory can be indicated under four headings.

Democracy

A broad distinction is made between formal and substantive democracy. The former includes: competition (through elections based on universal adult suffrage and involving multiple political parties) for political offices, at regular intervals, excluding the use of force; accountability of rulers to the ruled through modes of representation and the rule of law; civil and political liberties sufficient to ensure competition and accountability. Substantive democracy is all that plus genuine participation in rule by the majority of citizens. In class-divided societies this majority has less wealth, income, education, honour and (especially) power. Democracy has historically been about lessening the unequal distribution of power, about the empowerment of subordinate classes through the vote, representation, increased participation and so on in the collective political concerns of society. Whether or not a society moves toward democracy is 'fundamentally shaped by the balance of class power', and 'it is the struggle between the dominant and subordinate classes over the right to rule that – more than any other factor – puts democracy on the historical agenda and decides its prospects'.[8] Capitalist development changes class alignments and is therefore fundamentally important for democratic prospects.

Class power

Historically, democratization has been both resisted and pushed forward by the changing dynamics of class relations and different classes pursuing their separate interests. Subordinate classes have usually pushed for democracy, dominant classes nearly always have resisted it. There are other forms of social and economic inequality, including gender and racial divisions, but class inequality has historically been the most important for democratization so far.

Broadly, five classes are singled out, distinctions between their different interests made, and their different orientations to democratization identified on the basis of the authors' comparative history analysis. *Large landlords* as a class have historically been the most anti-democratic force in society (a confirmation of Barrington Moore's finding). One reason for this is that they have been dependent on a large supply of cheap labour, and since democratizaton has tended to improve the position of rural workers (making their labour no longer cheap) landlords have perceived democracy as incompatible with their interests in making adequate profits from their land. Democratization has been resisted where large landlords have been powerful, particularly when they have been closely allied with the state apparatus; democratic prospects have been improved where landlords were weak. The *peasantry and rural workers* as a class have had an interest in democratization but have acted rarely on their own in support of it. They have not always been passive spectators, however, for peasant rebellions have occurred and some plantation proletariats have been well organized and powerful. On the whole, though, the peasantry have been disorganized and comparatively weak as a force for democratization. The *urban working class* has historically been an important force pushing for extension of the suffrage, union rights and other aspects of democratic advance. Capitalist development can strengthen the working class and weaken the landed class, such developments being structurally favourable to the development of democracy. In this way, democracy can be said to emerge out of the contradictions of capitalism. The role of the *bourgeoisie* has been less clear. They have not been as anti-democratic as the large landlords, but neither have they been known to press for substantive democracy. Indeed, there are plenty of cases where the bourgeoisie have supported the crushing of democracy. Their role has varied a lot depending on the alignment of other classes, the position and power of the state, and transnational forces. The ambiguous position of the *salaried and professional middle classes* on democratization has been similar. It depends on the context. Where the working class has been comparatively weak, the middle classes have pushed for democratization to improve their positions. Where the working class has been strong, the middle classes may or may not have been as energetic.

The main general point is that the position of any one class on democratization cannot be considered in isolation from others. Various combinations and alliances of classes have occurred which have been more or less favourable to democracy.

State power

Together with the structure of classes, the role of the state has been utterly fundamental to the success or failure of democratization. For one thing, democratization in a nation-state has been impossible unless state power has first been consolidated, in the sense of the state apparatus and its managers laying claim to a monopoly on the use of violence and coercion in society as the basis for making authoritative decisions on a firm foundation and binding on all. A realm of state power separated from the array of classes in society has been a prerequisite for any democratization demands from subordinate classes being successfully accommodated and implemented in the society generally. For such accommodations to occur, the state must have sufficient power to make them stick, and also must have at least some autonomy in relation to dominant classes, so that it can act against dominant interests when responding to subordinate class demands. A very powerful and almost entirely autonomous state in relation to social classes and groups has provided a most uncongenial setting for democratization. This has been so especially where the military and the police have been strong within the state apparatus. Democratization has had more chance of success in the middle ground between too much and not enough state power. As Rueschemeyer, Stephens and Stephens remark, 'processes of democracy, then, must steer between the Scylla of a dependence of the state on the dominant classes that is incompatible with democracy and the Charybdis of a state machinery too strong to be democratically tamed'.[9]

Capitalist development has historically led to the emergence of a denser civil society. This phenomenon can increasingly provide a counterweight to state power by enhancing the predilections of people in subordinate classes to organize for collective action. The state can also, however, shape civil society for its own purposes by co-opting groups and associations. One type of association is especially important: political parties have been at the interface between civil society and the state, both mobilizing and mediating democratization pressure from groups within subordinate classes, usually in a manner that does not fundamentally threaten dominant class interests. Dominant classes are more likely to accommodate democracy where the party system includes a strong party of the right; where such a party is lacking or no longer able to protect their interests, such classes have been readier to appeal to the military to end democratic rule.

Transnational power

State and classes in any one society have been shaped historically by transnational structures of power. The importance of the transnational can vary depending on the size of the country concerned, its proximity to a world (or important regional) power, the nature and timing of its colonial experience, the extent of its economic dependence within the global economy and so on. Sequence and timing are crucial in determining the effects of such transnational power relations for the democratization prospect. The effects can also be equivocal. Export-led growth based on primary products from plantations may provide a setting for the political organization of workers, but such growth can also strengthen large landowners. Economic dependence generally can delay industrialization and keep the urban working class small, thereby weakening the pro-democracy forces. 'Late' development can involve heavy state interventions and inhibit democracy. Geopolitical dependence can also be unfavourable for democratic consolidation if massive military and economic aid strengthen the state apparatus unduly in relation to the balance of class forces. In this context, the relaxation of international tension and the end of superpower confrontation may improve the democratic prospect. The relation between war and democracy, however, has not been straightforward, and has varied depending on other factors. Military defeat by a foreign power has led to the imposition of democracy, as in Japan. The national mobilization of men and, perhaps especially, women for war or in the face of external threat has also historically led to extensions of the franchise and other democratic advance. Yet war also has strengthened the military in society and within the state, and in the absence of other countervailing forces severely threatented the democratic prospect. Autonomous colonial states dominated by transnational structures of power were the antithesis of democracy, and democracy can for that reason be precarious for countries recently emerged from colonialism (but different types of colonialism, such as British or French, can make a difference).

Transnational ideological and cultural flows can also enhance the democratic prospect. Democracy as a 'good idea', particularly following the end of communism in Eastern Europe and the break-up of the Soviet Union, has through improved communication networks percolated everywhere, even into societies dominated by repressive states and reactionary classes. It also suited the economic interests of the US government, the World Bank and others involved in the global capitalist system in the early 1990s to put 'democratization pressures' on authoritarian regimes.

I have summarized bluntly a complex theory set out and used with great care in a rather large book. No doubt the theory appears heavily deterministic as presented here, and that is to some extent misleading. The roles of leadership, cultural values, chance, error and so on inevitably come into the explanation as contingent factors in particular circumstances, but democratization is finally shaped by the changing structures of class, state and transnational power driven in certain countries by a particular history of capitalist development. There are of course problems with any theory pitched at this level of generalization, and one must always beware of using such propositions in a mechanical way without careful attention to how they work out (and sometimes do not work out) in unique ways in individual cases.

Asian Political Terrain

Bearing in mind such general propositions about class, state and transnational structures of power, the first thing that strikes one about Asia this century in a general way is the prevalence of colonialism, war, authoritarian state power, large (and mostly disorganized) peasantries and comparatively small organized working classes – not a congenial setting for democracy. Indeed, there have been few democracies in Asia until recently, and even they have struggled.

Much of Asia this century was ruled by colonial states until the 1940s (or later). Most of colonial Asia then collapsed suddenly in 1941-2. The Japanese invaded Pearl Harbor on 7 December 1941, they were in Hong Kong by 25 December, Manila by 2 January, Kuala Lumpur by 11 January,

Singapore by 15 February and Rangoon by 7 March; by the end of April 1942, western colonial power had completely gone in South-East Asia, the Japanese were launching an attack on India in the jungles of Assam and engaged in a major war on the Chinese mainland. The Asian War of 1941–5 was a momentous transnational event that all of Asia, uniquely, shared directly or indirectly. The war had a number of political consequences, mostly negative in terms of democratic prospects. For example, Japanese military administrations demonstrated throughout Asia the principle of army participation in politics and they encouraged the formation of indigenous military and paramilitary forces, which formed the core of post-war national armies. Western security forces also encouraged the formation of clandestine, armed underground forces; for example, Ho Chi Minh in Vietnam. Towards the end of the war the Japanese attempted to build indigenous support for the war effort in the occupied countries by making concessions to, and building up, nationalist groups and leaders. Another consequence of the war: the legitimacy of colonial rule was completely undermined. Sjahrir in Indonesia remarked that 'all layers of society came to see the past in another light. If these barbarians [the Japanese] had been able to replace the old colonial authority, why had that authority been necessary at all?'[10]

The Asian War of 1941–5 ended even more abruptly than it began – with Hiroshima on 6 August, Nagasaki on 9 August, and Japanese unconditional surrender on 14 August. Japanese overlords and occupying forces across Asia immediately vanished. No one saw this sudden denouement coming, least of all the former European colonialists. Into this temporary power vacuum stepped armed Asian nationalist leaders and groupings, including socialist ones. The stage was set for subsequent violent conflicts in the 1940s and 1950s between assertive nationalist movements which had already experienced 'independence' and returning colonialists attempting to reimpose their rule in changed circumstances.

South Asia had a less traumatic experience. India and Ceylon mobilized for the war, but avoided military occupation by the Japanese. British colonial states continued to rule there throughout the war, with civilian control of the military within the apparatus of the state firmly maintained. India and Ceylon established democracies after the war which, most unusually for Asia, have endured (more or less). The only other enduring democracy in Asia dating from the 1940s is Japan; significantly for this discussion, the military was virtually abolished when the conquering Americans imposed democracy there. Three other enduring democracies have been Malaysia (given independence by the British in 1957), Singapore (breaking free from Malaya in 1965) and Papua New Guinea (granted independence by the Australians in 1975).

All the other twenty-six political regimes in Asia had never been a democracy or had only fairly brief acquaintances with it. By the beginning of the 1980s, there were: the six enduring (formal) democracies; seven military dictatorships or regimes controlled by a civilian party beholden to the military – Pakistan, Bangladesh, Burma, Indonesia, Taiwan, the Philippines and South Korea; five royal autocratic or colonial regimes – Brunei, Bhutan, the Maldives, Nepal and Hong Kong; two other authoritarian regimes – Afghanistan (in flux at the time) and Thailand (a regime in which there was a sort of trade-off between the military, the bureaucracy, the royal court and certain democratically orientated groupings and parties, with the military tending to be the final arbiter in the balances that had been periodically struck); and six communist party mobilization regimes pursuing a socialist model of development – China, North Korea, Mongolia, Vietnam, Laos and Kampuchea (Cambodia). Generally, then, the Asian political terrain was marked in the early 1980s predominantly by autonomous, heavily armed authoritarian states. Their presence owed much to a history of colonialism and war, not only the 1941–5 war but subsequent war and revolutionary violence – in Korea, Malaysia, Vietnam, Cambodia, the Philippines, Indonesia and East Timor, Afghanistan, Sri Lanka, India and Pakistan, and so on and on. Asia had probably been, during the period 1940–80, the most violent region in the world, and this stoked the persistence of authoritarian states, and the importance of the military and the police within them. The presence of such concentrations of state power in most of Asia bedevilled the struggle for democracy there. Such states continue to pose a problem for democratization.

The problems such states have posed, however, have not been insuperable. By the early 1990s there had been an important development. Seven of those twenty authoritarian regimes had started on the road to democracy – Pakistan, Bangladesh, Nepal, the Philippines, Taiwan, South Korea and Mongolia. That this occurred underlines the importance of considering state power not on its own but in relation to class and transnational power. Doing so can suggest possible explanations of why these states were moving in that direction.

Explaining (Capitalist) Democratization

Precisely how state, class and transnational power structures have combined to shape capitalist development in a democratic direction will clearly vary from case to case depending on many factors, including the unique characteristics of the particular political economy concerned. The combinations also vary depending on the point at which a regime is located on the route to democracy. In the early 1990s, for example, Indonesia had not yet begun democratization, South Korea had definitely started on the route, and India had been on it since the 1940s. In this section I want to look briefly at these three examples and what some of the theoretical propositions suggest regarding explanations of their recent democratization experiences.

Indonesia and South Korea are examples of Asian countries in which capitalist industrialization has been flourishing within authoritarian state structures. As that process spreads and deepens, the changing character of class, state and transnational structures of power can drive the regime in a democratic direction, for a sequence of reasons Robison[11] and others have suggested:

1 The rapid development of (late) industrial capitalism in Asia created new and initially fragile capital-owning classes; and these developments were nurtured by authoritarian (frequently military-dominated) states.

2 Such authoritarian states were appropriate agents for undertaking a number of vital political and economic functions essential to the growth of (late) capitalism: these included the suppression of reformist or revolutionary threats from workers and peasants, supplying essential investment for heavy industry and economic infrastructure, providing cheap credit and tariff protection for capitalists, enforcing trade monopolies, making lucrative contracts with capitalist entrepreneurs for supply and construction work needed by the state, helping to provide skilled and disciplined low-wage labour, and so on.

3 There developed what amounted to a 'pact of domination' between leading capitalists and the military-bureaucratic leaders of the state apparatus based upon a 'complex conjuncture' of common interests. Together, state and class drove forward late capitalist development.

4 As capitalist industrialization proceeded, however, the authoritarian state gradually came under increasing pressure from the growing power of the capital-owning and middle classes, who found the economic and social controls of the authoritarian state increasingly irksome. This weakened the pact of domination, set up complex contradictions and conflicts between the dominant classes and the state, and weakened the social basis of authoritarian rule.

5 Those domestic structural transformations were reinforced by transnational structures of power as the country became more integrated into the international division of labour and moved into a phase of

export-orientated industrialization. The freer movement of goods, labour and capital tended to be easier in democratic or semi-democratic regimes, and it was in the interest of transnational capitalist enterprises to advocate some form of democracy as a way of 'opening up' the markets of exclusionary authoritarian regimes to foreign goods and services. Democratization was increasingly seen by important people in the country as a necessary ticket for membership in the 'advanced' international club to which they aspired, and this also provided a strong incentive for economic and political liberalization.

6   A contingent factor in the 1980s was the weakening of authoritarian states due to growing economic crises. Growing balance of payments deficits, debt, inflation and fiscal crises encouraged such states to hand over economic responsibility for development to the urban bourgeoisie. Democratization was a way of spreading and sharing responsibilities, and defusing the mobilization of discontent.

There is nothing automatic about (late) capitalist development of this kind leading in a democratic direction. Both Indonesia and South Korea, for example, can be said to have been 'on' the earlier stages of that route. State and class drove capitalist development forward with impressive speed in both countries. South Korea's average annual growth rate of 6.8 per cent (GNP per capita) between 1965 and 1988 was the highest in the world (after Botswana), and only a handful of countries had a higher growth rate than Indonesia's (4.3 per cent); accompanying such growth was an extraordinary burst of capitalist industrialization – the industrial sector as a percentage of GDP leaping up in both countries between 1965 and 1988 (13–36 per cent in Indonesia, 25–43 per cent in South Korea).[12] Both countries also had authoritarian state structures. Yet South Korea had started democratization by the early 1990s and Indonesia had not. Why the difference?

One important reason was that by 1990 about 70 per cent of South Korea's population were concentrated in the towns and cities, providing the workforce and service sector for that industrial burst, in a comparatively compact country; compact, that is, compared to Indonesia, where there were more than four times as many people in a dispersed country, less than 30 per cent of whom were concentrated in urban areas. In such circumstances, one might expect the working class in South Korea, if it were organized, to be a more powerful force for democratization than its counterpart in Indonesia, and this indeed has been the case. A remarkable study of the Korean labour movement by Ogle has documented how Korean workers, both men and women, have provided cheap labour but also fought repeatedly for union rights, in the teeth of terrible repression by the authoritarian Korean state backed by the US government; and by the late 1980s, as democratic accommodations began to be made, a 'new egalitarianism took shape and became institutionalized in what has come to be called the *minju nodong oondong*, or the democratic labour movement', which now confronts the official state-sponsored Federation of Korean Trade Unions and which 'creates new possibilities for South Korea to move beyond the militarized authoritarianism' that has been dominant.[13] Mass action by organized workers, the formation of many new unions and of other associations of workers demanding an improvement in their conditions of work has been an important ingredient in South Korea's democratic beginning. Capitalist development is also contributing to the increasing vigour of civil society in the countryside.[14]

A mobilized working class pushing for democracy *vis-à-vis* South Korea's authoritarian state and dominant bourgeois class has been buttressed by the more pro-democracy character of transnational power. For one thing, the lessening of military tension with North Korea has increased the sense of physical security for most South Koreans, and this, together with greater economic security for many people due to rising living standards, has meant that 'gradually the central concern of an increasing number of people [in South Korea] has shifted ... to the quality of life, especially political life'.[15] More particularly, the posture of the US government changed from one consistently supporting the succession of authoritarian regimes in South Korea to one advocating limited democratization along Japanese lines with which capitalists would be comfortable. In the late 1980s, for example, the American Embassy in Seoul was 'proffering to the men who rule South Korea' a model of democracy with 'one-party rule, with a legitimate but impotent opposition – a labour party of some sort to accommodate the urban working class and render it politically docile'.[16] This change in orientation was not due to the sudden conversion of the US government to the intrinsic desirability of democratization; it was based on US economic interests – some democratization in South Korea would mean a rise in wages for the workers, which would make Korean exports to the US less competitive. Authoritarian governments in Korea had held wages down. Some democratization would also open up Asian markets to American goods and service industries.

The Americans had also had a hand nearly forty years earlier in clearing the Korean countryside of a backward-looking landlord class, whose continuing existence could have made democratization even more difficult than it was. Japanese colonialism earlier in the century had grounded the centuries-old landlord class in Korea even more firmly in the agrarian structure, in order 'to extract rice and keep peasants quiet'.[17] Then, in the late 1940s, the Americans urged radical land reform, but no redistribution occurred before the North Koreans occupied most of the South in the summer of 1950 and landlords were summarily dispossessed. When the South was cleared of these revolutionaries, the Americans insisted that the landlords not be allowed back on the land; they 'received state bonds convertible to industrial wealth'.[18]

Indonesia, like South Korea, experienced similar pro-democracy pressure from the US government and transnational capitalism, and it also had no large landlord class. Unlike South Korea, however, there was no powerful, mobilized working class pressing from below for democracy, and the peasantry were either scattered on numerous islands or not well organized. State power had been unyielding and was widely known throughout Indonesia to be capable of ferocious repression; the force used in East Timor has been very heavy indeed and the mass slaughter of Indonesian communists in late 1965 was still a vivid reminder to those who lived through that period. In the circumstances it has not been surprising that considerable attention has been given to the possible role in democratization of the salaried and professional middle classes. But it seems that in the early 1990s they were divided in that the

> trading and manufacturing element of the middle class will, as long as it remains relatively small and comparatively rich in a sea of poverty, not endanger its position of privilege and is more likely to ally itself to the political elite, while the much stronger salaried middle class has a vested interest in maintaining its own power in what is essentially a bureaucratic polity.[19]

A substantial capital-owning class (including many former military personnel) has gained in importance and has been nurtured by, and accommodated within, the authoritarian state. Pressure from abroad and from sections of the bourgeoisie and middle classes (including Indonesian technocrats trained in the US, especially the 'Berkeley Mafia') has not yet 'opened up' the polity and produced a democratic beginning, but if rapid economic growth and reduced transnational tensions persist, then domestic and international pressures on the authoritarian state are likely to intensify.

'Strong' states have provided formidable opposition to (capitalist) democratization in Indonesia and South Korea. Strong states have also figured centrally in analyses of the struggle for democracy in other Asian regimes; for example, Taiwan,[20] the Philippines,[21] Thailand,[22] Myanmar (Burma),[23] Bangladesh,[24] Pakistan,[25] and Nepal.[26] Even the (comparatively few) more established Asian democracies have been distinguished by a fairly 'heavy' state presence (Papua New Guinea is an exception). For example, Japan's economic success owed much to administrative guidance; that is, the authority of officials in the various ministries 'to issue directions (*shiji*), requests (*yōbō*), warnings (*keikoku*), suggestions (*kankoku*), and encouragements (*kanshō*) to enterprises or clients within a particular ministry's jurisdiction'.[27] Penalties for non-compliance were never specified, but since such guidance was normally couched in the national interest few objections were raised. The Japanese press used to cite the case of a bank executive who called on the Ministry of Finance to protest that his bank could not absorb the full quota of government bonds assigned to it by administrative guidance. A ministry official replied, 'So you think your bank can survive even after Japan collapses? Go back and tell your president exactly what I said.'[28]

Together with a fairly 'heavy' state presence in Asian democracies there has been a tendency for political competition and accountability to be narrowed somewhat. Although there have been multiple parties contesting elections, one dominant party has tended to prevail and repeatedly form governments. This has been the case in Japan[29] with the LDP (Liberal Democratic Party), Singapore[30] with the PAP (People's Action Party), Malaysia[31] with the various alliances dominated by UNMO (United Malays National Organization), and Sri Lanka[32] since 1973 with the UNP (United National Party). Such one-party dominance can also compromise somewhat the political accountability that periodic elections are meant to provide. India's federalism has been perhaps a hybrid case, in that the country's national politics has tended until recently to be one-party dominant, with the Congress regularly forming governments despite winning a minority of the votes cast, while the individual states in India's federalism have been very competitive.[33] Papua New Guinea, the exception, has been fully competitive since it was granted independence in 1975, with a high turnover of MPs and changes of government produced by regular elections with competitive party activity and high voter turnouts.[34]

What about civil and political liberties? In an abstract world of pure values the protection of such individual liberties is widely regarded as the *sine qua non* of democracies. In Asia, the state, even in democratic regimes, has been pretty rough on individuals opposed to its rule. Assessments of the prevalence of individual liberties in different societies are notoriously varied, but the Dutch PIOOM Reports (Projects for the Interdisciplinary Study of Root Causes of Human Rights Violations), in measuring what they called 'violations of the integrity of the person', came up with the data for 1980 and 1988 for sixteen Asian countries that are set out in table 17.1.

TABLE 17.1 Observance of integrity of the person in selected Asian countries, 1980 and 1988

Country	AI 1980	SD 1980	AI 1988	SD 1988
Afghanistan	5	5	4	5
Bangladesh	3	3	3	3
Burma/Myanmar	–	3	5	5
China	3	3	3	3
India	4	3	4	4
Indonesia	4	3	3	3
Japan	–	1	2	1
Kampuchea	3	3	3	4
Laos	3	3	3	3
Malaysia	2	2	2	2
Pakistan	3	3	3	3
Philippines	4	3	3	3
Singapore	3	3	2	2
South Korea	3	3	3	2
Thailand	3	3	2	3
Vietnam	3	3	3	3

AI = based on reports of Amnesty International
SD = based on reports from the US State Department

Level 1: Countries live under a secure rule of law, people are not imprisoned for their views, and torture is rare or exceptional. Political murders are extremely rare.

Level 2: There is a limited amount of imprisonment for non-violent activity. However, few persons are affected, and torture and beating are exceptional. Political murder is rare.

Level 3: There is extensive political imprisonment, or a recent history of such imprisonment. Execution or other political murders and brutality may be common. Unlimited detention, with or without trial, for political views is accepted.

Level 4: The practices of level 3 are expanded to larger numbers. Murders, disappearances, and torture are a common part of life. In spite of its generality, on this level terror affects primarily those who interest themselves in politics or ideas.

Level 5: The terrorism of level 4 has been expanded to the whole population. The leaders of these societies place no limits on the means or thoroughness with which they pursue personal or ideological goals.

Source: derived from data in *PIOOM Newsletter and Progress Report*, 2:2 (Autumn 1990), pp. 18–20.

These data suggest two things of importance. First, with the exception of only two or three countries the integrity of the person and political rights generally were more or less severely compromised (levels 3–5) in the 1980s throughout Asia. Indeed, comparative evidence from other regions of the world suggests the state was generally tougher on the individual in Asia than elsewhere.[35] Second, there was no consistent association between levels of toughness and formal democracy. Japan and Malaysia (and Singapore in 1988) were on levels 1 and 2, but India, perhaps the best-known democracy in the so-called developing world, was on level 4. Regimes starting on a democratization route, like the Philippines, South Korea, Bangladesh and Pakistan, tended to be on level 3. Non-democratic regimes were also on level 3, except for Afghanistan and Burma (in 1988) on level 5. The four Communist Party mobilization regimes in table 17.1 – China, Kampuchea, Laos and Vietnam – were all on level 3 and on a par with much of the rest of Asia.

Despite the authoritarian 'edge' to Asia's few democracies, they have endured as democracies for some time and in three cases for nearly half a century. India has been perhaps the outstanding example. How does one explain India's democratization in terms of class, state and transnational structures of power?

Barrington Moore did it many years ago (although he neglected the transnational) and it is useful to summarize his answer. Moore's comparative analysis generally identified three historical routes to the modern world. Democracy, as in England and France, emerged in conditions where a strong and independent bourgeoisie came into being in opposition to the past regime and managed to exert its control over national policy, while at the same time a rough balance was maintained between the landed upper classes and the state, and where the influence of the peasantry was negligible or non-existent because they were transformed or destroyed by lords and others engaged in the commercialization of agriculture. Fascism, as in Japan and Germany, emerged in conditions where the urban bourgeoisie was comparatively weak and relied on the dominant landed upper classes to sponsor the commercialization of agriculture through their domination of the state, which enforced labour discipline among the peasantry. Communist revolution, as in China, occurred in conditions where the urban bourgeoisie was weak and dominated by the state, the link between the peasantry and the landlords was weak, the landlords failed to commercialize agriculture, and the peasantry was cohesive and found allies with organizational skills. India, for Moore, was a rather special case. Capitalist development had been stifled up to the 1940s because the colonial state had protected the landed upper classes and enabled them to pocket much of the economic surplus generated by the peasants, rather than directing that surplus towards industrial growth. The urban bourgeoisie was therefore weak, the landed upper classes saw little incentive to commercialize agriculture, the peasantry lacked the cohesion and leadership for political actions, and none of these classes had made a revolutionary break from the past. For Moore, this was an unpromising structural framework for

democratization, given his 'route to democracy' indicated above, yet
democracy did emerge. Why?

Moore's answer is complex but he summarizes it like this:

> British rule rested mainly on the Indian upper classes in the countryside, native
> princes and larger landowners in many, but not all, parts of the country ...
> Some major political consequences of the tendency to rely on the upper strata
> in the countryside deserve to be noticed right away ... This tendency alienated
> the commercial and professional classes, the new Indian bourgeoisie, as it
> slowly put in an appearance during the course of the nineteenth century. By
> splitting the landed upper classes from the weak and rising urban leaders, the
> English presence prevented the formation of the characteristic reactionary
> coalition on the German or Japanese models. This may be judged a decisive
> contribution towards the eventual establishment of parliamentary democracy
> on Indian soil, at least as important as the osmosis of English ideas through
> Indian professional classes. Without at least some favourable structural condi-
> tions, the ideas could scarcely have been more than literary playthings. Finally,
> the British presence drove the Indian bourgeoisie to an accommodation with
> the peasantry in order to obtain a massive base.[36]

Thus some of the conditions in the more general route to democracy
were there in India, but others were not (for example, no commercialization of agriculture or transformation of the peasantry, no vigorous and
dominant indigenous bourgeoisie). That is why Moore believed that
India's new formal democracy was rather precarious.

By the early 1990s it was not, perhaps, quite so precarious.[37] The
princes and large landlords had mostly gone as a consequence of the
implementation of various land reform and other measures in different
regions. They were gradually replaced by a new class of owner-
cultivators, or 'rich peasants'[38] or 'bullock capitalists',[39] who formed a substantial minority of the rural population. The dominance patterns in
which they were involved varied considerably from region to region.[40] In
most areas, however, this class became well represented in state
legislatures within India's federalism, was influential in relation to the
local state bureaucracy including the police, and was supportive of the
formal democracy locally that served its interests. Women, poor peasants,
agricultural labourers, ethnic and religious minorities and other
oppressed peoples in the countryside could vote periodically, but otherwise were not genuinely accommodated within the democratic formalism
of the local state (West Bengal and Kerala were partial exceptions). It
would be very misleading, however, to portray the rich peasant class as
totally dominant in relation to a supine rural underclass; there were complex arrays locally of conventional modes of participation involving the
underclass, sometimes organized by local elites in non-governmental
organizations (NGOs) and other associations in civil society, and some-

times not.[41] There were also myriad forms of collective action and protest.[42] In many areas, the system operated to provide local elites (not only from the rich peasantry) with a stake in the formal democracy of the local state, giving a certain resilience to India's democracy.[43] Recently, local elites in many areas (including thugs in Bihar and elsewhere) with little patience for, or need of, democracy have come more to the fore in local politics, and levels of state repression and social violence in the countryside have been increasing, leading some scholars to argue that 'a grave systemic crisis is in progress'.[44]

At the national level, particularly by the early 1990s, the indigenous capitalist class had become far more vigorous and powerful *vis-à-vis* the national state and the ruling Congress Party.[45] Industrial licensing controls had been loosened, restrictions on foreign collaboration eased, a variety of supports for the private corporate sector of the economy introduced, and other measures implemented which hastened capitalist development and strengthened the growing power of capital. Like the 'bullock capitalists', the capitalist class supported the continuation of the formal democracy nationally that broadly served their interests. Organized interests from below, like the industrial working class, urban trade associations, professional groups and civil servants, comprised only about 10 per cent of the population of the country and tended to be fragmented nationally.[46] As the state became less autonomous in relation to the dominant classes, it also became more brutal in its handling of communal (religious, caste, ethnic) conflicts and political opposition;[47] tougher repressive legislation has been passed and implemented by central and state governments to suppress or silence permanently political dissidents, labour leaders, civil rights activists and other opponents of the regime, especially in Punjab, Assam and Kashmir (thus India's place in level 4 in table 17.1). The danger for democracy is that the Indian state nationally and locally is gradually losing its autonomy in relation to dominant classes while becoming too impervious to democratic demands from increasingly restless political movements grounded in subordinate classes.

Communist Party Regimes

In Asia's Communist Party mobilization regimes, competition and accountability and the maintenance of civil and political liberties have been severely circumscribed. Communists argue that in classless societies competitive elections have a different and more limited function, and that in any event political competition in bourgeois democracies is itself profoundly compromised because the workers and peasants cannot vote not to have capitalism, and capitalism serves the narrow interests of an exploiting class. Hoang Tung, director of the Committee of Social Sciences in Hanoi, put the issue this way in 1982, when Kathleen Gough challenged him to answer the charge that elections to the National Assembly in Vietnam were rubber-stamp affairs:

> 'Capitalist democracy has its own characteristics', he said. 'You have some limited mass media of the proletariat, and some right of debate with the bourgeoisie, but the bourgeoisie still has full control of the electoral process. They will never let the communists win the elections, and they select the main candidates . . .
>
> When the proletariat comes to power, it does the same. It will not let the remnants of the former forces play a strong role. It's true that some candidates get 99 per cent of the vote, because there are no surviving classes.
>
> The main point is that *before* the provinces and cities select the candidates . . . [they] have group discussions with all the mass organizations. In this way they ensure that workers, peasants, intellectuals, women, and ethnic minorities are all represented. During the actual campaign there is not much debate, but the internal discussions before the candidates are selected are very intense. It's not entirely democratic, but it's very much so. The final voting *is* mainly ratification, to show that the candidates have the people's trust, and to see who has the most trust. But the voters do cross out the names of some candidates . . . The main idea is internal negotiations and arrangements that have a democratic character'.[48]

Of the 496 members elected in 1981, for example, 20 per cent were industrial workers, 18 per cent peasants, 22 per cent technicians, scientists, artists and academics, 24 per cent political cadres working in government service, the armed forces or mass organizations, and 15 per cent members of ethnic minorities from several walks of life. Twenty-two per cent were women. Only 16 per cent were Communist Party members. The Assembly met twice a year in the 1980s, each time for two to four weeks. The Assembly normally ratified legislation and ministerial appointments proposed by the Council of State, the Central Committee and the Political Bureau of the party. However, some draft laws, directives and actions gave rise to sharp conflict and, occasionally, storms of protest. They were then modified. Vietnamese communists suggest on the basis of such activities that there has been somewhat more competition and accountability in Vietnam than has been generally recognized by western critics.

As for civil and political liberties, the four communist regimes in table 17.1 were all placed on level three, better than India in the 1980s but worse than Asia's other formal democracies. Prominent in communist regimes was the utter denial of political liberties to capitalists and others opposed to socialist development.

As one would expect in mobilization regimes, participation in political life tended to be fuller than in formal democracies elsewhere. 'China's democracy involves participation without influence', a major study ...ncluded.[49] In Vietnam, the Peasant Union, the Trades Unions, the Women's Union and other mass organizations and their local branches were also tied into the decision-making structures of the party, and although these organizations were usually considered by critics as only manifestations of political mobilization, there was no doubt that they also debated policy proposals vigorously and frequently modified them, even important policies. Numerous examples are described in Kathleen Gough's remarkable study of Vietnam's political economy, in which she concluded that Vietnamese citizens 'probably have more chance than do the bulk of US citizens of complaining to local authorities (People's Councils and Committees, People's Control Commission and mass organizations of various kinds) about supplies, marketing, housing, employment, welfare services, education, public safety, theft, corruption, wife-beating, and a host of other problems'; and on such national issues as 'farm policies, welfare institutions, social security, family legislation and the rights of women, it seems that ordinary Vietnamese influence their government more than do Americans'. For example, Vietnamese women 'have claimed and won free day care, health care, maternity care, a six-month paid maternity leave, and even a one-day paid holiday during menstruation, rights still unavailable to most US women workers'.[50]

So, Asian Communist Party regimes have not been formal democracies in terms of competition, accountability and political liberties, even though participation has been extensive and citizens have got used to voting periodically in local elections. Given the 'democracy contagion' triggered by what has happened recently in Eastern Europe and else-where, what are the prospects for democracy in the Asian communist world? It is tempting to retreat from this question on the ground that no one really knows, and invoke the Vietnamese proverb: 'if you know something, speak, but if you don't know, lean against the pillar and listen.'[51]

One thing, however, is clear: it is a mistake to lump together all Communist Party regimes and assume roughly that what happened in Eastern Europe yesterday will happen in Asia tomorrow. Even scholars on the left, like Miliband, have tended to assume that all Communist Party regimes now share a common crisis.[52] The simple point is that each Communist Party regime is quite distinctive, even in Asia as between, for example, China,[53] North Korea,[54] Vietnam[55] and Laos.[56] In Mongolia,[57] a pro-democracy movement in 1990 launched the political slogan

'Mongols, mount up!' (there were about 2.2 million horses in Mongolia at that time, on average just over one per head of population), and this movement led quickly to multi-party elections being held that year for the first time. But Mongolia is not a good indicator of how democratization in other Asian Communist Party regimes may proceed. An important factor in Mongolia's Communist Party regime had been the presence of Soviet troops, and their departure in 1990 probably assisted democratization, but the presence or absence of Soviet troops is of no consequence in other Asian communist regimes.

China certainly cannot be lumped together with other communist regimes. It has unusual prominence within Asia, and its sheer size rules out any speedy conquest by capitalism. Furthermore, within an Asian context China's model of development has had fairly impressive results, despite enormous problems and setbacks; for example, its average annual growth rate (GNP per capita) between 1965 and 1988 was 5.4 per cent, higher than Japan (4.3 per cent), Indonesia (4.3 per cent) and Malaysia (4.0 per cent), and of course far higher than the US (1.6 per cent) or the UK (1.8 per cent).[58] While this was occurring, China was moving from a command economy towards a form of market economy more successfully perhaps than other Communist Party regimes have done so far, and it was doing it in its own way without being overwhelmed by expert advice from the management schools of the capitalist world. Economic reforms together with serious economic problems continued in the early 1990s. Deng Xiaoping told an audience in Shenzen special economic zone in January 1992 that 'reforms and greater openness are China's only way out' and 'if capitalism had something good, then socialism should bring it over and use it'.[59] Economic reforms were also prompting certain political developments; for example, the National People's Congress was gradually taking on a more powerful role in the political system, increasing its legislative involvement in, and oversight of, political decisions by the state and the party.[60] If Deng's 'reforms and greater openness' persist, it has been suggested that China just might offer favourable terrain for the working out in due course of some hybrid form of substantive democracy, an essentially 'non-capitalist but complex and self-governing society'.[61]

Other Communist Party regimes are more vulnerable to wholesale capitalist penetration. If one analyses them in terms of class, state and transnational structures of power, then democratic prospects look distinctly unpromising, at least in the medium term. Take Vietnam. Class and state structures? Roughly, Vietnam in the early 1990s had no capitalism, no capitalist class (to speak of), no landlord class, a powerful state apparatus controlled primarily by a combination of party and state elites together with economic elites managing state enterprises, considerable participation in economic, political and social life by workers and peasants in party-linked mass organizations, but a weak civil society with few autonomous associations of any consequence. Transnational structures? Global capitalism was not only about to break in but Vietnam was reaching out to engage with it. For example, American business interests were keen to begin serious economic activity there and Vietnam had approached the World Bank for help, as reduction of economic assistance from Eastern Europe and the former Soviet Union was presenting formidable economic problems. At the same time, transnational structures of power were shifting within Asia in new ways, as Asian countries were reshaping economic, political and security ties through ASEAN (Association of South-East Asian Nations) and in other ways. In early 1992, for example, Vietnam and Laos were on the point of signing the ASEAN treaty of friendship and cooperation as a first step toward membership of the association (which included Brunei, Indonesia, Malaysia, the Philippines, Singapore and Thailand), and there were plans to put together an East Asian Economic Caucus linking an enlarged ASEAN with Japan, Korea and Taiwan. The opening up of Vietnam and the reappearance of capitalism and capitalists there are likely consequences. The combination of a fragile capitalist class closely aligned to a powerful state apparatus with a weak civil society does not look a promising structural context for democratization.

The great unknown, however, concerns civil society. Communist Party regimes in Asia have been noted for the extent to which workers and peasants, women and ethnic minorities and other disadvantaged groups have participated in political life through party-linked mass organizations and other associations. As such regimes are 'opened up' and party discipline over such organizations relaxes, several scenarios are possible. Such mass organizations may wither, become moribund, and die out. But it is also just possible that they may remain active and in a changing political context become vigorous forces pushing towards substantive democracy. Capitalist development has been intrinsically inegalitarian everywhere, incapable of allowing anything more than formal democracy. Perhaps mass organizations and participative modes of political life in post-communist regimes in Asia will prosper and be able, within the context of an initially more fragile capitalism, to push democracy further.

Conclusion

I am painfully aware that various important issues have been ignored during this rapid tour throughout the Asian political terrain aimed at suggesting why democratization has struggled there. I want to mention two such issues by way of conclusion. First, I have not hesitated to use an explanatory framework grounded in western concepts such as 'capitalism', 'class', 'state' and 'transnational structure of power'. Some orientalists would object to these concepts on the grounds that they fail to capture the uniqueness of particular Asian social and cultural forms. My position is that, although there is value in studying the uniqueness of particular cultures, there is also value in addressing general questions requiring transnational comparative analysis, and the meanings of indigenous Asian concepts of a more general nature required for such an analysis are very close to the meanings of the general western concepts used here. Second, there are large issues around the relationships between capitalism and democracy. The particular Asian evidence surveyed in this chapter may appear to support the general argument that capitalist development (and its internal contradictions) is a necessary condition for democratization. But any such proposition is surely too narrow. Capitalist development can change class, state and transnational structures of power towards alignments more favourable to democratization, but so can the development of other economic forms. What matters for democratization, and the move from formal towards more substantive forms of democracy, is the alignments themselves, which involve (among other things) the break-up of overwhelming concentrations of economic and political power, the growing power of men and women in subordinate classes, and the development of more egalitarian social and economic relations throughout society.

NOTES

1 L. Diamond, J. Linz and S. Lipset (eds), *Democracy in Developing Countries: Asia* (London, Adamantine Press, 1989). There are companion volumes on Africa and Latin America.
2 B. Moore, *Social Origins of Dictatorship and Democracy: lord and peasant in the making of the modern world* (Boston, MA, Beacon Press, 1966).
3 D. Rueschemeyer, E. Stephens and J. Stephens, *Capitalist Development and Democracy* (Cambridge, Polity Press, 1992).
4 I have discussed Moore's book at length, with particular reference to India, in D. Potter, *Lords, Peasants and Politics* (Milton Keynes, Open University Press, 1974). The best critical review, of the hundreds that have appeared, is by T. Skocpol, in *Politics and Society*, 4 (1973), 1–34.
5 G. Therborn, 'The rule of capital and the rise of democracy', *New Left Review*, 103 (1977), 3–41.
6 T. Skocpol, *States and Social Revolutions: a comparative analysis of France, Russia and China* (Cambridge, Cambridge University Press, 1979).
7 G. O'Donnell, P. Schmitter and L. Whitehead (eds), *Transitions from Authoritarian*

Rule: prospects for democracy (Baltimore, MD, John Hopkins University Press, 4 vols, 1986).

8 Rueschemeyer et al., *Capitalist Development and Democracy*, p. 47.

9 Rueschemeyer et al., *Capitalist Development and Democracy*, p. 66.

10 Cited in C. Thorne, *The Far Eastern War: states and societies, 1941–45* (London, Unwin Paperbacks, 1986), p. 301.

11 R. Robison, 'Authoritarian states, capital-owning classes, and the politics of newly industrialising countries: the case of Indonesia', *World Politics*, 26 (1988), 52–74.

12 World Bank, *World Development Report 1990: Poverty* (Oxford, Oxford University Press, 1990), pp. 178–9 and 182–3.

13 G. Ogle, *South Korea: dissent within the economic miracle* (London, Zed Books, 1990), p. 158.

14 M. Moore, 'Economic growth and the rise of civil society; agriculture in Taiwan and South Korea', in G. White (ed.), *Developmental States in East Asia* (London, Macmillan, 1988), pp. 113–52.

15 Chong-min Park, 'Authoritarian rule in South Korea: political support and governmental performance', *Asian Survey*, 31 (August 1991), p. 759.

16 B. Cummings, 'The abortive abertura: South Korea in the light of Latin American experience', *New Left Review*, 173 (1989), p. 34.

17 Cummings, 'Abertura', p. 11.

18 Cummings, 'Abertura', p. 12. For a critique of Cummings and the general approach taken here on South Korea, see J. Cotton, 'Understanding the state in South Korea: bureaucratic–authoritarian or state autonomy theory?', *Comparative Political Studies*, 24 (1992), 512–31.

19 U. Sundhaussen, 'Indonesia: past and present encounters with democracy', in Diamond et al., *Democracy: Asia*, p. 459.

20 L. Liu, 'Self determination, independence and the process of democratization in Taiwan', *Asian Profile*, 19 (1991), 197–205; D. Hickey, 'Tiananmen's tremors: the economic, political and strategic impact of the Democracy Movement on Taiwan', *Issues and Studies*, 27 (1991), 36–57.

21 R. Tiglao, 'March of pluralism: democracy takes root despite hazards and obstacles', *Far Eastern Economic Review*, 153 (5 Sept. 1991), 16–18; C. Landé, 'Manila's malaise', *Journal of Democracy*, 2 (1991), 45–57.

22 K. Hewison, 'The state and capitalist development in Thailand', in J. Taylor and A. Turton (eds), *Sociology of 'Developing Societies' in Southeast Asia* (London, Macmillan, 1988).

23 R. Taylor, *The State in Burma* (London, Hurst, 1987); see also R. Taylor, 'Change in Burma: political demands and military power', *Asian Affairs*, 32 (1991), 131–41.

24 B. Crow, 'The state in Bangladesh: the extension of a weak state', in S. Mitra (ed.), *The Post-Colonial State in Asia* (Hemel Hempstead, Harvester Wheatsheaf, 1990), pp. 193–223.

25 H. Alavi, 'State and class', in H. Gardezi and J. Rashid (eds), *Pakistan: the roots of dictatorship* (London, Zed Press, 1983); see also D. Taylor, 'Parties, elections and democracy in Pakistan', *Journal of Commonwealth and Comparative Politics*, 30 (1992), 96–116.

26 A. Hall, 'Constructing democracy: progress and prospects in Nepal', *Journal of Commonwealth and Comparative Politics*, 30 (1992), 85–95.

27 C. Johnson, *MITI and the Japanese Miracle: the growth of industrial policy, 1925–1975* (Stanford, Stanford University Press, 1982), p. 265.

28 *Mainichi Daily News* (8 Jan. 1976), cited in Johnson, *MITI*, pp. 266–7.

29 B. Eccleston, *State and Society in Post-war Japan* (Cambridge, Polity Press, 1989); T. Ishida and F. Krauss (eds), *Democracy in Japan* (Pittsburgh, University of Pittsburgh Press, 1989).

30 G. Rodan, *The Political Economy of Singapore's Industrialization* (New York, St Martin's Press, 1989).

31 F. von der Mehden, 'Malaysia in 1990: another election victory', *Asian Survey*, 31 (1991), 164–71.

32 M. Moore, 'Retreat from democracy in Sri Lanka?', *Journal of Commonwealth and Comparative Politics*, 30 (1992), 64–84.

33 P. Brass, *The New Cambridge History of India. Vol. IV.I: The Politics of India since Independence* (Cambridge, Cambridge University Press, 1990).

34 D. Lipset, 'Papua New Guinea: the Melanesian ethic and the spirit of capitalism, 1975–1986', in Diamond et al., *Democracy: Asia*, pp. 383–421.

35 Comparative evidence from other parts of the world is reported in *PIOOM Newsletter and Progress Report*, 2:2 (Autumn 1990), pp. 18–20.

36 Moore, *Social Origins* p. 354.

37 Another, different explanation of India's democratization, which emphasizes political leadership, political culture and the party system, is J. Manor, 'How and why liberal and representative politics emerged in India', *Polical Studies*, 38 (1990), 20–38.

38 T. Byres, 'Agrarian structure, the new technology and class action in India', in H. Alavi and J. Harriss (eds), *Sociology of 'Developing Societies': South Asia* (London, Macmillan, 1989), pp. 46–58.

39 L. Rudolph and S. Rudolph, *In Pursuit of Lakshmi: the political economy of the Indian state* (Chicago, University of Chicago Press, 1987).

40 F. Frankel and M. Rao (eds), *Dominance and State Power in Modern India: decline of a social order. Vols 1 and 2* (Delhi, Oxford University Press, 1989, 1990).

41 For case studies see R. Holloway (ed.), *Doing Development: government, NGOs and the rural poor in Asia* (London, Earthscan, 1989). More generally, see J. Clark, *Democratizing Development: the role of voluntary organizations* (London, Earthscan, 1991).

42 A. Basu, 'State autonomy and agrarian transformation in India', *Comparative Politics*, 22 (1990), 483–500; G. Shah, 'Grass-roots mobilization in Indian politics', in A. Kohli (ed.), *India's Democracy: an analysis of changing state–society relations* (Princeton, NJ, Princeton University Press, 1988), pp. 262–304.

43 S. Mitra, 'Room to maneuver in the middle: local elites, political action, and the state in India', *World Politics*, 43 (1991), 390–413.

44 Brass, *Politics of India*, p. 336.

45 J. Harriss, 'Indian industrialization and the state', in Alavi and Harriss, *Sociology of 'Developing Societies'*, pp. 70–90.

46 Rudolph and Rudolph, *Lakshmi*, pp. 22 and 277–80.

47 R. Kothari, *State Against Democracy: the search for humane government* (New Delhi, Ajanta, 1988); see also A. Kohli, *Democracy and Discontent: India's growing crisis of governability* (Cambridge, Cambridge University Press, 1990).

48 K. Gough, *Political Economy in Vietnam* (Berkeley, CA, Folklore Institute, 1990), p. 256.

49 A. Nathan, *Chinese Democracy: the individual and the state in twentieth century China* (London, Tauris, 1986), p. 227.

50 Gough, *Vietnam*, p. 292.

51 D. Steinberg (ed.), *In Search of Southeast Asia: a modern history* (Sydney, Allen and Unwin, revised edn, 1987), p. 472.
52 R. Miliband, 'Reflections on the crisis of communist regimes', in R. Blackburn (ed.), *After the Fall: the failure of communism and the future of socialism* (London, Verso, 1991), pp. 6–17; R. Miliband, 'What comes after communist regimes?', in R. Miliband and L. Panitch (eds), *Socialist Register 1991: Communist Regimes: the aftermath* (London, Merlin Press, 1991), pp. 375–89.
53 G. White (ed.), *The Chinese State in the Era of Economic Reform* (London, Macmillan, 1991); H. Harding, *China's Second Revolution: reform after Mao* (Washinton, DC, Brookings Institution, 1987); P. Nolan and D. Fureng (eds), *The Chinese Economy and its Futures: achievements and problems of post-Mao reform* (Cambridge, Polity Press, 1990).
54 J. Cabestan and E. Seizelet, 'La Corée du Nord entre l'orthodoxie et l'ouverture: un communisme dans l'impasse', *Politique Etrangère*, 55 (1990), 863–87.
55 Gough, *Vietnam*; C. Joiner, 'The Vietnamese Communist Party strives to remain the "only force"', *Asian Survey*, 30 (November, 1990), 1053–65.
56 G. Evans, 'Planning problems in peripheral socialism: the case of Laos', in J. Zasloff and L. Unger (eds), *Laos: beyond the revolution* (London, Macmillan, 1991), pp. 84–130.
57 A. Saunders, 'Mongolia 1990: a new dawn?', *Asian Survey*, 22 (1990), 158–66.
58 World Bank, *World Development Report 1990*, pp. 178–9.
59 Reported in *The Guardian* (30 Jan. 1992), p. 13.
60 K. O'Brien, *Reform Without Liberalization: China's National People's Congress and the politics of institutional change* (Cambridge, Cambridge University Press, 1990).
61 R. Blackburn, 'Preface', and 'Fin de siècle: socialism after the crash', in Blackburn, *After the Fall*, pp. xiii and 237.

18

THE PROSPECTS FOR DEMOCRACY IN THE MIDDLE EAST

Simon Bromley

Considered as a specific, historically contingent form of rule, the question of 'democracy' cannot be addressed in the absence of a more general treatment of those social transformations which provide its structural preconditions. The central argument of what follows is that capitalist democracy is a form of rule that is specific to a determinate pattern of surplus appropriation. At this level of analysis, there are two essential conditions for capitalist state formation to take a democratic form.[1] In the first instance, the state apparatus must be able to uphold its authority and monopoly of coercion against other sites of political command, to such a degree that the general, public functions of society become decisionable by a single body of rule-making and coercive enforcement, or else democratic control of the state draws it into particularistic, violent struggles. And secondly, there must be a significant degree of separation between the institutions of rule and the mechanisms by which the surplus labour of the direct producers is appropriated, thus uncoupling the material basis of the power of the ruling class from the formal exercise of state-political power, otherwise the dominant class has a direct material stake in opposing democracy. Taken together, the emergence of a sovereign public sphere in conjunction with the privatization of command over surplus labour provide the basis for a form of rule in which the state apparatus is formally responsible to elected decision-makers who are chosen by means of a universal and equal franchise.[2]

The social transformations which make this possible involve changes in which the means of public administration -- a centralized monopoly of

Many thanks to Paul Cammack, Vanessa Fox, Fred Halliday and Justin Rosenberg for helpful comments on an earlier draft.

coercion, fiscal basis, monetary order and the sanctioning of state decisions by a unitary legal apparatus – become general, public forms consistent with, indeed providing the presuppositions of, private forms of appropriation set free from major communal functions. But in all pre-capitalist formations the means of administration and of appropriation are not so differentiated. It follows that those complexes of social power which organize political command and surplus appropriation in the pre-modern era stand as an obstacle to the development of new forms of economy and polity. The transition from pre-capitalist to modern forms of rule must therefore involve a change in the social location of these complexes. Furthermore, where social forces seek to resist the transition to modernity, or where there is opposition to the particular course of modern development, then this is likely to cohere in forms of organiza-tion based on these older complexes. Thus any account of projects of capitalist state formation and economic development must attend to the precise matrix from which these were launched.

Once the conditions outlined above are present, democracy does not necessarily follow. Whether democracy is consolidated or not depends also on the political economy of class coalitions and competition located within historically specific patterns of development.[3] At the broadest level, landed classes dependent on repressive modes of controlling labour oppose democracy. The dispossessed classes generally favour democratic rule when they are able to exercise their potential power through collective organization. Given the difficulty of peasant or tribal organiza-tion, it is the labour movement that is central in this context. The posi-tion of the capitalist class is altogether more ambiguous. While in a broad range of conjunctures the capitalist class favours a degree of liberal gov-ernance, its support for democracy is both more hesitant and more dependent on the behaviour of the subordinate classes. A full account of the prospects for democracy must also attend to these questions.

In order to analyse the extent to which the societies of the Middle East meet the criteria for capitalist democracy, it is necessary to examine the historical evolution of the region's social structure. Most importantly, how have the patterns of surplus appropriation found in these societies been recomposed by the conjoint impact of integration into the world market and state system and the projects of state-building and economic development launched by indigenous forces? It is this pattern of com-bined and uneven development that I try to sketch below. I propose to undertake this task in four stages. To begin with I identify the character of the pre-capitalist social formations in the region. Here I focus on the combination of tributary and tribal-nomadic forms together with their modes of articulation with Islam. Next, I outline the ways in which the internal decline of the Ottoman and Safavid empires interacted with the pressures of European imperialism and colonialism to produce a distinct pattern of class formation. In combination, these features provided the environment in which projects of state formation have been undertaken, and this forms the third area of focus. This theme is developed by taking the path of state formation, and the subsequent transition towards democracy, in Turkey as both a model and a measure of political change in the region. On this basis, I then sketch some of the main variants seen in Egypt, Iraq, Saudi Arabia and Iran. Finally, I conclude with some general reflections on the prospects for democracy and the causes behind the rise of 'Islamic fundamentalism'.[4]

Tributary Appropriation, Tribal Nomads and Islam

The central and overriding fact of the Ottoman state was its tributary character.[5] With the exception of *waqf* (or religious) lands, all land was the patrimony of the sultan. Both Islamic law and Ottoman practice classed land as belonging to the state *(miri)*. Peasant families with rights of access to the land constituted the main units of production and consumption, and these were organized into wider village communities. Peasants farmed the land for tax payments to the state. The sultan's household was staffed by ex-Christian slaves taken as tribute and by the Islamic stratum of *sipahi* cavalry, based on the *timars* (benefices) granted by the sultan in return for military service. (When the cavalry gave way to a salaried army, so the grants became tax-farms.) In marked contrast to the position of the nobility within feudalism, such grants neither were heritable nor connoted any rights of jurisdiction over the direct producers, and the revenues attached to them were set by the sultan's treasury. This state of affairs applied most fully in the empire's Anatolian (Turkish) and Rumelian (Balkan) core. By contrast, in some of the outer regions, such as Egypt, Iraq and Arabia, there were no *timar* lands; instead these were garrisoned by *jannissary* troops and paid taxes to the treasury. Profits from guild regulation of markets and customs dues also went to the urban-based intermediaries of the state. It was this urban location and tributary form of surplus appropriation, together with the high levels of tax levied on the cultivators, that dictated the absence of any long-term interests geared towards agricultural improvement: urban consumption, not productive innovation, was the mission of the ruling class.

Formally speaking, the official corps of Sunni theologians, judges and teachers ran parallel to this tributary structure. This religious hierarchy performed important administrative functions and filled the leading civil and judicial posts of the state. In the provinces, personnel recruited from the *ulema* formed the basis of administration. But what was the precise role of the Sunni *ulema*? Dating from the Abbasid period in Sunni Islam, *madrasa* (theological and legal colleges), endowments and fees constituted the clergy as a major group of surplus takers, and on this basis they extended their functions to charity, education, justice and informal social and political leadership. By contrast, the Turkish conquerors, of nomadic stock and backed by slave armies, had little or no experience of sedentary agriculture and imperial administration. Thus the *ulema* could organize society but they could not suppress banditry and parasitic disorder, while the new overlords could supply order but could not rule. The happy conjunction has been well summarized by Ira Lapidus:

> Faced with military elites unfamiliar with local traditions, the 'ulama' emerged, on the basis of religious prestige and educational and judicial authority as a new communal notability. The 'ulama' married into established merchant, administrative, and landowning families, and merged with the older local elites to form a new upper class defined by religious qualifications. The 'ulama' assumed the functions as well as the status of the former elites. They took charge of local taxation, irrigation, judicial and police affairs, and often became scribes and officials in the Saljuq succession states. While conquerors and regimes came and went, Islam became ever more firmly and widely entrenched as the basis of the social and political order.[6]

This was the pattern that was reproduced throughout the Ottoman empire. The Turkish overlords, whether state officials or military personnel, lived off the land and resided in the towns, and often did not learn the language of the local notability and peasantry. The tacit cooperation of urban forces, especially the merchants and the *ulema*, was therefore necessary. Merchants required the overlords to maintain order and the networks of trade and finance, and their largest customers were often the central tributary authorities. The *ulema* were even more significant to social control than the merchants, for they provided more general social cohesion and regulation. They too depended on order and became dependent on state finance.

But beyond the compass of the urban Sunni clergy and Ottoman military power lay the tribal forces that remained outside central control. Here we are in the world of Ibn Khaldun.[7] In these regions the tributary state was unable to control the rural areas, essentially because of the greater weight of pastoral nomadism with its mobile means of production, armed populations and absence of urban growth. Tribal pastoralism permitted neither any significant development of the forces of production nor any lasting social stratification or political authority within the community. The tribal nobility was not reproduced by regulated intermarriage and it had no power to tax, control or command. And even if tribal warfare precipitated the temporary emergence of a confederation, the paucity of the available surplus meant that state formation was unthinkable. Where this tribal cohesion survived it proved to be destructive of development as such, for in so far as nomads accumulated surpluses at all this was by means of parasitic plunder from sedentary agriculture or from the siphoning of tribute from trade routes.

Under these circumstances popular (Sufi) Islam was called on to play a very different role from the literate practice of justice and administration found in the urban centres of surplus appropriation. What Ernest Gellner calls 'folk' Islam, and in particular its array of saints, performed the following roles:

> Supervising the political process in segmentary groups, e.g. election or selection of chiefs. Supervising and sanctioning their legal process, notably by collective oath. Facilitating economic relations by guaranteeing caravans and visits to the markets of neighbouring tribes; trade and pilgrimage routes may converge. Providing spatial markers for frontiers: a saintly settlement may be on the border between lay groups. Providing temporal markers; in a pastoral society, many pasture rights may be bounded by seasons and require rituals for their ratification. What better than a saintly festival for such a purpose? Supplying the means for the Islamic identification of the tribesmen ... All these factors clearly conspire to one end: the faith of the tribesmen needs to be mediated by special and distinct holy personnel, rather than to be egalitarian; it needs to be joyous and festival-worthy, not puritanical and scholarly; it requires hierarchy and incarnation in persons, not in script. Its ethic is one of loyalty not of rule-observance.[8]

Of course, folk Islam was present among the settled, rural peasantry as well, since they were also illiterate and had need of its ability to facilitate the interaction – material and symbolic – between otherwise hostile communities. This folk Islam, the religion of the majority of the population, was independent of the state, and often the urban tributary power sought to suppress Sufi orders, seeing them as a threat to its own position.

Finally, there was Shi'i Persia. 'Twelvers' (by far the largest grouping in Shi'i Islam and the predominant form of Shi'ism in Persia) take their name from following the twelve infallible imams. The line began with Ali, who was the cousin and son-in-law of the Prophet, and it ends with Muhammad al-Mahdi, who is believed to have gone into occultation in AD 874. The theoretical basis of the Shi'i *ulema*, articulated at a time when temporal political power resided with Sunni Moslems, lies in the notion that they are the collective deputies of the Occulted Imam. After the Safavid conquest of Iran, however, Shi'ism was proclaimed the religion of the state. The latter was composed of a tributary structure similar to that of the Ottoman empire, though the control of the central state was weaker to the extent that its army was composed of tribal levies. This reflected the greater presence of pastoral nomadism and thus tribal organization within post-Mongol Iran. The peasantry had already flocked to Sufi orders. While the empire lasted, the Shi'i *ulema* supported Safavid power against the Ottoman adversary and the Safavids deferred to the *ulema* on a range of issues. Ira Lapidus has noted that by the late Safavid period, 'Shi'ism had duplicated the whole complex of religious sensibility already found within Sunnism. It thus became a comprehensive alternative vision of Islam'.[9] Shi'i jurists argued that the canonical alms, the *zakat*, were to be collected and distributed by the clergy, thereby legitimating one of the material bases of the clergy (the others being the money paid for services to the merchants, the religious endowments and the *madrasa*).

Post-Safavid Iran was subject to a series of warring dynasties, and by 1779 the Qajars had defeated their main rivals, the Zand, to establish a dynasty that lasted until 1924. In this period, the central authority diminished and the corresponding power of tribal leaders and landowners increased, and the *ulema* were able to develop a further autonomy through establishing their own religious courts, private armies and bodies of students. In addition, the location of the most important Shi'i shrines in Iraq, especially the symbolically central site of Karbala,[10] further augmented the distance of the clergy from the state. Taken together, these features meant that the Shi'i *ulema* constituted a powerful grouping of surplus takers, and were able to establish a much greater degree of independence from the central tributary structures than the Sunni clergy of the Ottoman domains.

In sum, Islam has been, and to a marked yet uneven extent continues to be, central to the nature of Middle Eastern societies. In fact, until the modern period of state-building and economic development began, during the 1920s in Turkey and the 1950s elsewhere, Islam was in part constitutive of the social formation as a whole. However, the role played by Islam cannot be understood either as an enduring, recalcitrant tradition, a cultural form operating separately from other social and historical determinations, or in terms of the theological power of the Islamic clergy (the *ulema*), holding a mystical sway over ignorant masses. As Ernest Gellner has cogently argued, 'the *differentiae* of Islam seem institutional rather than ideological'.[11] As a form of religious identification and a culture of signification, Islam remains rooted in broader sets of social and material practices, and thus its changing forms must also be related to the historically given organization of economy and polity.

As noted, by the time of the consolidation of the Ottoman and Safavid empires in the sixteenth century, it is possible to distinguish a range of different societies within the Middle East, in each of which the articulation of Islam took its own distinctive form: the heartlands of the Sunni Ottoman empire in urban areas linked to sedentary agriculture; those regions of the Ottoman domain where the centre's writ was more attenuated, either as a result of stronger tribal organization or because of logistical distance from the Anatolian core; and Shi'i Persia (Iran). Throughout the region, then, Islam was much more than the predominant style of religious belief. In a direct, material sense it regulated social reproduction and articulated relations of authority, and it is this role which has given it such a persistent, and indeed potent, presence. And while in the urban centres of the Ottoman lands the Sunni *ulema* were organized in parallel to the tributary structure of the state, for the mass of the population 'folk' Islam, or in the Iranian case the Shi'i clergy, was socially and materially independent from the state. Looking forward, this was to mean that the creation of 'modern' forms of surplus extraction and political rule would necessarily involve a radical reconstitution of the social location of Islam. Where this has failed, it is scarcely surprising that political protest has taken an Islamic form.

Tributary Decline, European Expansion

Turning now to the first of the two major processes which have reshaped the region, I consider the pattern of indigenous decline and external control that took hold in the nineteenth century. Once territorial expansion ceased, the Ottoman polity began to disintegrate as an increasingly counterproductive form of surplus extraction set in. There is little doubt that the fundamental causes of Ottoman decline derived from its tributary structure.[12] This dynamic obtained in all of the Islamic land empires (Ottoman, Safavid and Mughal) during the eighteenth century and was itself a critical precondition for the establishment of European global preponderance, complementing the hold already established on the Atlantic seaboard. Moreover, the incorporation of these regions into the capitalist world played an important role in shaping the pattern of their future subordination. In fact, there was something akin to a 'general crisis' of the Moslem land empires in the eighteenth century.[13] The Mughal and Safavid empires were destroyed by 'tribal breakouts', India falling to outright conquest and Persia maintaining an uneasy, if largely formal, independence; and in the Ottoman empire there was a growing regionalization of political power as landed classes began to consolidate and internal and external trade continued to expand. In Qajar Iran central tributary power was never recuperated, and formal independence coexisted with informal domination by Britain and Russia. And in the Ottoman domains the authority of the Porte was challenged by the rise of provincial rulers – military *pashas* in Egypt and Syria, *derebeys* (valley lords) in Anatolia, *ayans* (dynastic notables) in Rumelia, and *Wahhabi* tribes in Arabia – and European imperialism.

The rulers in Turkey and Egypt sought to modernize their armies by adopting weaponry and tactics from the west and replacing mercenaries by conscripts, and this required increased taxes. The attempt to raise revenue by abolishing tax-farming, appointing salaried officials and regularizing legal administration exacerbated conflicts between the central administration and local rulers. Additional resources were also required for educational reform to staff the expanding military and administrative posts. As long as the centre held (in the Ottoman core until the First World War, under Muhammad Ali in Egypt from 1805 to 1848), the resulting loss of local power had the effect of drawing the state into a closer infrastructural role, strengthening rural security, and thereby laying the basis for sustained economic progress. In Turkey military reorganization was a result of European pressure, whereas in Egypt it was motivated by a desire for independence from the Ottoman centre. In both cases, however, it was the need of the state for revenues which laid the grounds for the formation of a settled, agrarian capitalist class, rather than pressure from landed and commercial elements. The onerous loans contracted to finance modernization had the effect, secondly, of leading to growing financial penetration by the west. Before long, the failure of the reforms to generate sufficient growth and revenues resulted in the bankruptcy of the state (1875 in Turkey and 1876 in Egypt), followed by direct European supervision of the public finances. In the case of Egypt, European influence produced revolt and this, combined with its strategic position, led to outright occupation by the British in 1882.

Nevertheless, the degree of economic change should not be over-stated. For example, the Anatolian economy remained dominated by peasant production and, under the control of landlords, industry continued to be confined to foodstuffs and textiles. Still, in some regions, pastoralism and communal or tribal forms of land tenure were replaced by settled agriculture and the creation of landed estates. Charles Issawi has summarized the results as follows:

In Iraq and Syria the settlement of titles was carried out in conditions that transferred huge amounts of tribal and village lands to sheiks and other notables; in Egypt Muhammad Ali laid the basis of a large landlord class; and in

North Africa a large proportion of the land was acquired, mainly by expropriation or chicanery, by European settlers.[14]

The steady commercialization of tributary appropriation and rule also
laid the basis for a rapid expansion of trade with Europe during the nineteenth century, facilitated by falling transport and communication costs
arising from steamships and the building of telegraphs, railways and
ports. Large amounts of European capital were also invested in the
region and a financial system emerged to cope with the foreign trade,
much of which was handled by local but minority intermediaries –
Greeks, Jews, Armenians, Syro-Lebanese Christians – and Europeans.
Considerable settlement occurred in Palestine, Egypt and North Africa.
Increased connections with Europe drove many indigenous manufacturers out of business and encouraged the expansion of cash-crops.
Economic activity concentrated on the building of infrastructure and the
provision of irrigation. In addition, the plague disappeared at the start of
the century and later there were improvements to public health. But
most of the increased rural surplus was either consumed or channelled
into urban political activity.

In sum, the economic growth of the Middle East in the nineteenth
century was shaped by the expansion of the European market for agricultural products, on the one hand, and the reactive construction of
strong, centralizing regimes in Istanbul and Cairo, on the other.[15] In the
process, the Europeans came to dominate the economies of the region by
a mixture of capitulations and consular or mixed courts, by control over
public revenue and expenditure, or by direct occupation; minorities acted
as the lubricators of trade and investment; and the Moslem population
produced the growing surpluses. As Charles Issawi comments: 'By 1914,
Europeans held all the commanding heights of the economy except for
landownership in the Middle East, and the minority groups occupied the
middle and some of the lower slopes.'[16]

State Formation

Finally, in the context of declining tributary societies, riddled with
European economic penetration and political control, projects of state-
building were launched. The dismemberment of the Ottoman empire, in
conjunction with the nationalist and revolutionary legacy of the First
World War, marked a major turning point in the evolution of the modern
Middle East.[17] The Eastern Question, namely the means by which
property relations and forms of rule in the Middle East were to be

recomposed by, and then incorporated into, the capitalist market and state system of the west, was now formally at an end. Yet this long decline and incorporation was precisely the epoch in which, first, the distinction was forged between the advanced and the underdeveloped world and, secondly, the capitalist world market and a small number of rapidly industrializing states established their global dominance. Thereafter, all development was dependent development.

Specifically, the background to the Eastern Question was given by the expansion of European capitalism, on the one hand, and the process of Ottoman decline, on the other. But the fortunes of North-Western Europe and the lands of the Porte were not simply uneven, capitalist dynamism as contrasted with pre-capitalist stagnation, they were also combined. The dynamic of colonial expansion and aggrandisement was itself critically determined by the 'general crisis' of these land empires in the eighteenth century. Equally, the reformist impulses and recuperative powers of the periphery played an active role in its own incorporation into the world economy and state system. Through this process of combined and uneven development, then, a systemic antagonism between capitalist nation-states and a tributary empire was worked out in which the former achieved a decisive victory by virtue of its economic vitality and military power.

At the core of the empire a new state, Turkey, emerged, while in the former Arab regions a number of dependent states were created – in Lebanon and Syria by France, and in Iraq, Jordan and Palestine by Britain. The Gulf sheikdoms remained, in effect, British protectorates, and in Saudi Arabia and North Yemen new states developed. In Iran also a new state was forged. Egypt remained under British control and in North Africa French influence persisted. Despite this continued predominance, the terms of imperialist rivalry in the region were altered by the growing importance of the region's oil, together with the entry of the US into the picture. At the same time, the balance of social conflict was changed by the spread of nationalist movements, as well as the existence of a state socialist regime in the Soviet Union. Finally, with the Balfour Declaration (1917), and more importantly the incorporation of the Zionist pro-gramme into the British mandate for Palestine (1920), the seeds of future Arab–Israeli antagonism were sown by the consolidation of Jewish settler colonialism.

But naturally the formation of new states in the region did not produce stable forms of rule and economic progress. Drawing lines on the map, appointing rulers, developing forms of bureaucratic administration and taxation, even training and equipping armies, do not by themselves create durable state forms. The projects of state-building launched after 1918 had to work with the inheritance of tributary formations in decline and the overriding presence of classes whose mission consisted in facilitating dependent incorporation and the consumption of any accumulated surplus.

Viewed in these terms, on the eve of independence the region could be differentiated roughly as follows: in Turkey the Ottoman bureaucracy dominated surplus appropriation (though with the support of rural notables in the west and Kurdish tribes in the east), while the Sunni clergy was dependent on the state and thus lacked an autonomous base of operation; in Egypt, Syria and Iraq urban-based absentee landlords dominated the land and surplus appropriation and gained support from the relevant foreign powers, and there was a Sunni *ulema* (there were also significant ethnic or religious minorities, especially in Iraq and Syria); in Arabia the elite was tribal (and owed its continuing position to British support), and much of the population was nomadic; and in Iran absentee landlords, tribal peoples and a powerful Shi'i clergy coexisted with a weak polity. It is to these particularities, with their divergent implications for democratic development, that I now turn.

Turkey

In many respects Turkey provides a model for the rest of the region, and can thus serve as a standard to which developments elsewhere may usefully be compared. This is so because, by virtue of the positions of the Moslem state bureaucracy and the Sunni clergy, the consolidation of state authority was relatively unproblematic, if extremely violent, and because once a degree of industrial development had been launched a certain separation of the institutions of rule and surplus appropriation developed. Together with a favourable external environment, these facts have pushed Turkey further along the road towards the structural conditions for democracy than any other society in the Middle East.

Amidst the disintegration of Ottoman rule, the Hamidian regime was overthrown by the Young Turk revolution of 1908 – a movement composed of junior army officers and minor bureaucrats in which the army was the chief beneficiary. The Committee of Union and Progress finally ended the ensuing uncertainty and seized power in a coup (23 January 1913). The CUP continued the formula of Ottomanist reform for the empire: a secular system of law and education, a liberal constitution, a strengthened army and administration, and more emphasis on economic development. But given the reality of secession under protection from Christian powers and dependent incorporation under the aegis of a non-

Moslem bourgeoisie, the Turkish national movement increasingly assumed a dictatorial and Moslem-nationalist form, as Ottoman identity proved incapable of providing a unifying framework for programmes of renewal. (Ottomanism had become simply the formula for disintegration, the Sunni *ulema* a bulwark of reaction.)

The Kemalist revolution from above was carried through by the Moslem state bureaucracy, the main axis of surplus appropriation.[18] After the dispossession, expulsion and extermination of minority commercial classes during and shortly after the First World War, the state stood centre-stage in the economy of what became the Turkish Republic. The continuity of the ruling class from the Ottoman to the Kemalist era may be seen in the fact that 93 per cent of staff officers and 85 per cent of civil servants retained their positions under the Republic. (As late as 1964 one half of senior officials came from bureaucratic and military families.) By the time of the inter-war depression, Kemalist forces had been able to fashion a single-party dictatorship, comprising an organizational framework that owed more to Durkheimian corporatism and European fascism than to Islam. A protected economy, with a strong element of state direction, and the creation of parastate organizations of social control, steered Turkish development until the end of the Second World War. (This framework did not extend to labour, which was rigidly excluded from all forms of collective organization.) The state and party elite merged in the Republican People's Party. As Caglar Keyder has argued, the Turkish model pioneered under Kemalist forces set a pattern of nationalist state-building and capital accumulation that was later repeated in much of the Third World.[19]

In relation to Islam the Turkish experience was also pioneering. Kemalism was the exemplary instance of modernization *against* Islam, a fact arising from the imbrication of Islam with the discredited old order and the dependence of the Sunni *ulema* on the state. This is not gainsaid by the fact that 'the Turkish national movement was essentially a Moslem protest against Christian assertion'.[20] In fact, the militant secularism of the state amounted to rigid state control over religious life, and a strict laicism in public affairs, rather than the institutional separation of church and state. After all, in the new state 98 per cent of the population was Moslem (a majority Sunni), 85 per cent spoke Turkish (10 per cent Kurdish) and 80 per cent were dependent on agriculture.

In the Second World War Turkey remained neutral, finally joining the Allied side in February 1945. Cold War tensions and Turkey's strategic location resulted in the massive provision of US economic and military aid after the Second World War. In part responding to the liberal ideology of the time, the Turkish state announced the need for a party of opposition. The rival Democrat Party opposed the statist order on the grounds of freedom of the market and of religion. The continuing weight of the peasantry and the *petit bourgeoisie* meant that a populist ideology of the market had considerable appeal, and the Democrat Party won power in 1950. Wider use of market forces, rapid economic development, urban growth and populist mobilization ensued. But the failure of this model to provide stable accumulation led to the military coup of 1960, which inaugurated a national capitalist programme of import-substituting industrialization combined with an expansion of welfare entitlements.

Unfortunately for Turkish democracy, the 'limited weight of organised labour within the working class, and the small proportion of the working class within the total population'[21] frustrated the transformation of the RPP into a social democratic party. As the strains of increasing inequality and political mobilization increased in circumstances of acute economic crisis and social breakdown, the military once again intervened (1980). This time the military regime was the occasion for the introduction of a programme of social stabilization and export-led growth, involving structural adjustment and economic liberalization. The military regime encouraged Islam to combat the left, but the conservative, modernizing, urban elites have employed the state to maintain a firm control over religious forces and to channel them in regime-supporting directions.

Precarious and largely formal though it may be, Turkish democracy has been the outcome of early and successful consolidation of state authority under Kemal, relatively impressive levels of industrialization and with it a degree of organizational independence in civil society, and state control over religious forces. On this basis, a 'restricted democracy' has developed on the basis of the 1982 constitution, and, given reasonable economic growth and the ambitions of the Turkish ruling class for membership of the European Community, a stable parliamentary system has a fair chance of developing.

Egypt

In some measure the situation in Egypt resembled that of Turkey, with a Sunni clergy subordinated to the state, a settled peasantry transformed into share-croppers and wage labourers by the consolidation of private property rights in land, and some limited industrial development. There was also a similar degree of religious and ethnic homogeneity. Two important differences should be noted, however: first, the decline of central authority at the end of Muhammad Ali's rule created a stronger notable class and a weaker state than that which existed in Turkey, including a small, Egyptian commercial and industrial class; and secondly, the strategic position of Egypt meant that financial collapse brought with it British occupation in 1882. For these reasons, the notable classes and imperialist controls were able to persist until after the Second World War. But once the anti-imperialist and anti-landlord revolution began in 1952, in its broad outlines the pattern of state formation and import-substituting industrialization in Egypt replicated many features of the Turkish experience.

Nationalist revolt in 1919 resulted in a reassessment of imperial strategy by the British: the protectorate was renounced but control over defence and foreign policy, the security of the Suez Canal, the government of the Sudan and the future of the capitulations remained in British hands. Around this time, over 90 per cent of the population was Moslem (nearly all Sunni), and about 70 per cent was based in agriculture. Industry was dominated by an urban-based notable class who engaged in the politics of patronage *vis-à-vis* the state. The capacity of this class to prosecute development can be seen in the fact that per capita income did not increase between 1910 and 1950, while the class distribution of income widened.

Against this background, the Egyptian revolution of 1952 had two main features:

> The first was the replacement of the old landed urban notables who had dominated the political system of Egypt since the nineteenth century by a new ruling elite, composed initially of military officers and subsequently of a mixed military–civilian class of state functionaries. The second was a major shift of political, economic and social power to the state.[22]

Agrarian reform had already been proposed by the US and the United Nations, and it had some support among the big bourgeoisie. The project of state-led, industrial development had long been the aim of the national bourgeoisie. Land reform was instituted, agricultural cooperatives were established and there was an extension of cultivatable land. Industrial growth was sponsored by the state and a programme of welfare reforms was initiated. The construction of the High Dam was an aid to irrigation, but its main importance was to provide the electricity needed for industrialization. The Suez Canal was nationalized in July 1956, and banks, insurance companies and commercial agencies in January 1957. Between 1959 and 1961 state control extended to Egyptian capital, foreign trade, labour organizations and agricultural cooperatives. In addition, progressive income taxes and confiscatory measures for personal wealth were adopted. Together, these policies were aimed at providing the resources and control necessary to launch a state-capitalist programme of import-substituting industrialization.[23] (Between 1952 and 1967 real wages rose by 44 per cent.)

The new, 'secular' regime also moved against the position of religion, seeking to subordinate it to state control. In 1952 family *waqfs* were abolished, and the public ones brought under state control in 1957. The Shari'a courts were closed in 1956, Sufi brotherhoods were officially outlawed in 1961, and the orthodox *ulema* cooperated with the state. Finally, the political activity of the Moslem Brotherhood was suppressed.

Defeat in 1967 constituted a profound shock to the army and the regime, and it resulted in a shift in the balance of political and strategic alignments as the financial capital of the oil-producing states was increasingly tied into the international capitalist system. The power of Nasser's arch-rival, the Saudi monarchy, increased accordingly. Thereafter, and especially once the October War (1973) opened up the prospect of substantive negotiations with Israel, the prospects of peace and favourable treatment from the US in the fields of economic and military aid beckoned. However, the seriousness of the economic crisis, and the political resistance to the reform of subsidized basic goods drove the state towards a '*rentier* quest' to liquidate state capitalism, supply surplus labour to the oil states, and garner foreign rents from aid, oil, profits on the Canal and tourism. At the same time, the technocratic and managerial bases of the new regime 'were interested in the prospect of Islamic law being appropriated to the state in a possibly expanded way, but not in a serious extension of influence by the clerical estate who are seen rather as a useful adjunct to the apparatus and ruling strata'.[24] (In the early 1980s, it was estimated that perhaps one-third of the adult, male population belonged to Sufi brotherhoods.)

For much the same reasons as in the Turkish case, a highly regulated experiment with a severely curtailed democracy has been taking place since 1976. The Egyptian polity comprises a strong presidential regime in which the parliament has little real power. In 1981, for example, Sadat arrested virtually every critic of the regime. But some parties have been allowed to form, the press is freer than at any time since 1952, and the judiciary has increasingly asserted both its independence and the need for constitutional propriety. Yet the elections of 1984, 1987 and 1990 were not free and were conducted under the State of Emergency legislation imposed after the assassination of Sadat. A dual problem of reform persists. On the one hand, the depth of economic crisis, together with the relatively short duration of state controls over religion, has produced a corresponding problem of Islamist opposition. And on the other, the very presence of the state in the economy (still some 70 per cent of GNP) and the continued power of the military and security services frustrate further democratization. The role of Egypt in the recent Gulf War strengthened its position in the Arab world, improved its standing in the west and, perhaps most importantly, facilitated the write-off of tens of billions of dollars of debt. The underlying problems, however, remain largely untouched.

Iraq

Of all the major states in the Middle East, Iraq faced the most formidable obstacles to state formation. While the presence of a notable class, British control, and a Sunni bureaucracy and *ulema* suggests some parallels with Egypt, the sheer arbitrariness of its formation, together with the absence of any developed tradition of state stability and its religious and ethnic heterogeneity (both a sharp contrast with Turkey and Egypt), produced an extremely refractory inheritance for state-building. In addition, as a major oil producer during the critical period when the state's authority was finally imposed, the *rentier* aspects of the Iraqi polity further increased its ability to opt for coercion over less brutal forms of the mobilization and control. The consequence has been the creation of the most controlled and repressive society in the Middle East.

After the First World War the British faced a dilemma. Could control of Iraq be maintained by the usual recipe for dealing with tribal magnates, a mixture of fraud and force, gold and silver for bribery and RAF bombs for coercion, as proposed by British India? Or was the Arab Bureau of the Foreign Office correct to suggest that the wartime mobilization of the region made 'nation-state building the wave of the future'?[25] The era of Lenin and Wilson argued for a new method of European control through the indirect colonial rule of the League's mandate system. When the French ousted Faisal from Syria, and as conflict raged between Ibn Saud and Hussain, the Arab Bureau's strategy of backing the Hashemites seemed dangerous. But the spread of revolt in Iraq cast doubts on the methods of British India. The solution agreed at the Cairo Conference was to install Faisal as head of an Arab government in Iraq. Tribal revolts were pacified through the vicious use of (low-cost) air power. A client government was established in which the British maintained effective control over military, fiscal and judicial matters. Internally, the British continued the privatization of land rights that had begun in the late Ottoman era and encouraged the new Iraqi army to suppress tribal revolts. The newly constituted Turkish Petroleum Company operated in the Mosul and Basra fields, now with US participation, and bolstered the fiscal base of the state.

Faisal defined the problem of state-building as follows in 1933: 'In Iraq there is still ... no Iraqi people, but unimaginable masses of human beings, devoid of any patriotic ideal, imbued with religious traditions and absurdities, connected by no common tie, giving ear to evil, prone to anarchy, and perpetually ready to rise against any government whatsoever'.[26] If we can excuse the contemptuous tone from one whose own ancestry should surely occasion a greater respect for such people (the qualities listed were those of his father, Hussain), then Faisal's depiction is accurate enough. Sunni Arabs made up one-fifth of the population, Shi'i Arabs about one-half, and Kurdish tribes one-seventh. Much of the population was tribal and perhaps 5 per cent was literate. Sunni notables and bureaucrats, installed under Ottoman rule and strengthened by the British, supported the Hashemite monarchy; and tribal sheiks were an important source of support at provincial level. Land-ownership was extremely concentrated and the position of the direct producers was wretched. The Iraqi army was composed of ex-Ottoman and ex-Sharifian forces, and was therefore almost exclusively Sunni. During the 1930s the army broke the military power of the tribes, except in Kurdistan. (In 1933 the tribes were estimated to have 100,000 rifles as against 15,000 in the army.)

During the Second World War struggles over relations with the imperial power, Britain, intensified. The anti-imperialist and anti-landlord revolution of 1958 overthrew the monarchy and instituted a republic. The landed political class was replaced by an elite based in the civil and military bureaucracies of the state. Yet for a decade there was no real consolidation of state authority. At first Qasim relied on the Iraqi Communist Party, which played a dominant role in the mass organizations of workers and peasants. In 1963 Arabist and Ba'athist groupings attempted to seize power, but the disunited Ba'athists were soon expelled from government. In 1968 the Ba'athist coups were successful and a pattern of mobilization and organization familiar from state-led industrialization in dependent economies was inaugurated. The mobilizing ideology of the Ba'ath, Arab nationalism, was little more than the vehicle of Sunni, later Takriti, assertion in a state where they were significantly outnumbered. Land and welfare reform followed the Egyptian model, but the former was poorly executed due to political disruption and the absence of trained personnel.

Oil became central to the economy and the state; and intense levels of repression characterized the political order, especially after Saddam Hussein consolidated his power through the security apparatus of the Ba'ath. This regime straddles a society of considerable ethnic and religious diversity. Its narrow social base is located in the (huge) security services and elements of the military, and is linked to a highly centralized and brutally repressive political order. In the absence of an indigenous bourgeoisie and also given the physical extermination of most of the left, oil revenues and terror have been the mainstays of Ba'ath rule. The massive costs of the war against Iran had resulted in the cancellation or delay of much-needed economic development, and the anticipated post-war reconstruction had proved disappointing. The crisis was clearly spreading into the public sector and even into the state apparatus itself. Under these circumstances, Saddam appears to have decided on an aggressive policy of annexation in Kuwait to garner oil assets and bolster support throughout the (non-Gulf) Arab world. While the Gulf War led to the destruction of much of the civilian and military infrastructure of Iraq, Saddam Hussein remains in power and the levels of internal repression have scarcely diminished.

Saudi Arabia

Saudi Arabia provides a striking contrast with the regimes dealt with so far. Three facts account for this: modernization and state formation *with*, rather than *against*, Islam; the absence of a landed notable class; and the huge abundance of oil in relation to population. Ernest Gellner has pointed to the important fact that Islam's 'traditional internal differentiation into the folk and scholarly variants was actually helpful in effecting adjustment. The folk variant can be disavowed, blamed for cultural backwardness, or associated with the political machinations of colonial powers, whilst the "purer" variant can be identified all at once both with pristine origins and with a revived, glorious, modern future.'[27] This is precisely what happened in puritan, Wahhabi Saudi Arabia. After 1900 the Ikhwan recovered some control in eastern Arabia and Ottoman authority had been eclipsed by 1914. Ibn Saud increased his power aided by British subsidy and weapons. However, the role of Hussain as ruler of the Hijaz and thus controller of the pilgrimage, and as head of the Hashemites (his sons Faisal and Abdulla were installed by the British in Iraq and Transjordan, respectively), constituted a threat to the authority of the Saudis. Fortunately for the latter, Hussain undermined his own position through heavy taxation of merchants and pilgrims. Before long, Hussain was defeated militarily by Ibn Saud and the Ikhwan. After this, Ibn Saud signed the Treaty of Jidda with the British in 1927 and then used the provision of mechanized weaponry by the latter to suppress the Ikhwan. Founded on the Wahhabi–Saudi movement, the Kingdom of Saudi Arabia was thus established in 1932.

In general, the ecology and pattern of cultivation in Arabia did not lend itself to the consolidation of large estates, and the 'wealth and power of traditional notables had derived less from land and more from tribal authority, religious status, and trade. In Arabia the great destructive force of land reform had little on which to work.'[28] By contrast, Arabia and the Gulf states had oil in abundance, and it was this – together with the outside support which it soon attracted – which enabled tribal elites to hang on to power. In the process, states which were formed to distribute oil rents facilitated the transformation of ruling families into ruling classes. (It was only in South Yemen that a notable class fell with the retreat of the colonial power that had fostered its original formation.)

In the oil-based, *rentier* states, state-led industrial development, urbanization and the creation of a middle class of welfare workers, military personnel, bureaucrats and professionals went along with generous welfare provisions. Most manual and low-grade service sector work has been carried out by migrant labour from the non-oil Arab states and the Indian subcontinent. Political democracy is non-existent and the (foreign) labouring classes are excluded from all forms of participation. The orthodox Sunni *ulema* have by and large backed the rule of tribal families, most obviously in the case of Saudi Arabia, where the 1926 constitution stated that 'all administration is in the hands of His Majesty King 'Abd al-'Aziz ibn Sa'ud. His majesty is bound by the laws of the Shari'a.'[29] While the beginnings of a private-sector, capitalist class can be seen, the prospects for democratic reform are scarcely visible.

Iran

Iran differed in a number of ways from the states considered so far. In comparison with the sedentary Ottoman lands, the central state was much weaker, the weight of pastoralism greater and the power of the nobility more extensive, even extending to foreign policy. The Shi'i *ulema* had carved out a position of substantial autonomy. Iran also escaped formal colonial control. The period of state strengthening and industrial development coincided with, indeed was made possible by, the arrival of oil rents. The resulting pattern of development led to an event unique in modern history: a modern revolution carried out under clerical leadership.

In 1906 a constitutional revolution took place. Largely a Tehran affair, the deadlock between the Qajar government and the Majlis was ended by the shah's coup in 1908. Yet no real government, let alone state, was established. The British D'Arcy concession of 1901, which formed the basis of the Anglo-Persian Oil Company's power in Iran, had excluded the five major northern provinces precisely because of Russian claims in the region. After the war, the British Foreign Office sought to establish a semi-protectorate with the Anglo-Persian agreement of 1919, involving the supply of British financial advisers for the state, the retraining of the army and the provision of engineers for railway construction. However, Britain was not willing to assist in quelling internal revolts. The military nationalist leader, Reza Khan, continued to consolidate his rule and, after abolishing the Qajar dynasty, crowned himself Reza Pahlavi Shah in 1925. British influence remained extensive by virtue of its position in the Gulf, its oil concession and its links with tribal chiefs in the south.

During the 1920s and 1930s, Reza Shah sought to settle nomadic tribes, bolster the power of landowners *vis-à-vis* the clergy (while confiscating land and becoming the largest landowner himself), strengthen the army, and sponsor industrial development. However, while state controls over education and law, together with restraints on the material bases of the clergy, were established, development was limited. Agriculture was ignored, and attention focused on import substitution and infrastructure. The limited internal resources of the state derived from indirect taxes and state monopolies in tea and sugar.

Allied occupation during the Second World War served to compound the internal struggle for power, and only after the coup of 1953 did stability return. The Tudah Party, with its base in Tehran and among the oil workers in Khuzistan, demanded a national democratic revolution. Under Mossadeq's leadership (1951-3), the Majlis refused to ratify the oil agreement covering the Anglo-Iranian Oil Company's (AIOC) operations and demanded the nationalization of the oil industry. Religious protests also increased. Mossadeq and other nationalist landowners wanted to expel the AIOC and to reduce the powers of the Shah, but his reliance on the streets alienated the landowners and the *ulema*. After the coup, the Shah smashed the Tudah and the National Front. The army was enlarged and SAVAK founded. Outside the rapidly expanding repressive apparatus of the state, the shah's power depended on the conservative landowners who dominated the Majlis and the clergy who serviced the bazaar.

Notwithstanding rising oil revenues, the shah needed greater resources to finance military expansion and economic development. In 1963 he launched the White Revolution, the centre of which was a programme of land reform. Other elements included an attempt to reduce the power of the clergy and policies to win the support of industrial workers and women. The oil-backed industrial development, and the US-backed military aggrandizement, resulted in huge social dislocations because of their highly uneven character. Rapid urban expansion was combined with widening patterns of inequality. At the same time, the base of the Iranian state in oil rents, together with its politico-military links to Washington, permitted an expansion of its compass without the development of corresponding mobilizing or representative institutions. It was this *rentier* character of the polity, in combination with the uneven pattern of state capitalist integration into the world market and the material durability of the Shi'i *ulema*, that rendered the state vulnerable to overthrow from below. These features also account for the paradoxical character of the Iranian Revolution noted by Fred Halliday: namely, that it 'was the first contemporary instance to be religious in orientation, [and] was also the first ever "modern" revolution'.[30]

The *ulema* resisted the changes of the White Revolution as it impinged directly on both their material interests and their ability to articulate the wider process of social reproduction, especially the activities of the bazaar. (Some estimates suggest that as late as the 1950s the revenues paid to the clergy exceeded those paid to the state.) It was this social and material location of the Shi'i clergy in Iran which gave the revolution its Islamic character. In theological terms, Shi'i Islam can equally legitimate positions ranging from quietist aloofness from politics, through support for the government, to militant opposition.[31] Indeed, despite the mobilization of the urban masses, and commitments to land reform, to income redistribution and to the nationalization of foreign trade, the socio-economic content of the revolution has been limited. In fact, in many respects the Iranian experience is better compared to examples of third world populism than to examples of social revolution. Ervand Abrahamian has drawn attention to the following similarities between the Iranian and Latin American situations:

> 'economic rather than political dependency on the West; informal rather than formal subjection to imperialism; an upper class that included the comprador big bourgeoisie; an anti-imperialist middle class; an industrial working class unorganized by the Left; and a recent influx of rural migrants into the sprawling shantytowns.'[32]

Khomeini's social and political thought, and especially his reworking of the doctrine of *velayat-e faqih* (legal guardianship) to include the clerical supervision of affairs of state, breaks radically with Shi'i thought, and in other respects the constitution of revolutionary Iran owes more to the French Fifth Republic than to any model of classical Islam.

Conclusions

Now that I have reviewed the pattern of political change in a range of Middle Eastern states, I will attempt to summarize the problematic fortunes of democracy in the region. We have seen that the late Ottoman era (the Qajar period in Iran) and the brief interlude of European colonialism created an urban-based class of private appropriators who monopolized political power. At the same time, the intermediaries of integration into the world market were in many cases local minority groups or Europeans. At first, political life was organized by the politics of clientelism in which patrons (notables) operated in the state in order to deliver benefits to their clients (tribes, peasants, urban workers).[33] In return, clients performed labour services and provided political support for their patrons. Thus even where a limited parliamentarism existed, this was combined with a largely unaccountable executive and notable dominance of the latter.

In the apparatuses of the newly formed states, however, the civil and military officials of the old orders found another site of organization, surplus appropriation and hence class formation. Across much of the region, the pattern of development has followed that pioneered by Turkey in the 1920s and 1930s, namely that of revolution from above against landed classes and foreign capital, albeit with important variations relating to the external room for manoeuvre, the relation of the landed class to the state, the ability of the state to consolidate its rule, and the social location of Islam. The strengthening of the repressive apparatuses of the state, land reform, the elimination of foreign capital, state-led industrial development, attempted state control or suppression of the clergy, and the fostering of a secular ideology drawing on pre-Islamic themes have been the main objectives of conservative and radical regimes alike. Politically and economically breaking the power of the notables, and thereby destroying the political form that this took, was a precondition for launching strategies of development: 'Land reform was the handmaiden of state-led industrialization strategies.'[34] Reformers expropriated their political enemies.

As the role of the state as the main site of accumulation and source of authority increased, so informal clientelism and parliamentary structures were either destroyed or strictly controlled by a mixture of populist mobilization under charismatic leadership, the emergence of state-based clientelism, and the imposition from above of bureaucratic forms of control organized by the party–military apparatus. Under whatever auspices, the primary functions of the state apparatus have been the consolidation of its rule over and against other principles of authoritative regulation and the mobilization of resources for economic development. As a result of its subordination to these twin functions, party organization has been weak, and where it has not been a direct creation of the state, it has been absorbed into the state apparatus. Corporatist forms have sought to contain class, ethnic and religious divisions.

Thus, the two fundamental preconditions for capitalist democracy – namely, a significant degree of separation between the institutions of rule and of surplus appropriation, and the ability of the state to uphold its authority against other sites of political command – have been absent from much of the region for much of the post-war epoch. More especially, the scale of resources devoted to the imposition of state authority has often blocked the potential for future democratization, and this position has been further aggravated in those instances where the expansion of the coercive apparatuses was financed by oil and strategic rents.

'Conservative' and 'radical' regimes may be distinguished by the model of state-led, dependent development adopted. In the conservative, state capitalist variant, the state seeks to mobilize resources and provide the infrastructure for capitalist development while transferring its own surpluses to the private sector (Turkey since 1950, Iran 1963–79 and Egypt since 1973). A second type exists where the state retains the surpluses on its own operations, captures a large share of those in the remaining private sector, and then attempts to secure for the state more or less complete control over resource mobilization, if not state control over all property (Turkey hesitantly in the 1930s, Egypt nominally after 1961 and Iraq since 1963). Other things being equal, the conservative regimes should provide a more fertile soil for capitalist democracy than the radical states, because of the centrality of the state to surplus appropriation in the latter. Equally, the state's role in surplus appropriation in the radical case may owe more to the need to consolidate its rule than to any desire to plan economic development.

In both cases, however, the prospects for democracy have been further attenuated by the fact that those classes which have historically pushed for liberalization – the private-sector bourgeoisie and the middle classes – and for democratization – the working class – have been numerically small for a given level of development,[35] and have emerged in circumstances where the state has been able to impose incorporative forms of political control. This reflects the general pattern of post-oligarchic rule in the semi-periphery identified by Nicos Mouzelis, namely a mixture of clientelist, populist and bureaucratic-military structures.[36] In those instances where a degree of capitalist development has occurred outside the direct control of the state apparatus, and has brought with it the tentative organization of a civil society by the bourgeoisie and the working class, some liberalization and controlled experiments in popular participation have emerged (Turkey, Egypt and even Iran). Where the state has maintained control of the organizations of civil society, then the prospects for democratic reform are more limited (the limit case being Iraq).

To a greater or lesser extent, most of the states in the Middle East are now entering a period of profound uncertainty as they adapt to pressures for structural adjustment and economic liberalization (*infitah*). Structural adjustment is a response to rising deficits in the public sector and on the foreign exchanges, together with the resulting inflationary pressures, and *infitah* results from the contradictions in state-led growth, the emergence of new class forces and the pressure from the advanced capitalist world mediated by the World Bank and the IMF. At the centre of this is the exhaustion of the nationally based strategy of import-substituting industrial development, and thus the political and ideological crises of the regimes which have presided over it. Foreign exchange was not generated but rather drained by the import of capital goods; agriculture fared poorly and food-dependence has increased rapidly; non-oil exporters could only cover the gap between domestic savings and invest-ment by borrowing abroad; operating losses contributed to the state's budget deficits, and when monetized this accelerated inflation; and state-led growth did not solve rural–urban disparities or other inequalities. Stagnant economies, growing problems of food security, a rapidly growing population, rising levels of urbanization and large numbers of unemployed and underemployed youth adds up to a recipe for continu-ing political instability. This will impose further strains on the already fragile prospects for democratic reform.

In sum, to the extent that circumstances have precluded a replication of the Turkish path, then the prospects for democratic patterns of political development have been similarly attenuated. The social location of Islam has likewise changed in different ways. In Egypt, the lack of any clear association between Islam and decline (imperialist control being a much easier target), in combination with the importance of Islam to Arabic culture, led to a weaker attack on the institutions of Islam. In Iraq, the ethnic and religious heterogeneity, combined with the minority status of the Sunni Arab elite, resulted in a strongly secular state, stressing Arab nationalist ideology. In Saudi Arabia, by contrast, modernization was *with* rather than *against* Islam and this produced a theocratic political order. And in Iran, the independence of the Shi'i *ulema* from the state, together with the depth of their penetration of social and material reproduction, contributed to the Islamic character of the revolution and Khomeini's populism. And where Turkish conditions could not be repeated, then what is mistakenly referred to as 'Islamic fundamentalism' has thrived. As Nikki Keddie has pointed out:

> The profile of countries with strong Islamist movements nearly always includes the following . . . one or more nationalist governments which tried to unify the country by relying more on national than Islamic ideology . . . rapid economic development and dislocations, which have brought rapid urbanisation and visibly differential treatment for the urban poor and the urban rich . . . virtually all have profited from oil economies at least at second hand . . . a longer and more radical break with an Islamically-orientated past government and society than is true of a country like Yemen. Most have experienced a heavy Western impact and control and Western and secularly orientated governments.[37]

Islamism, then, is a form of populist mobilization in which middle strata seek to mobilize the working class, and in particular the unorganized urban poor, against foreign influence and a failed political establishment. Drawing on charismatic leaders and the available symbols of popular culture, it does not question the status of private property, in fact it is generally pro-market, and it focuses on moral and political renewal. In the Middle East, populism takes a religious form not because it is an atavistic throwback but because Islam is constitutive not only of popular culture but also of many of the quotidian features of social life,[38] and because the failed regimes have been attempting to modernize under *secular*, nationalist ideologies. It is these refractory problems of state-building and economic development, rather than 'religion', 'oil' or 'neo-colonial' forms of control, which make the prospects for democracy in the Middle East so bleak. Sadly, the situation in Algeria in December 1991 and early 1992, involving the rapid mobilization and electoral success of the Islamic Salvation Front and the aborting of the electoral process and a related security crack-down, is only the most recent and dramatic example.

NOTES

1 I trust that it is obvious that these conditions are neither exhaustive nor without the usual *ceteris paribus* conditions.
2 The degree of real choice and the substantive control exercised over the state apparatus by elected forces are *empirical* not definitional questions.
3 For a recent comparative study of the relation between capitalist development and democracy, which while not considering the Middle East sheds considerable light on the whole topic, see D. Rueschemeyer, E. H. Stephens and J. D. Stephens, *Capitalist Development and Democracy* (Cambridge, Polity Press, 1992).

4   Because I am concerned with the pattern of state formation that developed as pre-capitalist forms came into contact with and were transformed by the world market and the modern state system, I do not consider the quite unique case of Jewish settler colonialism in Israel.

5   See P. Anderson, *Lineages of the Absolutist State* (London, New Left Books, 1974), pp. 361–94 and 496–520, and Chris Wickham, 'The uniqueness of the east', in *Journal of Peasant Societies*, 12 (1985), 166–96.

6   I. Lapidus, *A History of Islamic Societies* (Cambridge, Cambridge University Press, 1988), pp. 176–80.

7   This kind of society has been ably analysed by E. Gellner, *Muslim Society* (Cambridge, Cambridge University Press, 1981); but see also Y. Lacoste, *Ibn Khaldun* (London, Verso, 1984).

8   Gellner, *Muslim Society*, p. 41.

9   Lapidus, *A History of Islamic Societies*, p. 299.

10 The martyrdom of the third imam, Husayn, by the Umayyad armies of the caliph Yazid at Karbala (AD 680) is central to the symbolism of Shi'ism.

11 Gellner, *Muslim Society*, p. 6.

12 See Anderson, *Lineages of the Absolutist State*, pp. 378–94; and also E. Jones, *The European Miracle* (Cambridge, Cambridge University Press, 1981), pp. 175–91.

13 See C. A. Bayly, *Imperial Meridian* (London, Longman, 1989).

14 C. Issawi, *An Economic History of the Middle East and North Africa* (London, Methuen, 1982), p. 4.

15 This is the conclusion of R. Owen's fine study, *The Middle East in the World Economy 1800–1914* (London, Methuen, 1981).

16 Issawi, *An Economic History of the Middle East and North Africa*, p. 9.

17 The details of this story have been told elsewhere and will not be repeated here: see M. Yapp, *The Making of the Modern Near East 1792–1923* (London, Longman, 1987), and Yapp, *The Near East Since the First World War* (London, Longman, 1991); D. Fromkin, *A Peace to End All Peace* (London, Penguin, 1991); and E. Kedourie, *England and the Middle East* (London, Mansell, 1987).

18 While we may call the Kemalist project a 'revolution from above', the very limited development of a landed class within the Ottoman formation meant that there was little for Ataturk and his followers to dispossess. For a fuller discussion of these issues, see E. K. Trimberger, *Revolution From Above* (New Brunswick, NJ, Transaction Books, 1978).

19 See C. Keyder, *State and Class in Turkey* (London, Verso, 1987), and Keyder, 'Class and state in the transformation of modern Turkey', in F. Halliday and H. Alavi (eds), *State and Ideology in the Middle East and Pakistan* (London, Macmillan, 1988).

20 Yapp, *The Near East Since the First World War*, p. 15.

21 Keyder, 'Class and state in the transformation of modern Turkey', p. 215.

22 Yapp, *The Near East Since the First World War*, p. 211.

23 The main newspaper of the regime, *Al-Ahram*, translated and serialized chapters of Walt Rostow's *The Stages of Economic Growth*, with its headline taken from the book's sub-title, 'a non-communist manifesto'. See Marie-Christine Aulas, 'State and ideology in republican Egypt: 1952–82', in Halliday and Alavi, *State and Ideology in the Middle East and Pakistan*, p. 143.

24 M. Gilsenan, 'Popular Islam and the state in contemporary Egypt', in Halliday and Alavi, *State and Ideology in the Middle East and Pakistan*, p. 178.

25 L. Carl Brown, *International Politics and the Middle East* (London, I. B. Tauris, 1984), p. 114.

26 Quoted in Yapp, *The Near East Since the First World War*, p. 70.
27 Gellner, *Muslim Society*, p. 5.
28 Yapp, *The Near East Since the First World War*, p. 355.
29 Quoted in Yapp, *The Near East Since the First World War*, p. 189.
30 F. Halliday, 'The Iranian revolution: uneven development and religious populism', in Halliday and Alavi, *State and Ideology in the Middle East and Pakistan*, p. 35. The modernity of the Iranian revolution that Halliday refers to consists in the advanced nature of Iranian society, the urban location of the revolution, its prosecution through political rather than military conflict, and the absence of any significant external weakening of the state.
31 An excellent discussion of this can be found in M. Momen, 'Authority and opposition in twelver Shi'ism', in R. M. Burrell (ed.), *Islamic Fundamentalism* (London, Royal Asiatic Society, 1989).
32 E. Abrahamian, 'Khomeini: fundamentalist or populist?', *New Left Review*, 186 (1991), p. 118.
33 See S. N. Eisenstadt and L. Roniger, *Patrons, Clients and Friends* (Cambridge, Cambridge University Press, 1984), pp. 81–99.
34 A. Richards and J. Waterbury, *A Political Economy of the Middle East* (Boulder, CO, and San Francisco, CA, Westview Press, 1990), p. 151.
35 This seems to be a general feature of dependent development deriving from the leapfrogging of basic labour-intensive forms of industrial production by borrowing from the more advanced economies.
36 N. Mouzelis, *Politics in the Semi-Periphery* (London, Macmillan, 1986).
37 N. Keddie, 'Ideology, society and the state in post-colonial Muslim societies', in Halliday and Alavi, *State and Ideology in the Middle East and Pakistan*, p. 17.
38 For the continuing social articulation of Islam, see the fine study by M. Gilsenan, *Recognizing Islam* (London, I. B. Taurus, 1990).

INDEX

Numbers in bold type refer to main chapter pages